CAMBRIDGE
GUELPH & AREA

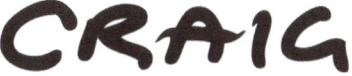

EDITOR

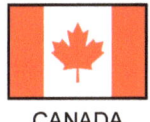

CANADA

Sedit qui timuit ne non succederet.

FOR LINKS TO PURCHASE THE BOOK OR SUBMIT ART TO THE NEXT
VOLUME, PLEASE VISIT:

TALENTNEXTDOOR.COM

IF YOU ARE AN ARTIST LOOKING TO BE PUBLISHED OR WOULD LIKE TO
FIND OUT ABOUT CRAIG'S OTHER BOOKS, PLEASE VISIT:

CRAIGMUSSELMAN.COM

TO SEE IF I AM MAKING A BOOK IN A GENRE THAT WOULD INTEREST YOU
OR HIRE ME.

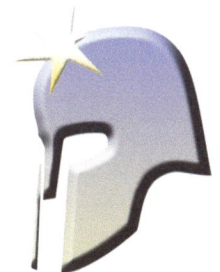

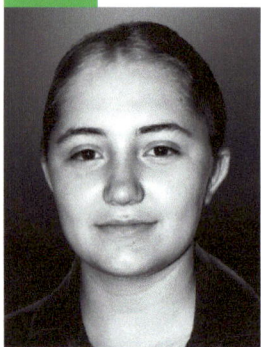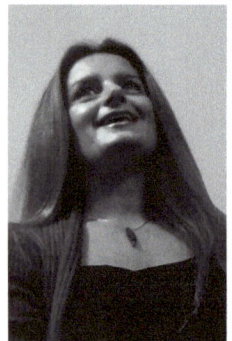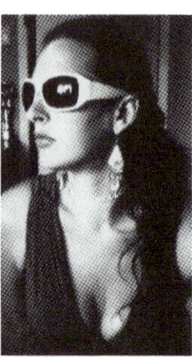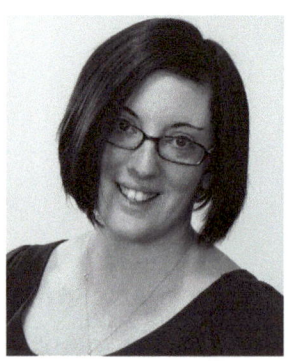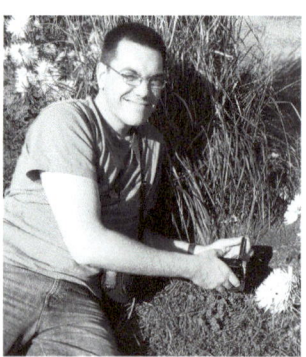

Meet the Jury

Last year I undertook an amazing project - without regard to social squabbling and politics, funding, or contacts, I set out to recruit every artist in the KW area and put them in one showcase art book. The result was Talent Next Door Vol 1. Volume 2 followed this year, so I expanded my recruitment net and sought out all the artists that I could find in the Cambridge and Guelph areas. The result of that call for submission is the book you see here.

All works (submitted before the deadline) were judged independently by a jury of five international and local artists (above from left): Zlatka Subotičanec (already a superstar in her teens), Sanela Dizdar (award winning painter), Angela Werstine (diva of black and white ink drawings), Alex Pominville (photography goddess), and of course my partner, muse and art critic - Joël Larose who puts up with me and the craziness at the deadline. I would like to thank the judges for a very difficult task. They were handed almost 400 pieces of art and told to "Just Pick the Best 5" - like that was possible. From that, they were to choose their favourite overall. The next 10 pages show a small sample of their own work with a list of their choices jury awards.

After taking in the works featured here, it is my hope that you use the listings on each page of the website to contact the artists, praise them, and find out how you can see (and BUY!) more of their work and invite them to exhibit in upcoming gallery shows. Everyone is also encouraged to submit their own work to the growing gallery on the TalentNextDoor.com website. If you are not in the book, there may be a next time. Feel free to email me at TalentNextDoorBook@gmail.com and join the facebook page (see the website) for updates.

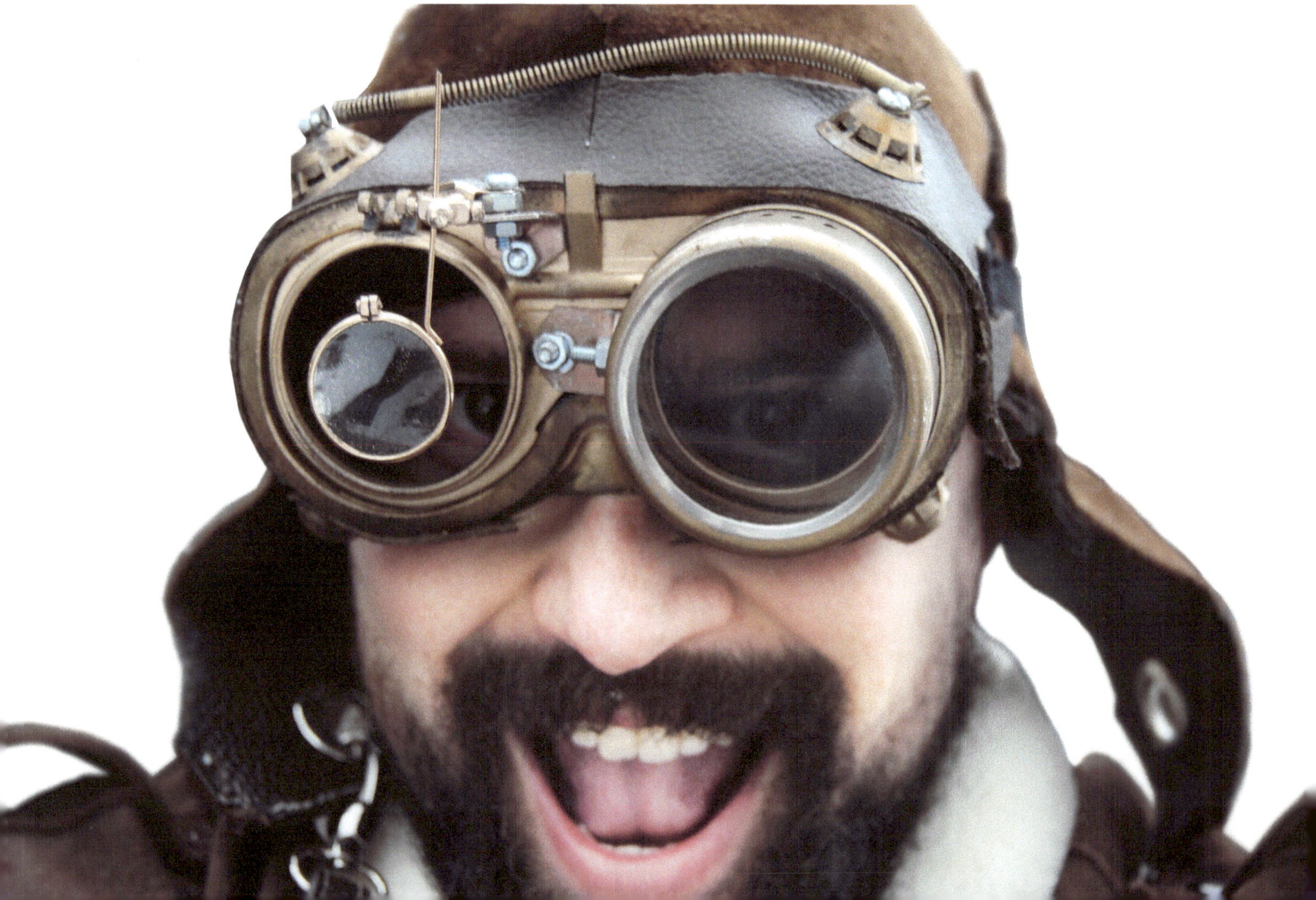

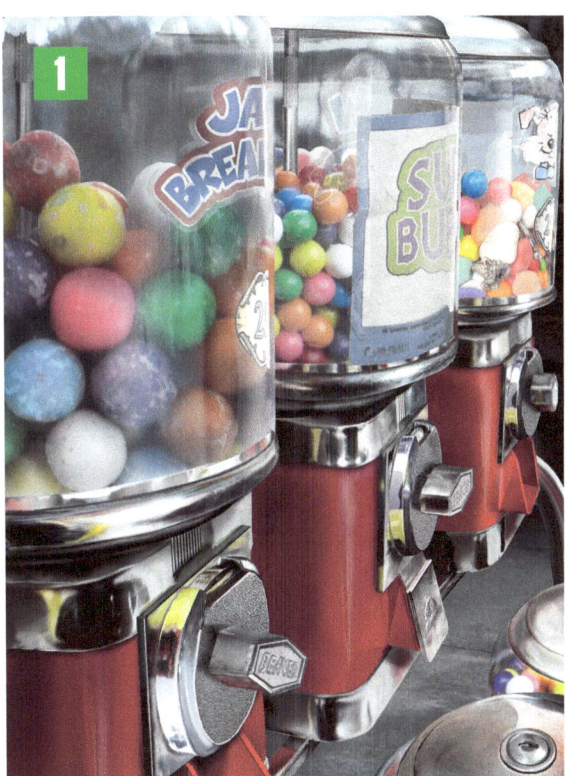

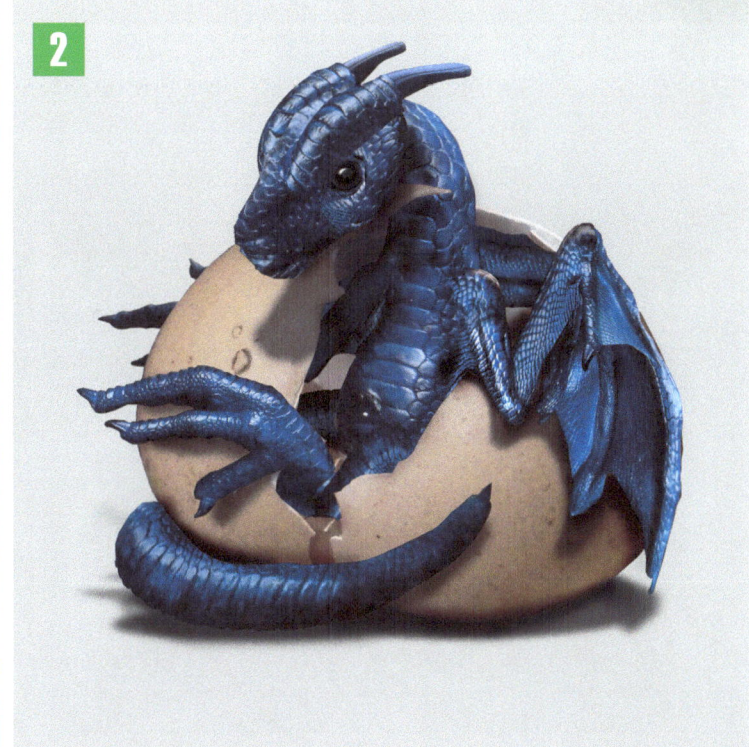

1 This Is Not A Gum Machine

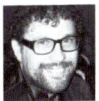 **3 Crab Apple Blossoms** 24x30" Acrylic on Canvas.

2 Baby Blue Photoshop Photo-manipulation constructions.

CRAIG MUSSELMAN

LOCATION: Waterloo

WEB: CraigMusselman.com, NightmareInShiningArmour.com MachinesAndMagic.com, TalentNextDoor.com, Steampunkart.ca, RealisticArt.org, ShootItFor.me

EMAIL: TalentNextDoorBook@gmail.com, Solipsism@innocent.com, MachinesAndMagic@gmail.com

Editor - Craig Musselman is an internationally award winning Artist and Graphic Designer, specializing in elaborate digital photomontage works of art, acrylic painting, and prop & costume design. He has been featured in Advanced Photoshop Magazine, ImagineFX Magazine, as well as co-authored a textbook on creative uses of Photoshop. His most recent book "Machines and Magic", features 91 Fantasy Sci Fi aritsts from around the world available now. He is also the founder and author of the TalentNextDoor.com series of books on local arts. Look for other books coming soon through his collection of websites: SteampunkArt.ca, RealisticArt. org, ShootItFor.me (his photo stock site) or CraigMusselman.com for the latest news and emails to submit to, or inquire about the books. For more about THIS book and helpful links visit: TalentNextDoor.com . Craig was born in 1970 & lives in Waterloo, with his longtime partner. Just look for his famous pink bicycle helmet.

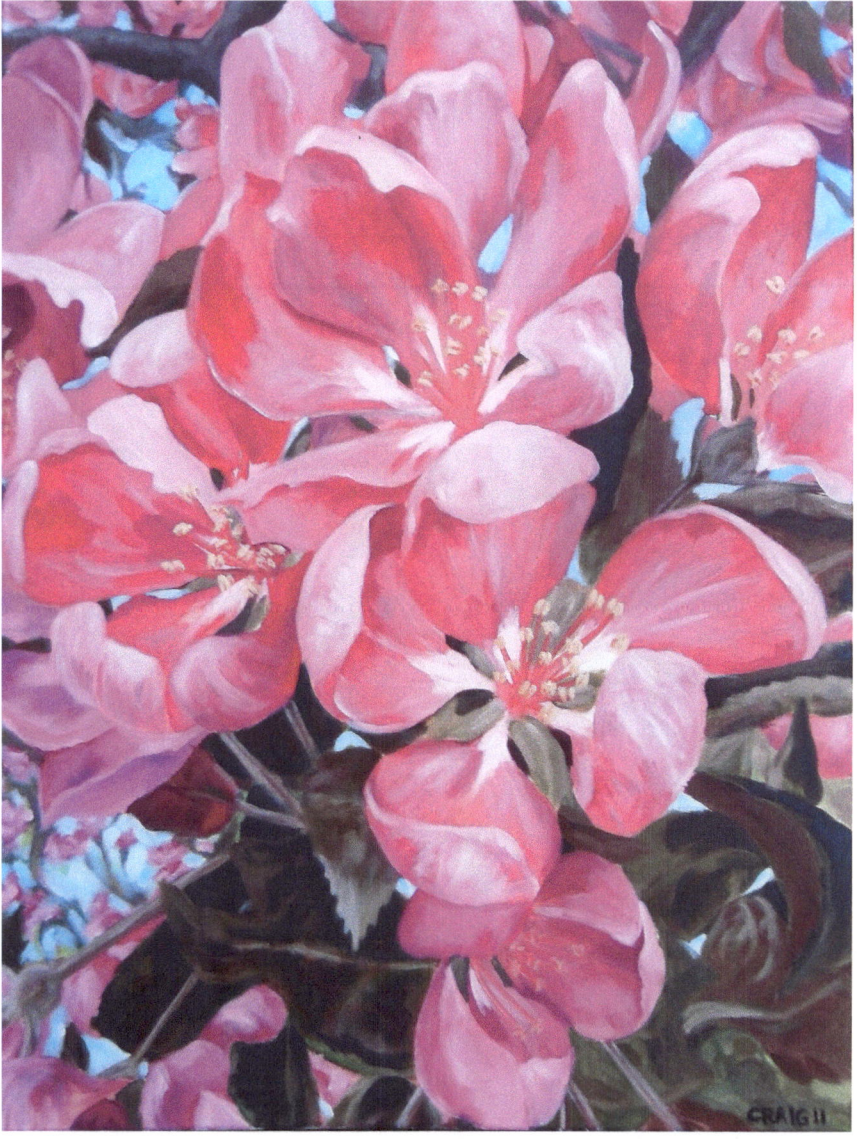

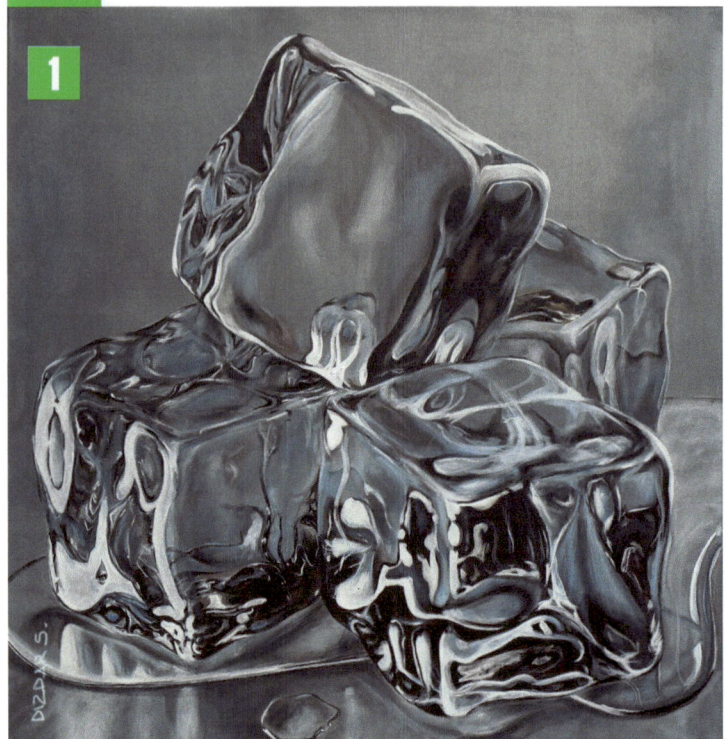

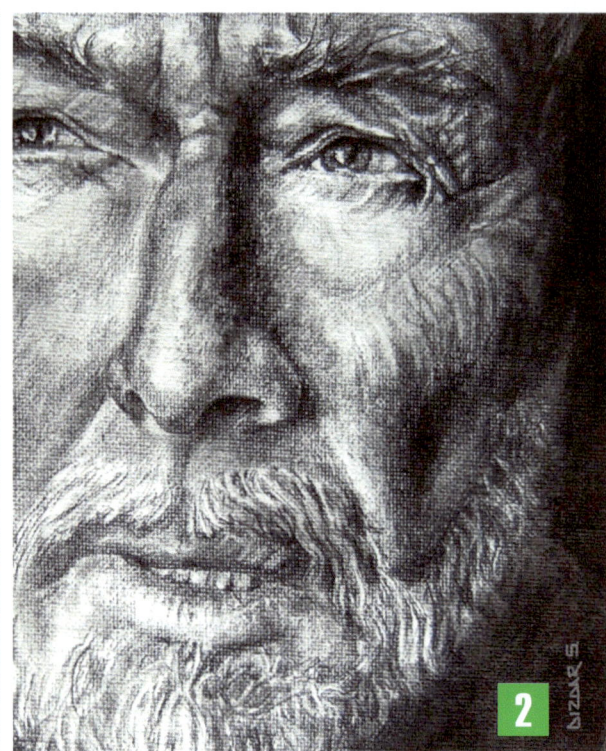

SANELA DIZDAR

LOCATION: Kitchener
WEB: SanelaArt.com
EMAIL: Sanela.art@gmail.com

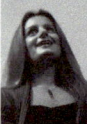

3 Sparkle Network 24x36 Acrylic on canvas.

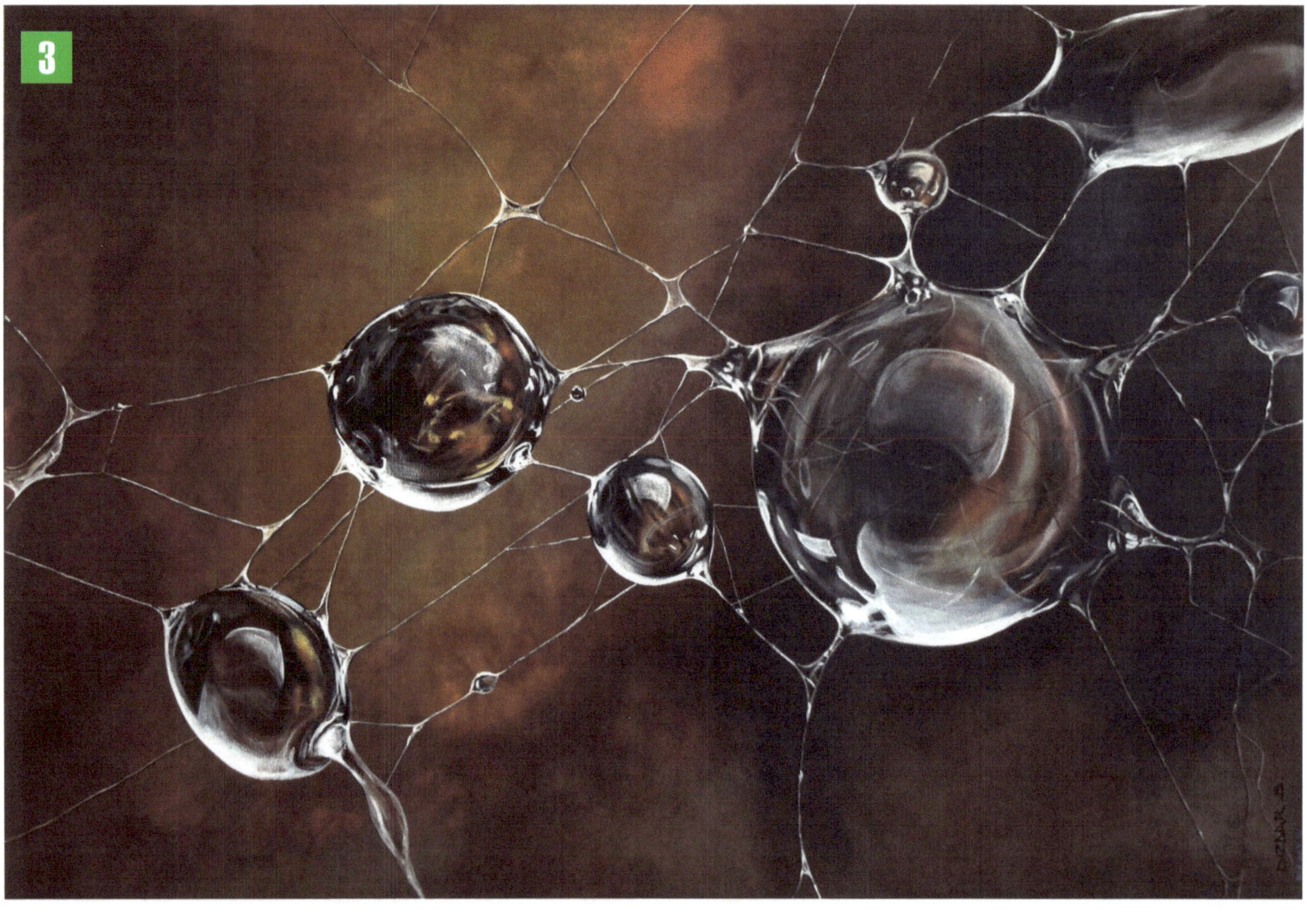

Sanela Dizdar is an artist and Graphic Designer. A constant self-challenger with her favorite tools of expression: graphics tablet, pastel, acrylic, oil and pencil/graphite. Her two challenges in art are painting water as alive and exploring human emotions. Sanela teaches drawing classes in Up-Town Gallery, Waterloo. Come and join her.

1 The Power of Positive Thought 30x30" Acrylic on canvas.

2 Part of the Face 16x24" Pencil on canvas.

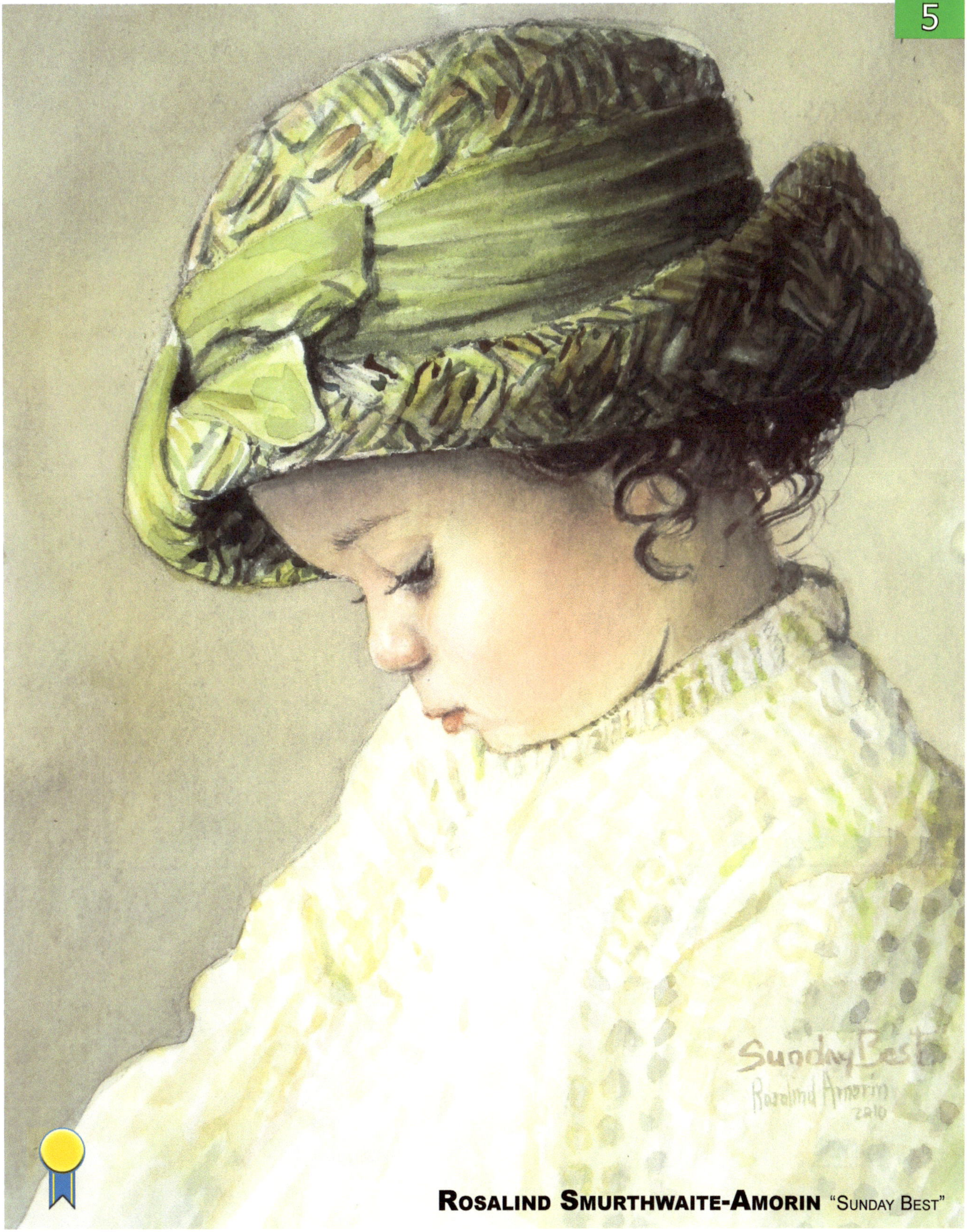

ROSALIND SMURTHWAITE-AMORIN "SUNDAY BEST"

SANELA'S SHORT LIST

ROSALIND SMURTHWAITE-AMORIN "SUNDAY BEST"
▶ **Helena Pravda** "MOTHER"
▶ **Nancy Yule** "EMERGENCE - CIRCLES"
▶ **Stacey Yacula** "JACK & PEEP"
▶ **Susan Strachan Johnson** "CLEAR WATERS"

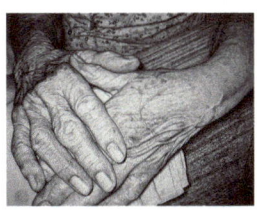
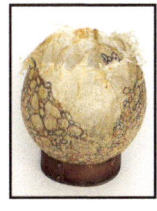
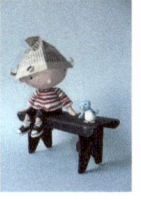
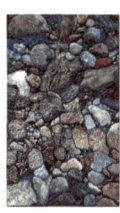

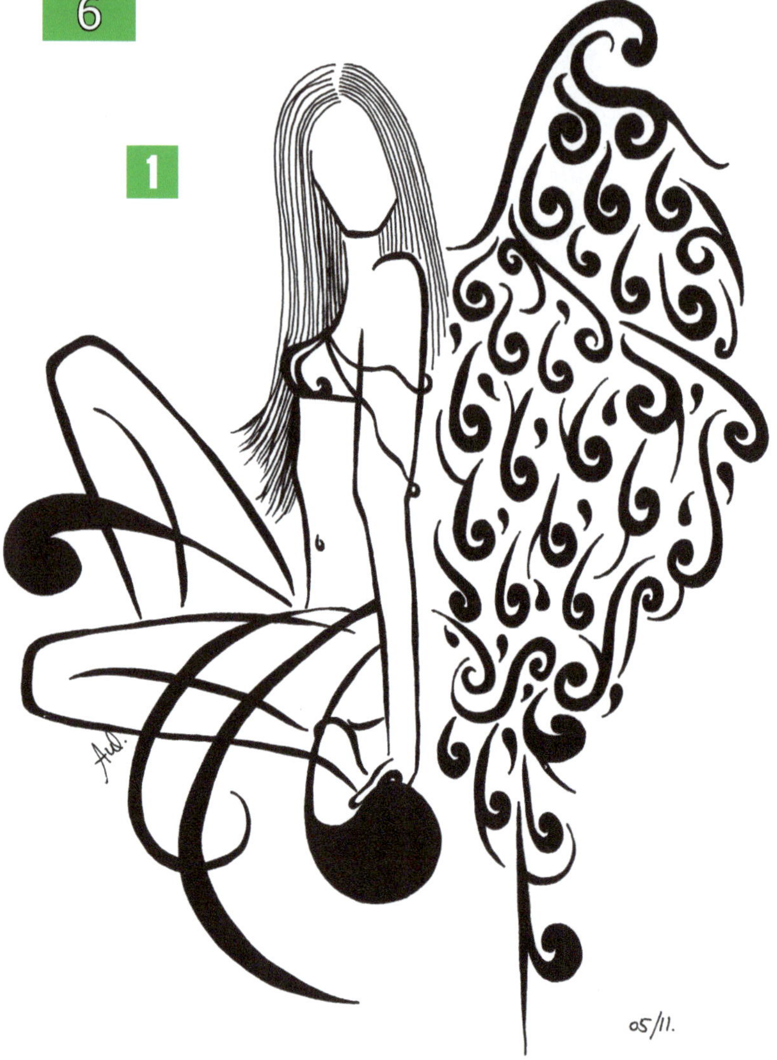

ANGELA WERSTINE

LOCATION: St. Jacobs
WEB:
www.facebook.com/Artist.Angela.Werstine
EMAIL: angela.werstine@live.com

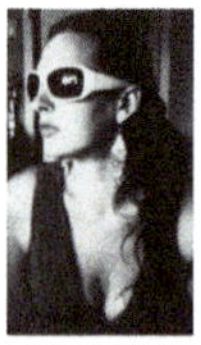

Angela Werstine's ink on paper work is sensual, erotic, beautiful, simple and elegant. Her drawings are evocative pieces that highlight the hips, legs, breasts and essential curves, and it makes sense that female beauty is the focus considering that Angela is a woman who is now able to celebrate her own body in a brand new way. Angela embellishes, accessorizes and infuses each piece with her own style and energy that perfectly reflects her new and lighter self. She uses as many lines as she sees fit, while celebrating the strength and beauty of the female body and spirit.

1 Butterfly Kisses 24x26" Ink on paper.

2 Atlantic 24x26" Ink on paper.

3 Metis Pride 24x26" Ink on paper.

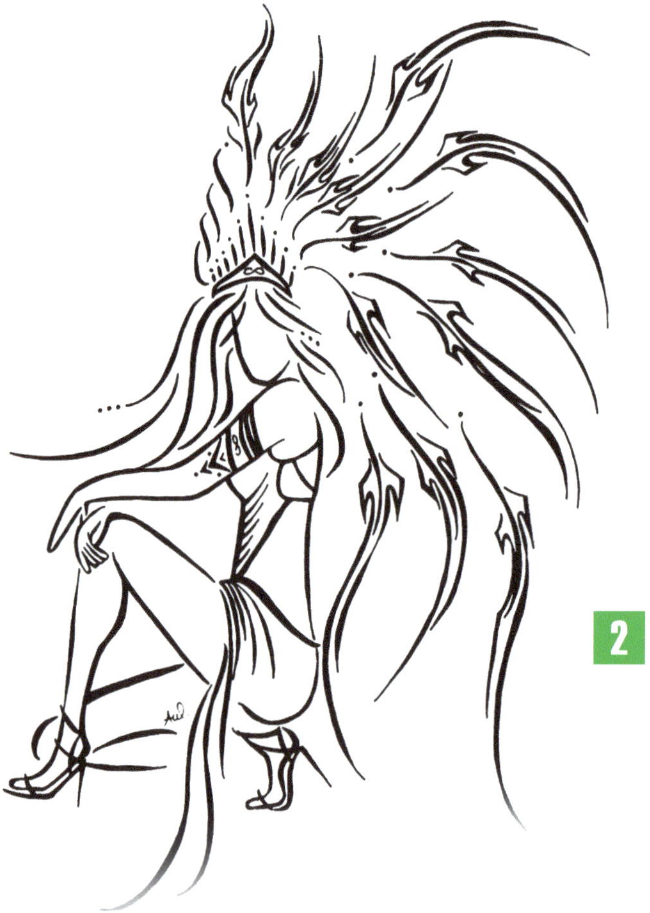

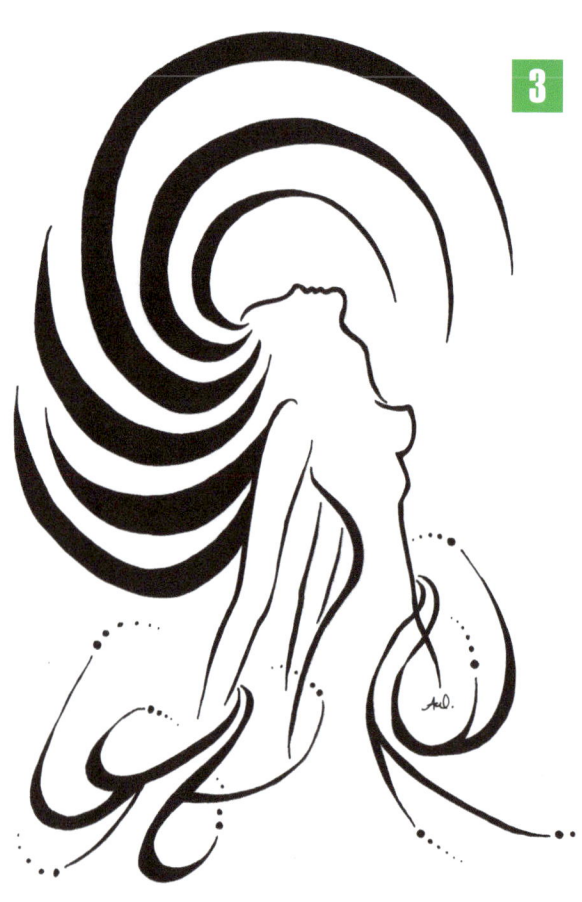

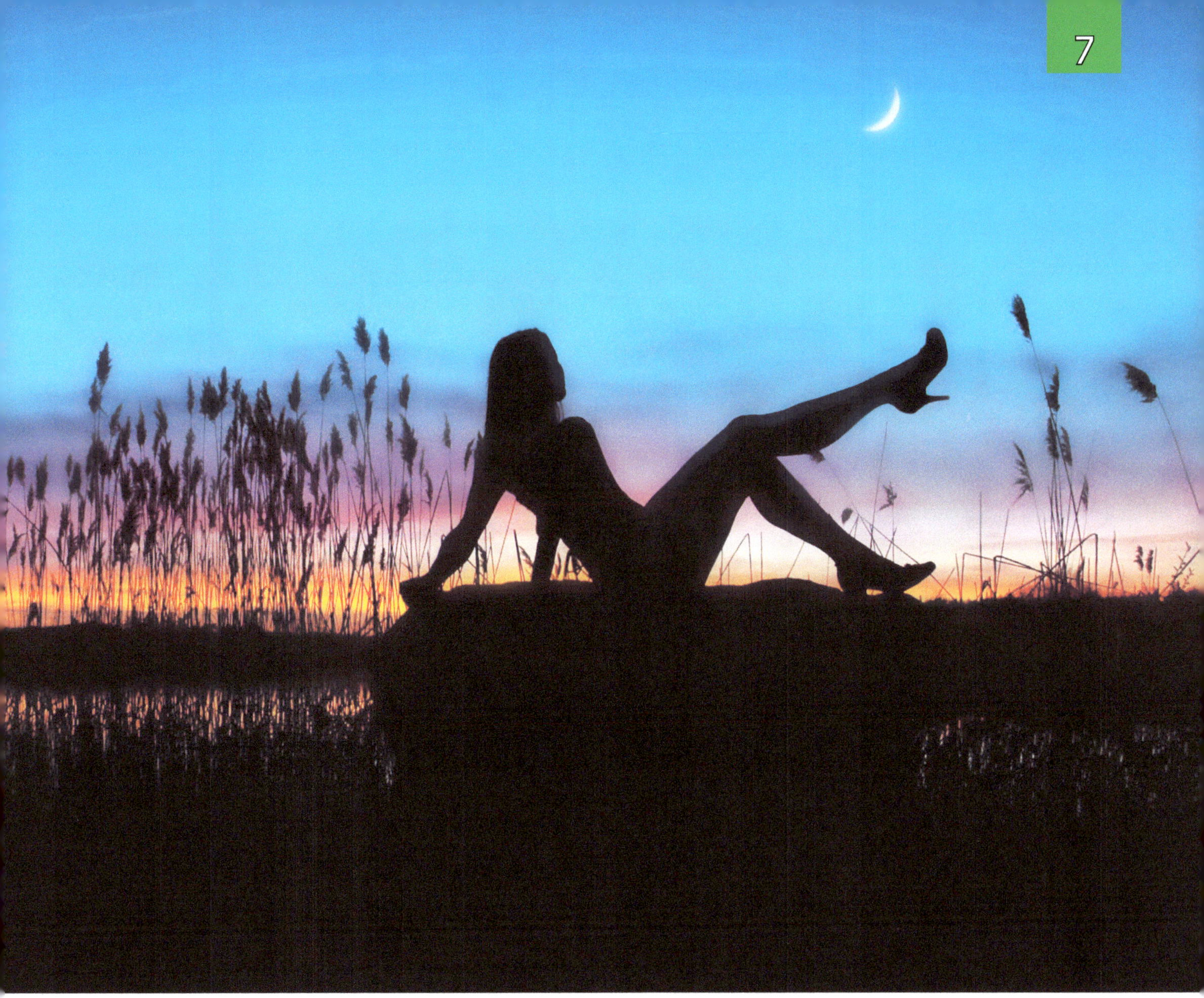

EMILY BEATTY IMAGERY "UNTITLED (PINUP)"

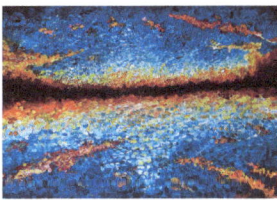 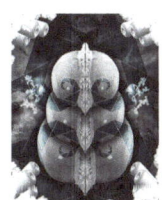 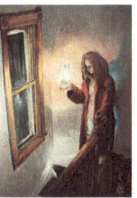 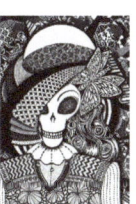

ANGELA's SHORT LIST

EMILY BEATTY IMAGERY "UNTITLED (PINUP)"
► **Michelle Ramalho** "ABSENT"
► **Cameron Stewart** "ALL FROM NONE"
► **Daisy Fresh** "POWERLESS"
► **Barbara Young** "BON TON #4"

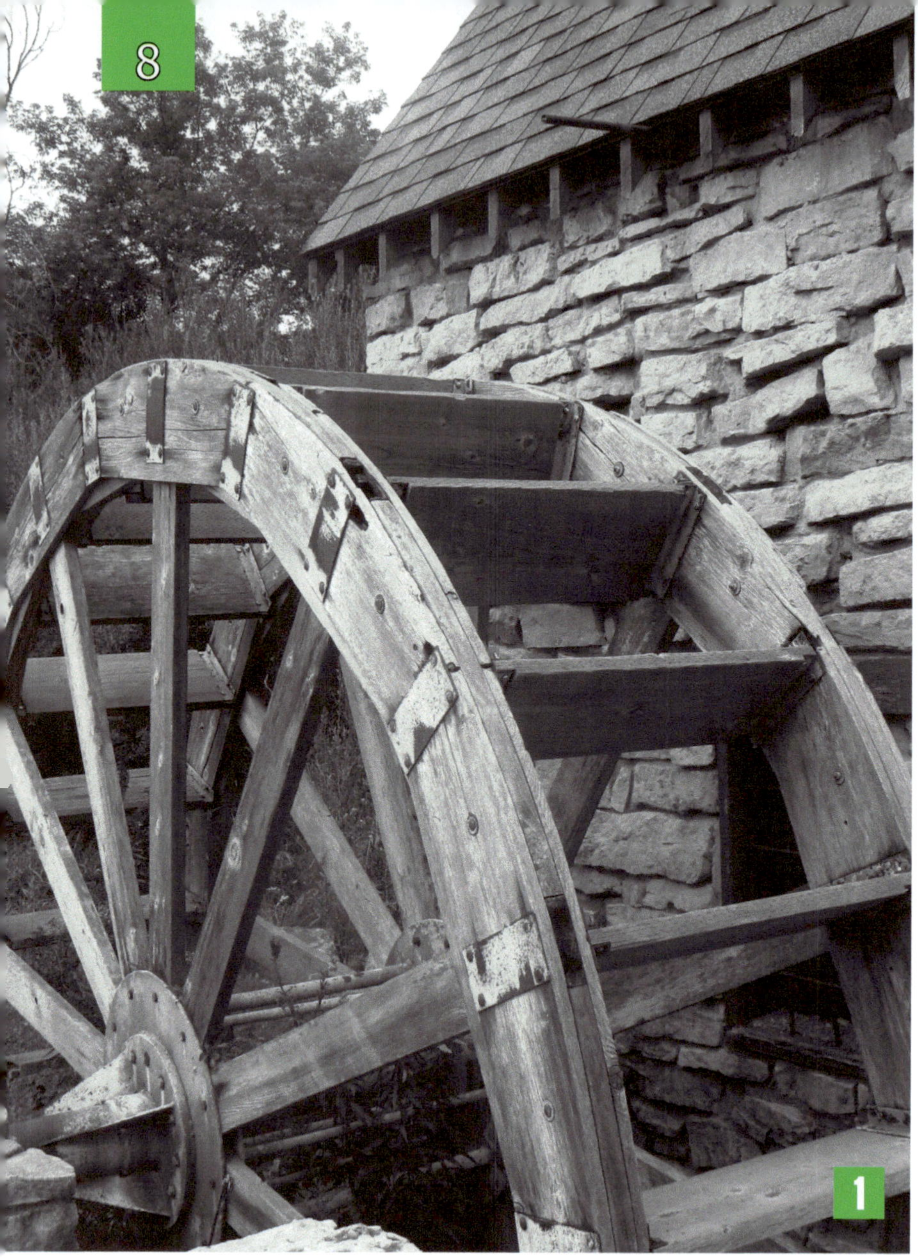

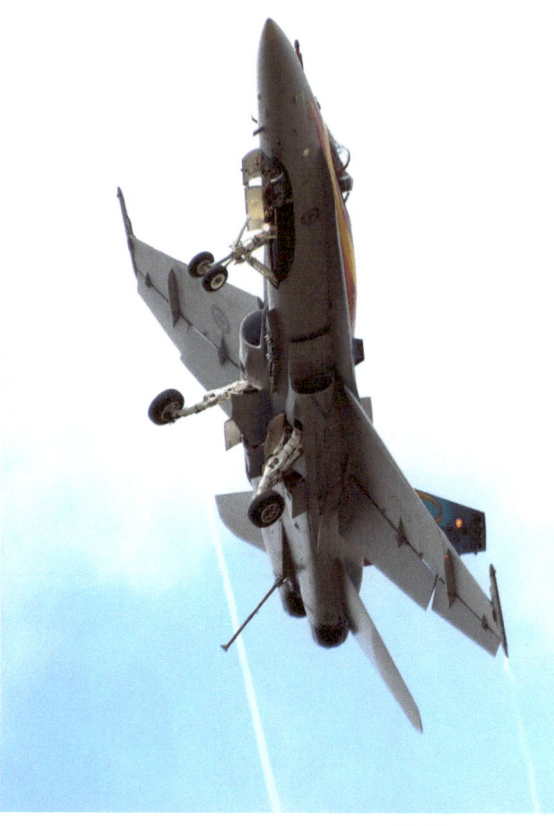

2 Flyby (Detail) Photo.

1 Waterwheel Photo.

ALEX POMINVILLE

LOCATION: Waterloo

WEB:
http://pominvillephotography.showitsite.com

EMAIL: pominvillephotography@gmail.com

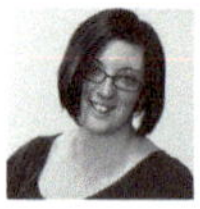

Alex started her business, Pominville Photography, in January 2010. Her photographs have been published and used in auctions for charity events. She enjoys photographing families, weddings, and large gatherings but she also has a passion for photographing the beauty in any situation. Alex finds inspiration and support through her children; Keean and Scarlett, and through her husband; Donald.

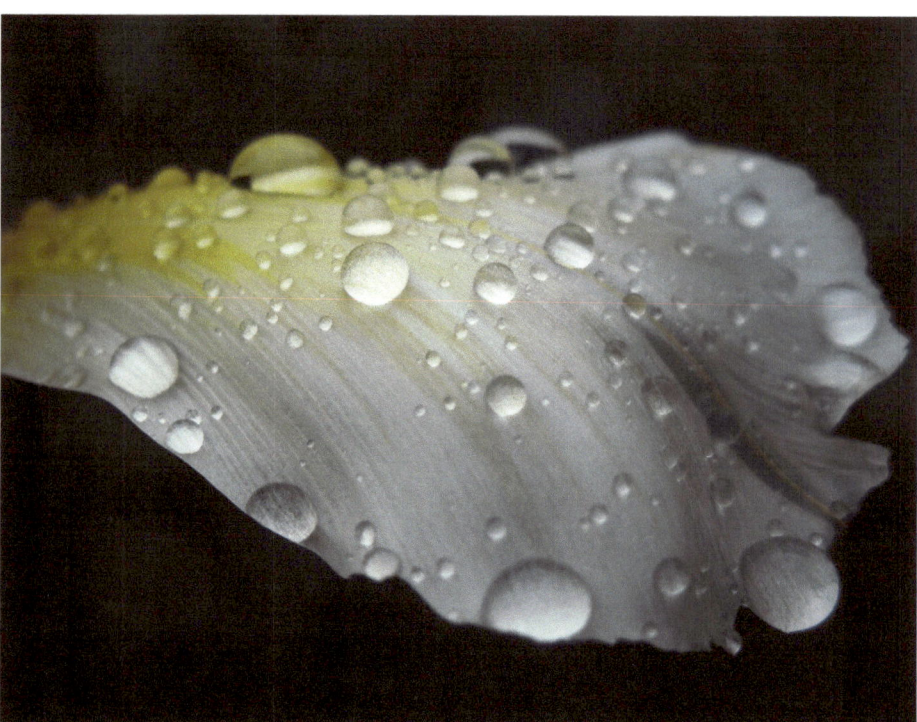

3 Sweet Rain Drops Photo.

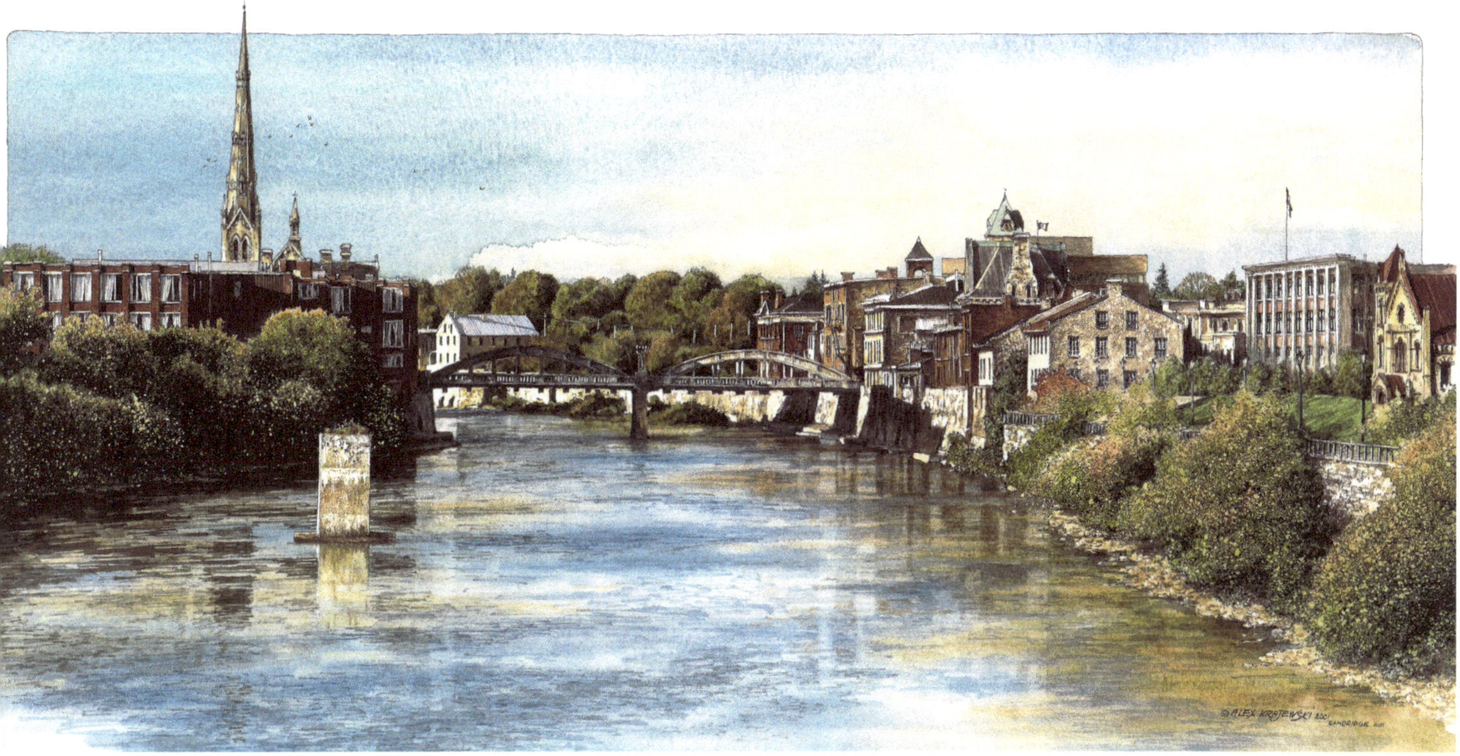

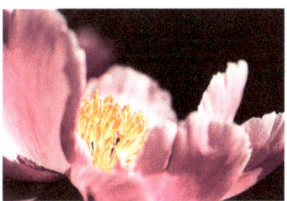

ALEX KRAJEWSKI "CAMBRIDGE"

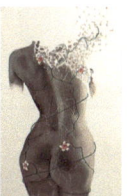 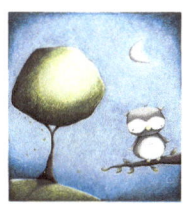 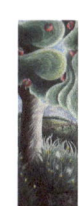

ALEX's SHORT LIST

ALEX KRAJEWSKI "CAMBRIDGE"
▶ **Ema Suvajac** "UNTITLED (PINK FLOWER)"
▶ **Carina Francioso** "GARDEN OF EDEN"
▶ **Stacey Yacula** "OWL BY MOONLIGHT"
▶ **Lisa Chandler** "UNDER THE APPLE TREE"

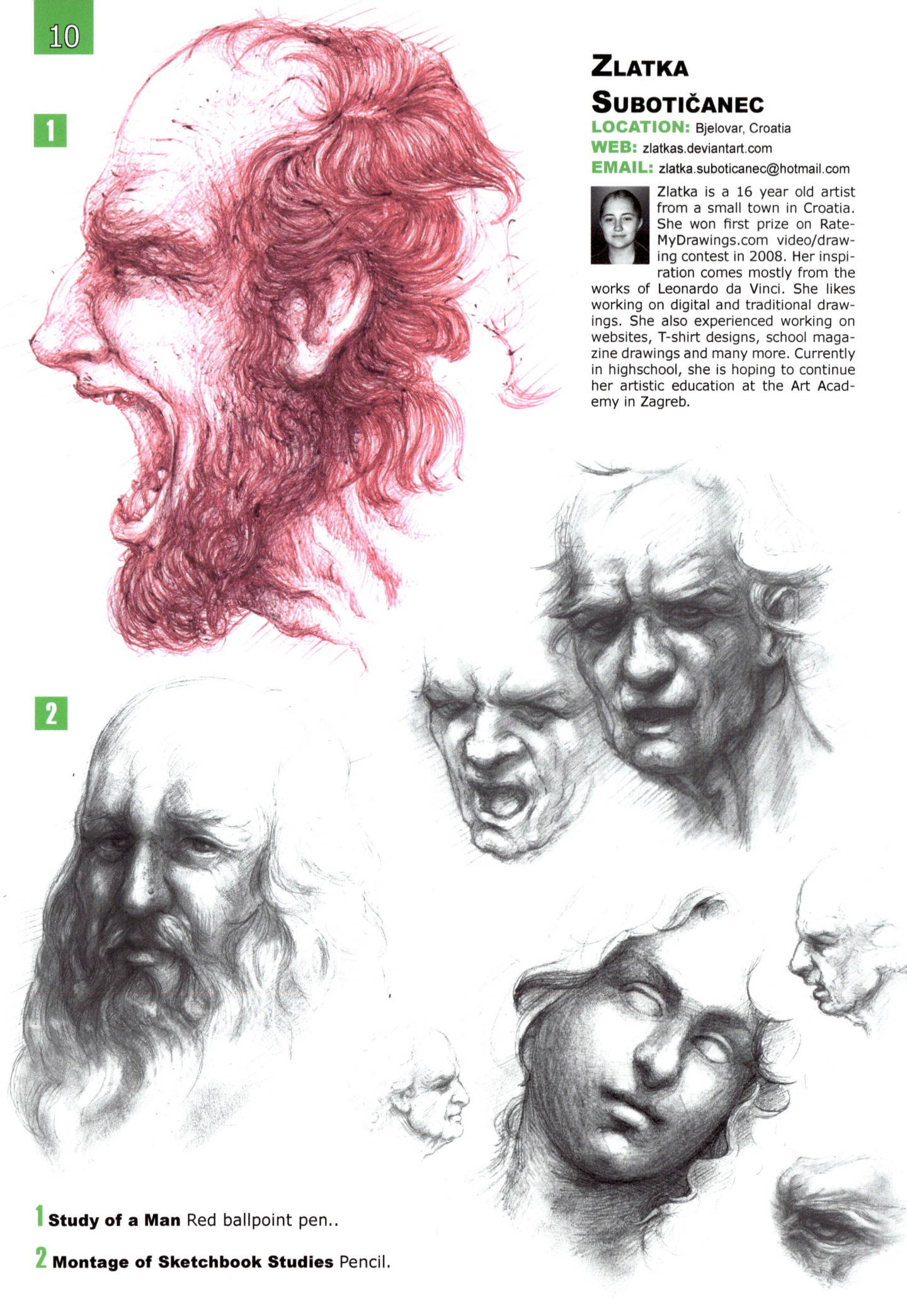

1

ZLATKA SUBOTIČANEC
LOCATION: Bjelovar, Croatia
WEB: zlatkas.deviantart.com
EMAIL: zlatka.suboticanec@hotmail.com

Zlatka is a 16 year old artist from a small town in Croatia. She won first prize on Rate-MyDrawings.com video/drawing contest in 2008. Her inspiration comes mostly from the works of Leonardo da Vinci. She likes working on digital and traditional drawings. She also experienced working on websites, T-shirt designs, school magazine drawings and many more. Currently in highschool, she is hoping to continue her artistic education at the Art Academy in Zagreb.

2

1 **Study of a Man** Red ballpoint pen..

2 **Montage of Sketchbook Studies** Pencil.

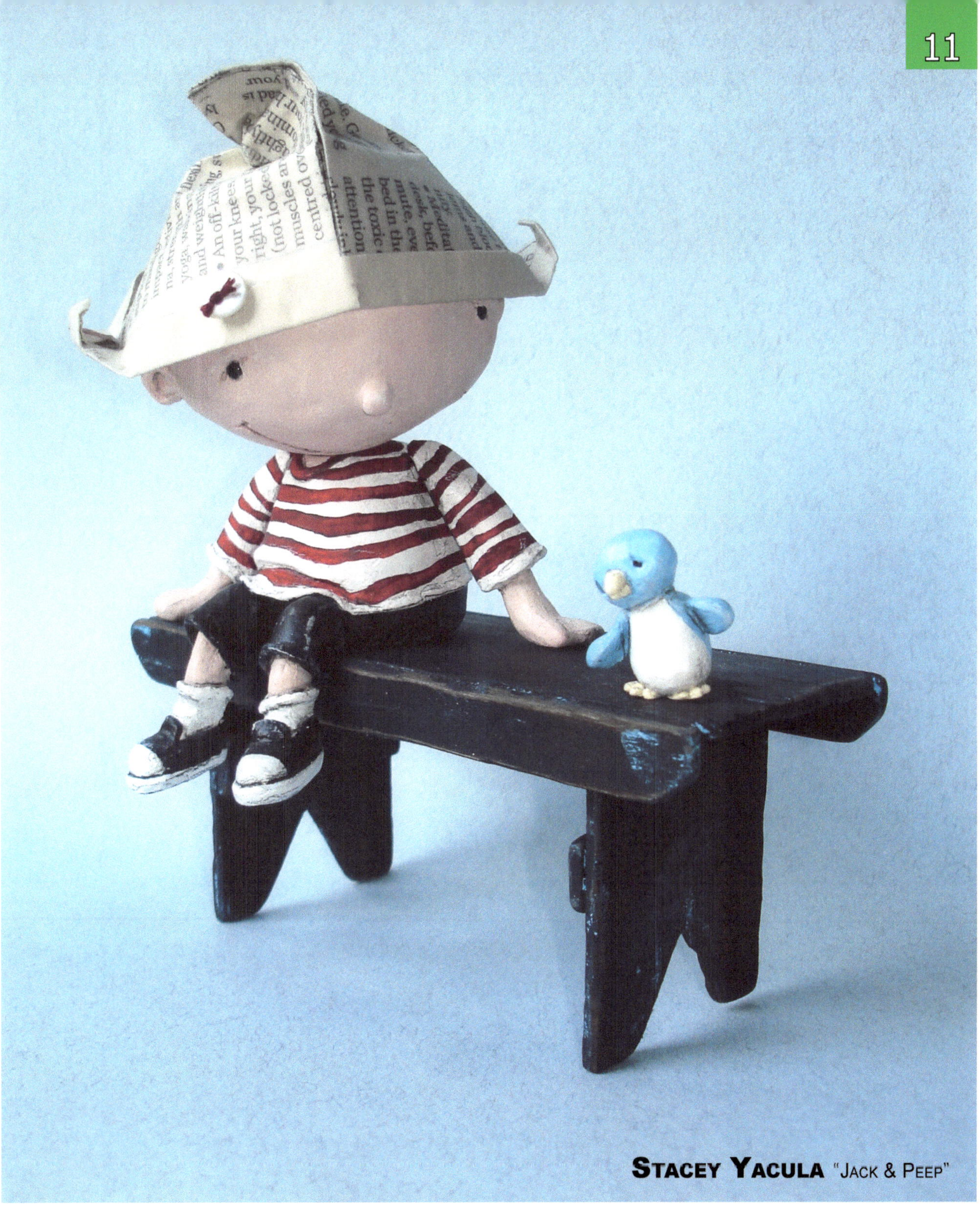

STACEY YACULA "JACK & PEEP"

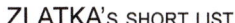

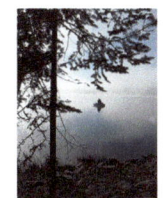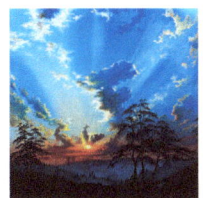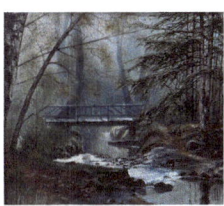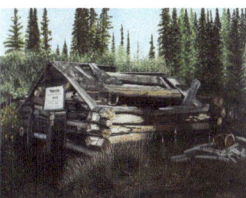

ZLATKA's SHORT LIST

STACEY YACULA "JACK & PEEP"
▶ **Sioux Thibodeau** ""STILL" FISHING"
▶ **Hanne Lore Koehler** "INSPIRATION"
▶ **Gerda Thibodeau** "MISTY SERENITY"
▶ **Beryl Dawson** "NORTH WEST MOUNTED POLICE POST 1898 - TAGISH - YUKON"

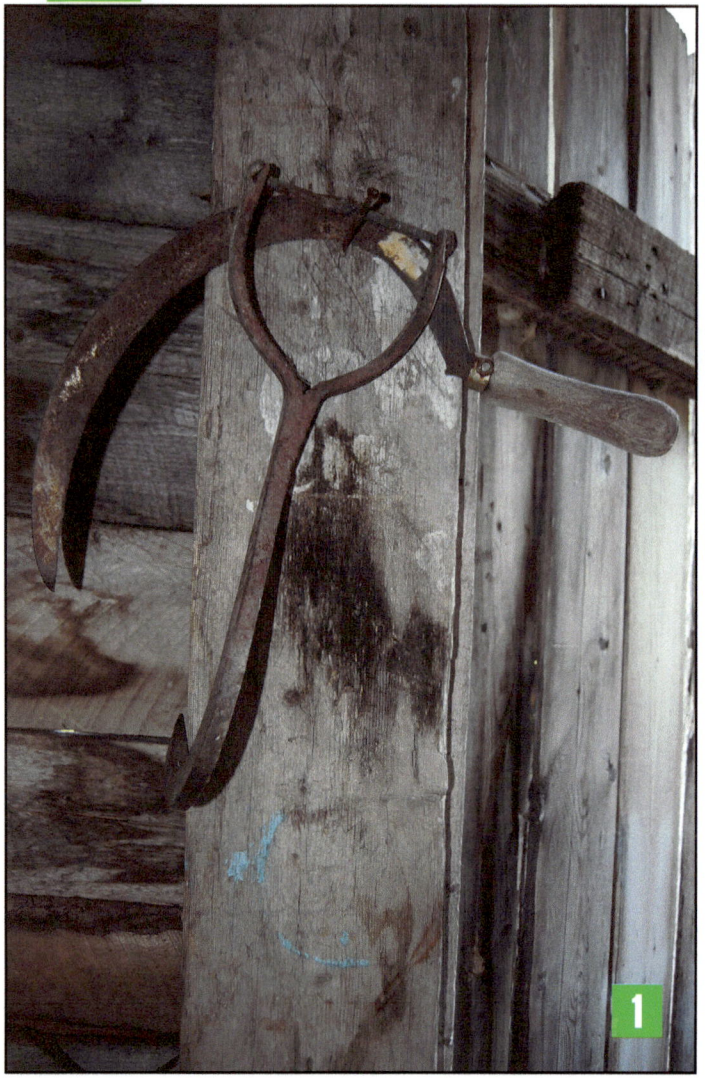

1 **Hook and Sickle** Photograph.

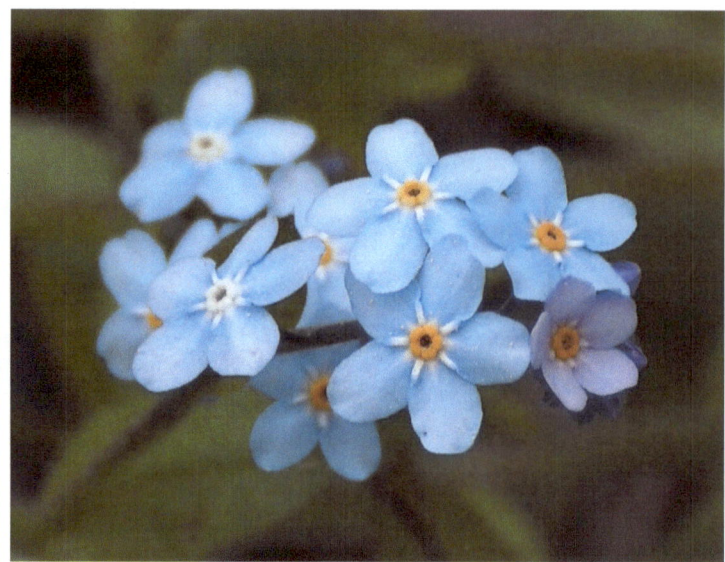

JOËL LAROSE

LOCATION: Waterloo
EMAIL: Joel.larose@gmail.com

Joël Larose is the partner and muse of the editor, who listens calmly to all his frustrations about publishing, and more importantly helps with decisions when late nights have taken their toll. He is a blackbelt martial artist, programs computers, and has extensive knowlege of Tarot symbolism, Astrology and ancient Japan. He is currently exploring the world of photography.

2 **10 Percent** Photograph.　　3 **Ant Oograh** Photograph.

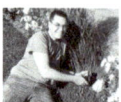

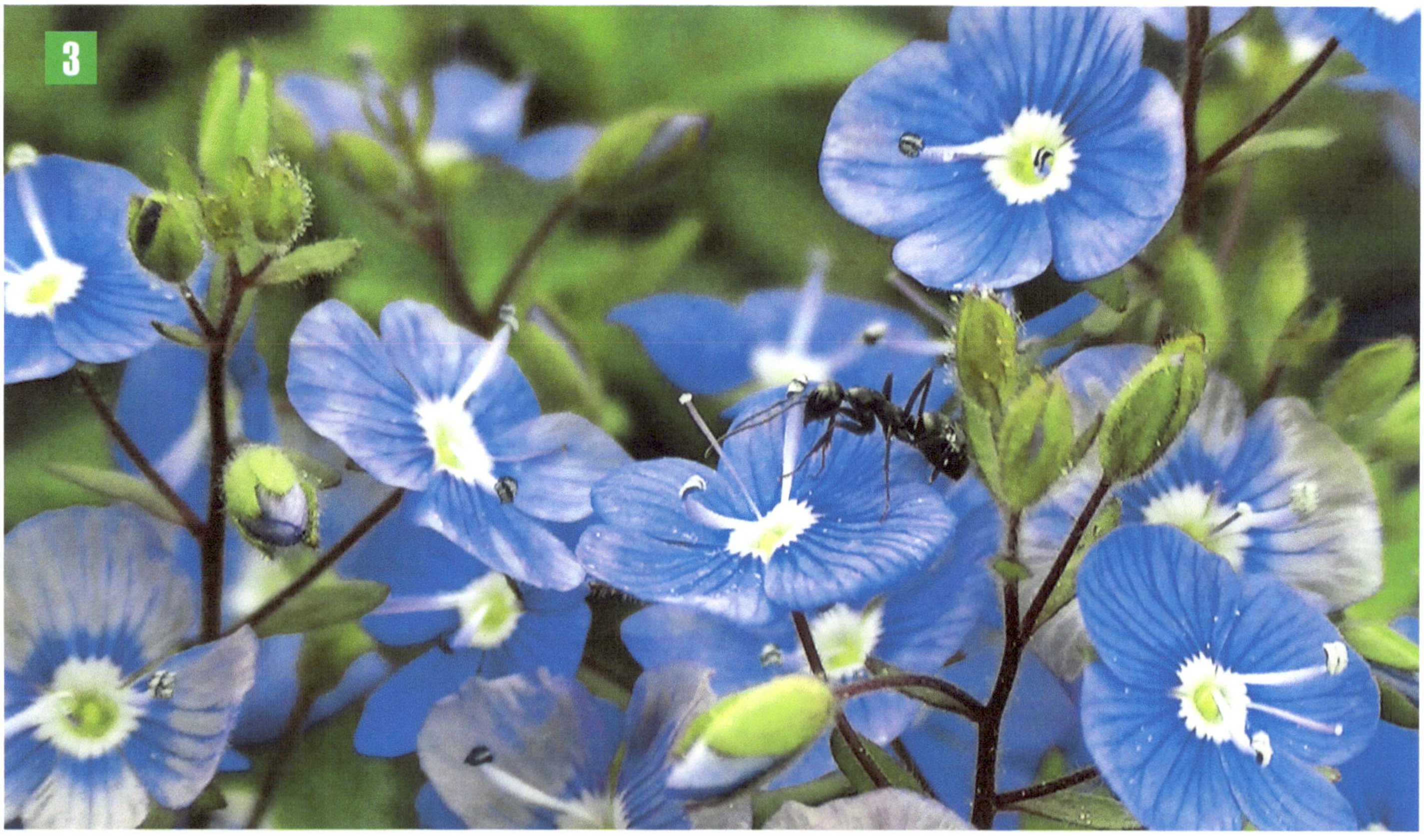

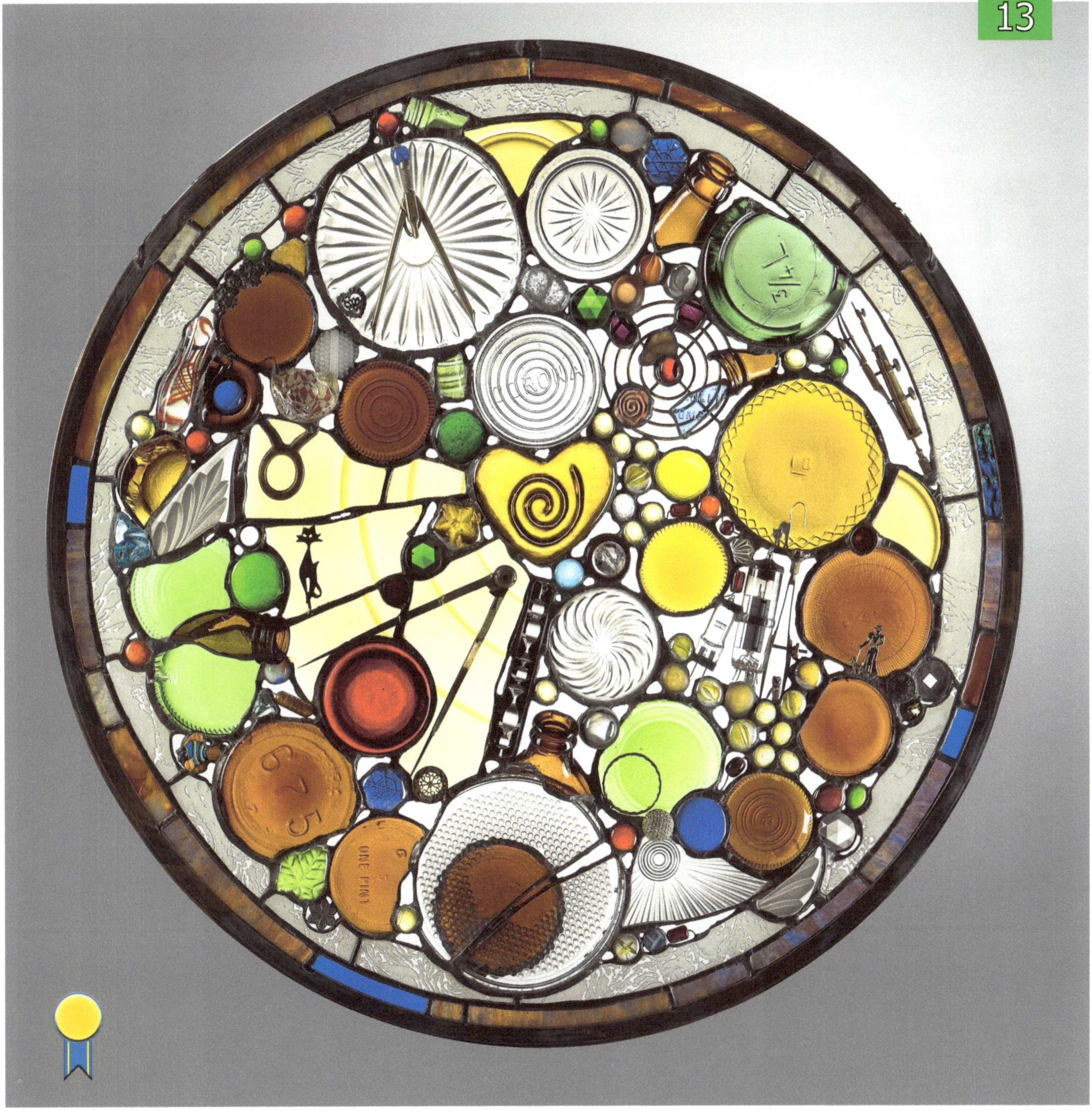

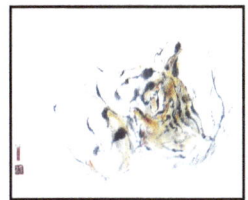

BARBARA BRYCE "3 CATS, 1 DOG, A FISH AND 4 COMPASSES"

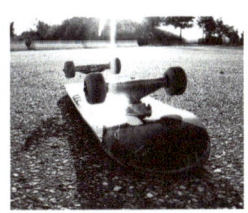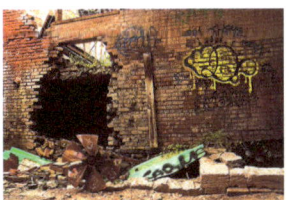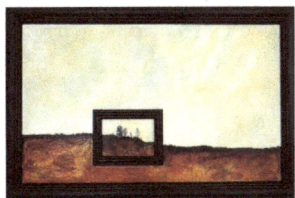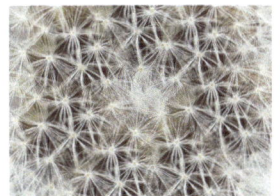

JOËL'S SHORT LIST

BARBARA BRYCE "3 CATS, 1 DOG, A FISH AND 4 COMPASSES"
▶ **Kevin W. Kreller** "SKATING"
▶ **Emily Beatty Imagery** "WONDERWALL"
▶ **Karin Silverstone** "FRAMED TREES"
▶ **Traci Cottingham** "SEEDS OF WISHES"
▶ **Roslyn Levin** "TIGER NAP"

**NOW ON
WITH THE
SHOW** ⇨

DEB JEFFERY

LOCATION: Baden
WEB: debjeffery.ca
EMAIL: debjeffery@rogers.com

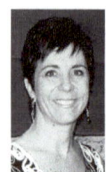

Deb is a physician who studied fine art as a mature student at the University of Waterloo. She paints out of her rural studio in Philipsburg. Using nature as her inspiration, Deb uses multiple media to create her mostly abstract paintings.

1 Allegro 19.5x24" Mixed media monoprint on paper.

2 Flamenco 19.5x"32" Mixed media monoprint on raw canvas.

3 Bridged 28x28" Acrylic and Oil on canvas.

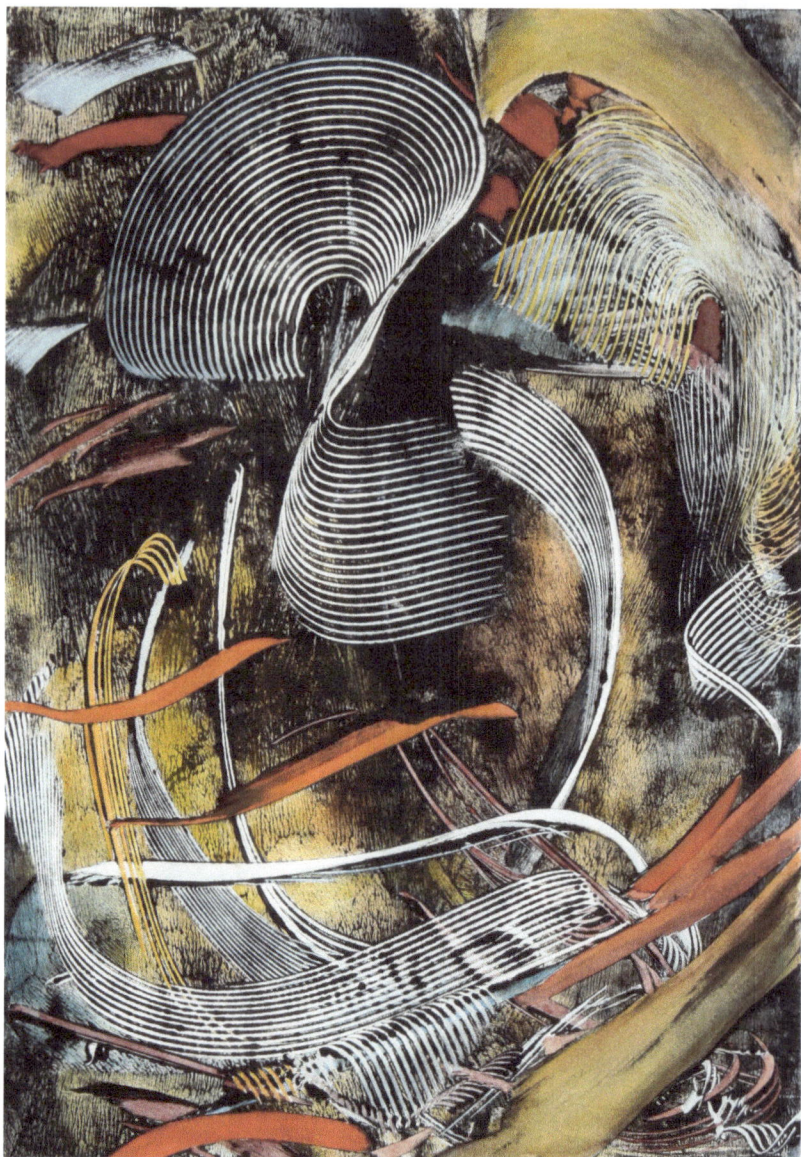

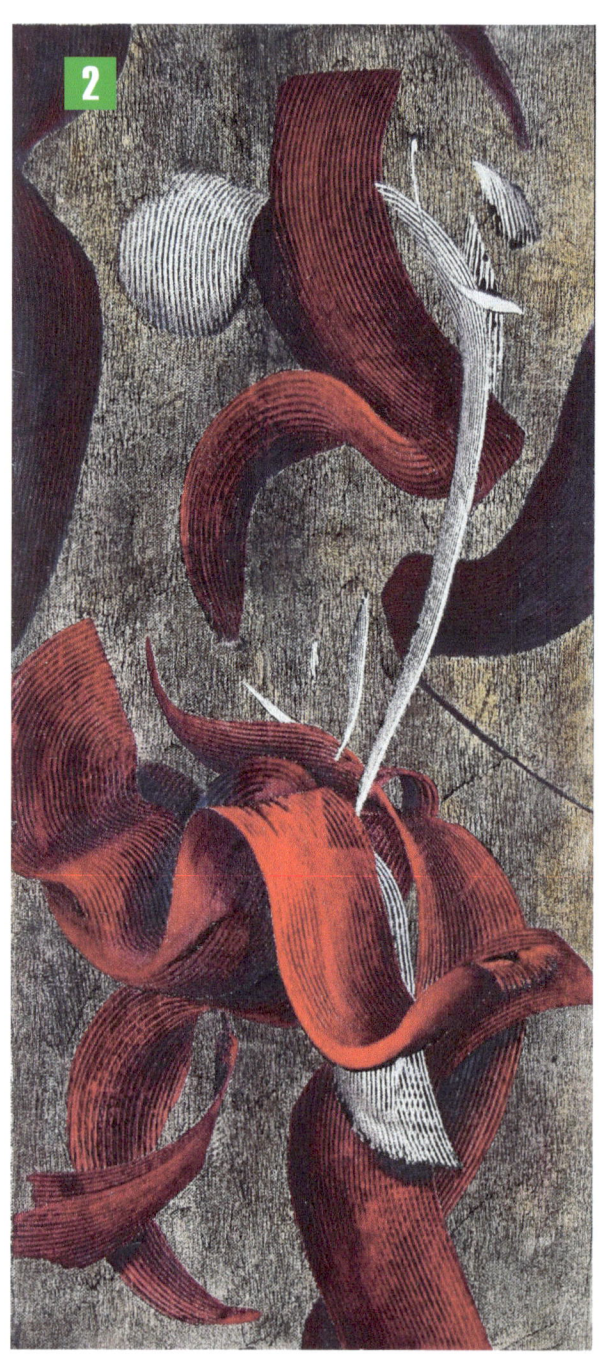

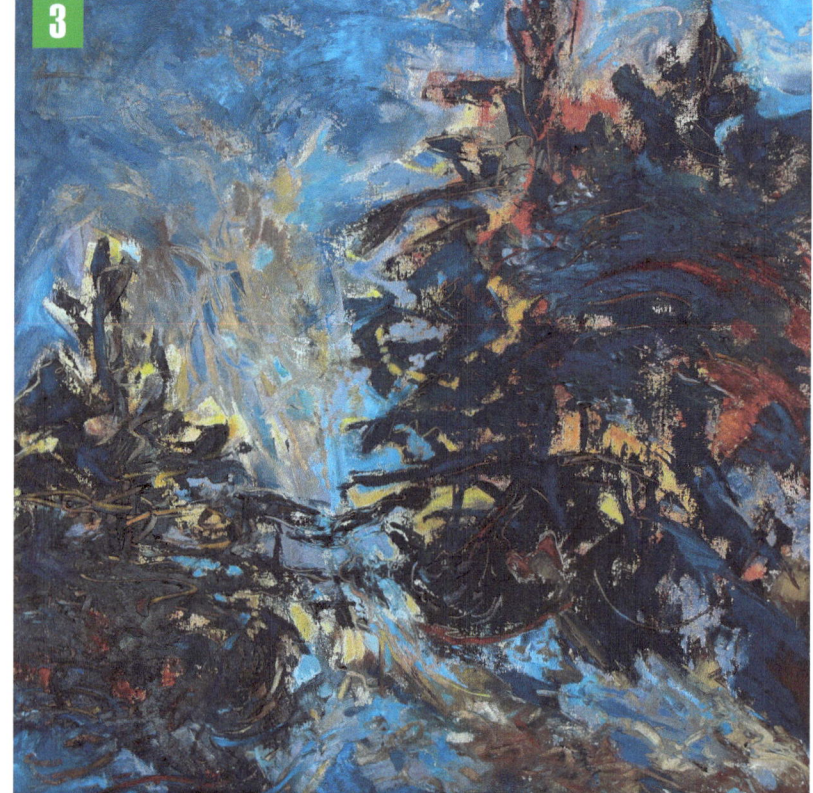

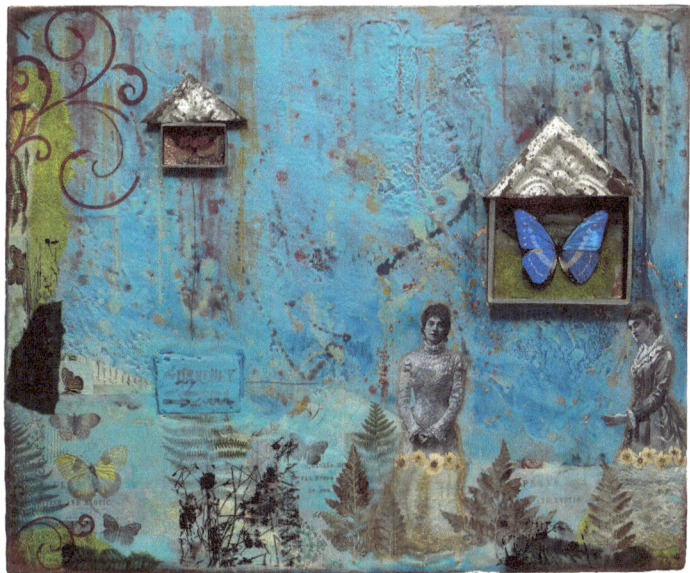

1 **The Journey** 30x24" Encaustic Mixed Media Collage, 2009.

2 **Taking Flight** 12x24" Encaustic Mixed Media Collage, 2009.

SUPRIA KARMAKAR

LOCATION: Fergus
WEB: supriasdesigns.com
EMAIL: info@supriasdesigns.com

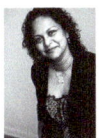
Raised in England and of East Indian heritage, Supria Karmakar has displayed an inclination to artistic creation from her childhood to her adult years. Inspired by diverse life experiences born of Eastern and Western cultures coming together, Supria uses the encaustic mixed media collage, as well as the altered book mediums as avenues to work out her musings about life's journey. The altered book and the encaustic mixed media collage medium is the perfect vessel for her work, as they unfold stories, contain depth, intrigue, vibrancy and the unknown.

"It is above all by the imagination that we achieve perception and compassion and hope." Ursula K.Le Guin

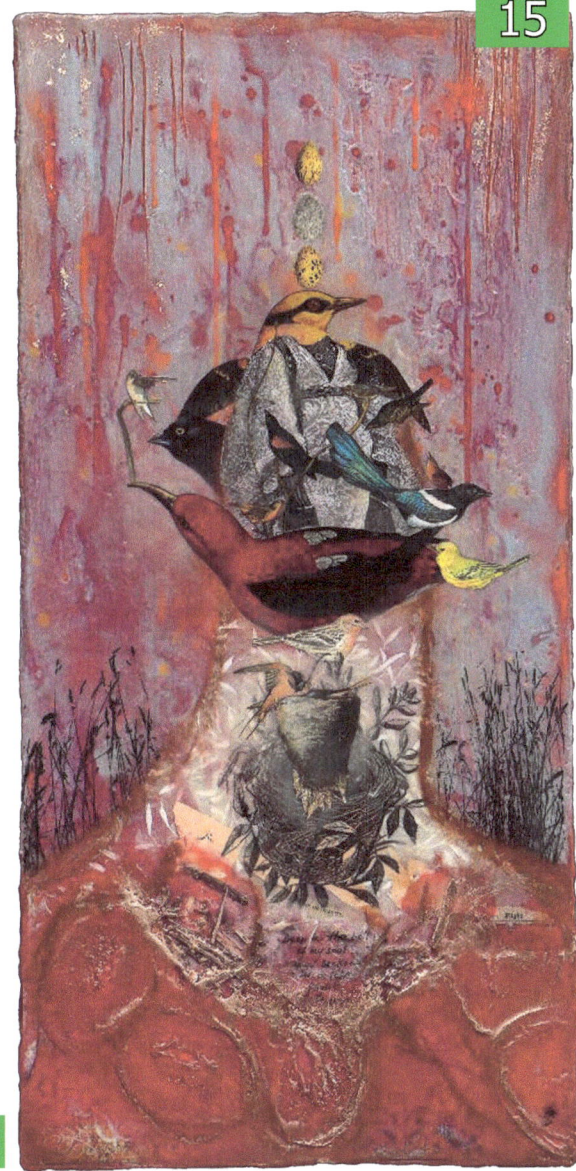

3 **Moon Dance** 34x18" Encaustic Mixed Media Collage, 2010.

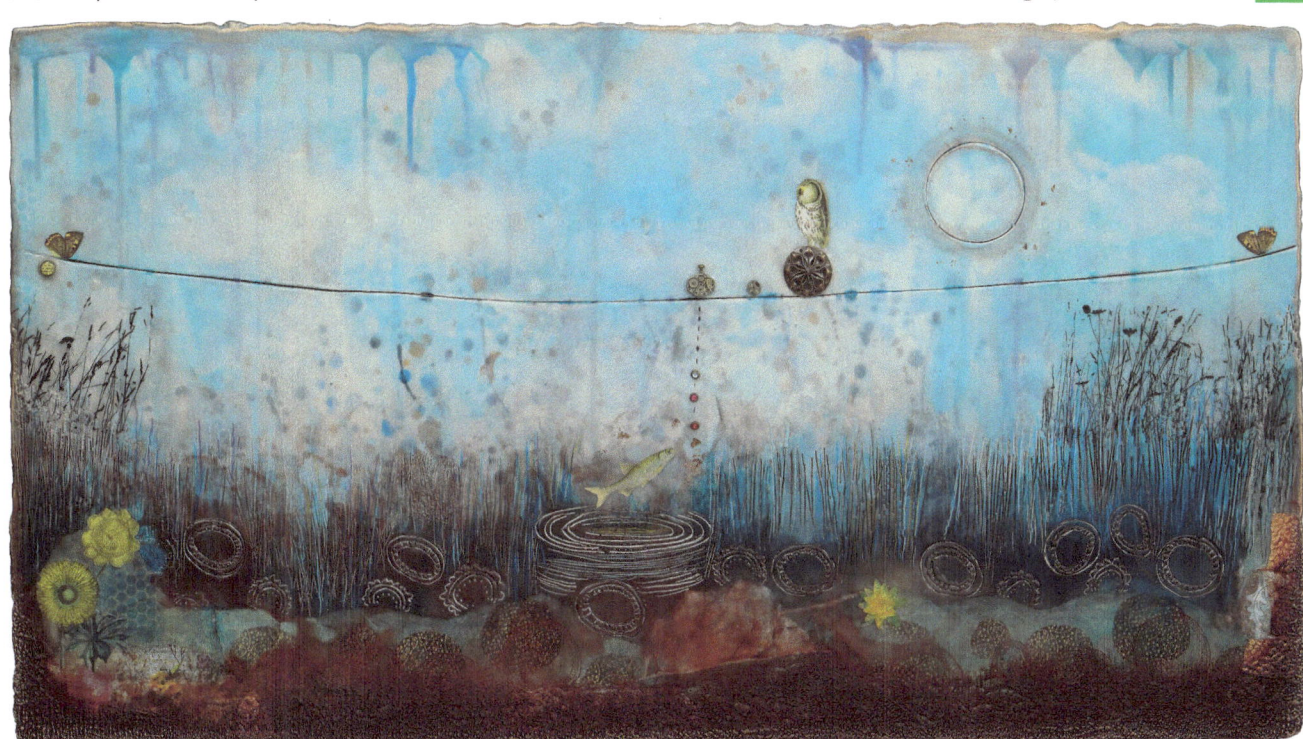

NANCY YULE

LOCATION: Cambridge
WEB: nancyyule.com
EMAIL: nancy@nancyyule.com

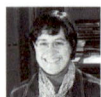

We all have an intimate relationship with fabric during our lifetimes. Life begins swaddled in a blanket and ends in a burial shroud. Although we take cloth for granted, I am enamoured with all of it's qualities. It's fluidity, texture, tactility, colour, the list seems endless. My artistry had developed through self-experimentation with fibre most of my life and I feel the journey has only just begun. Being an adventurous stitcher, I am always asking the questions: What if? Can I? What happens when I stitch paper to fabric? Can I stitch through metal? I experiment with different materials to create variations in texture. At the heart of each project, is my love for COLOUR! A magical union is when art meets function. My fibre artwork is often in the form of a fashion accessory or a vessel. My pieces have been purchased and sent around the world. What is my adventurous spirit pondering now? What would happen if I…. I invite the curious to come along to witness my journey with every stitch I create.

1 **A Real Jewel** Fabric collage, silk, copper.

2 **Emergence - Circles** Hog intestine and machine lace.

3 **Fragile Childhood** Tea bags, paper.

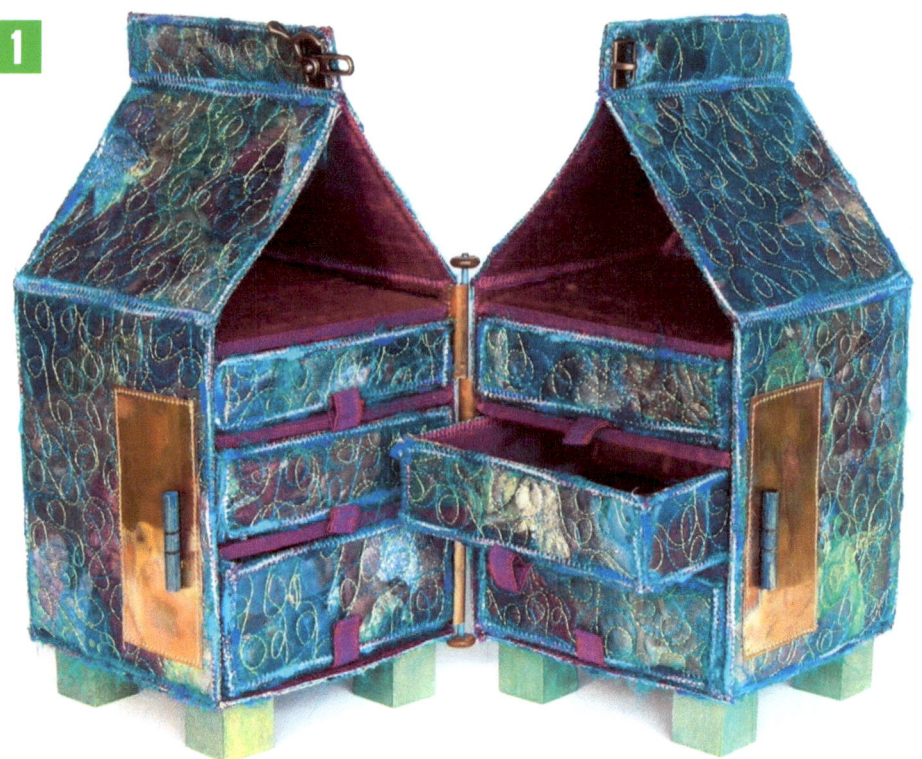

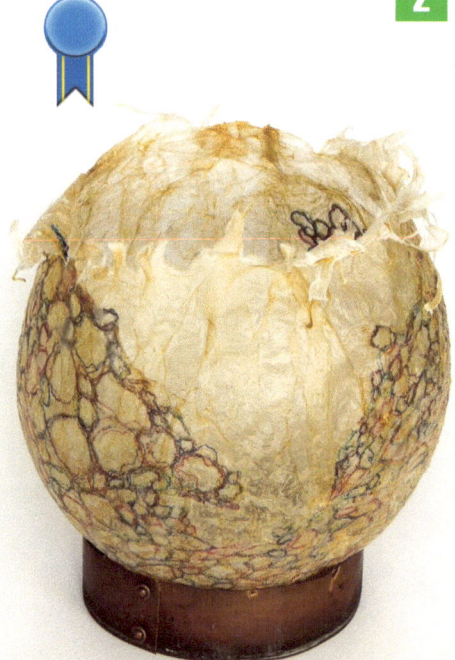

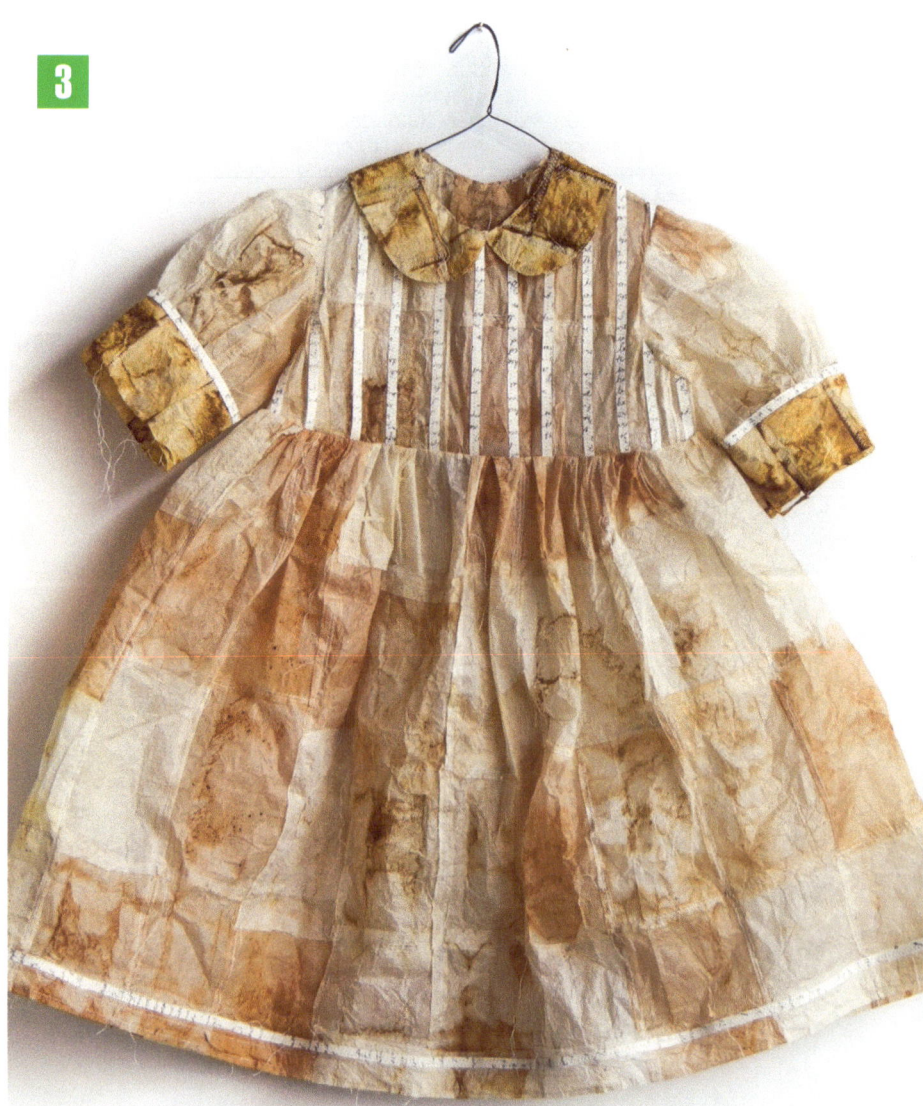

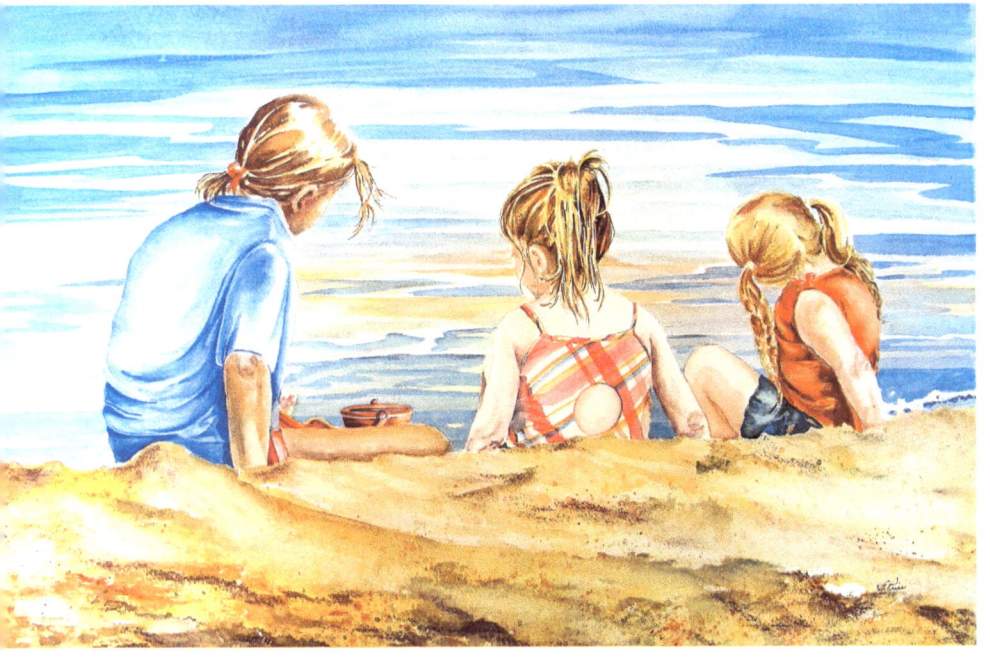

TIINA PRICE

LOCATION: Blair (Cambridge)
WEB: tiinapriceart.ca
EMAIL: tiinaprice@rogers.com

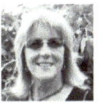

Tiina Price is a retired educator with a passion for watercolours. She combines her love of nature, of architecture, and of travel into translucent paintings. She is a member of the Kitchener Waterloo Society of Artists and Studio 30 in Cambridge; and has taken part in many group and solo exhibitions. Her home in the village of Blair (Cambridge), is her studio and her gallery. She also exhibits regularly at Gallery M in Cambridge and is a regular member of the Cambridge Studio Tour Show and Sale each September.

1 Sand Castles 20x27″ Capturing the feel of the sun, sand and childhood innocence was the challenge here.

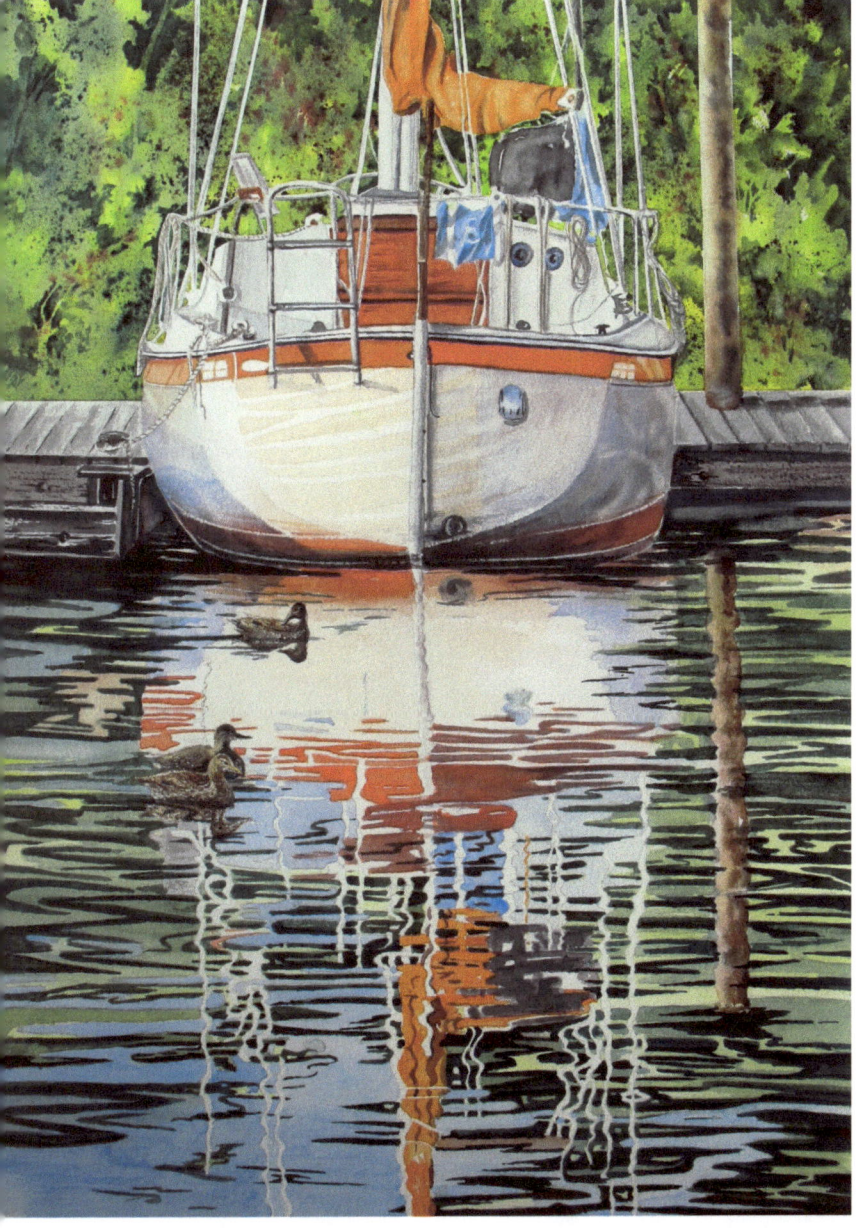

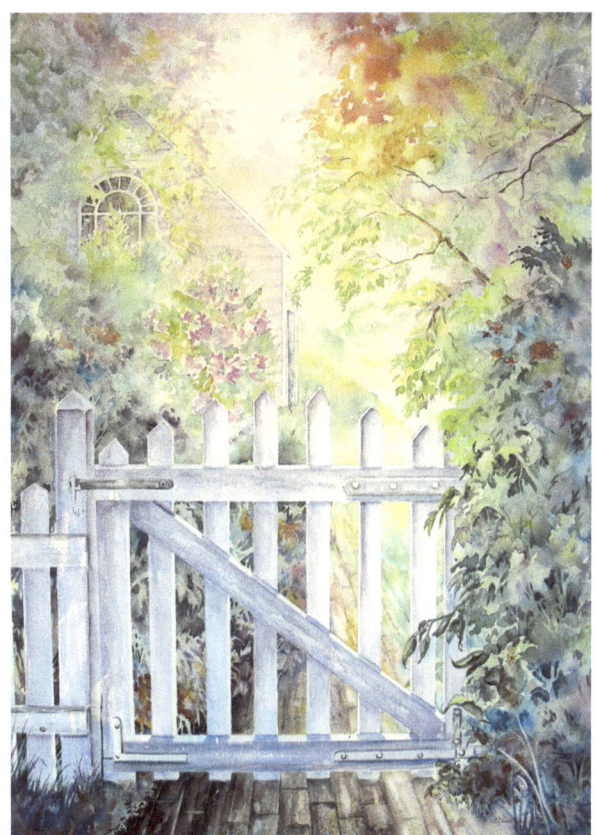

2 Tranquility Bay 31x25″ The light & reflections caught my eye in this quiet bay in Deep River, Ontario.

3 The Garden Gate 38x30¾″ Watercolour on 200lb watercolour paper. Early morning light at a friend's home in Virginia inspired this painting.

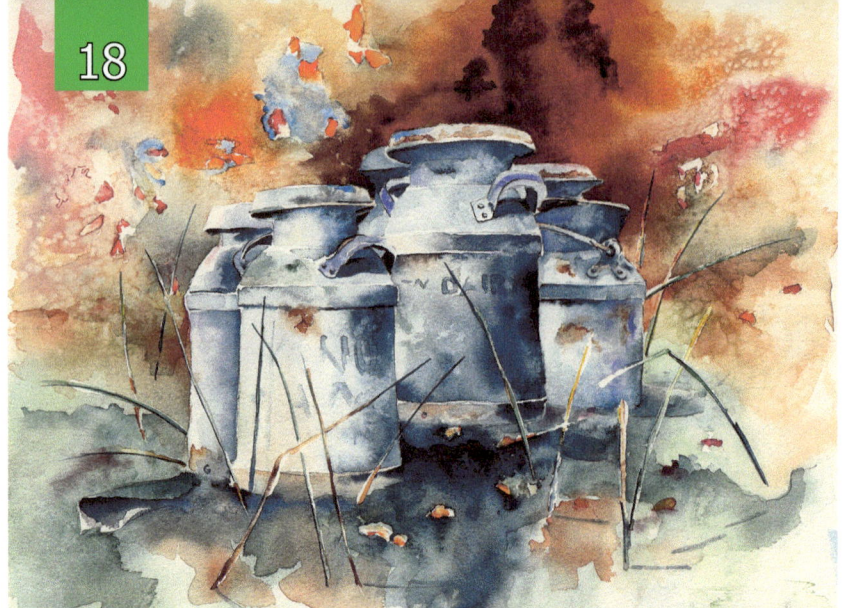

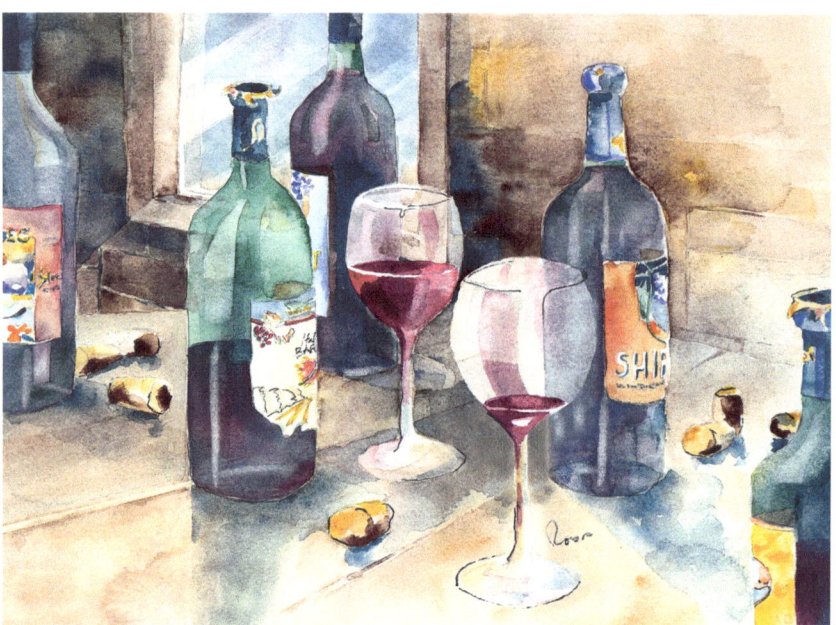

ROSS HAMILTON

LOCATION: Guelph
WEB: (N/A)
EMAIL: rosshamilton@rogers.com

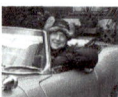

Ross Hamilton produces some rather exquisite photographs of automobiles and other interesting subjects. And if this isn't enough, Ross will then turn to his skills to produce some delightful works in the very challenging medium of watercolours. Living in Guelph, Ontario, a lovely community northwest of Metropolitan Toronto he never forgets what touches people's lives. Ross brings an understanding to his paintings that the viewer feels wonderfully caught up in a story. He has developed a sensitive style that is expressive, yet realistic. The viewer of his paintings will want to step right into the picture and share the moment. He is a member of the West Hills Art Group.

1 **Once Delivered** 10x14" Watercolour.

2 **Party of Three** 10x14" Watercolour.

3 **Control** 10x14" Watercolour.

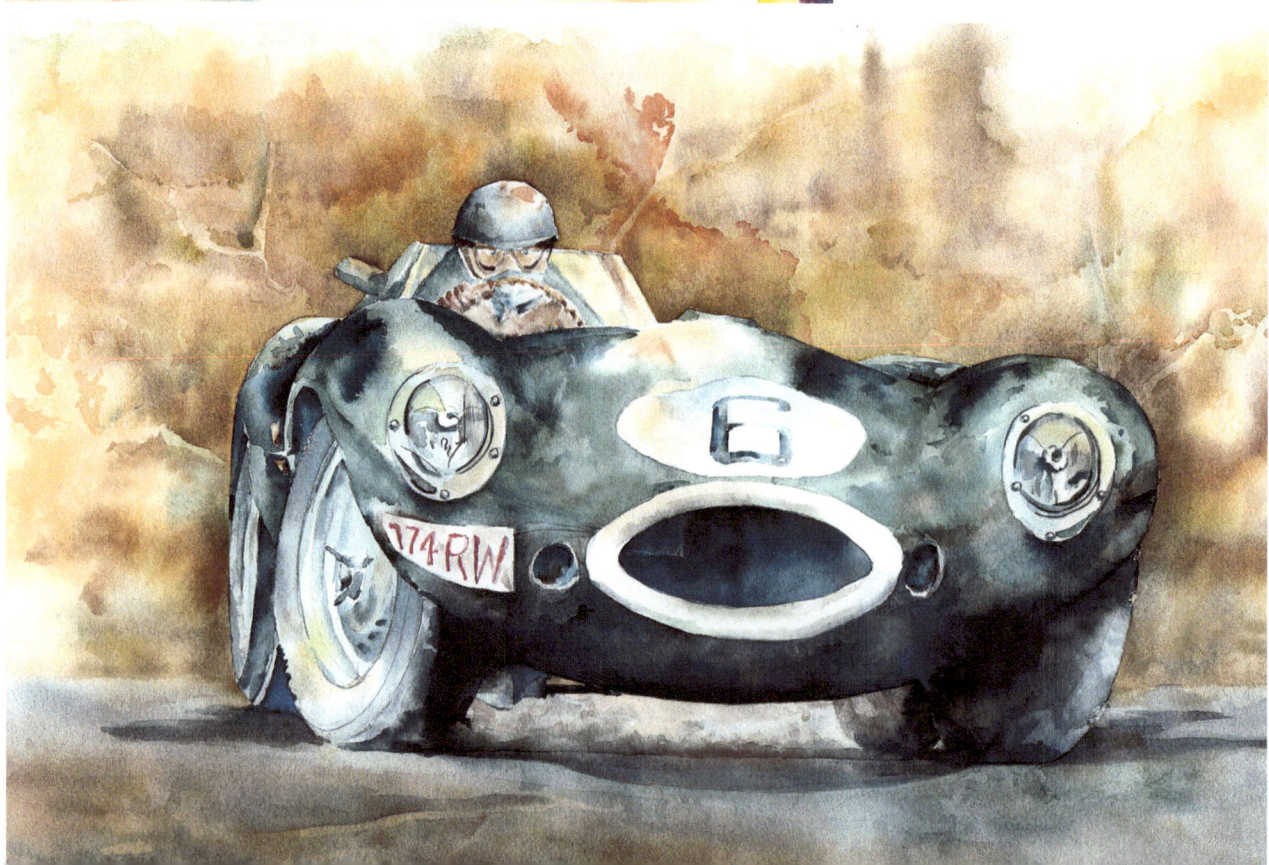

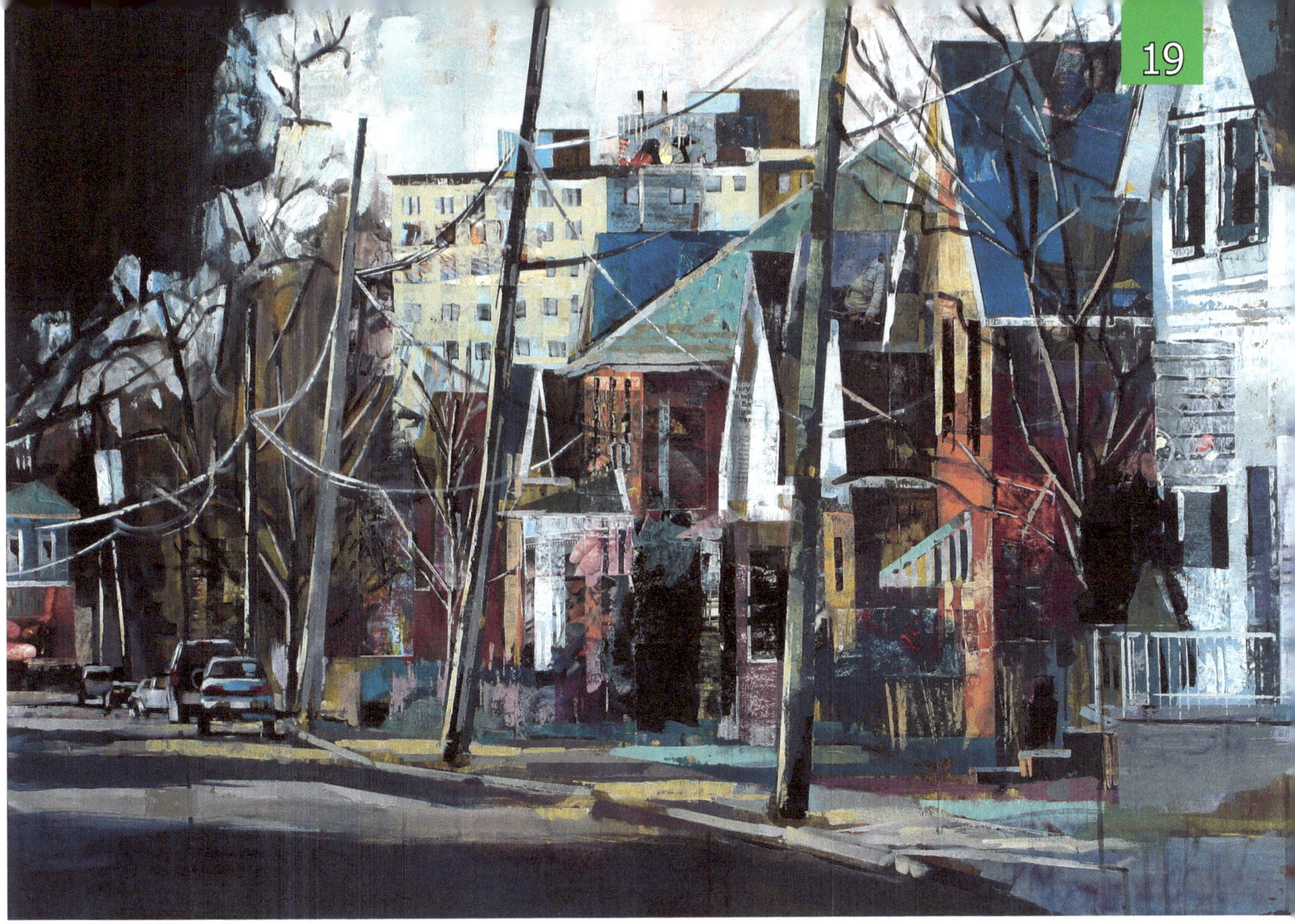

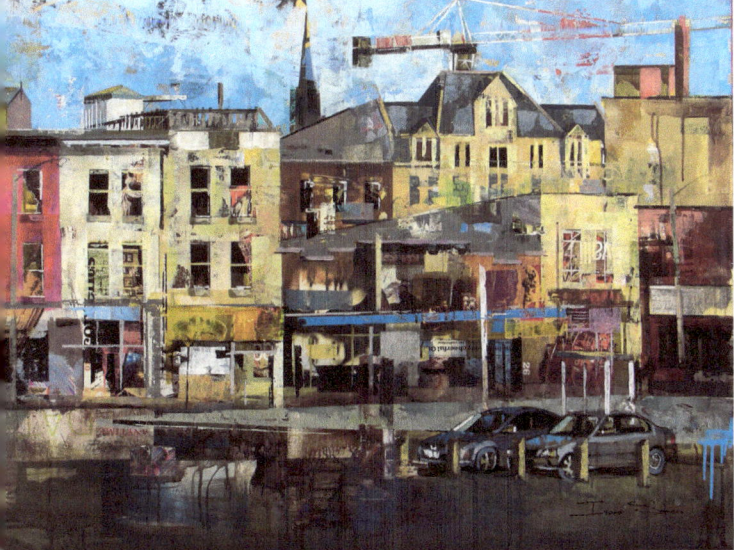

IVANO STOCCO

LOCATION: Guelph
WEB: ivanostocco.com
EMAIL: ivano_s@hotmail.com

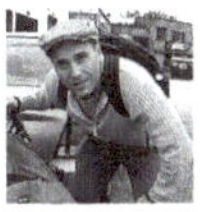

Ivano Stocco splits his time between Guelph, where he maintains a studio which was once a horse barn in his backyard, and Valencia, Spain. He is fascinated with urban landscapes and expressionism and paints in mixed media in a variety of formats, both in acrylic and oil. In Spain he participates in dozens of plein air painting contests per year and has won many recognitions and awards. In addition to being an artist, Ivano is a father, translator, and writer of prose fiction.

1 The Ward 45x35" Acrylic, oil, and collage on panel.

2 Wyndham 45x35" Acrylic and collage on panel.

3 First Day of Fall 39x28" Acrylic, oil, and collage on panel.

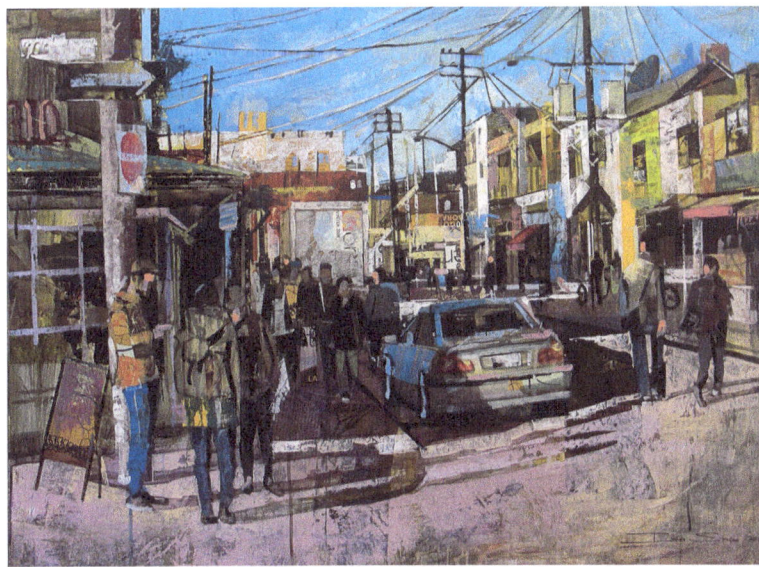

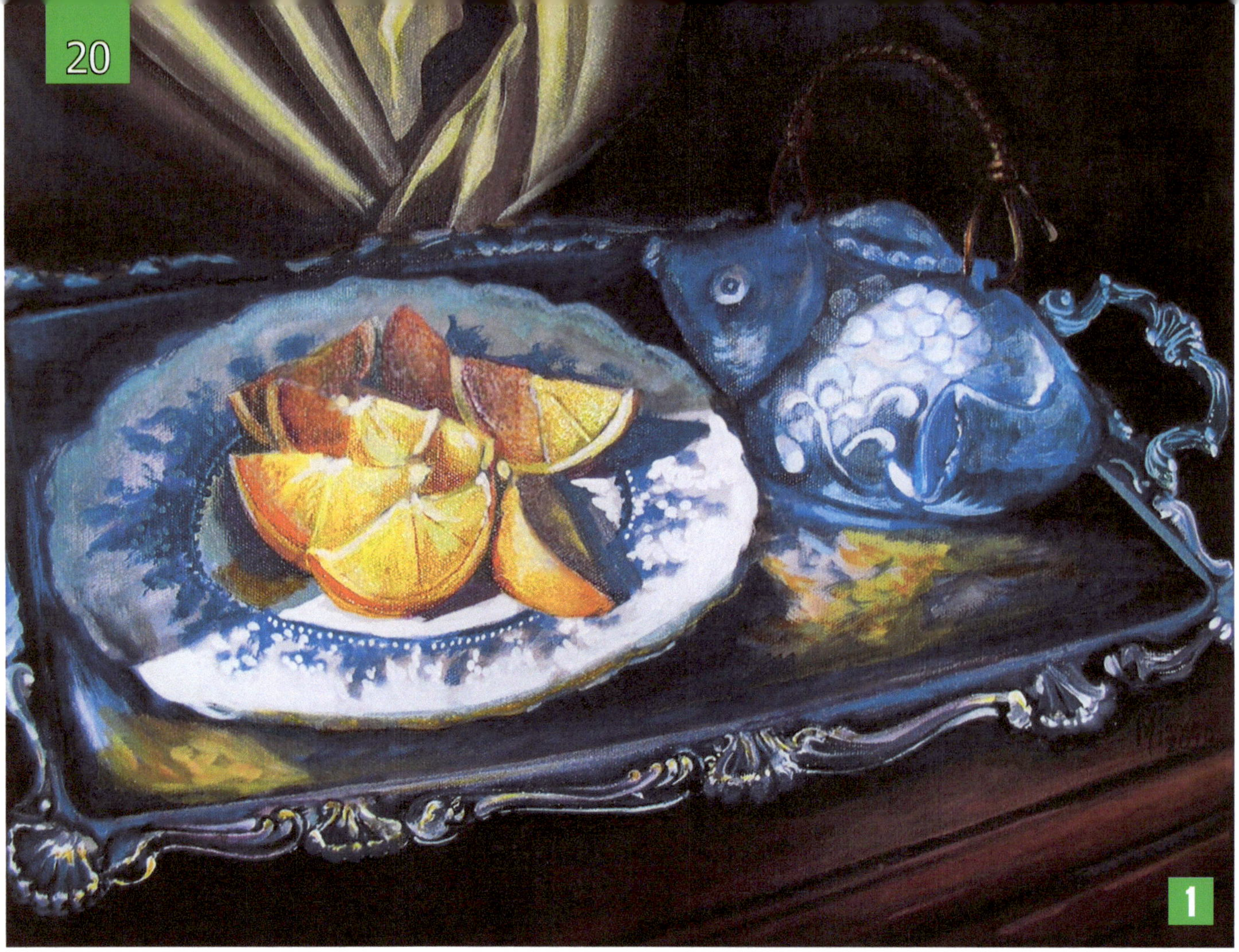

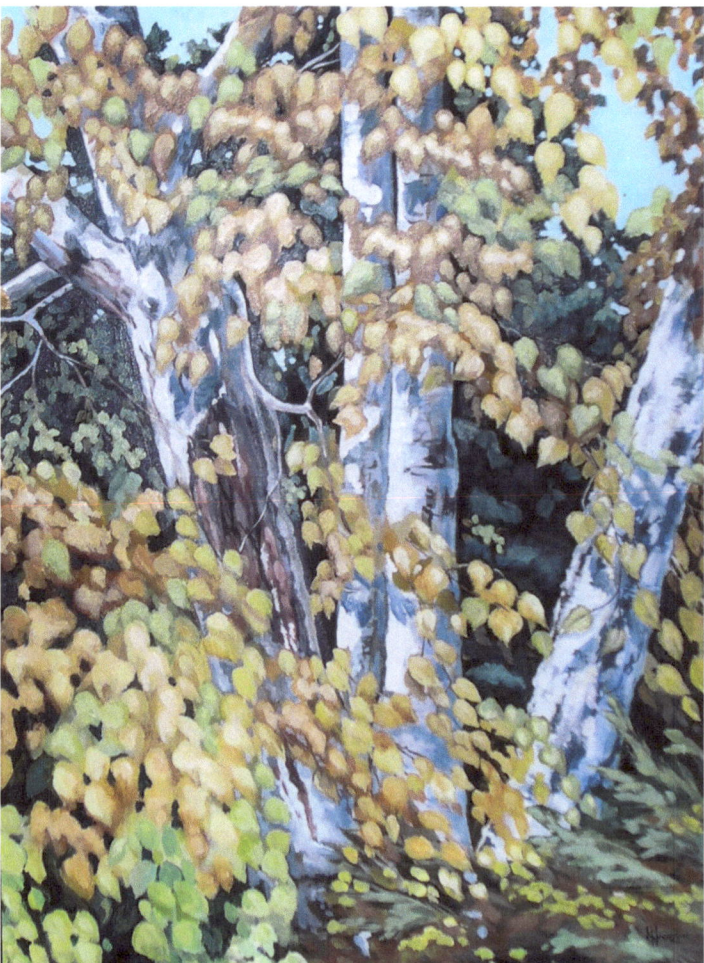

1 **Tea and Oranges** 14x18" Acrylic on Canvas.

2 **Chandelier** 48x48" Acrylic on Canvas.

3 **Autumn Birch** 24x31" Acrylic on Canvas.

MICHELE JONES

LOCATION: Cambridge
WEB: zhibit.org/michelejones
EMAIL: michelejonesartist@gmail.com

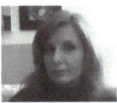

Michele graduated from O.C.A.D in 1990. She studied fine art and has worked as a mural artist in Toronto ever since. Moving to Cambridge in the last year has introduced her to an eclectic group of artist which has given her the inspiration to put brush to canvas. Discovering her new surroundings has provided a plethora of subject matter.

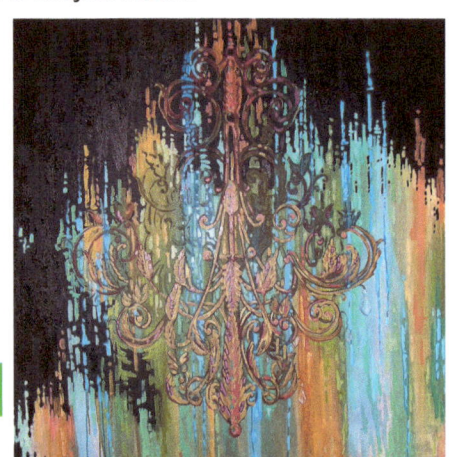

1 **Production Space** 24x36"
Digital media, acrylic.

2 **New Frontiers** 24x36" Digital
media, acrylic.

1

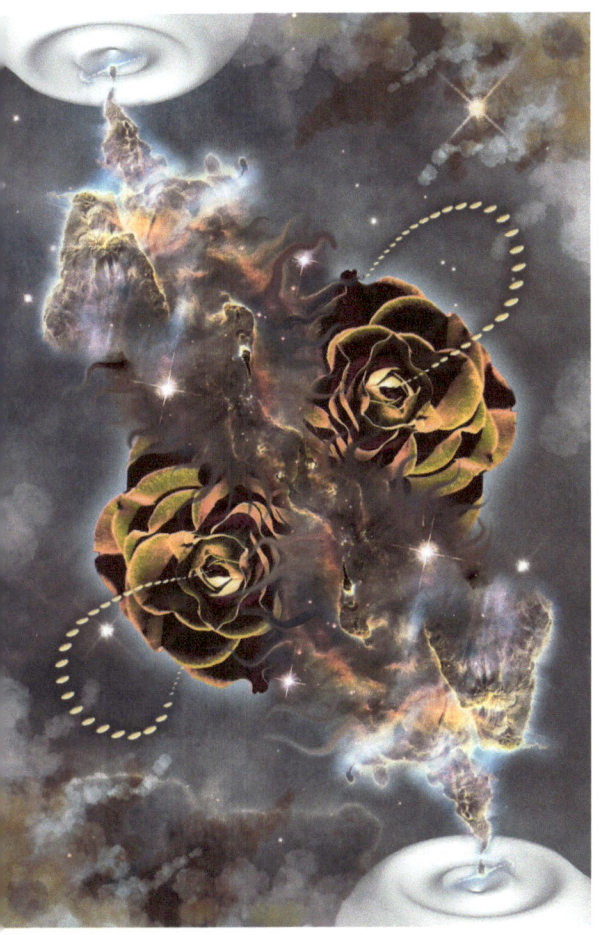

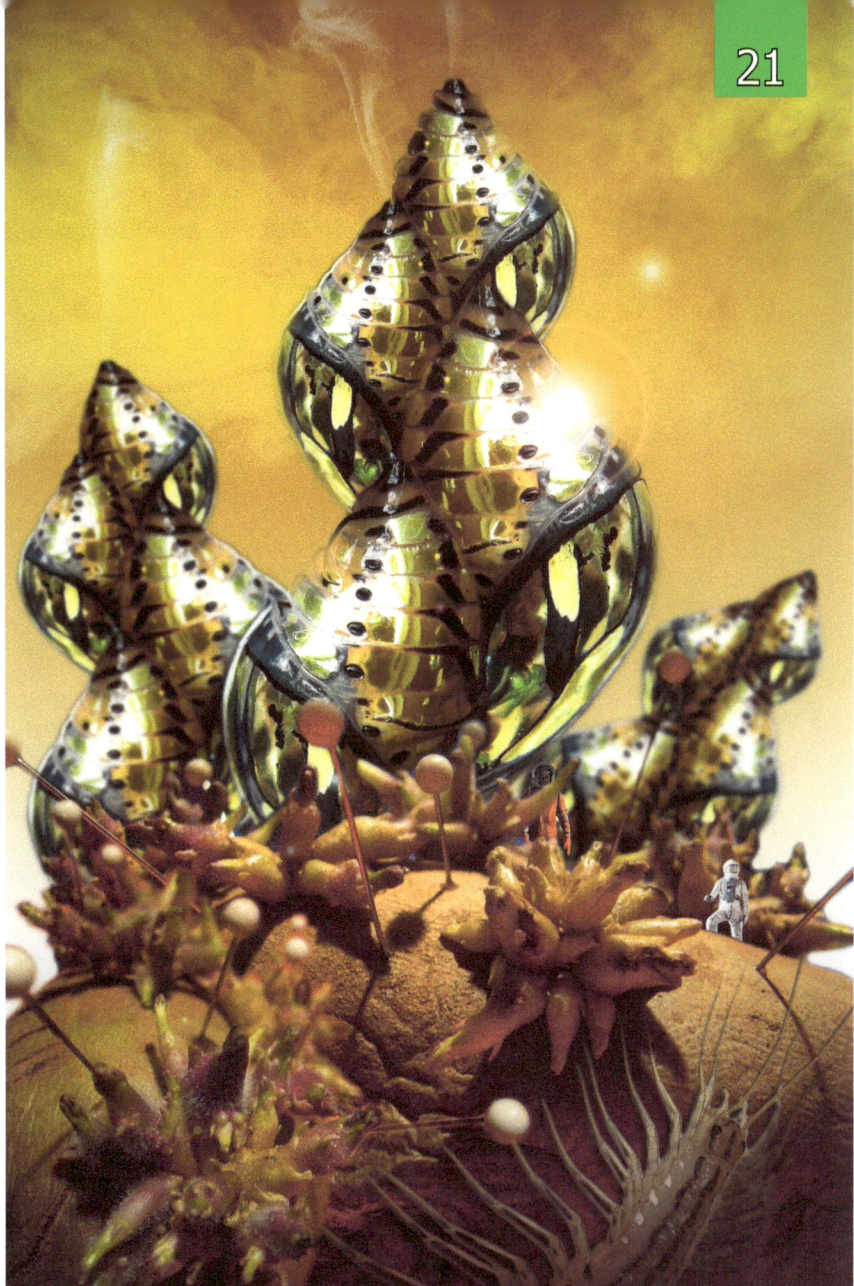

2

CAMERON STEWART

LOCATION: Guelph
WEB: cjsfolio.tumblr.com/
EMAIL: emptycentre@gmail.com

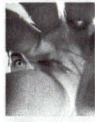 Cameron Stewart is an Artist/
Graphic designer and gradu-
ate of the University of Guelph
Fine Arts program, specializing in Sculpture & Digital
Media. His interests are in the
dichotomy of the natural world and the
emerging virtual landscape, and the ever
diminishing distance between them.
Through a recombination of computer
generated content and digital imagery
his work creates surrealist dreamscapes
that weave these natural and virtual en-
vironments into a new hybrid reality.

3 **All From None** 18.5x24"
Digital media, acrylic.

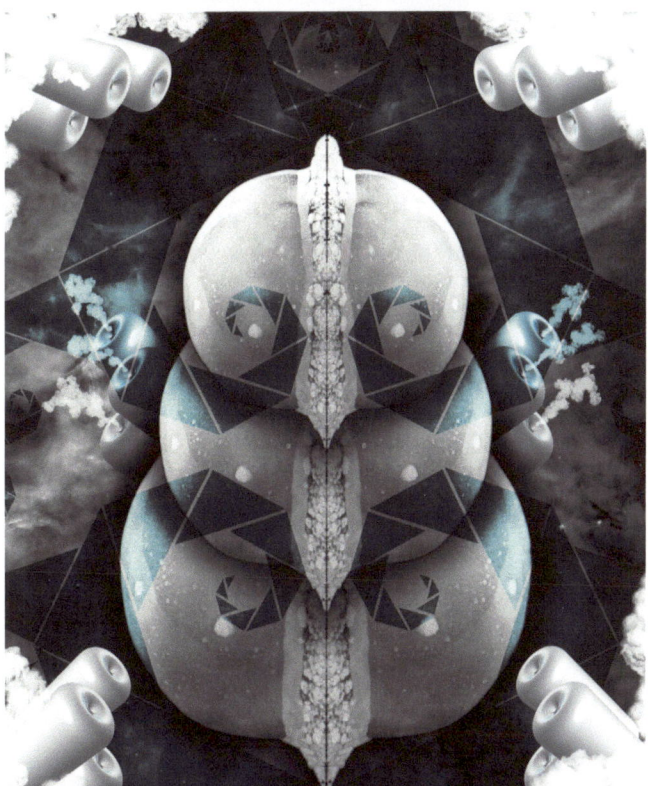

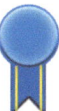

3

1 Garden of Eden 31x44"

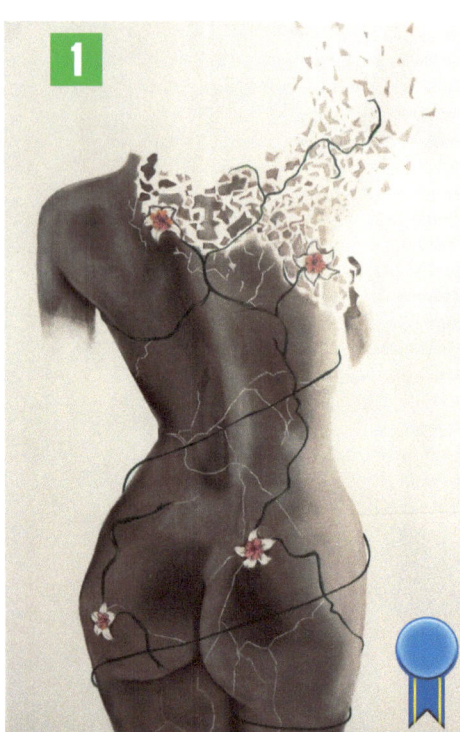

CARINA FRANCIOSO

LOCATION: Cambridge Guelph
WEB: (N/A)
EMAIL: carina@live.ca

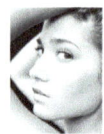

Several trips to Italy have helped Carina stay in touch with her Italian roots and she has always been intrigued by the fact that the cultural identity of her ancestors lies deeply rooted in the art and religion of the people. As a recent graduate of the University of Waterloo, with a major in Fine Arts and a minor in Italian Language, Carina strives to bring out the best elements of her heritage in the work she produces. From the beautiful and seductive form of the nude body that was loved and appreciated by the great masters, to the serene and romantic rooftops of the basilicas and cathedrals of Italy, Carina creates personal pieces from a culture that is widely accepted and loved around the world.

2 **Piazza Venezia, Roma** 30x40" My first architectural painting.

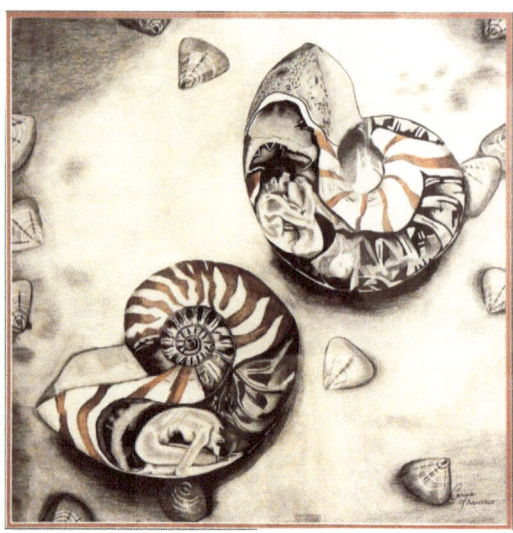

3

3 **Discovery** 25x25" Capturing the idea of Evolution. Where do we come from?

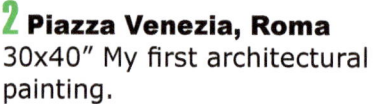

2

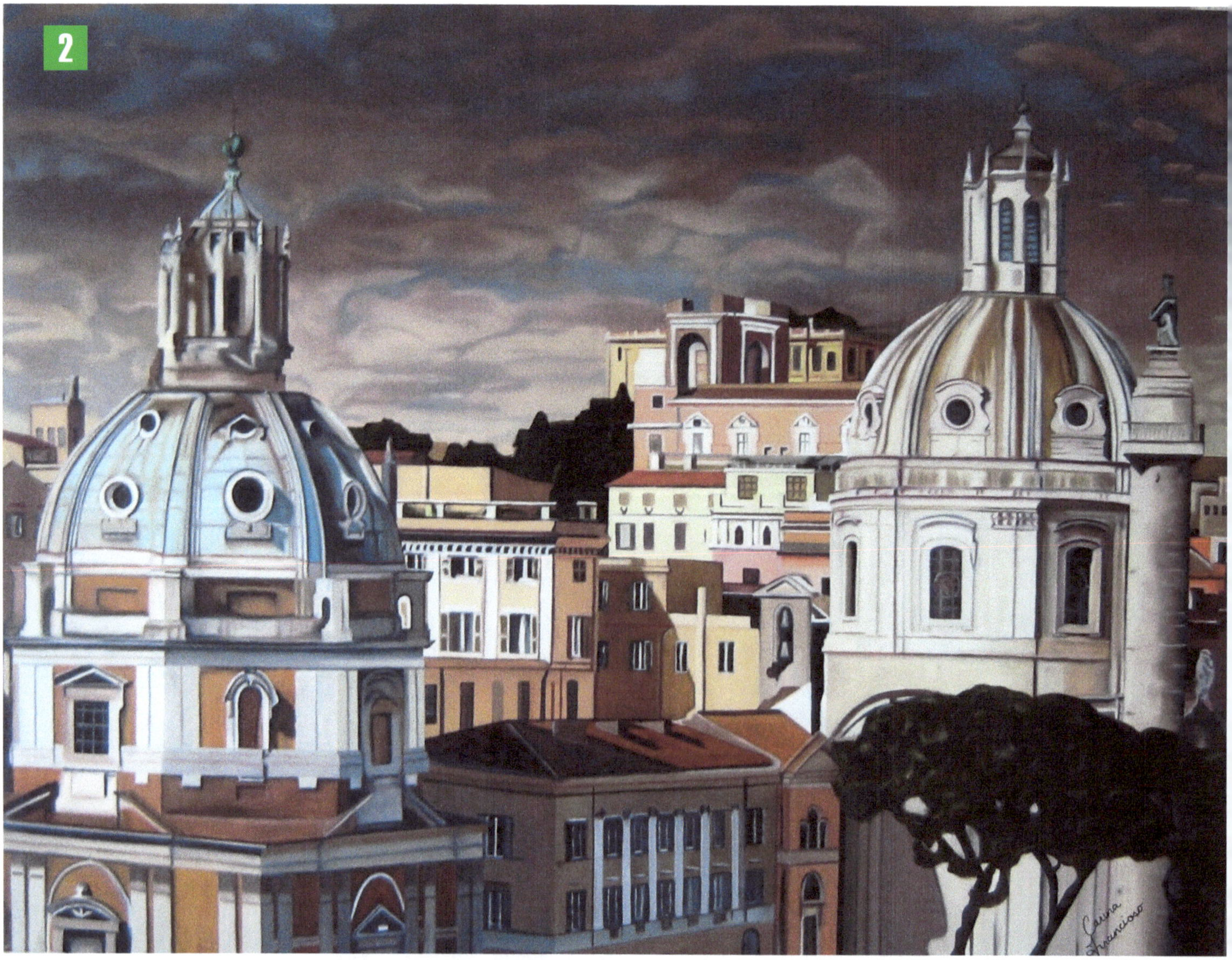

SUSAN STRACHAN JOHNSON

LOCATION: Everton
WEB: strachanjohnson.com
EMAIL: rooster@quican.com

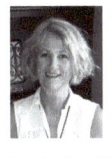

Originally trained as a painter, Susan has been working in fibre art since 2003, and her works are in private collections across Canada, the U.S., the U.K and Europe. Awards include Best in Show in Threadworks (2004), the Fibre Art award at Insights (2006), and Best in Show at Touched by Fire (2008). A member of Connections Fibre Artists since 2004, Susan has her Diploma in Stitched Textiles Design from the City & Guilds Institute, U.K. and teaches workshops in fibre art techniques throughout Southern Ontario.

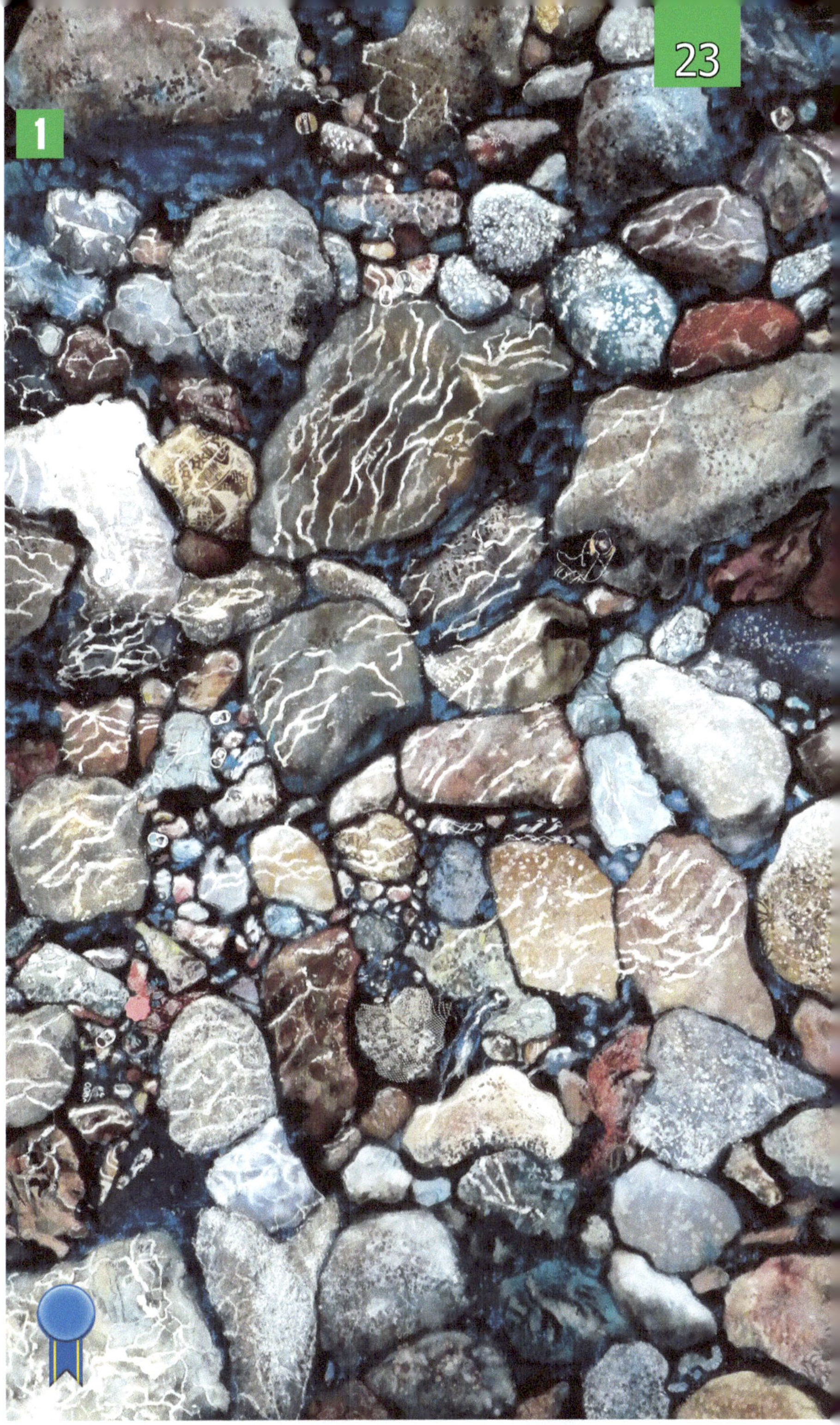

1 Clear Waters 40x66" Fabric scraps and recycled packaging on recycled denim jeans, painted stitched.

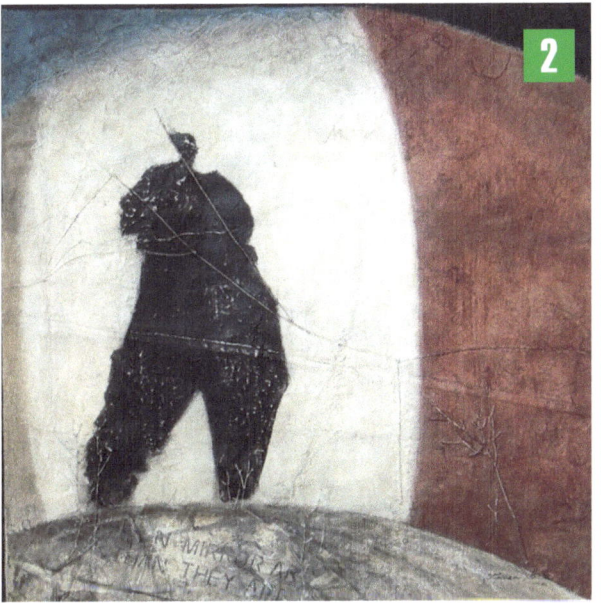

2 Closer Than She Appears 20x20" Paper collage, acrylic paint on distressed and repaired canvas.

3 Mother Universe 20x15" Paper collage and acrylic ink on distressed and repaired canvas, stitched.

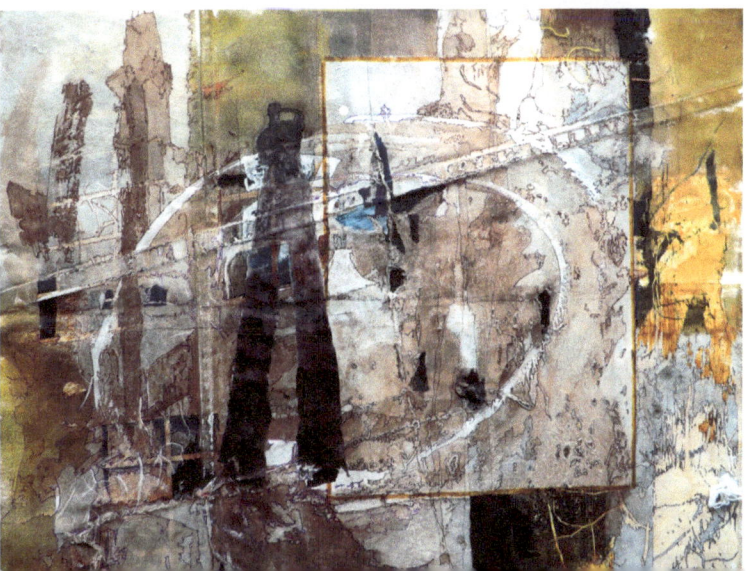

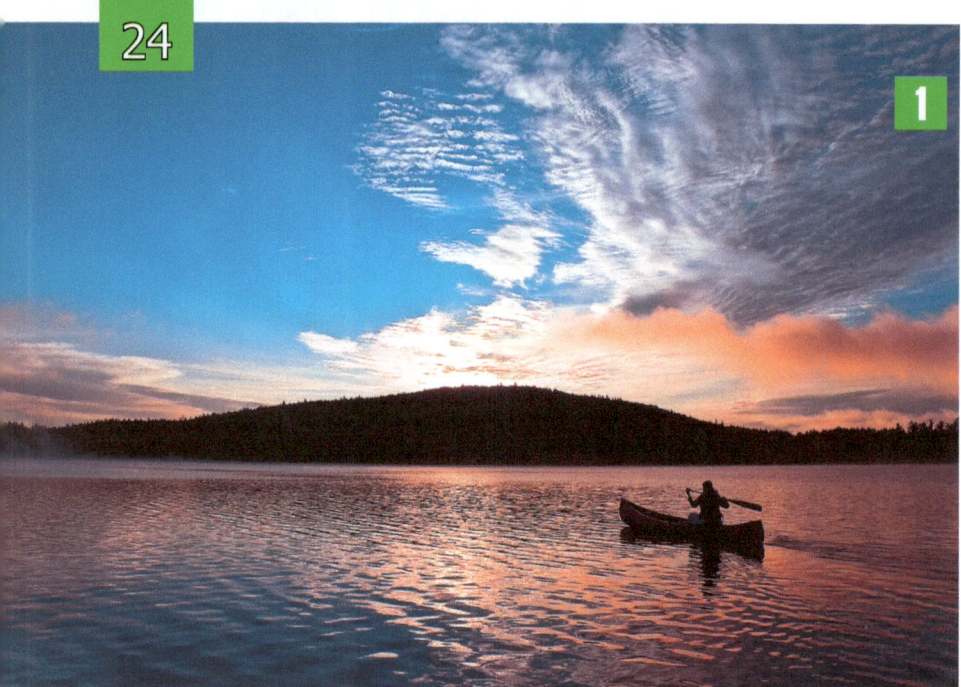

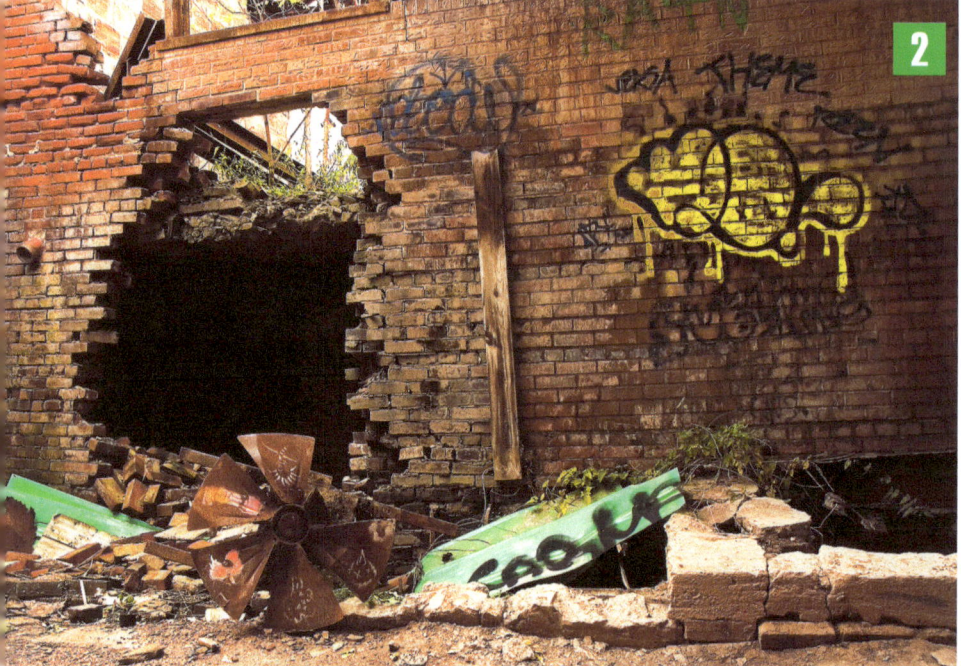

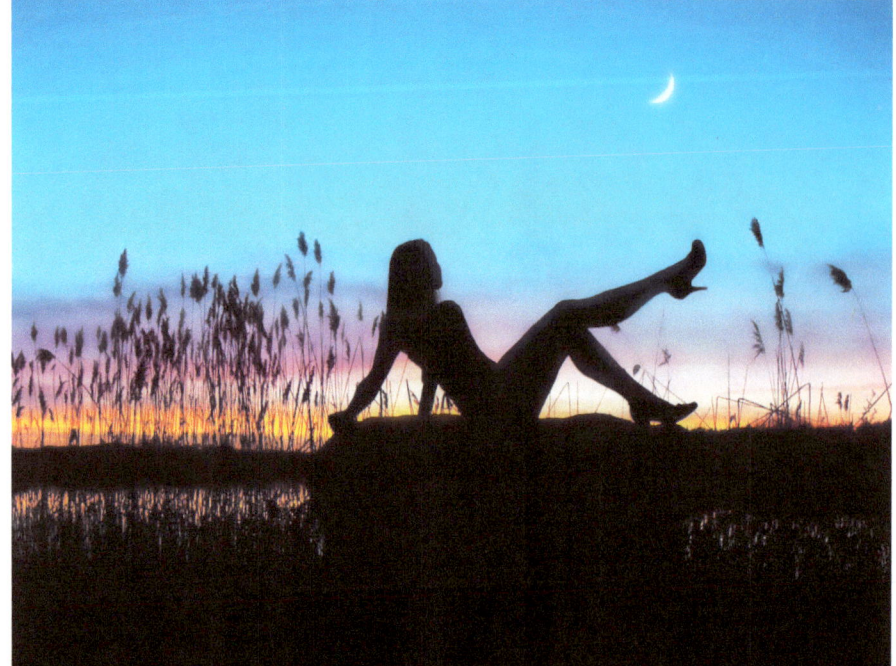

EMILY BEATTY IMAGERY

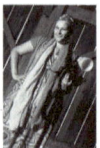

LOCATION: Belmont Village
WEB: emilybeatty.com
EMAIL: emilybeattyimagery@live.ca

Emily grew up in the country just outside of Maryhill, halfway between Guelph and KW. She has a Media Studies Degree from the University of Guelph and a Creative Photography diploma from Humber College. For her university thesis in 2006, Emily wrote about the effects that fashion photography have on women's perceptions of beauty and self esteem. Lately, she continues to explore these themes through boudoir portraits. When she's not photographing local ladies, Emily does fine art photography and traditional portraiture like wedding and family photos, as well as painting bright mixed media canvases. Her work attempts to bring viewers a sense of wonder and joy through bold, saturated compositions. She adores shooting vibrant colours, textures, and intriguing images of everyday items for local art shows and her business, Emily Beatty Imagery.

1 Dip Dip and Swing Photo 2010. A shot of the photographer's mother paddling a canoe at dawn in front of their Algonquin Park cottage.

2 Wonderwall Photo 2006. One of the photographer's favourite photos, taken at Brickworks in Toronto. A bittersweet development, this artists' playground is currently being renovated and restructured to house an organic farmer's market.

3 Untitled Photo 2008. The artist and her client snuck into an abandoned gravel pit after hours for this sunset pin-up shoot.

ZAK WHITFORD

LOCATION: Fergus and Kitchener
WEB: TheWorldThroughMyLens.ca
EMAIL: Zak@theworldthroughmylens.ca

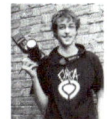

Zak started his photography business at the age of 16. Since then his work has been published in many magazines and newspapers. His goal is to keep his photography as authentic as possible making brilliant photos with minimal editing. He uses his skills as a photographer to create perfect photos with great attention to detail. Zak's services include commercial, real estate and outdoor portrait photography. He also uses his skills as a photographer to give back to his community and raises money for charity.

1 Innocence Photograph..

2 Reflection Photograph.

3 Snake Eye Photograph.

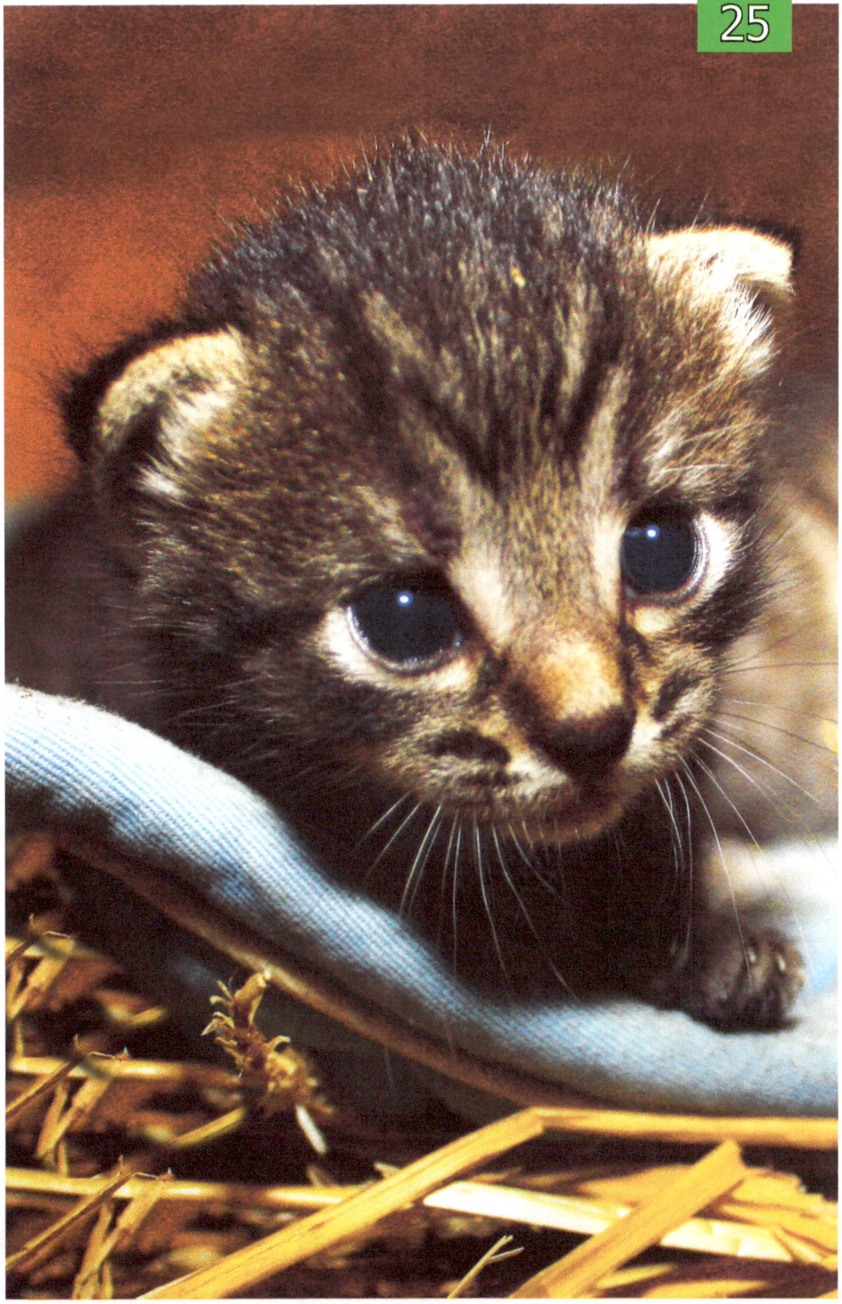

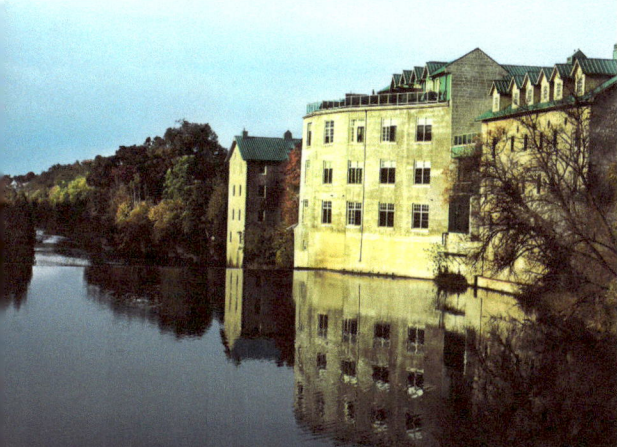

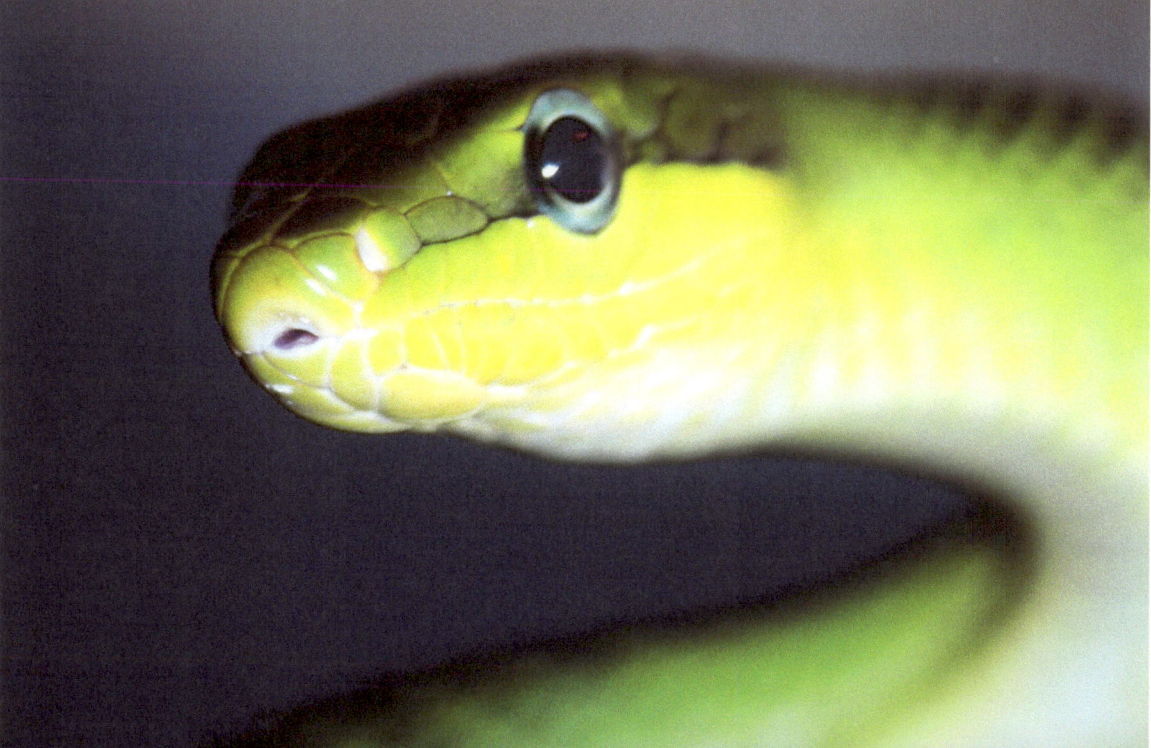

ANNA KRAJEWSKI

LOCATION: 63 Main St. Cambridge
WEB: annakrajewski.com
EMAIL: akrajewski@rogers.com

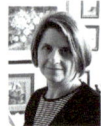

Anna Krajewski studied art at L'Ecole des Beaux Arts in Paris, France. Her theme includes whimsical interiors, floral and fruit arrangements. She paints in watercolour creating rich textures and colours by applying numerous watercolour washes, pastels and crayons. Her paintings have been featured in various magazines and licensed for a variety of products. Her art is represented by Krajewski Gallery in Cambridge, Ontario.

1 Flower Vase 20x14" Watercolour on paper.

2 Tulips and Pears 11x15" Watercolour on paper.

3 Porcelain Clock 30x12" Watercolour on paper.

1

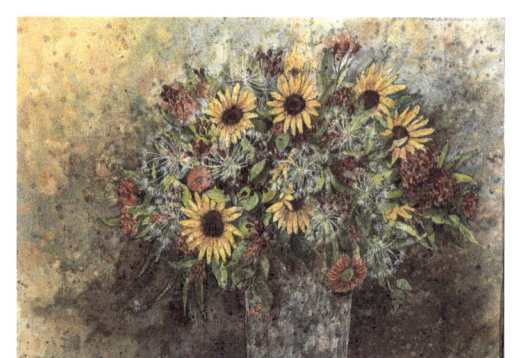

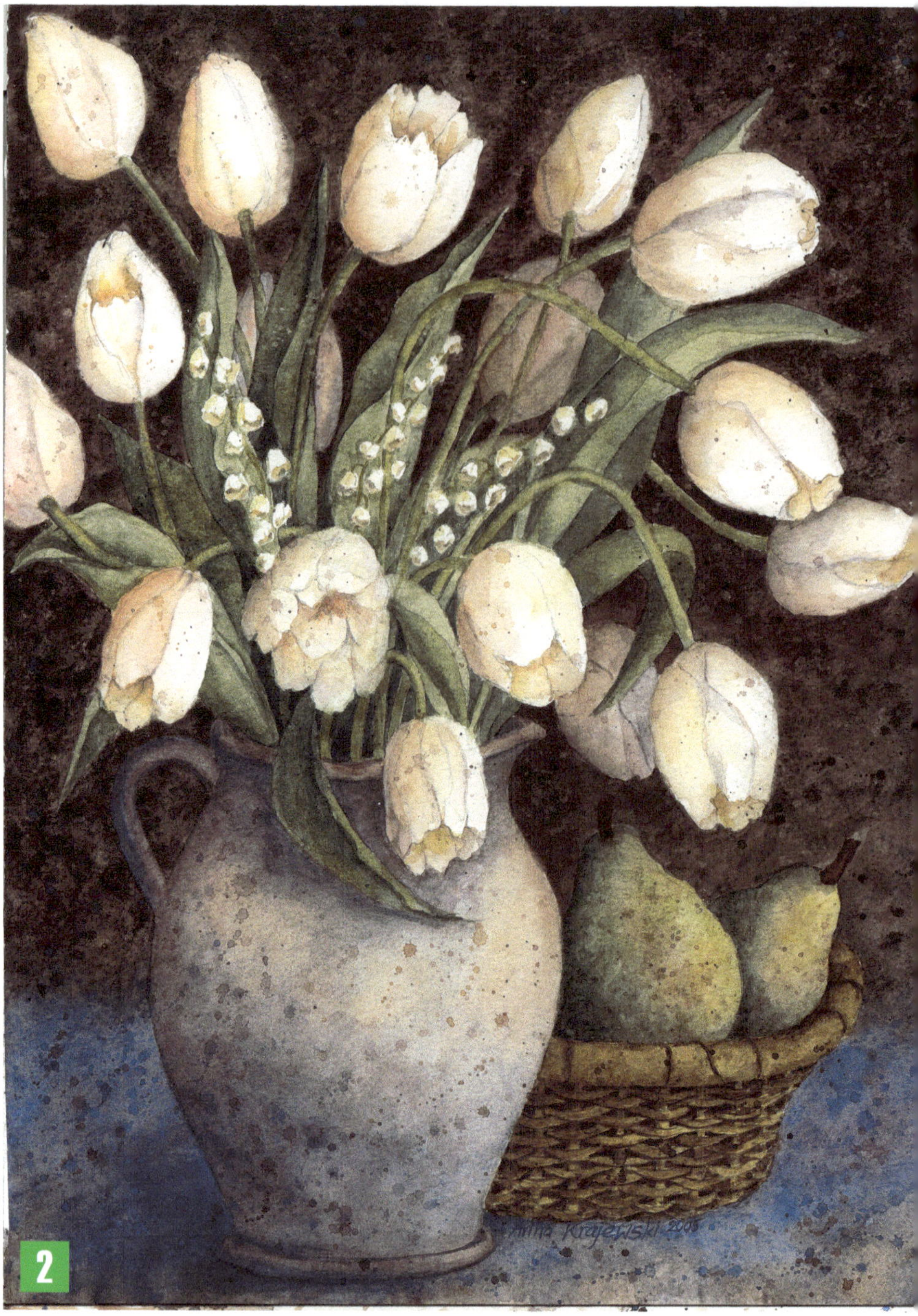

2

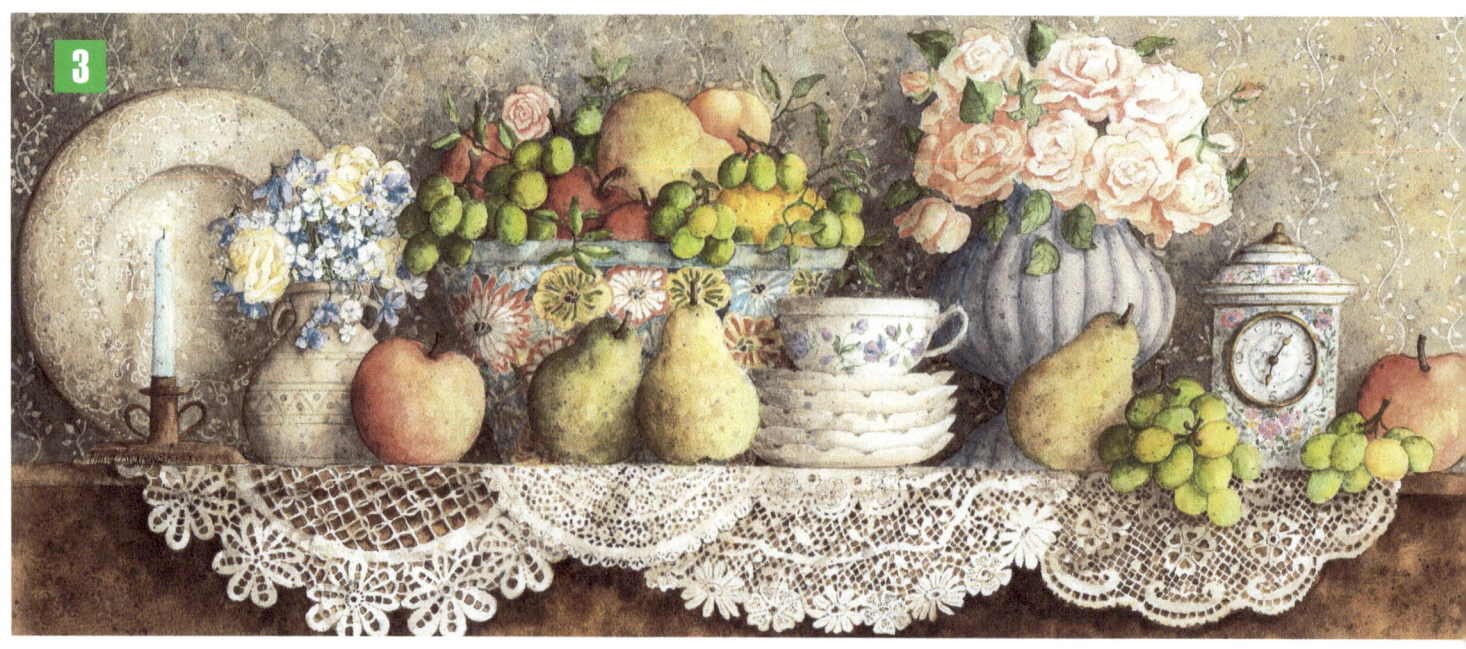

3

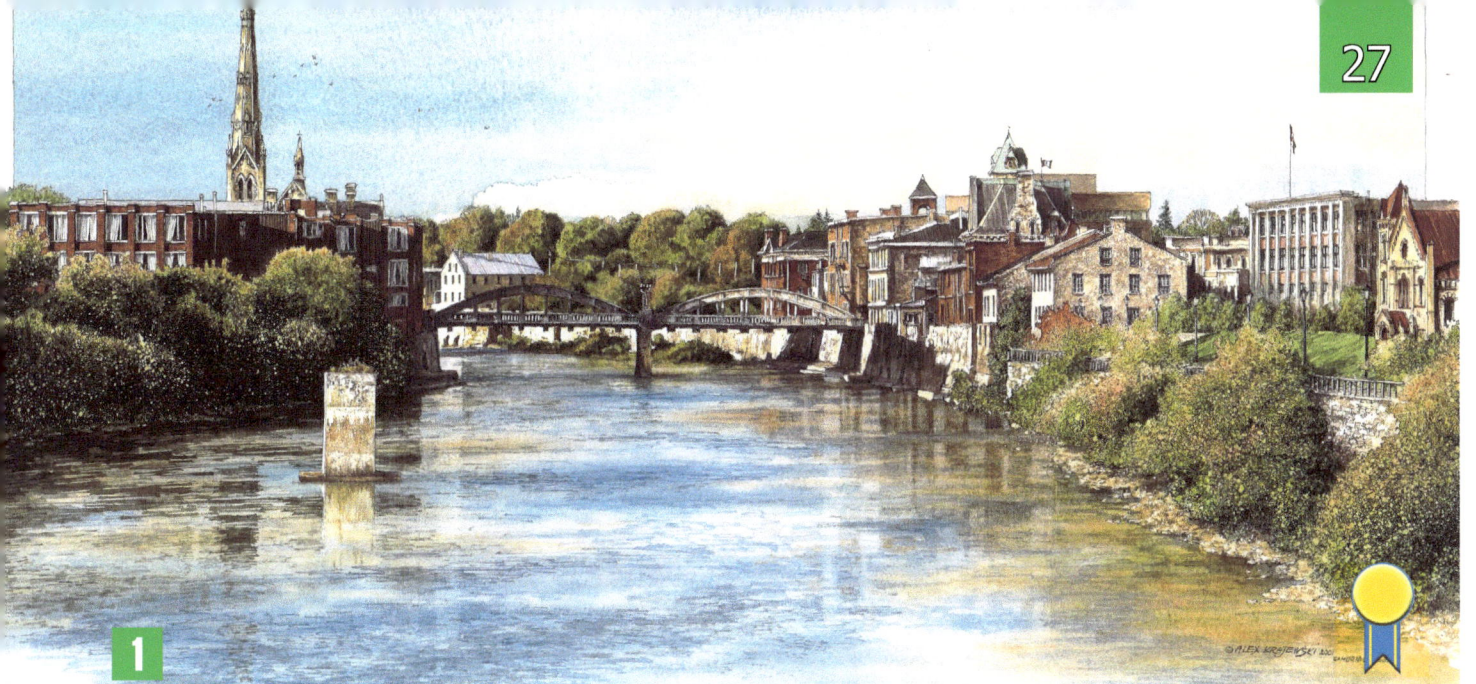

1

ALEX KRAJEWSKI

LOCATION: 63 Main St. Cambridge
WEB: alexkrajewski.com
EMAIL: akrajewski@rogers.com

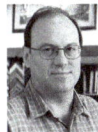
Alex Krajewski studied Architecture in Warsaw, Poland. He finds inspiration in North America and Europe. An active member of Cambridge Municipal Heritage Advisory Committee, Alex lends his knowledge and passion to the cause of preserving the precious monuments of our past. He paints in watercolours and also enjoys photography. Immortalized in Alex's images, precious architectural jewels become symbols of our culture and heritage and evoke in us a sense of belonging. Alex's art is represented by his own Krajewski Gallery in Cambridge, Ontario and numerous galleries in North America.

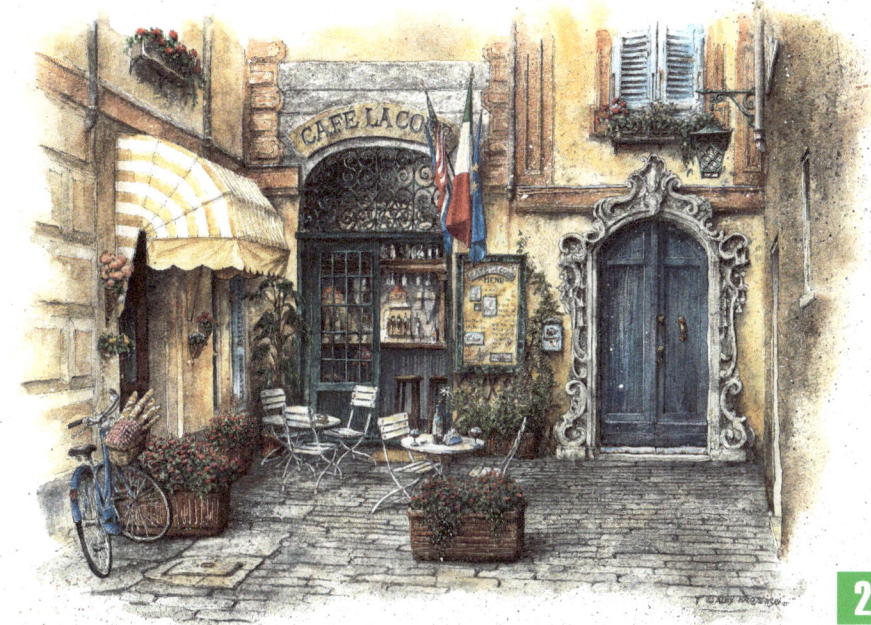

2

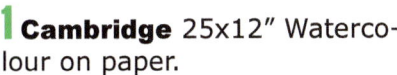**1** **Cambridge** 25x12" Watercolour on paper.

2 **Cafe la Cour** 30x21" Watercolour on paper. Portofino, Italy.

3 **Venetian Blue** 30x21" Watercolour on paper. Venice, Italy.

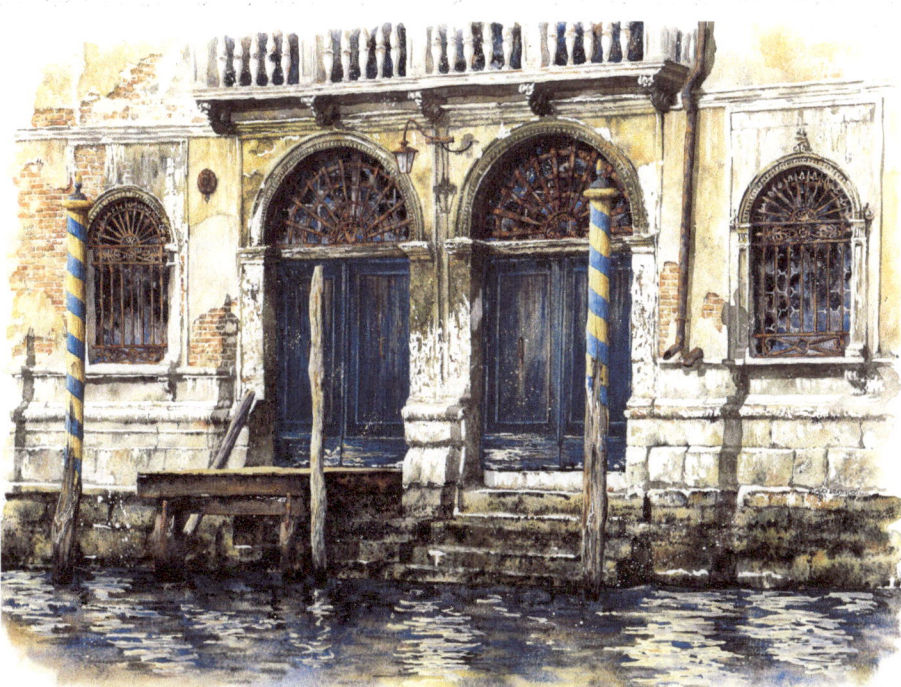

3

LAURA PERRIN

LOCATION: Cambridge
WEB: lauraperrinart.ca , artallies.com , riversideprintgroup.com
EMAIL: laurajeanperrin@googlemail.com

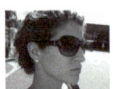

Laura is both an artist and art educator within the Waterloo Region. She studied at the University of Toronto and the Slade School of Fine Art in London, UK. Her interests are in print media, bookmaking, mixed media, and video/sound. Currently, her work investigates concepts and images surrounding the disappearance of the rural, and the expansion of the suburban in Southwestern Ontario.

1 Suburban Scatter 6x7' Etching on chine colle.

2 Desert Train Tracks 4½x8½" Aquatint etching on chine colle.

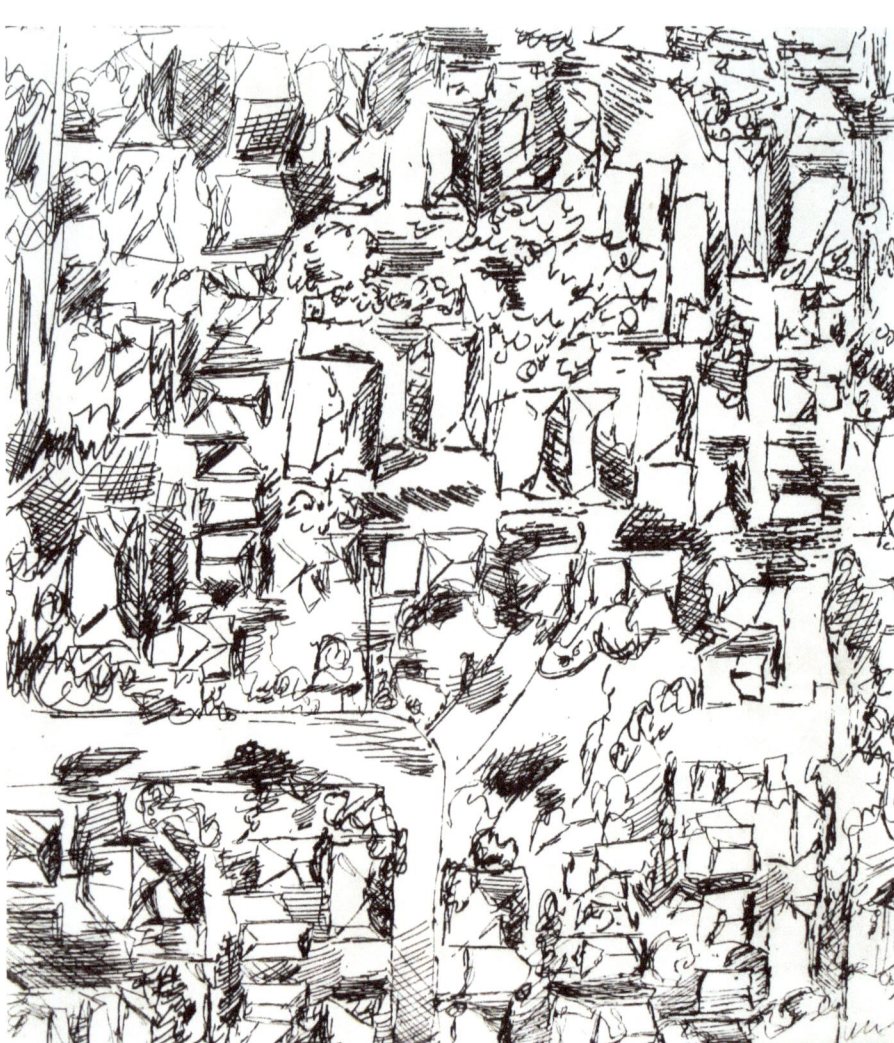

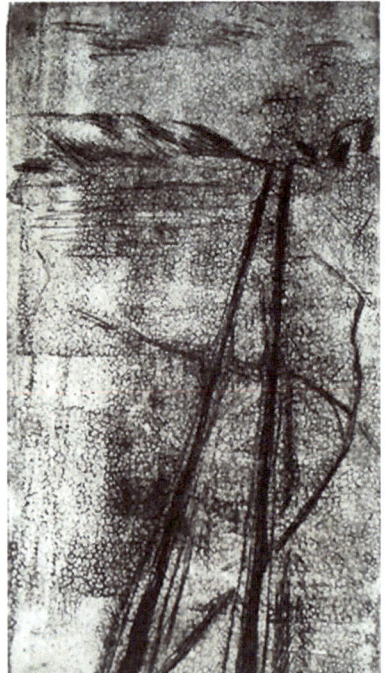

3 Aerial Landscape 6x 5½" Aquatint etching.

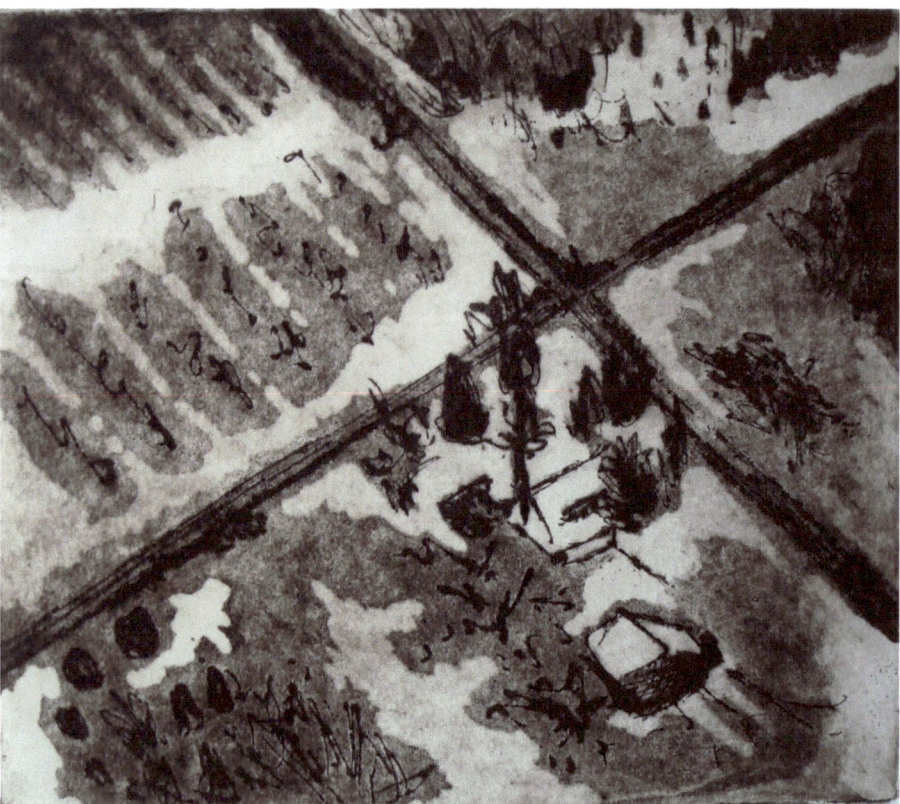

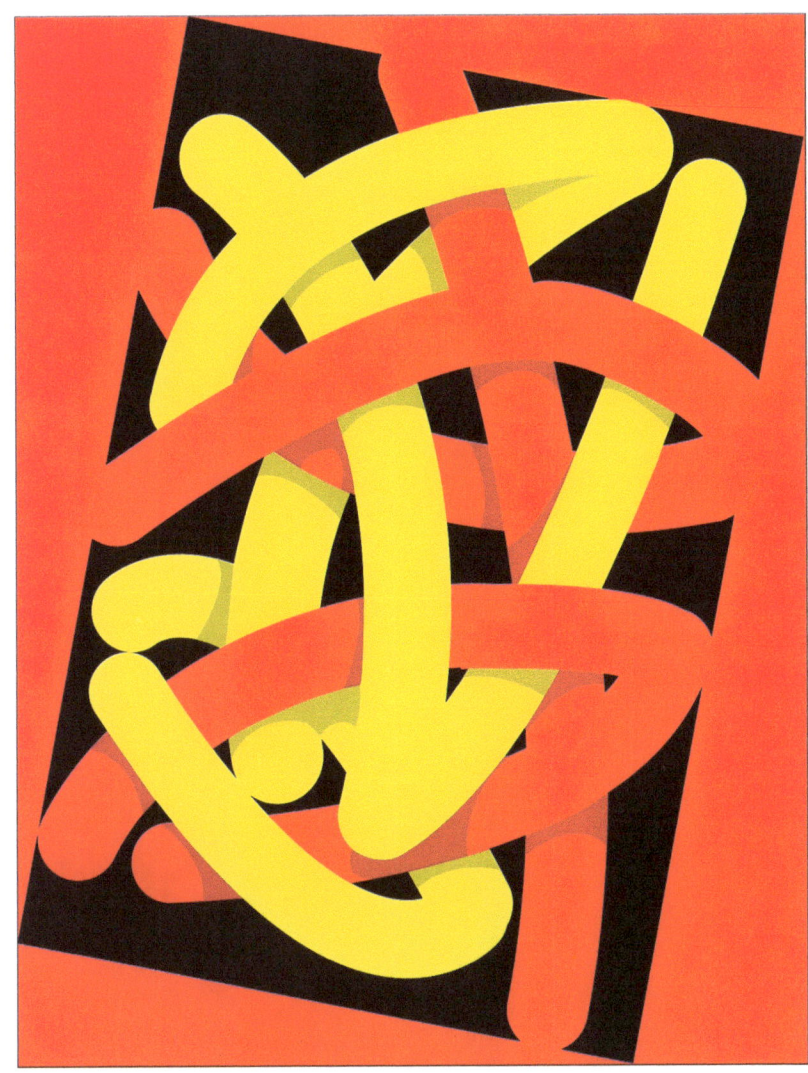

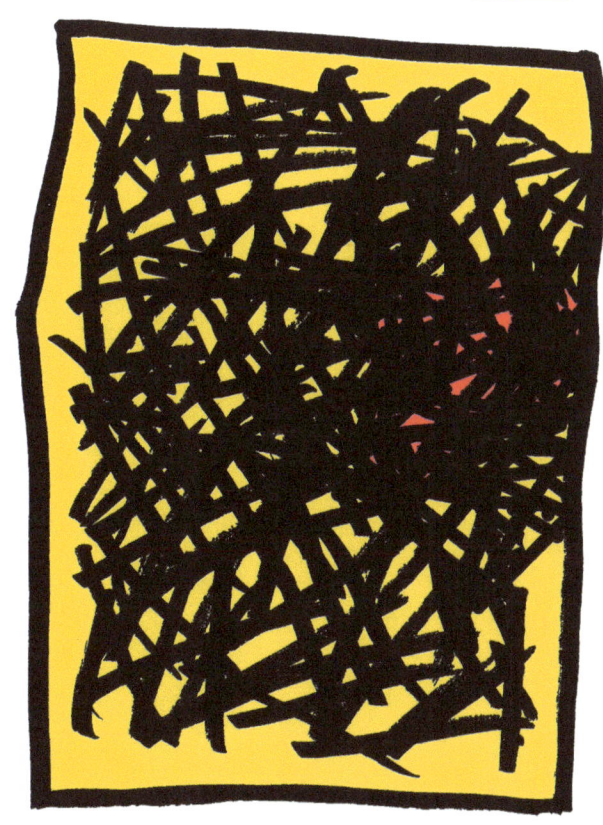

1 **Bedridden** 7x9" 3 colour engraving.

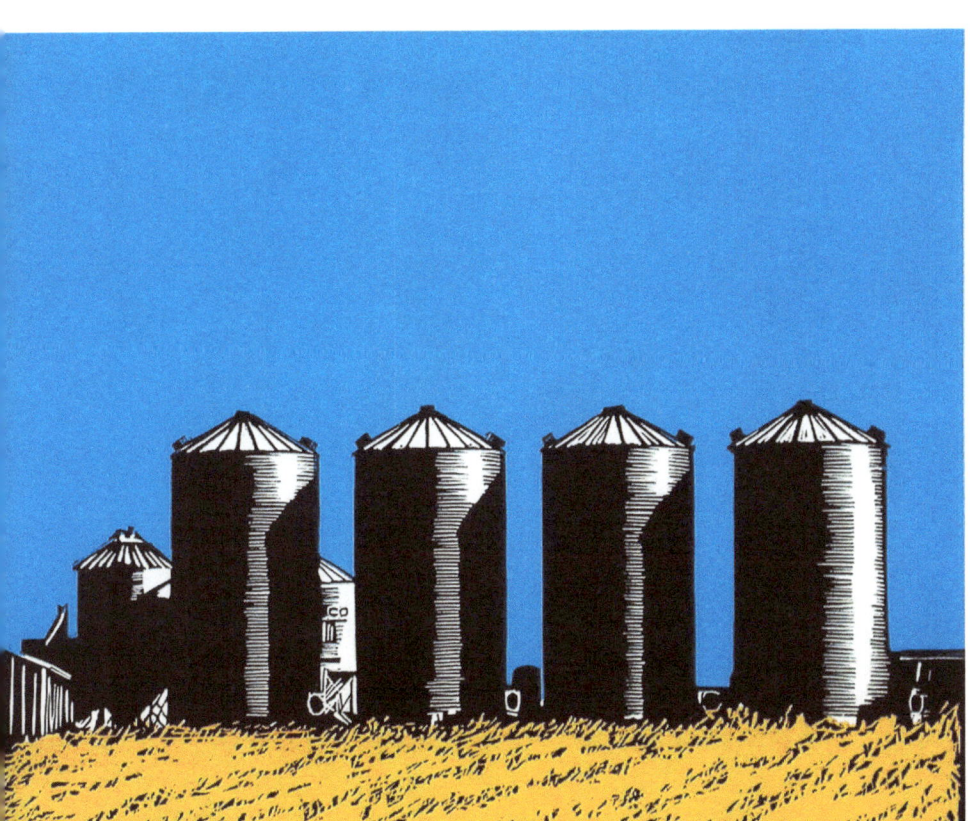

CLIVE LEWIS

LOCATION: Guelph
WEB:
http://clivelewisprintmaker.wordpress.com
EMAIL: l.clivelewis@gmail.com

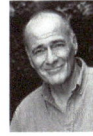 An OCA grad Clive became interested in letterpress printing and then engraving. His work encompasses landscapes and more abstract concepts; engraving and printmaking are still his primary focus.

2 **Impasse** 10x14" 4 colour engraving.

3 **Grain Henge** 9.5x11.5" 3 colour engraving.

1 **There Is Movement In This House: Part Three** 17x26" Oil on canvas 2011.

1

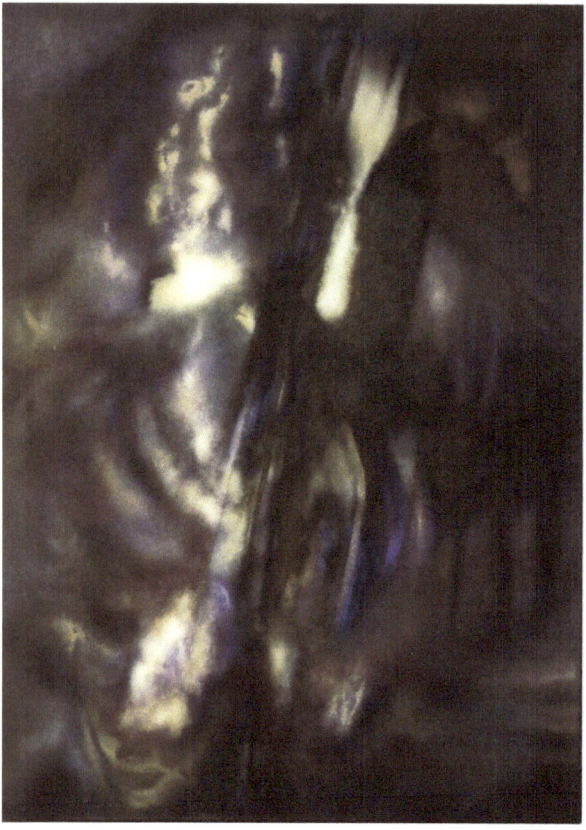

2 **Soulscape One** 66x48" Oil on canvas 2010.

2

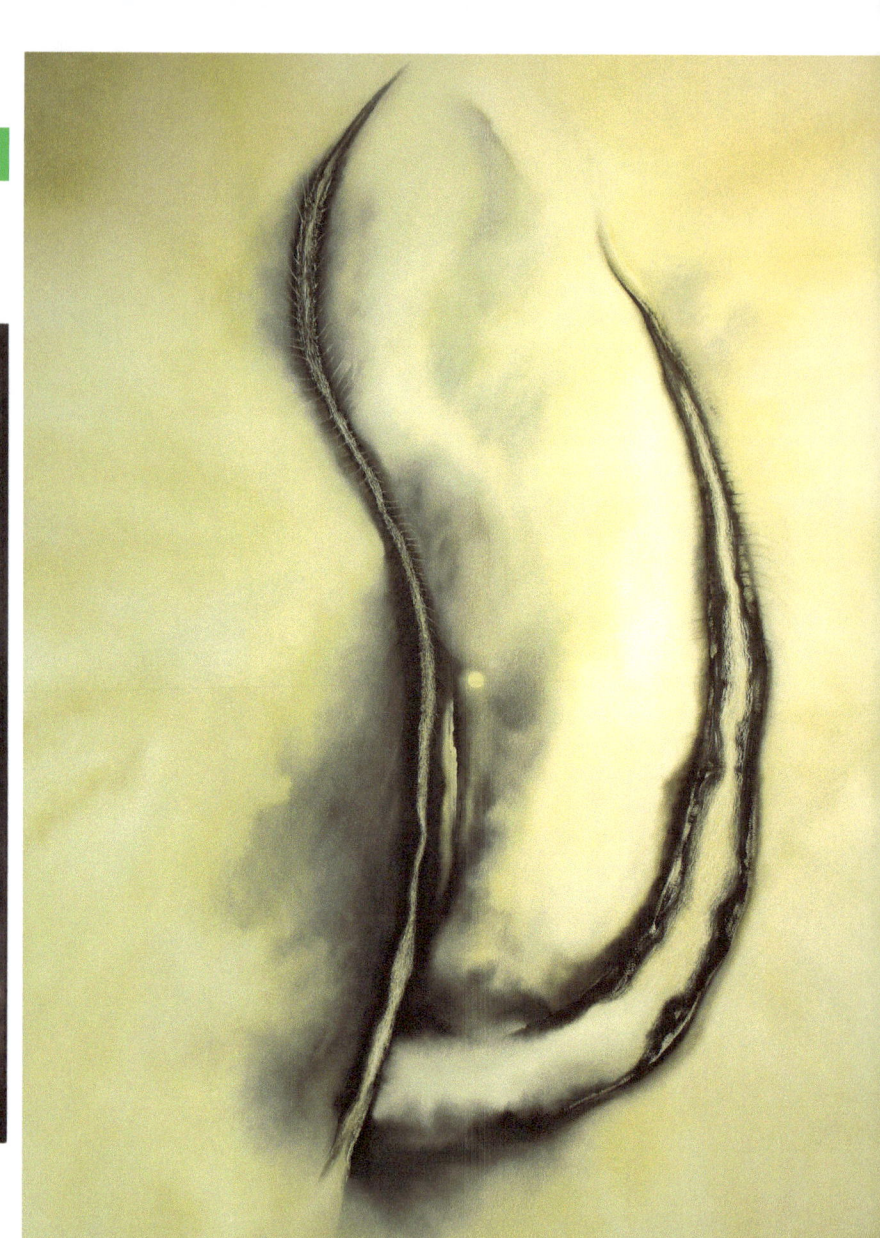

WILLIAM McRae

LOCATION: Cambridge
WEB: williammcrae.com
EMAIL: william.mcrae@rogers.com

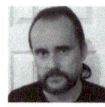 Originally coming from a graphic design background, William has been creating his own work for more than 25 years. Working in oil, wood and mixed media constructions, the pieces are based on social/political, music related, personal reminiscence or belief system themes. He has lived in Cambridge for the past seven years.

3

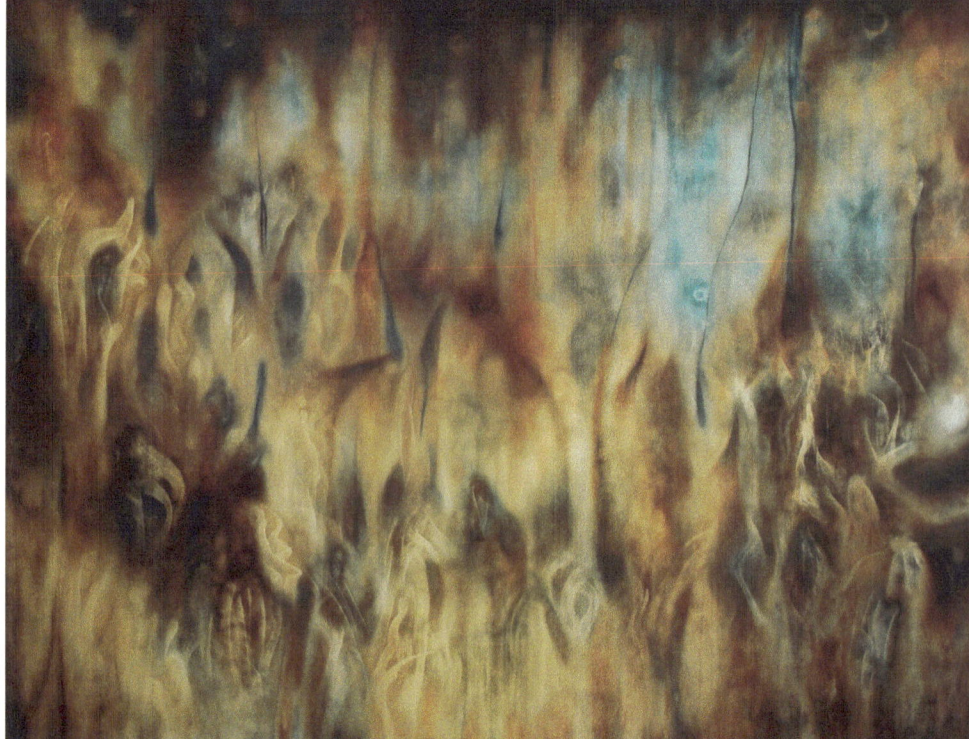

3 **New Pagan: Series Three** 54x72" Oil on canvas 2010.

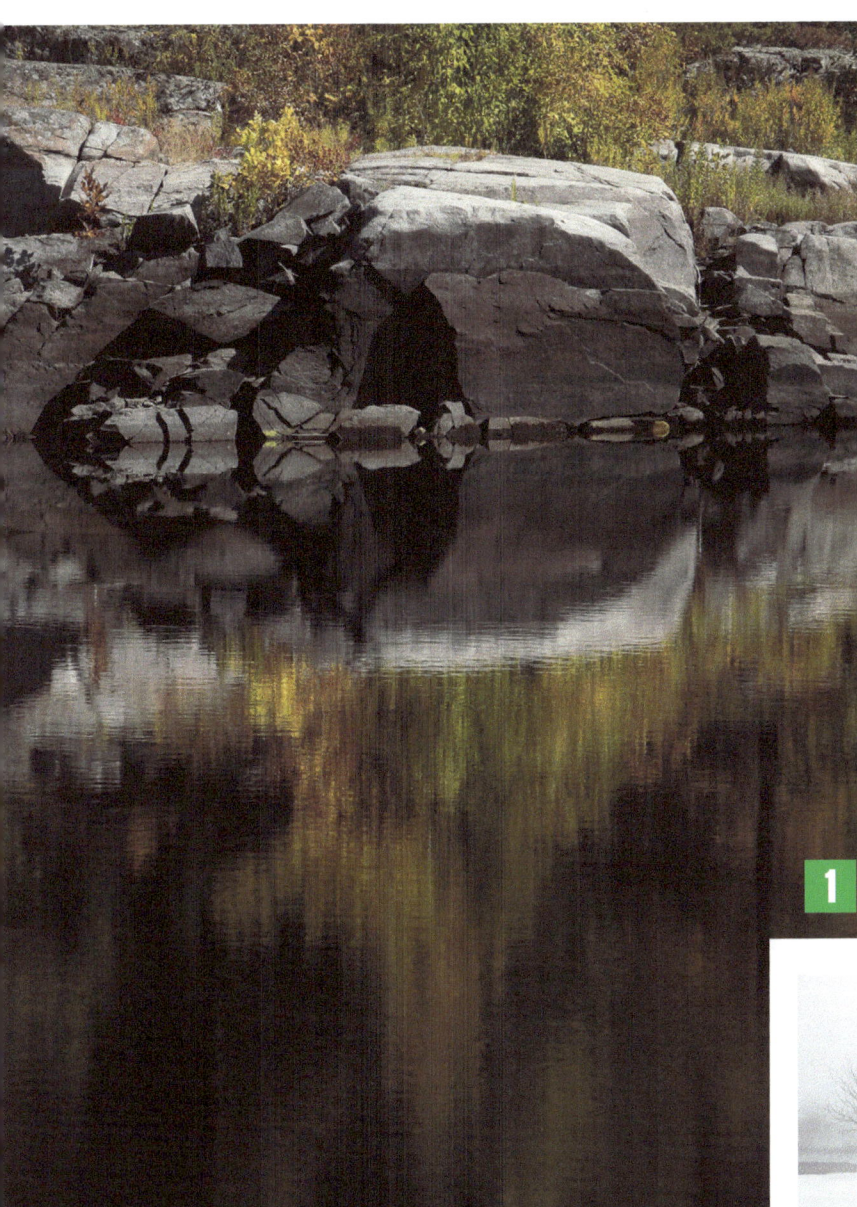

SYLVIA GALBRAITH

LOCATION: Fergus
WEB: sylviagalbraith.ca
EMAIL: info@silvercreekphoto.ca

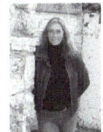

Sylvia Galbraith has worked with many mediums including clay, charcoal, watercolour and oils over the years, but found that the limitations and challenges of photography inspired her more than any other art form. Based in Fergus, ON, she is a recognized professional photographer whose work sells worldwide. She has shown her photographs in numerous galleries and shows over the past five years and has received several awards of merit. In the summer of 2009 she published a book of her images of the Grand River entitled "A Living River by the Door". The book has sold extremely well, and is in its third printing. She also teaches a popular series of photography workshops in Guelph & Elora.

1 **French River Reflection** 17x22" Photograph on bamboo fibre paper.

2 **Waterloo County Fog** 14x26" Photograph on bamboo fibre paper.

3 **Winter Afternoon With Willows** 15x26" Photograph on bamboo fibre paper.

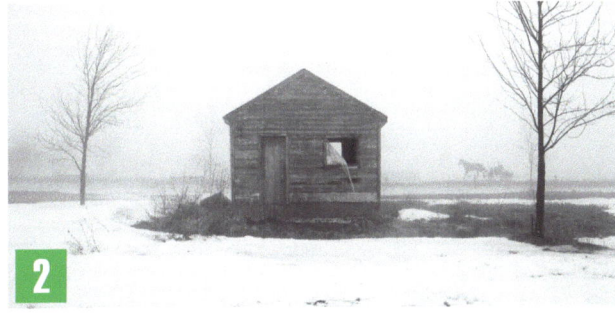

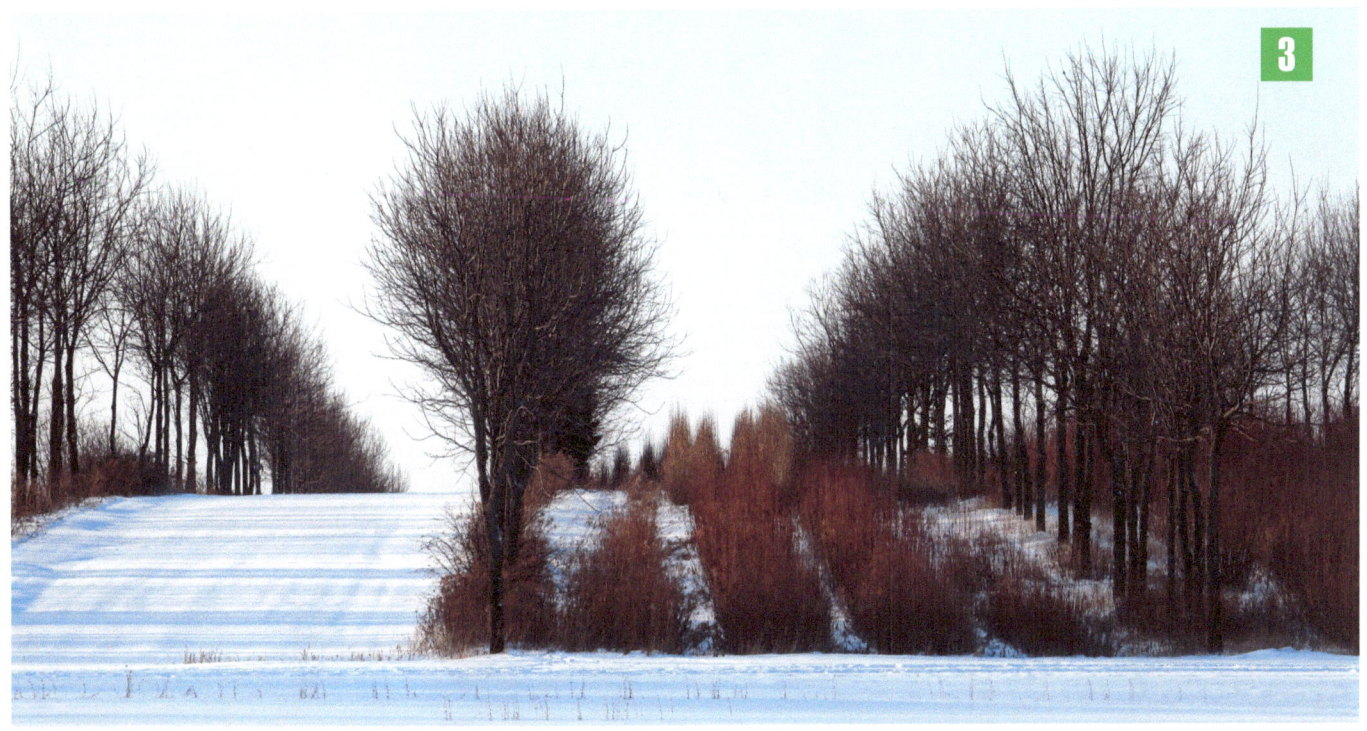

1 Danse de l Ombre 18x24" Oil on wood panel 2011.

2 Reflection at Little Lake 10x9" Coloured Pencil 2011.

3 Teacup Graphite 10x10" 2011.

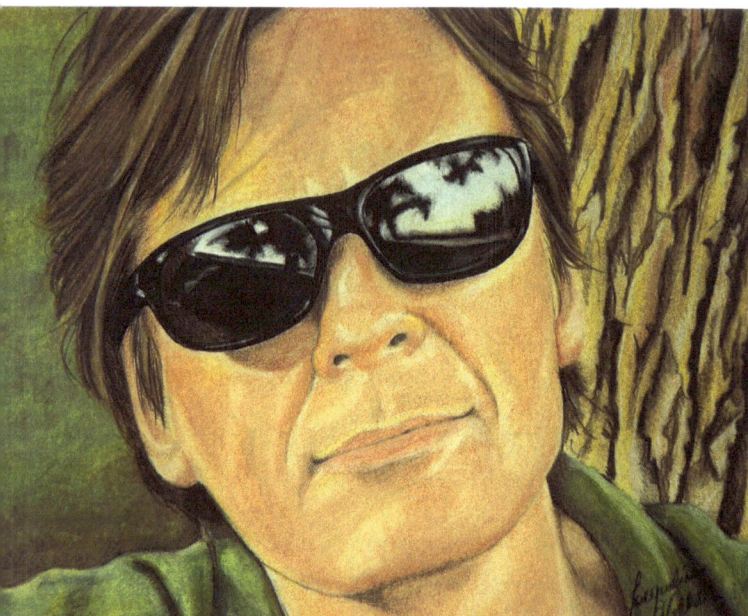

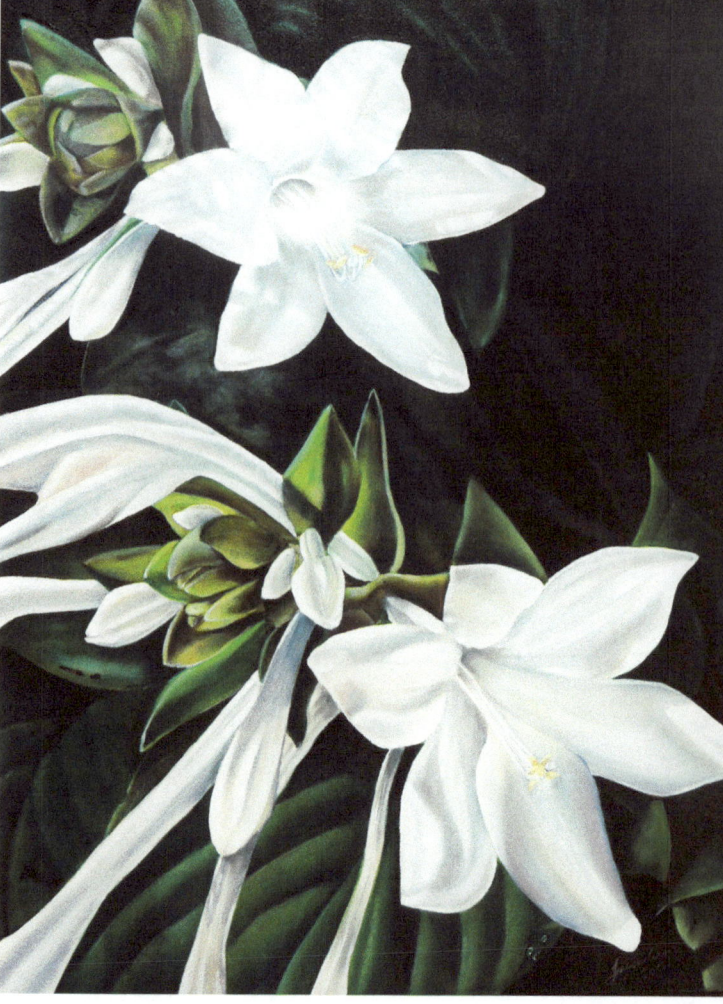

JACQUELINE VELTRI

LOCATION: Fergus Gallery
WEB: jacquelineveltri.ca
EMAIL: jacquelineveltri@hotmail.ca

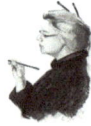

Born in France and raised in Canada, I knew from a young age that I wanted to be an artist & was encouraged by my family to do so. I would spend all my free time painting, finding inspiration in almost everything that surrounded me. A trip to France at age 16 resulted in a buying spree of art supplies that yearned to be transformed into works of art. The accolades for the resulting art work at my high school lead to several art awards. I attended the Ontario College of Art and Design where my love of painting was nurtured & introduced me to other mediums such as photography, intaglio and serigraphy which impacted on my painting sensibility. After graduating from OCAD, I primarily freelanced, doing graphic design and commissions, while raising a family. In recent years I decided to concentrate on my art & joined my local arts groups and began teaching there, eventually being elected to vice-president of Visual Arts Brampton. I began to exhibit with that group regularly. It was there that I was introduced to a new media - coloured pencil. After being accepted into the Colored Pencil Society of America's "Explore This! 7" exhibit, I joined that group as well. I became an exhibiting member of the Wellington Artists' Gallery in 2011. I have work in private collections in France, UK & Canada.

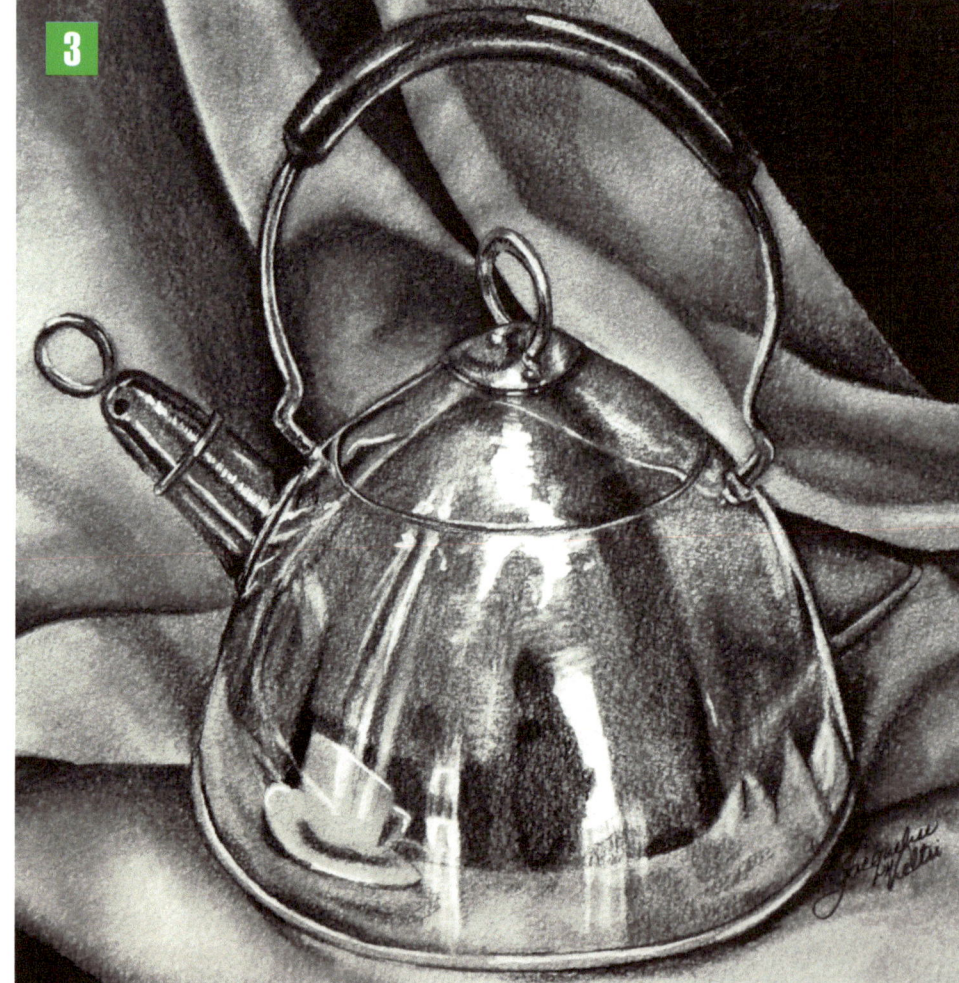

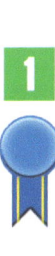

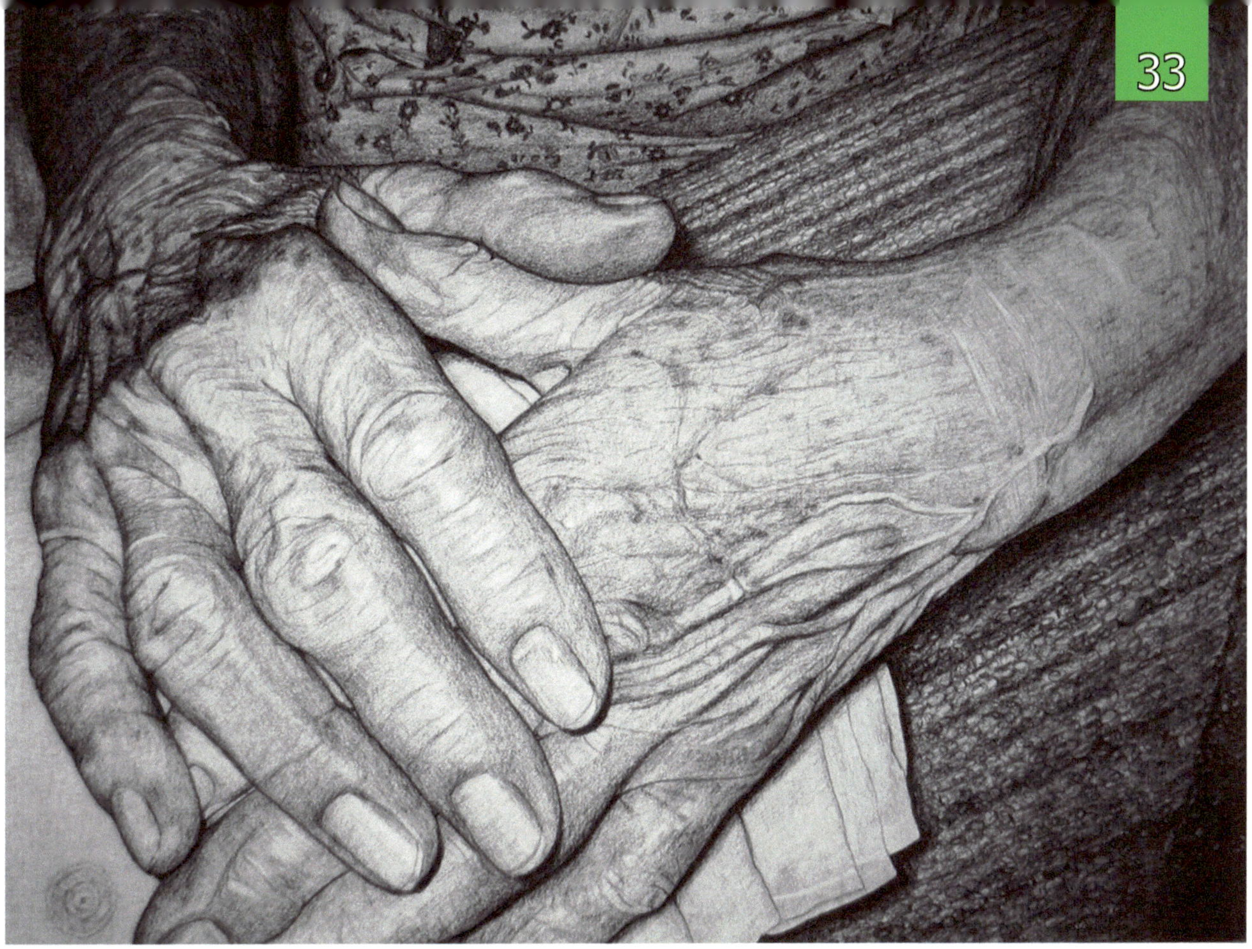

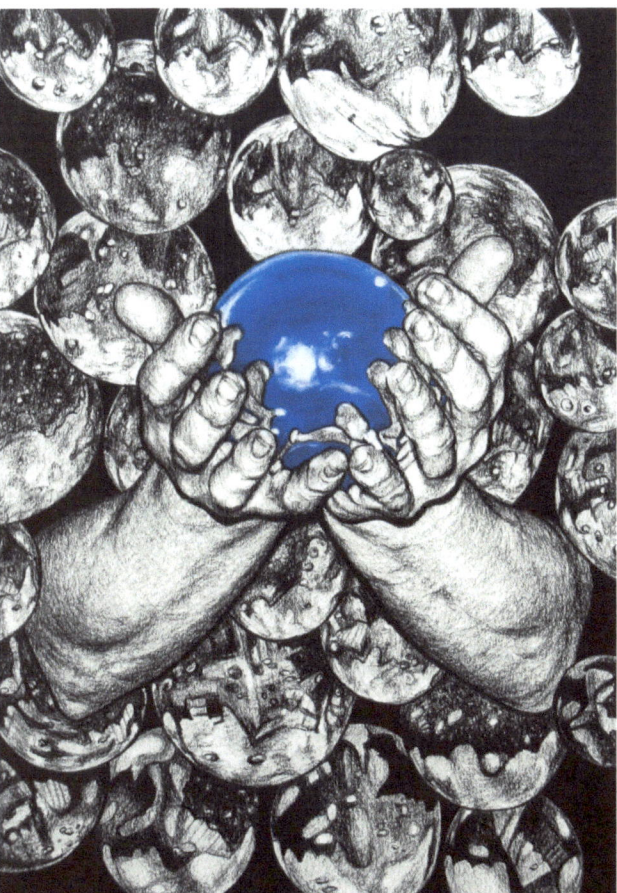

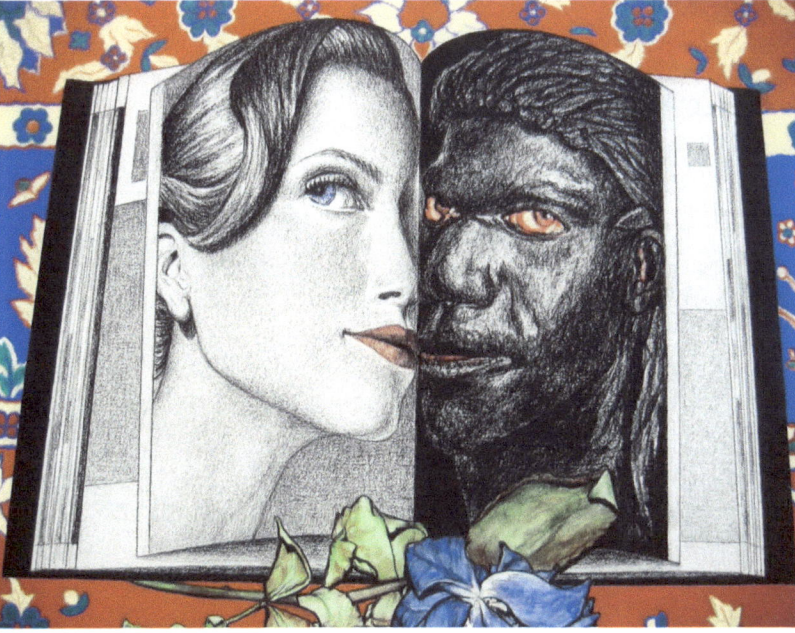

1 **Mother** 34x38" When "Mothers" get older.   **2** **Emerging** 26x20" Emerging of the Universe.

3 **Story of Life** 23x25 Story of Life or Beauty and the Beast?

HELENA PRAVDA

LOCATION: Cambridge
WEB: helenapravda.com
EMAIL: hpravda@gmail.com

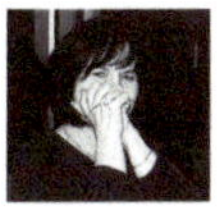

Helena Pravda was born in Brno in the Czech Republic, where she obtained a diploma from the College of Fashion and Design. After she moved to Kitchener, Ontario in 1983, she opened her own business and established her own fashion line. In 1999, she attended Wilfrid Laurier University, Waterloo, Ontario, to study psychology. In 2003, she graduated with a Bachelor of Arts degree in Psychology and Fine Arts, and applied to the University of Waterloo, Waterloo, Ontario, to further her studies in art. She graduated in the spring of 2005 with an Honours BA in Fine Arts, specializing in studio, drawing and painting.

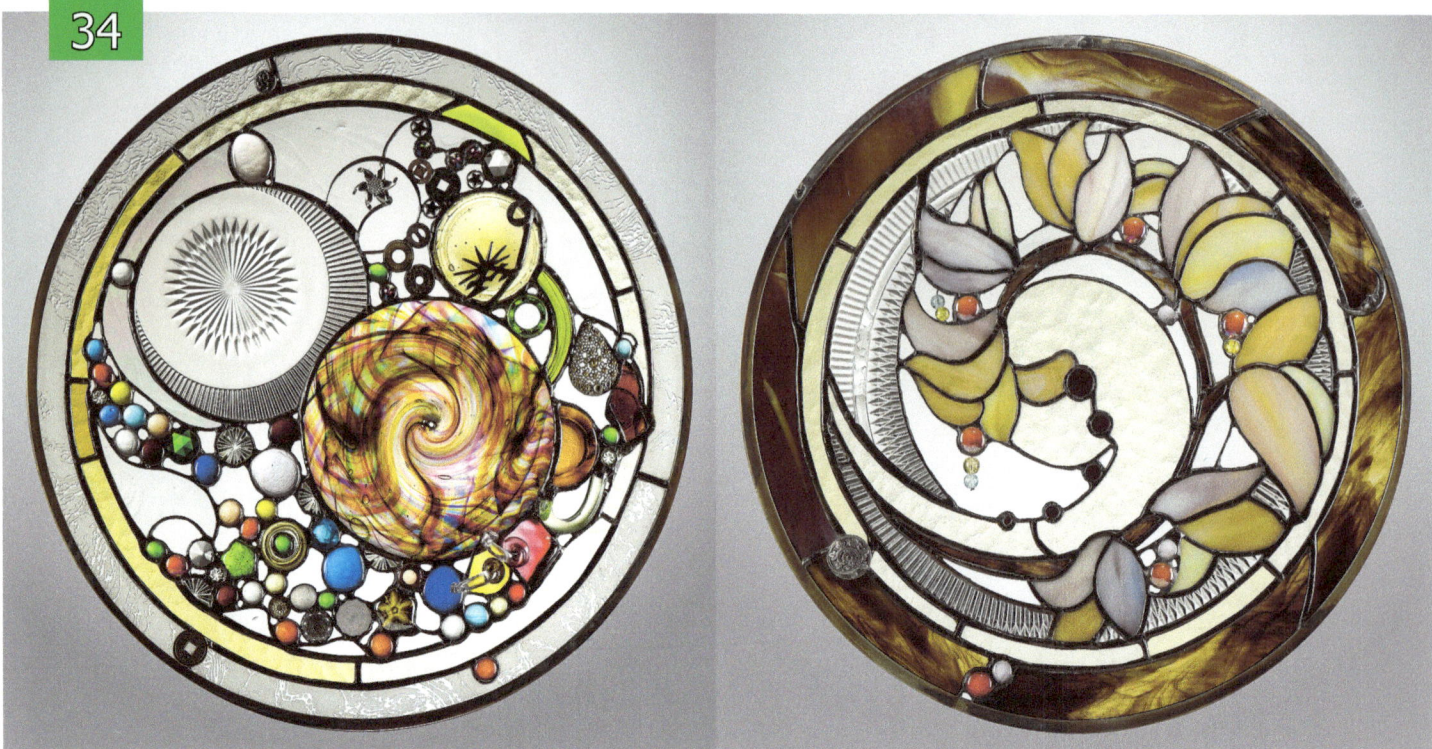

1 Flying Rainbows What would happen if a rainbow started to spin? I imagined flying colourful gravel. Find 10 buttons, 5 tokens and 2 moon star combinations.

2 Grace Fused leaves, canning jar lids and antique chandelier prisms, when I stood back and looked at this piece I said" Oh, this reminds me of my grandmother!. Her name was Grace.

BARBARA BRYCE

LOCATION: Guelph
WEB: sonicplayground.ca
EMAIL: barbara@sonicplayground.ca

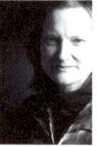

Barbara calls her work Improvised Art Glass because of the serendipitous process of finding materials and assembling them, often without a pattern. The work seems to design itself. Besides broken glass, Barb loves designing for Season Singers theatrical children's choir and she builds crazy musical instruments for the Sonic Playground.ca (www.sonicplayground.ca)

3 3 Cats, 1 Dog, a Fish and 4 Compasses Improvised art glass has a mind of it's own, this piece decided to be round. A good choice considering it contains 4 compasses a retired architect could never throw away.

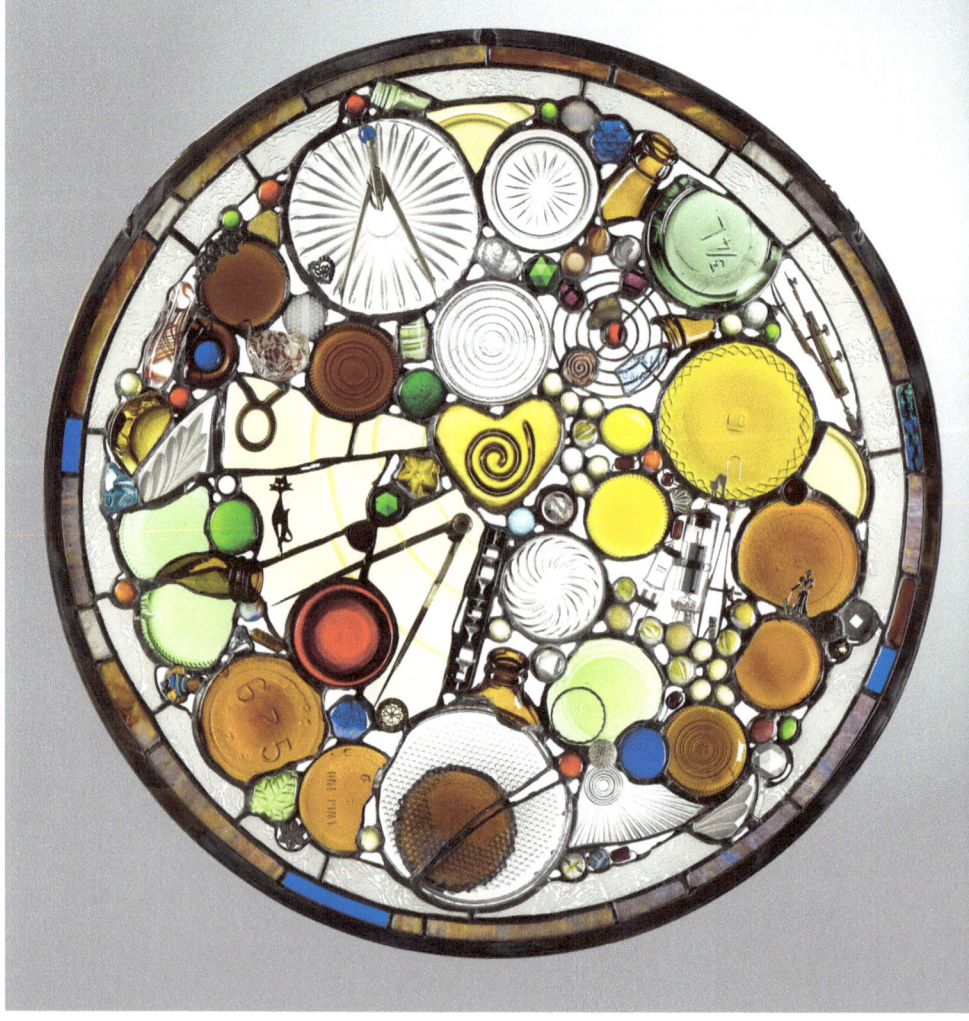

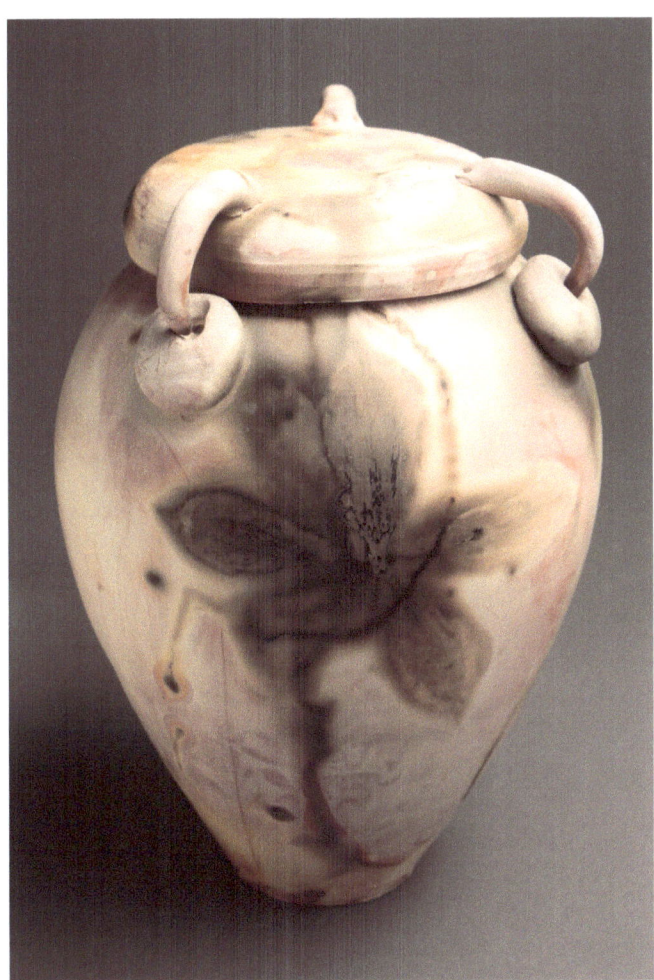

1

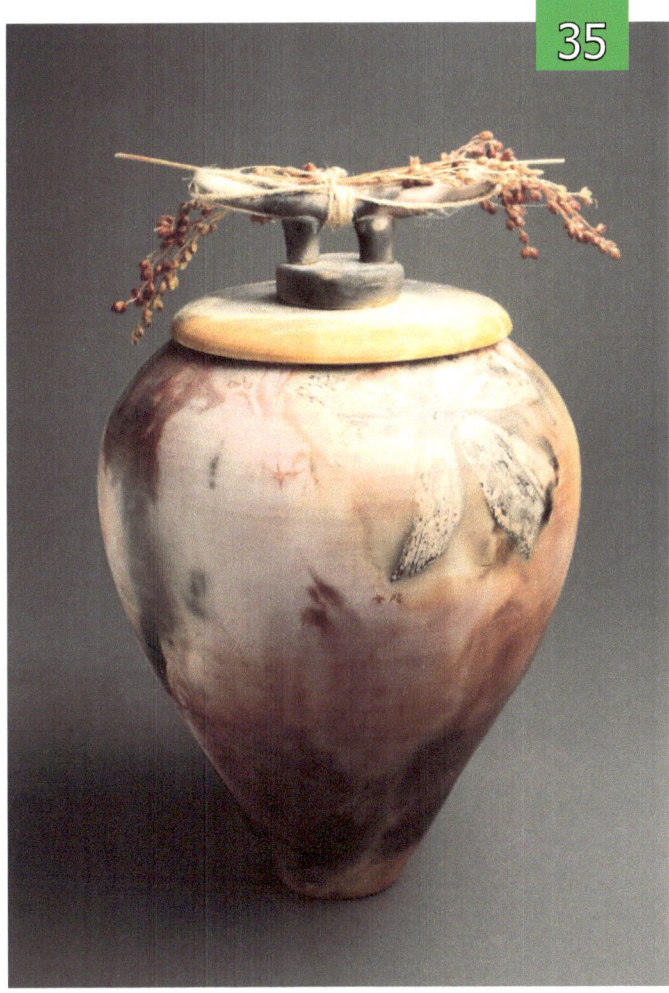

2

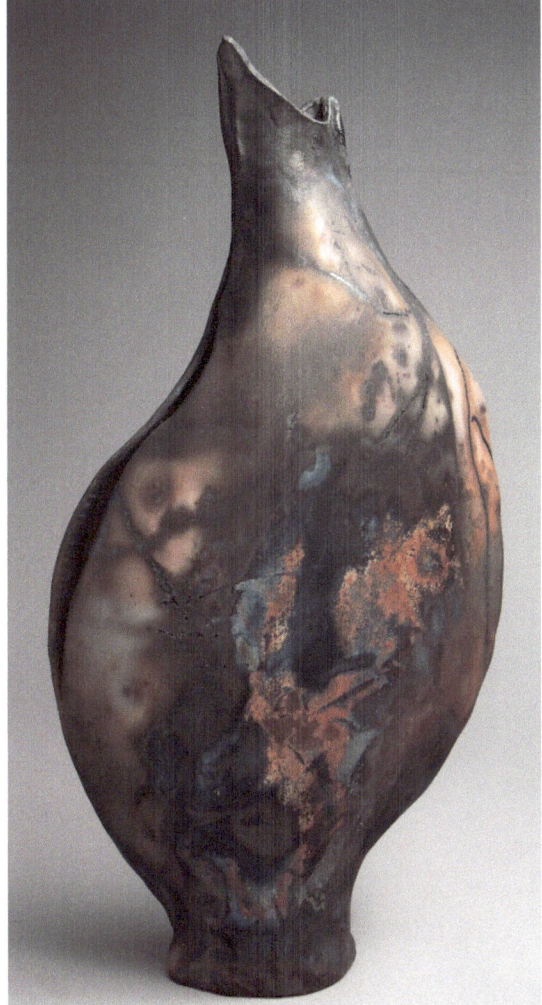

3

Natalie Prévost

LOCATION: Paris
WEB: thebarefootpotter.ca/
EMAIL: barefootpotter@hotmail.com

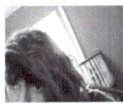 The start of a future smoke fire artist started in a small French community called Casselman. Natalie has apprenticed with many different potters in the area but is mostly self-taught. The Barefoot Potter studio was opened in 1998. The difficulties of these primitive firings is what has kept her fascinated with the art of clay and firing. Her Studio is located in Kitchener at Globe Studios where she teaches others the art of pottery!

1 Clematis Smoke fired clay (smoke firing is done in a garbage can or in a pit, using sawdust, wood, salt, oxides, plants, flowers & manure. The pots are burnished in different stages to make a soft surface. They fire for 10-12hrs. When finished the vessels are then polished with paste wax. There is no glaze on the pots the color is from the fire and additives.

2 Fleur Smoke fired clay.

3 Coloré Smoke fired clay.

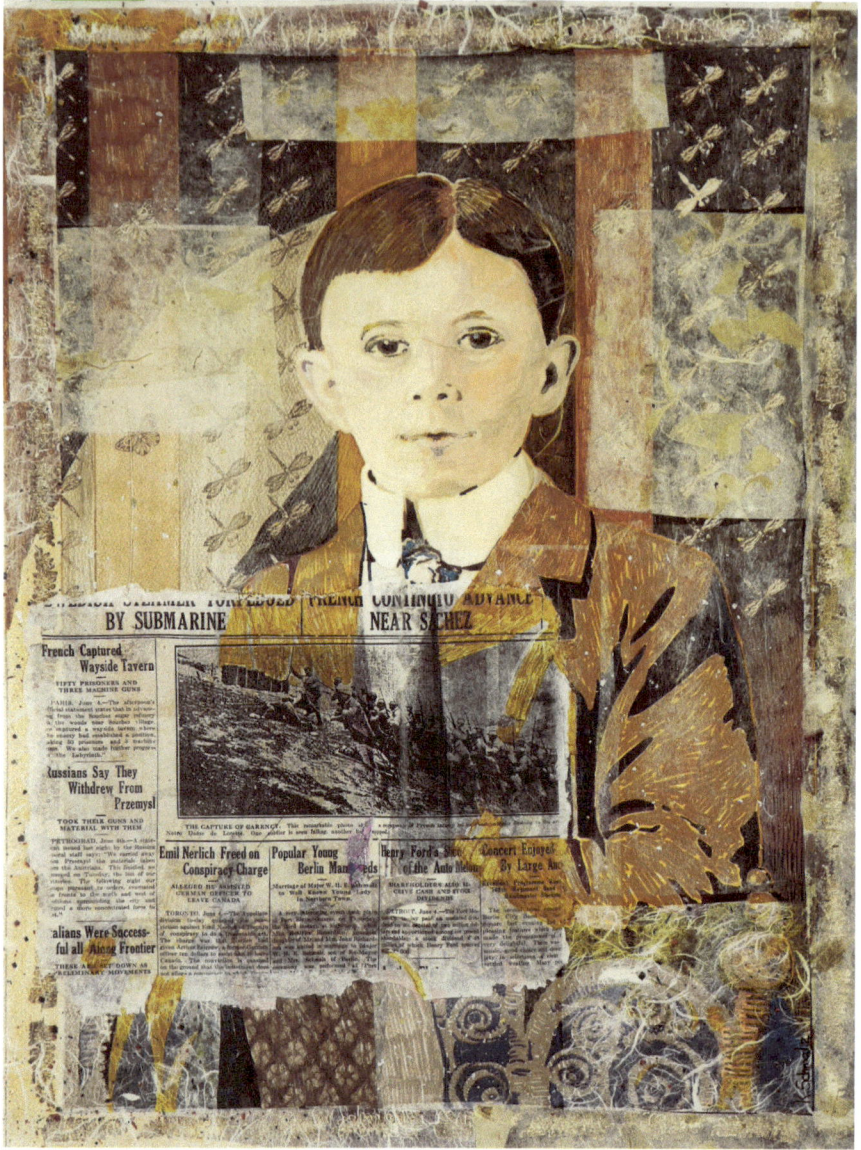

KATHLEEN SCHMALZ

LOCATION: Guelph
WEB: guelpharts.ca/kathleenschmalz
EMAIL: kathleen.schmalz@gmail.com

My interest in local history and architecture drew me to explore the interactions between historical research and the visual arts in my 2009 Doctorate of Visual and Performing Arts. To me everything is a story waiting to be told - from the laundry in the back yard to the historical buildings with 4 renovations. I paint in oil and acrylic as well as exploring fibre and photographic mixed media pieces. As an art educator, I am also interested in the stories other people, young and old have to tell through their art works. I teach painting in my Guelph studio and work with teachers and teacher trainees.

1

1 If... 26x20" Mixed media on water colour paper. Berlin Mayor's son - unable to serve as an officer in WW1 due to German name and residence location marries on day many die on the front.

2 Berlin, Ontario 30x40" Mixed media on water colour paper. The still-standing house on King St. of Berlin Mayor WH Schmalz, 1911 with attitudes towards German speaking residents changing over time.

3 City Halls 10x10" Process print. Both of Kitchener's prior city halls were taken down in flurries of controversy and the clock tower from the last, on the top layer of the print is now installed in Victoria Park.

2

3

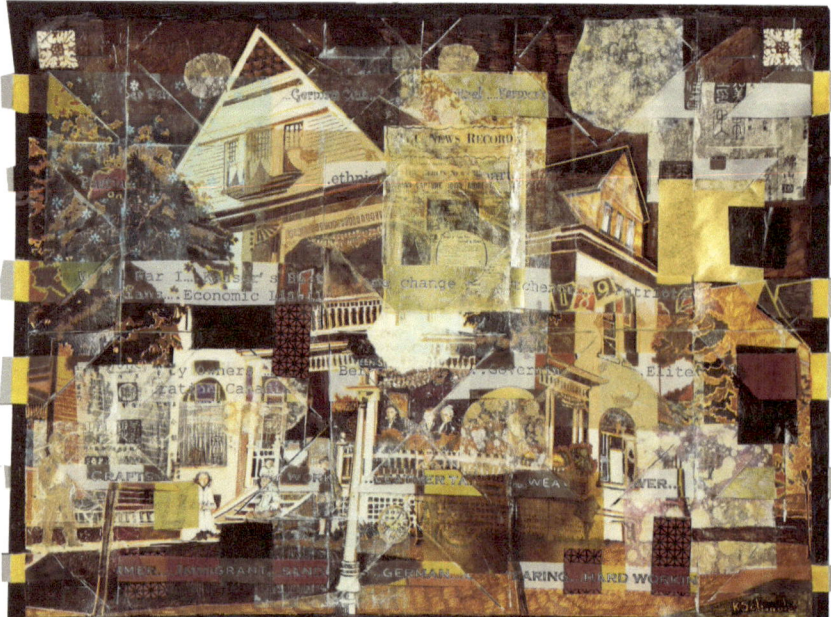

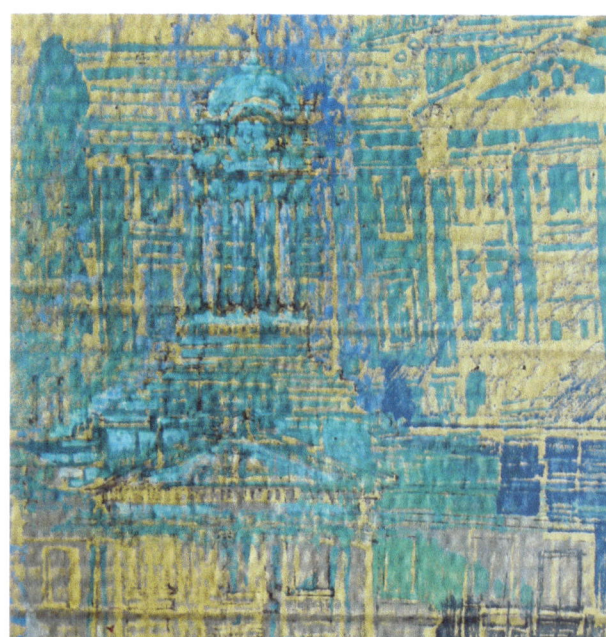

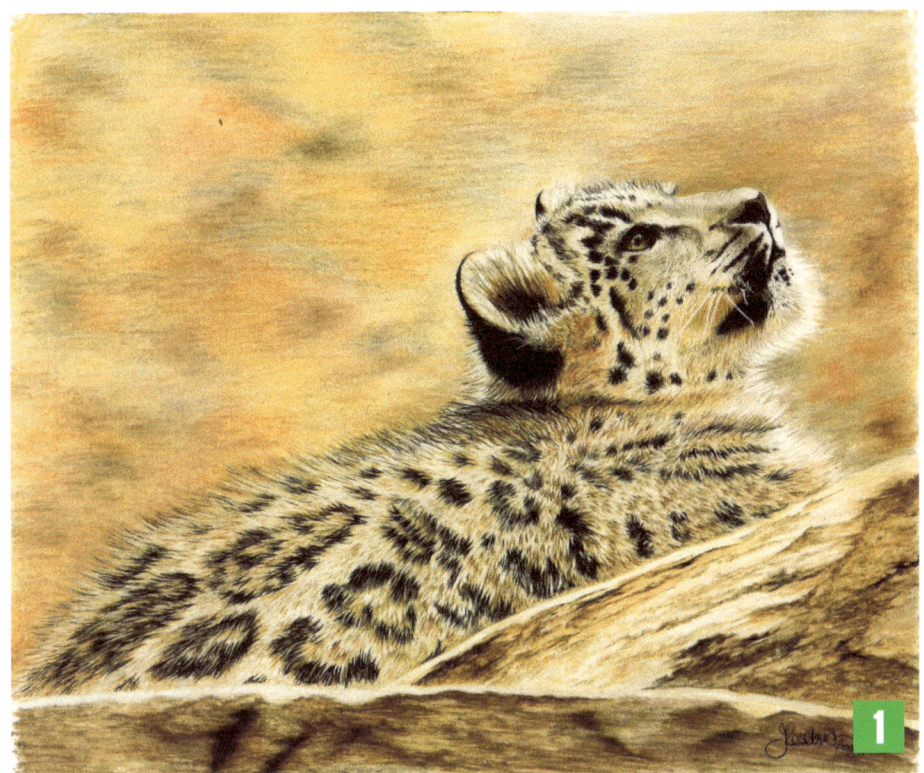

JENNIFER ROSEBUSH

LOCATION: Cambridge
WEB: jrosebushgallery.com
EMAIL: jen@jrosebushgallery.com

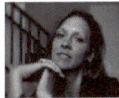

Jennifer is a self taught artist who loves working with all types of medium, but prefers graphite or coloured pencil on bristol paper. She loves to draw animals and wildlife, and always strives to keep her drawings as true to life as possible.

1 Lazy Afternoon Coloured Pencil on Bristol. I snapped a picture of this young Snow Leopard at the Toronto Zoo. I loved his eyes and his gaze up to the sky. It was the combination of that, along with the different textures - the soft looking fur against the rocks that made me want to put it on paper.

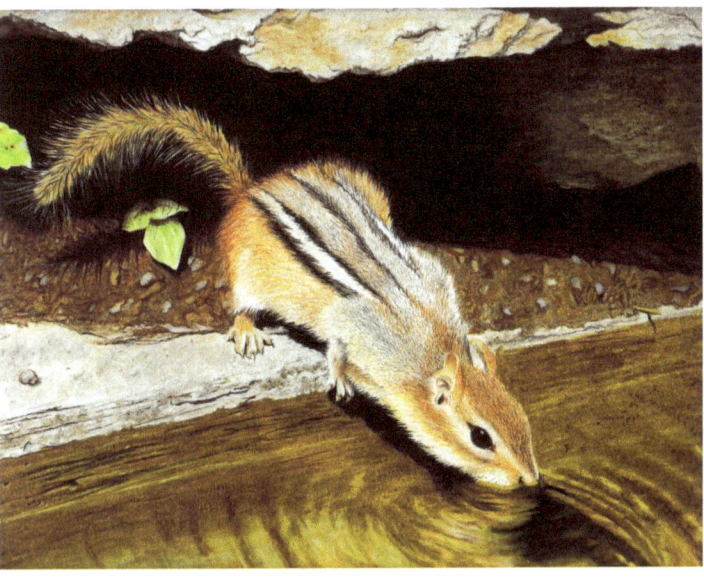

2 Chippy 11x14" Coloured Pencil on Bristol. I snapped a photo of this little guy at the Royal Botanical Gardens and named him after a childhood stuffed animal.

3 Corgies 8x10" Graphite on Bristol. This was a commission piece, it quickly became one of my favourites - and still is.

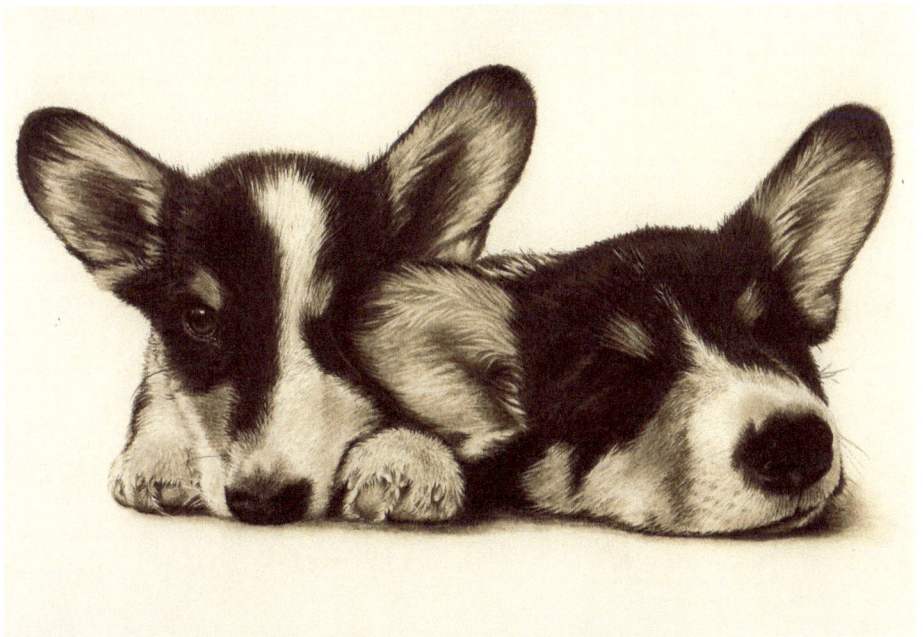

GRAYCE PERRY

LOCATION: Elora
WEB: grayceperry.com
EMAIL: grayceperry@gmail.com

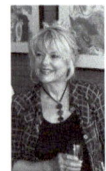

Grayce is an abstract artist living in Elora. Recently her focus has been on contemporary mixed media painting. She has been particularly drawn to the use of oil, graphite and charcoal on mylar. For Grayce, the process of painting has become a form of meditation. She works intuitively drawing from her own internal landscapes. The resulting imagery is sometimes ambiguous, appealing to the viewer to find their own insights into the work. She has come to realise that in painting as in life, anything can happen.

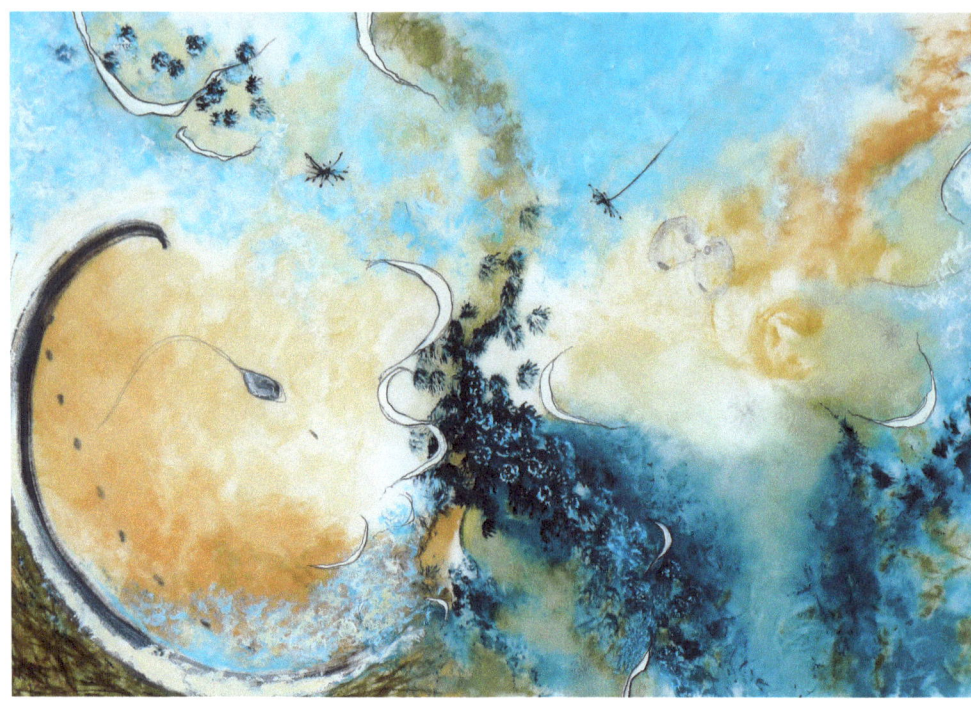

1 Poem to the Sea Oil and graphite on mylar.

3 Fragments and Memories Oil, graphite and charcoal on mylar.

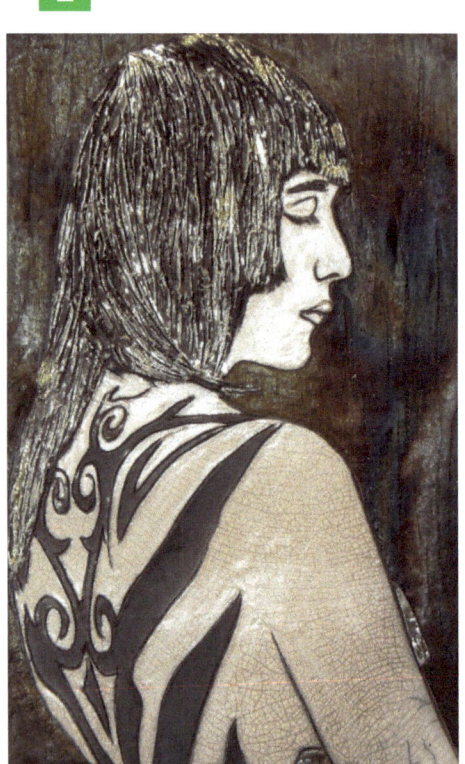

2 Erin Raku Sculpture.

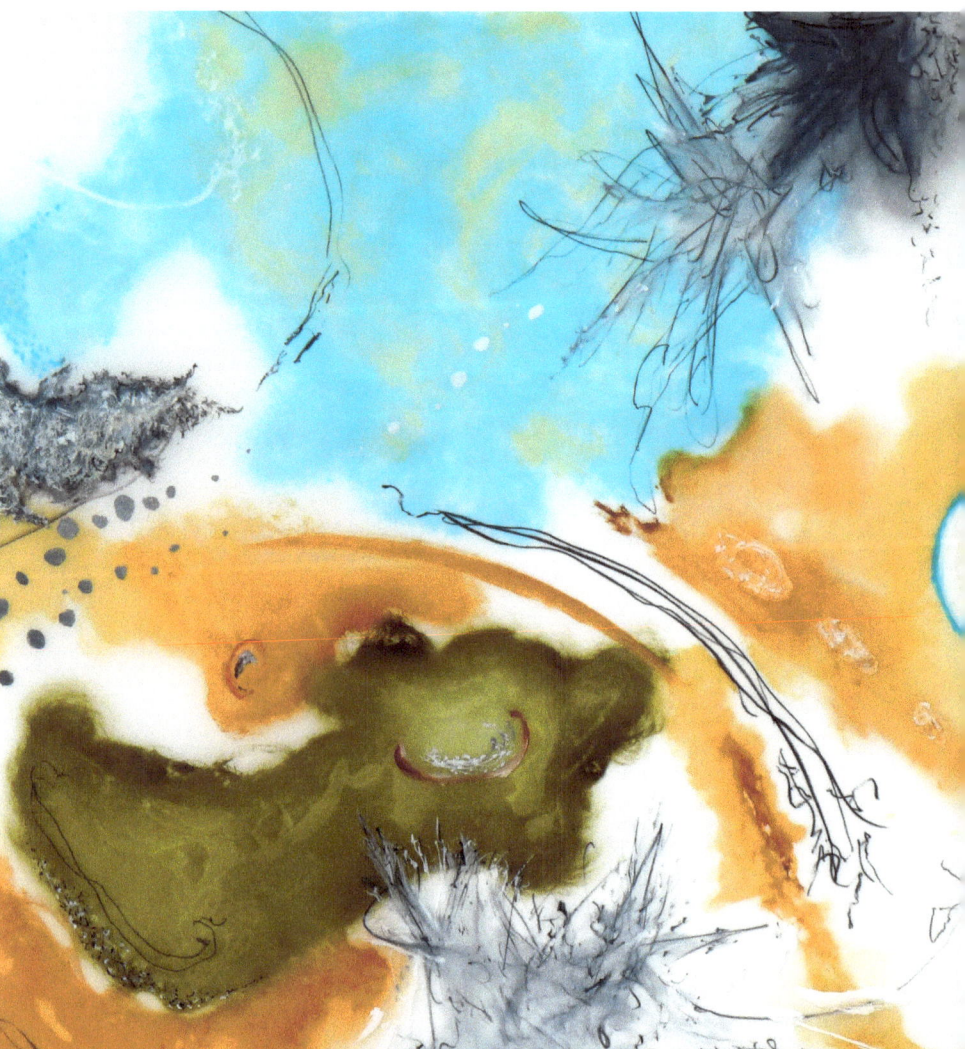

KEVORK GEORGE KASSABIAN

LOCATION: Guelph
WEB: georgekassabian.am
EMAIL: georgekassabian1@yahoo.com

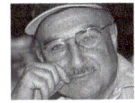

1967 Graduated Engineering, British Tutorial Institute. 1969 Graduated Computer Programming, B.M.T.I., Toronto. 1973 Graduated B.A. Fine arts, University of Western Ontario. As both a trained artist and engineer my work is a merging of science and art. I have always been interested by themes of space, mass and volume. I express myself through sculptures, paintings and photography.

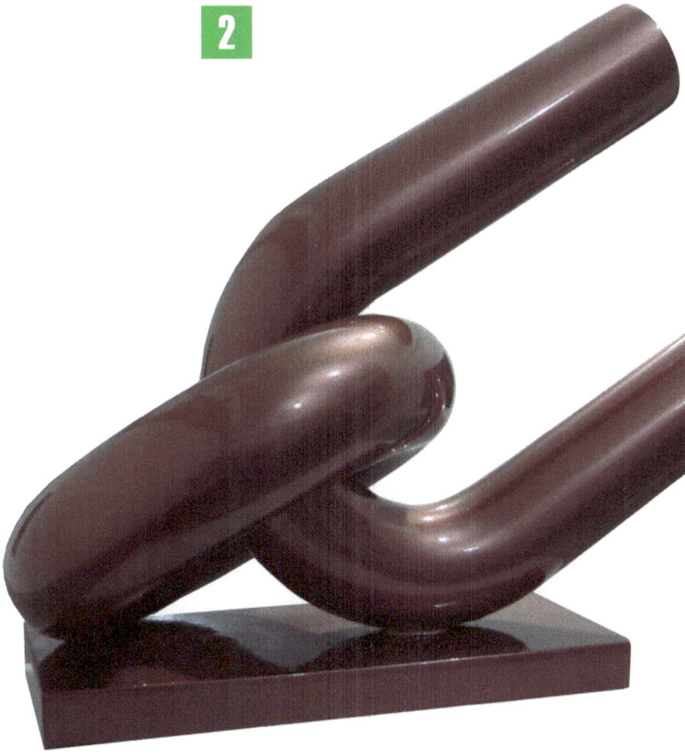

1 **The Blue Loop** 26x12x18" Auto metallic paint on metal. 2010.

2 **The Ring** 20x14x18" Auto metallic paint on metal. 2010.

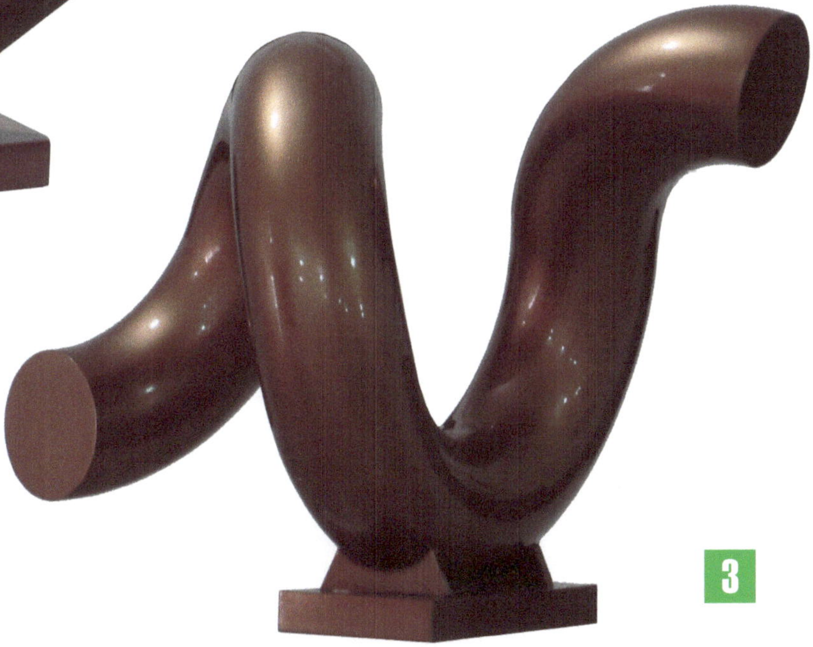

3 **The Golden Spiral** 38x24x20" Auto metallic paint on metal. 2010.

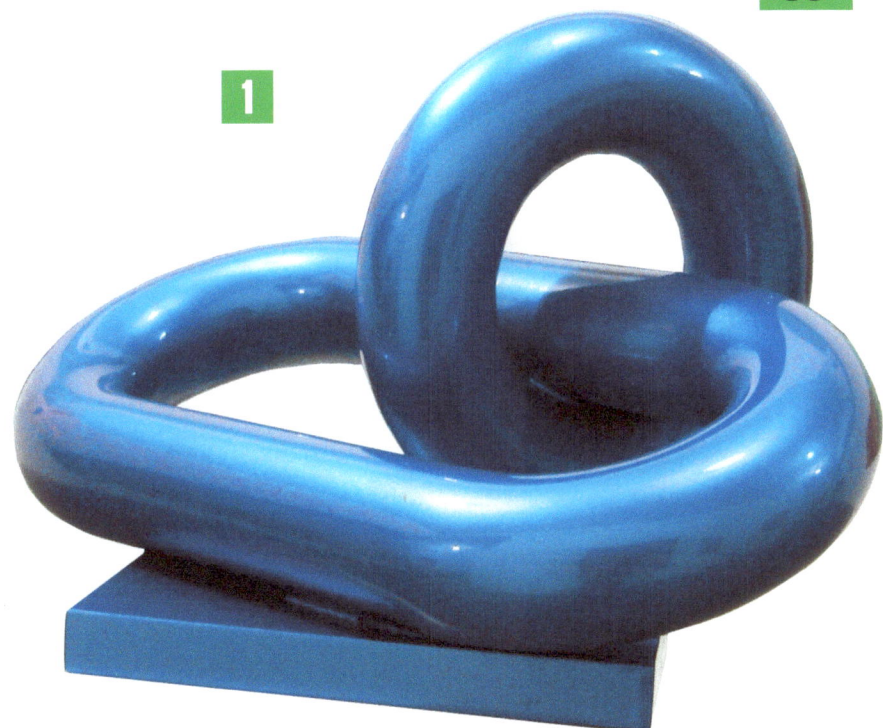

DORIS CLEMES

LOCATION: Guelph
WEB: (N/A)
EMAIL: (N/A)

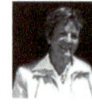

Doris' love and passion for vibrant creative painting has evolved over the 12 to 13 years. A member of the West Hills Art Group she enjoys painting with friends, taking workshops and painting outdoors. Doris has won numerous awards in juried shows, but her greatest reward is seeing a good number her paintings benefit charity.

1 Untitled

2 Untitled

3 Untitled

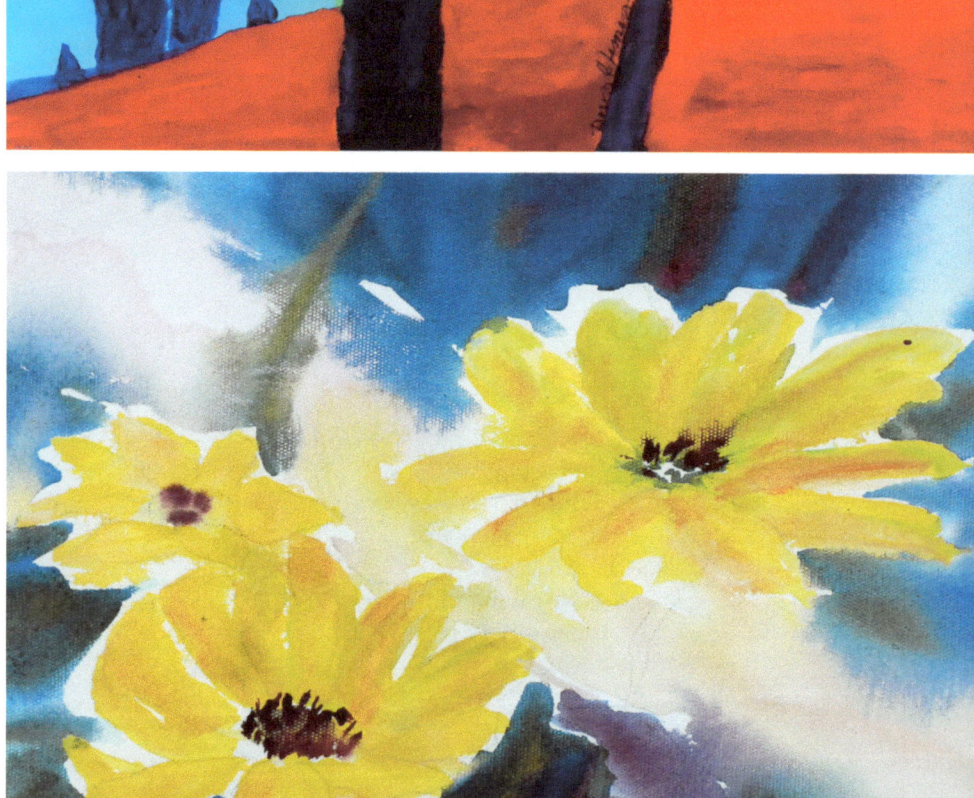

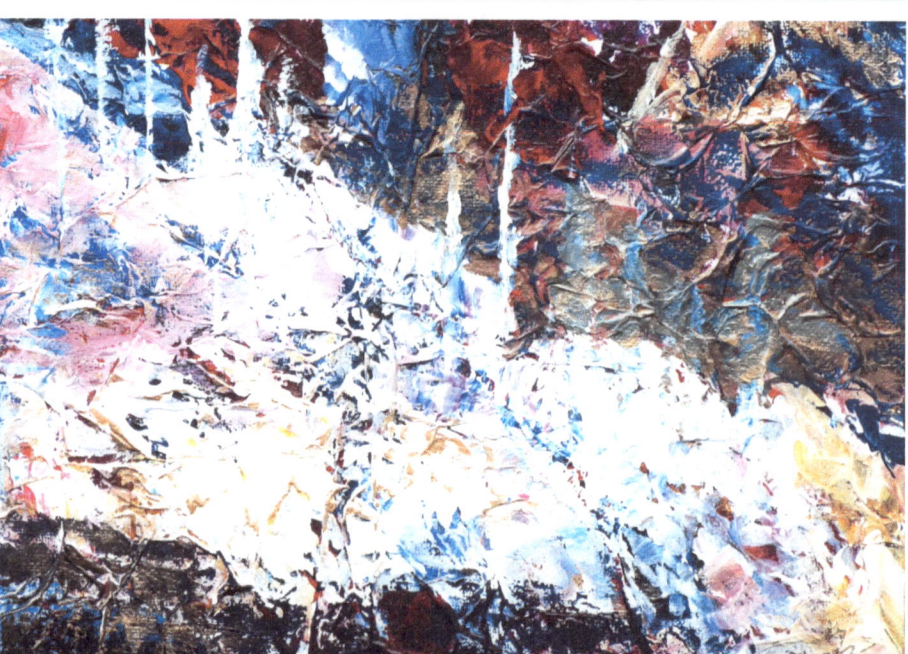

HANNE LORE KOEHLER

LOCATION: Cambridge
WEB: koehlerart.com
EMAIL: hannelore@koehlerart.com

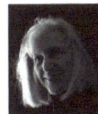

Born in Aachen, Germany, Hanne immigrated to Canada with her parents at the age of two. She grew up in Kitchener and married her childhood sweetheart. They live in Cambridge and have two children and two grandchildren who are the inspiration for much of her work. Next to her family, painting portraits, still life, landscapes, sports art, wall murals, illustrating and writing children's books are a constant joy in her life.

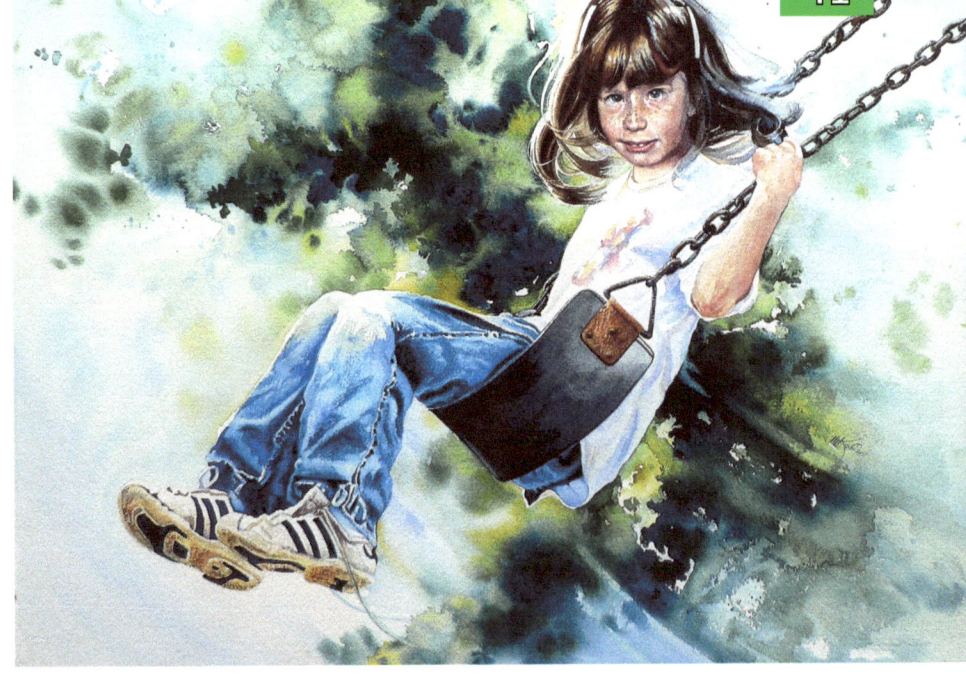

1

1 Tracy 22x30" Watercolour on paper. Portrait of girl on a swing.

2 Fish Tales 22x15" Watercolour on paper. Portrait of two young fishermen.

2

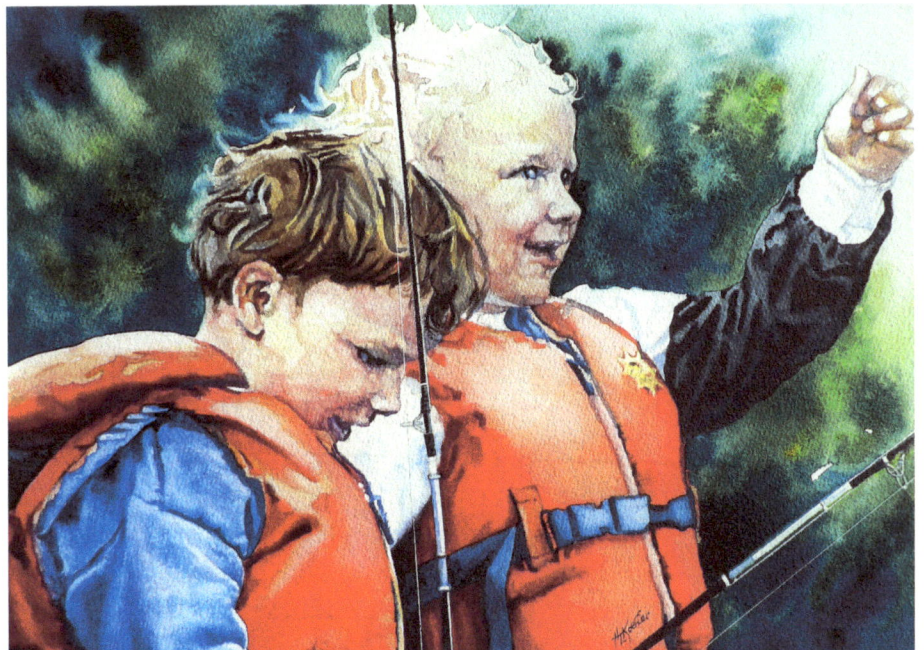

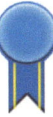

3 Inspiration 44x44" Oil on canvas. Algonquin autumn landscape.

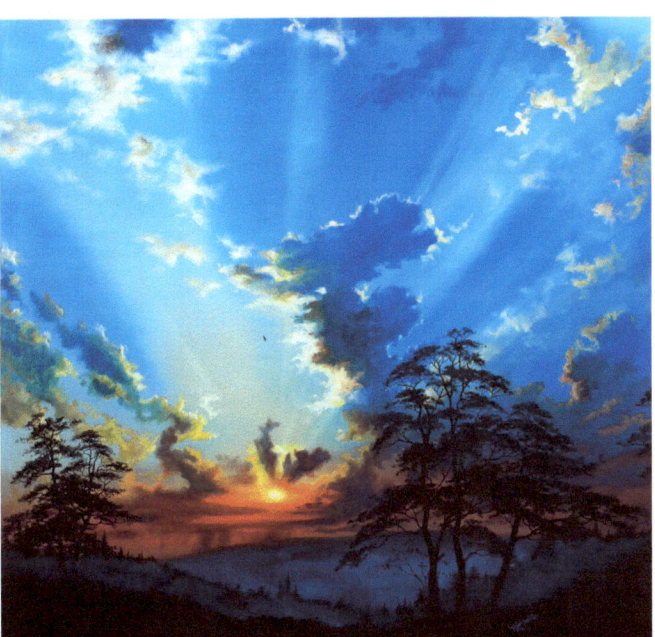

3

GINNY CARNEVALE

LOCATION: Cambridge
WEB: ginnycarnevale.com
EMAIL: ginnycarnevale@gmail.com

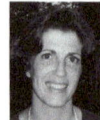

Ginny Carnevale lives in Cambridge, Ontario. She completed her Fine Art Degree at the University of Guelph, specializing in printmaking. Ginny spends her summer holidays in Northern Ontario surrounded by the landscape that inspires her work. After years of printmaking primarily in black ink, her focus in the last few years has been acrylic landscape painting using vibrant colour. Ginny has exhibited prints, pastels, pen & ink sketches and acrylic paintings in a variety of group shows since 1993.

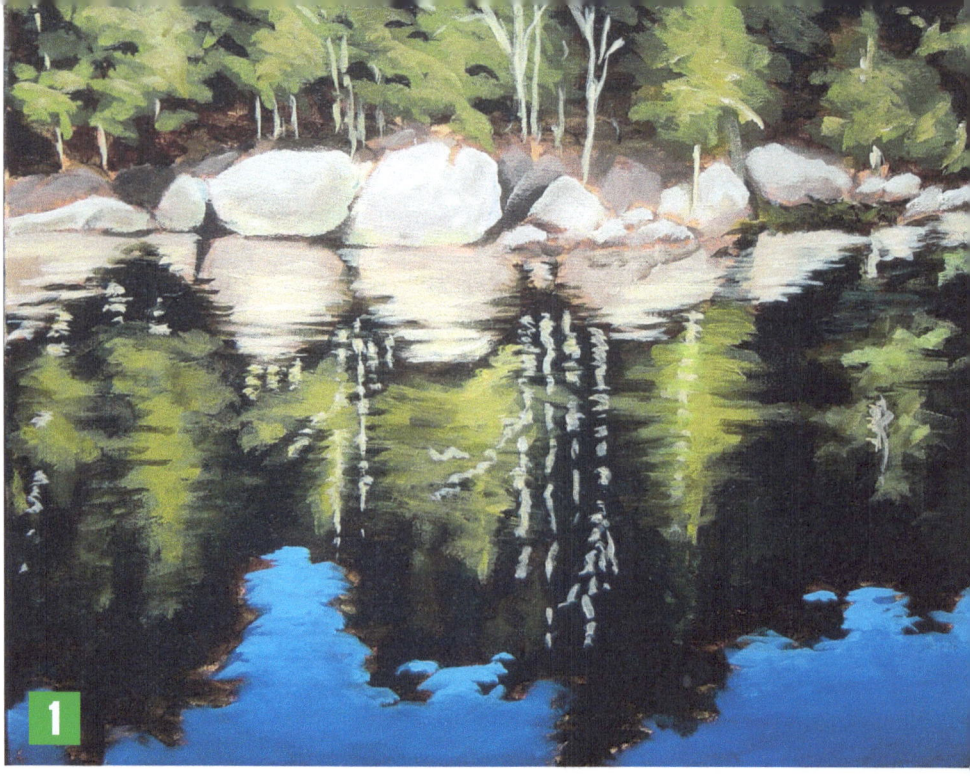

1 Clear Waters 16×20" Acrylic on canvas.

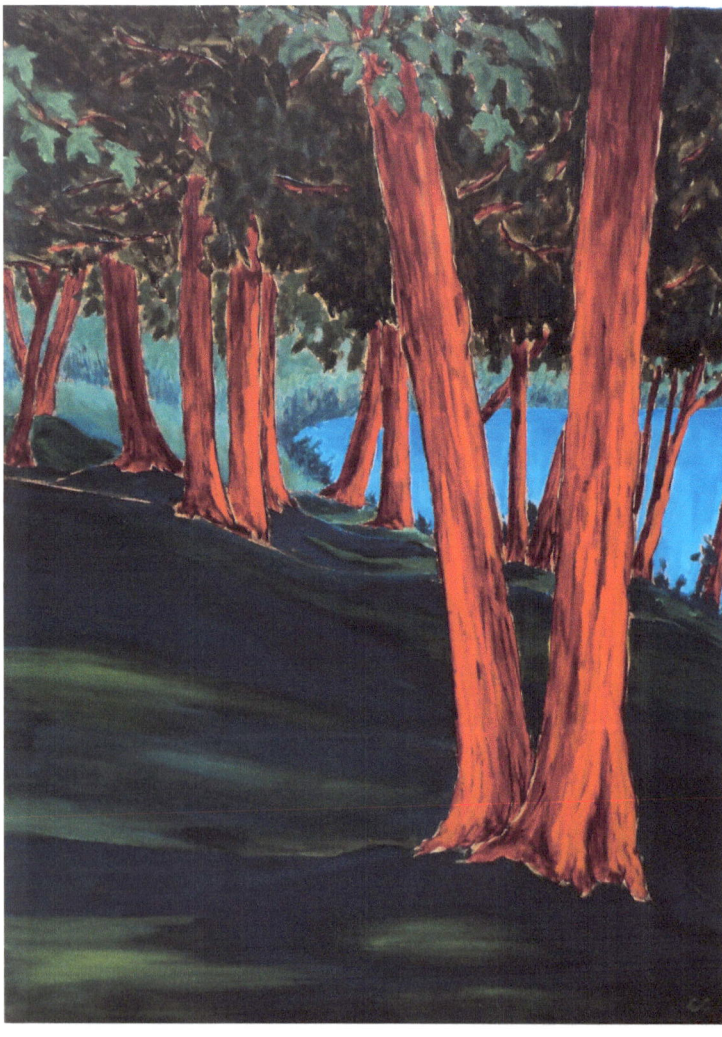

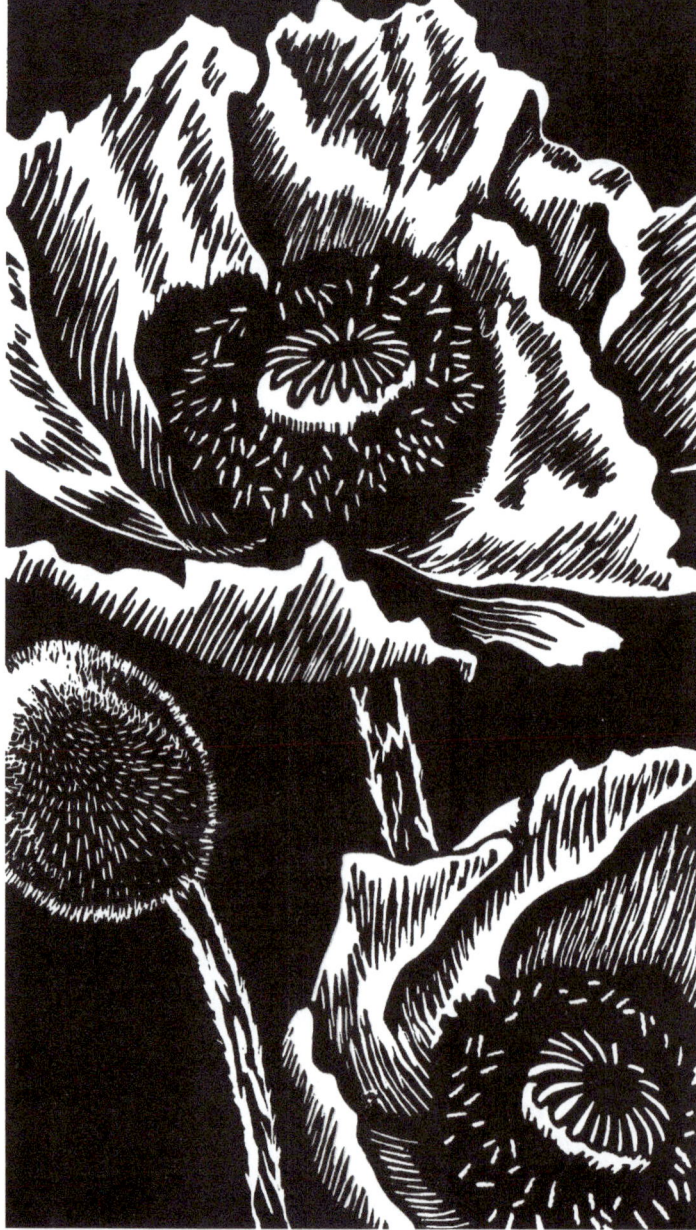

2 August Shade 31×41" Acrylic on canvas.

3 Poppies 5.5x10" Linocut print on paper.

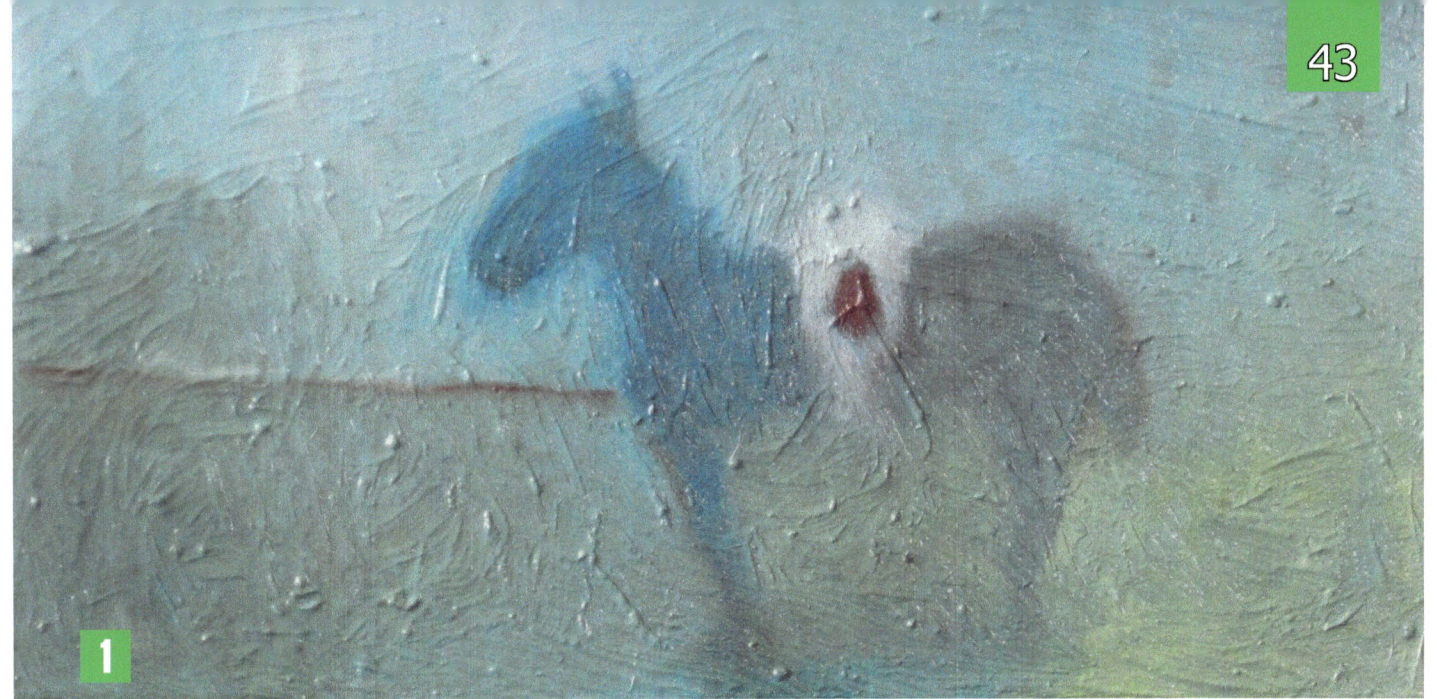

1 A Special Package 8x12" Oil on canvas board 2011.

CHRIS EVITTS

LOCATION: Guelph
WEB: chrisevitts.com
EMAIL: cevitts@rogers.com

3 Dream Catch 32x34" Oil on masonite board 2011.

2 We Rode Deep Into the Night 16x12" Oil on masonite panel 2011

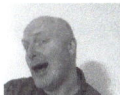

Born and raised in Toronto. I recieved my formal training at OCAD in Toronto. I pull my inspiration from many far flung corners, art, nature, symbolism ,myth, television, religion, psychology, dreams and the sub-conscious. All the works are spontaneous combustions, the paintings do evolve over time, with many acts of destruction leading to the final piece.

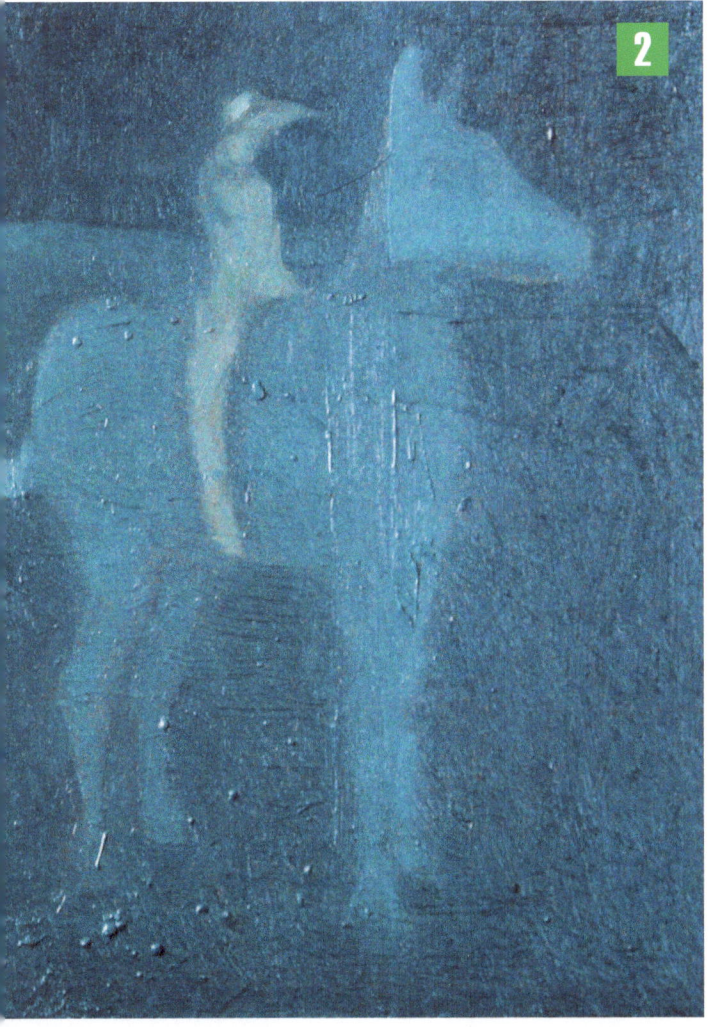

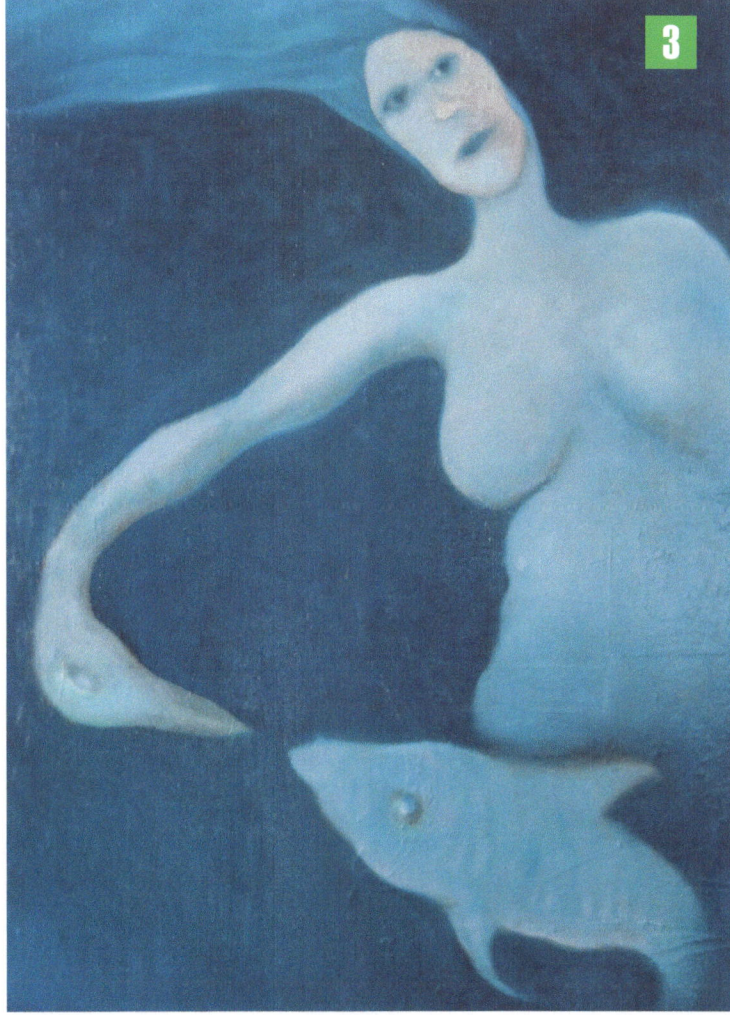

GRAY SCHILLING

LOCATION: Cambridge
WEB: (N/A)
EMAIL: gschills@hotmail.com

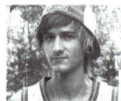

Gray Schilling is a self-taught mixed media artist, living outside of Cambridge, primarily creating abstract on canvas. But he plans on widening his horizons as time goes by.

1

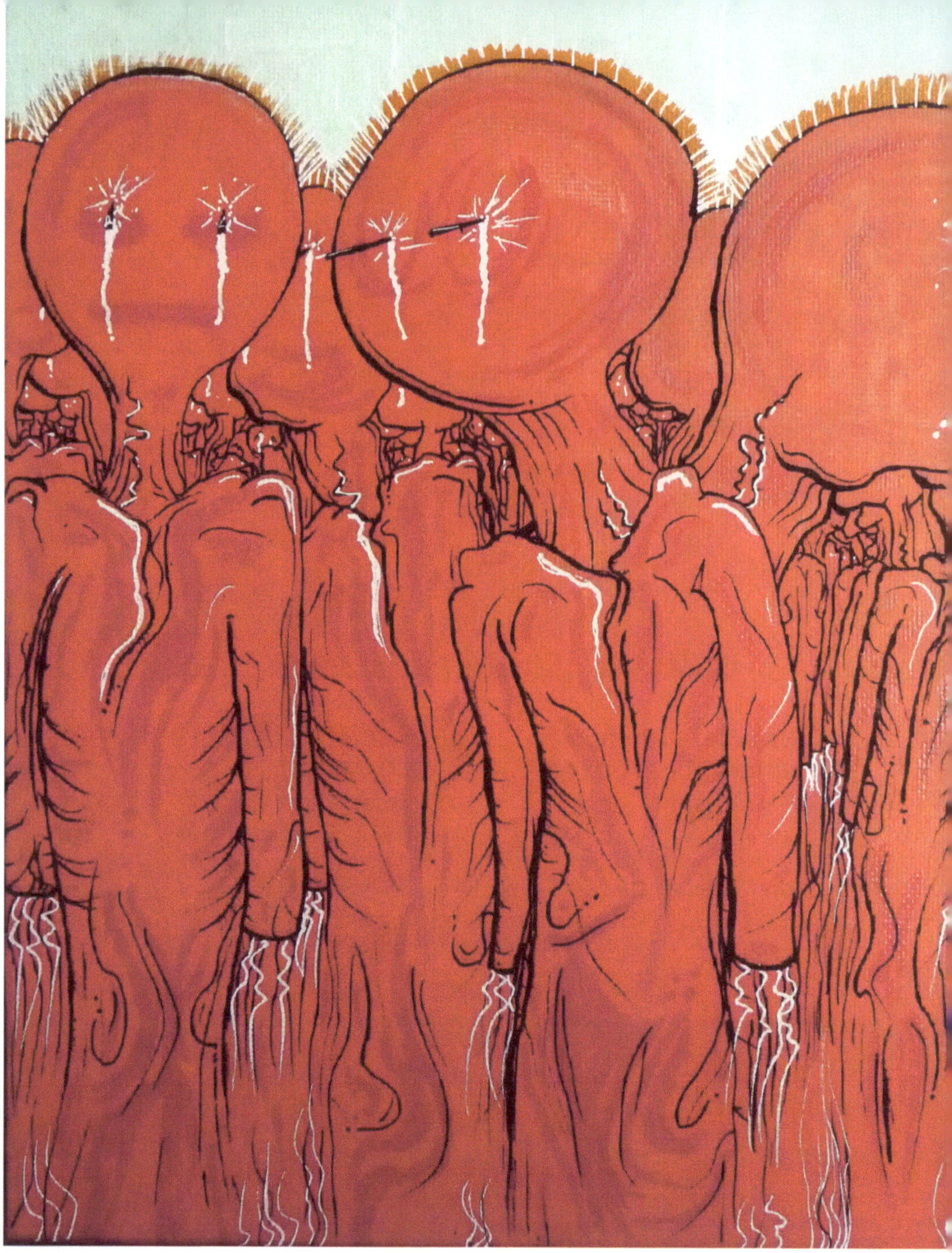

2

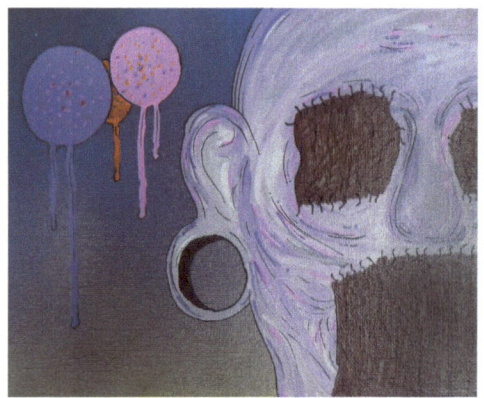

1 My Army II 8x10" Oil on canvas.

2 Gagged 8x10" Oil on canvas.

3 Feet, Clouds & Flowers 24x28" Oil on canvas.

3

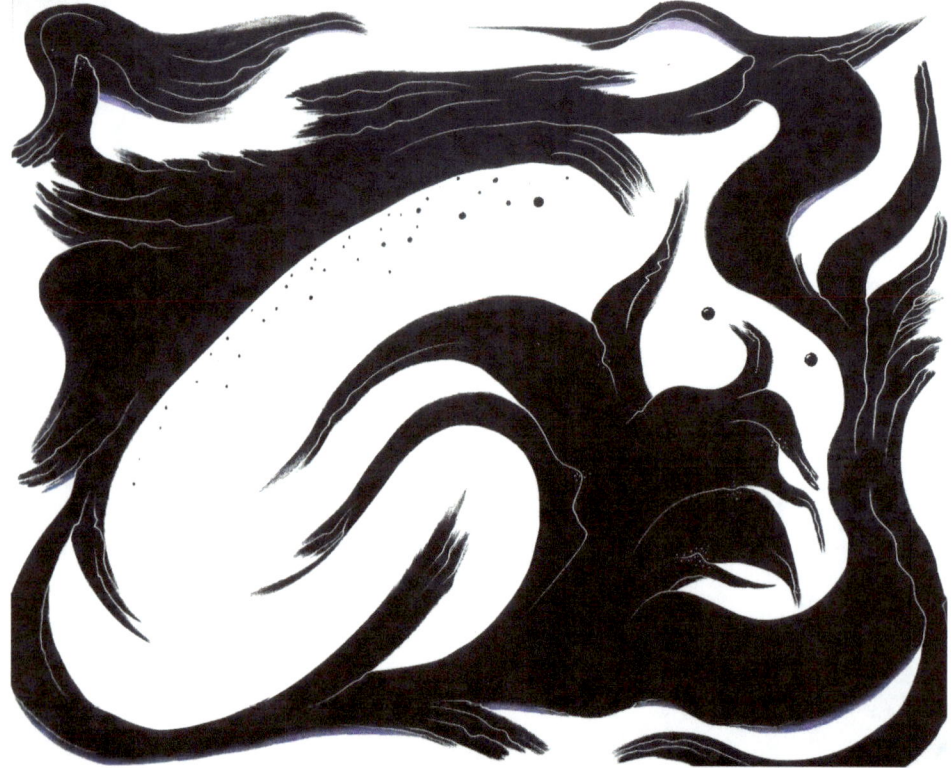

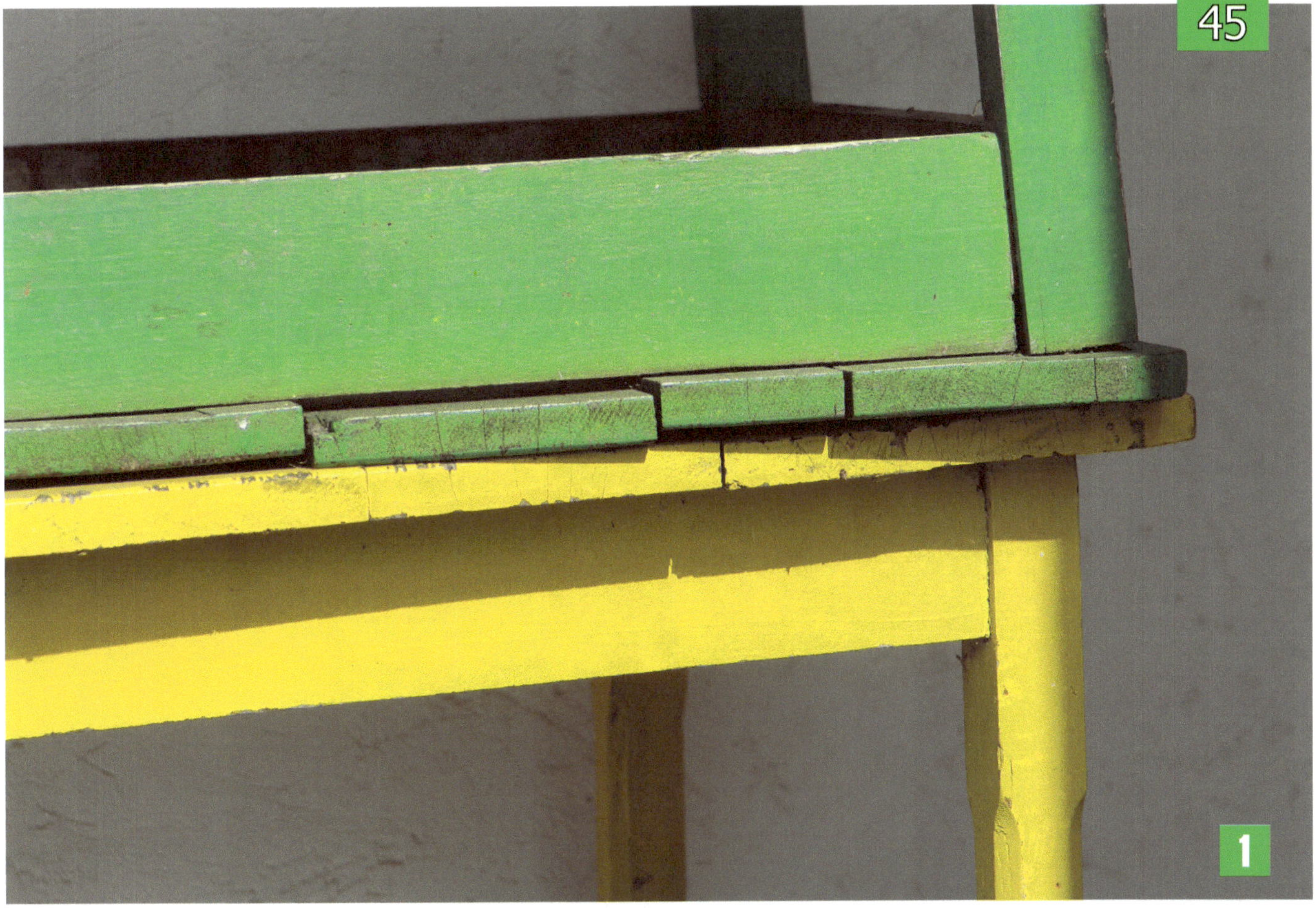

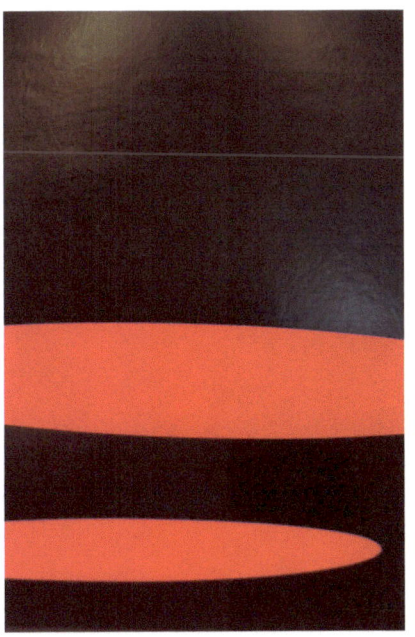

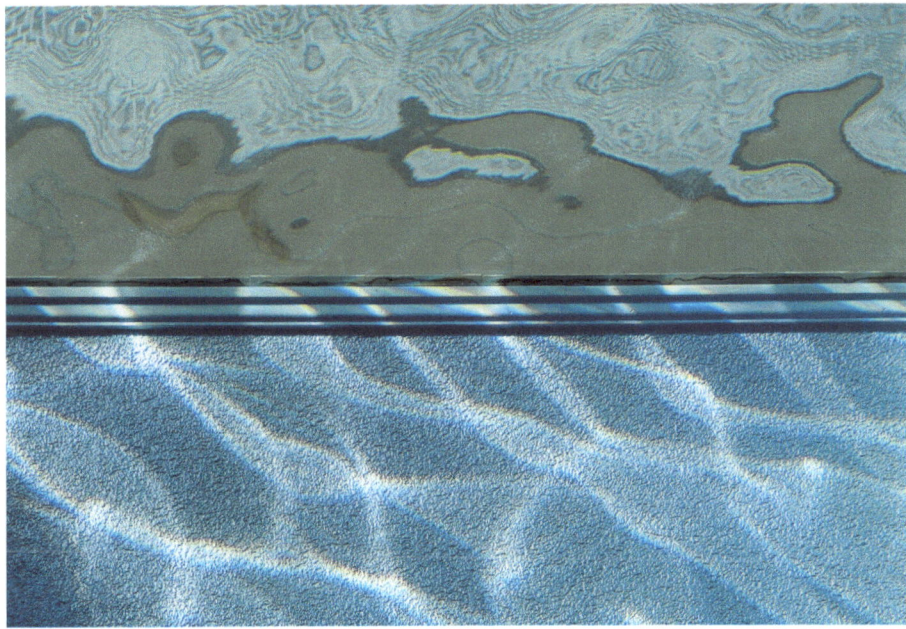

1 **Lost Table** Photograph.

2 **Black & Red** Photograph.

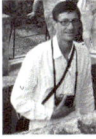

ALAIN GUILLOU

LOCATION: Cambridge
WEB: aguillou.com
EMAIL: ag5320@gmail.com

3 **Translucent** Photograph.

Alain Guillou sees the world through different eyes - those that have not been distracted by our fast moving modern world. At a young age, Guillou discovered photography. His quest for the perfect image is unending. He travels the globe, driven by a vigorous determination to capture the beauty that he sees & a profound respect for architecture. As a free artist he is unpredictable; his French background and his ability to see a different world through his lenses make his photography unique. He grew up in Normandy & got his education in engineering. He is a self-taught photographer.

CHRIS SMITH-DONISON

LOCATION: Guelph
WEB: art-in-the-basement.ca
EMAIL: chrissmith425@hotmail.com

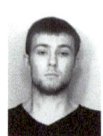

Though his paintings are sometimes animated or cartoon like, Guelph painter Chris Smith-Donison mainly thinks of himself as an abstract artist. He often draws inspiration for his paintings from graffiti. Chris usually paints on canvas, but enjoys working on old wooden boards (or whatever else he can get his hands on) most. Chris is a recent high school graduate who paints in his spare time, and plans to attend college for Art and Design.

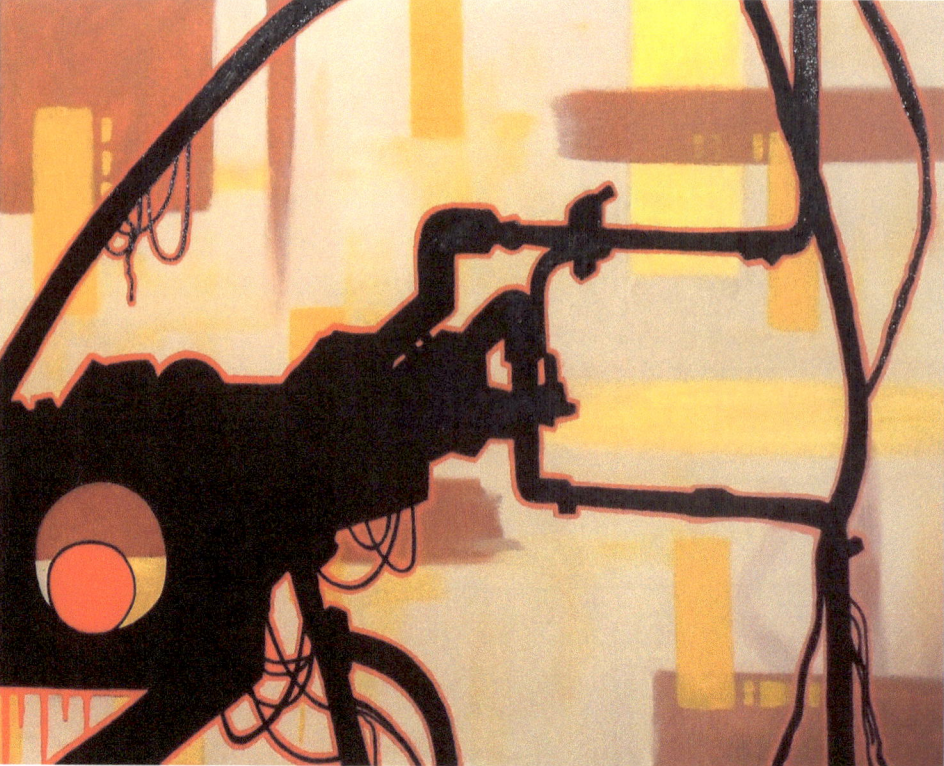

1

1 Untitled 30x24" Acrylic on canvas.

2 Untitled 10x10" Acrylic & Oil on board.

2

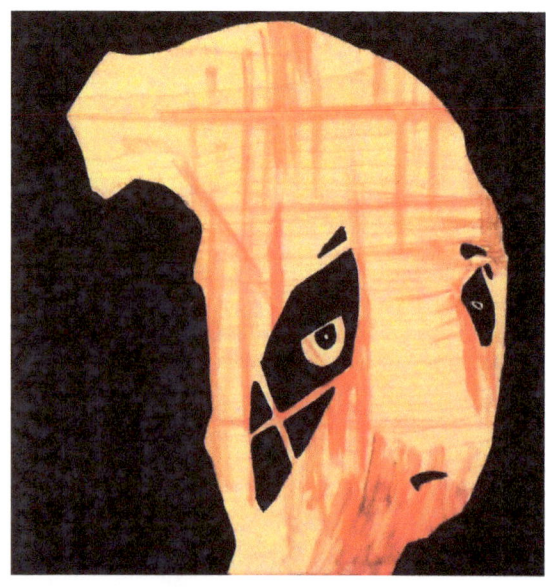

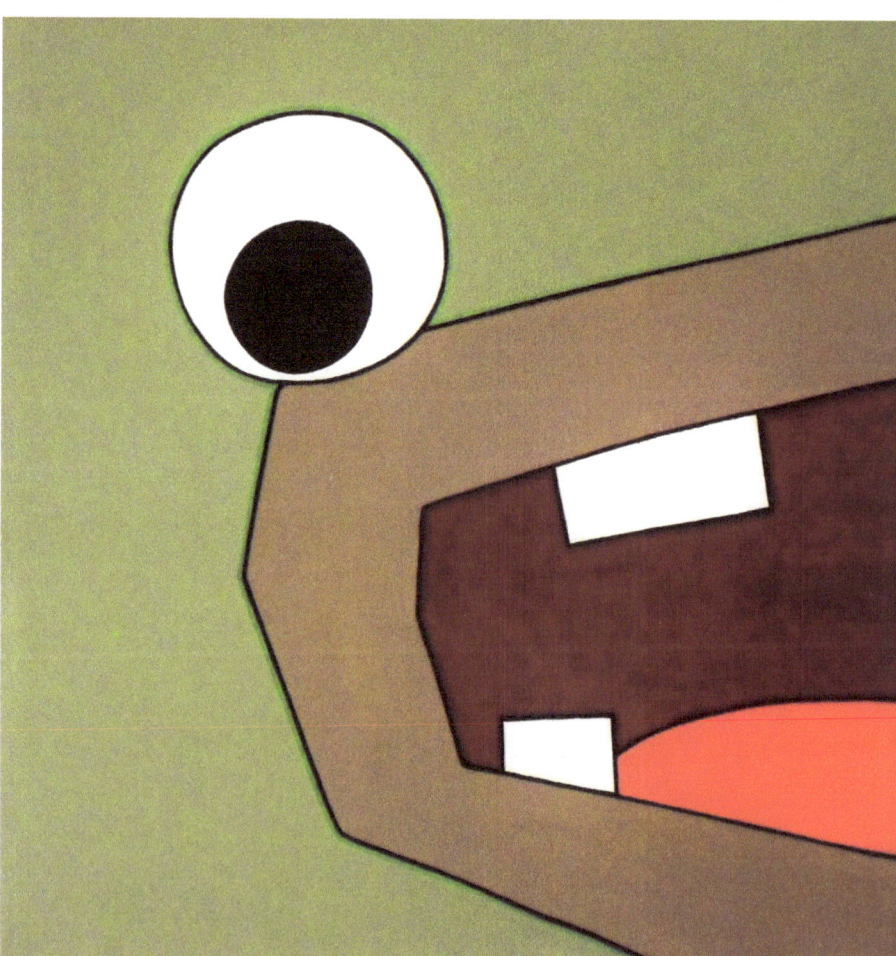

3

3 Untitled 16x20" Acrylic on canvas.

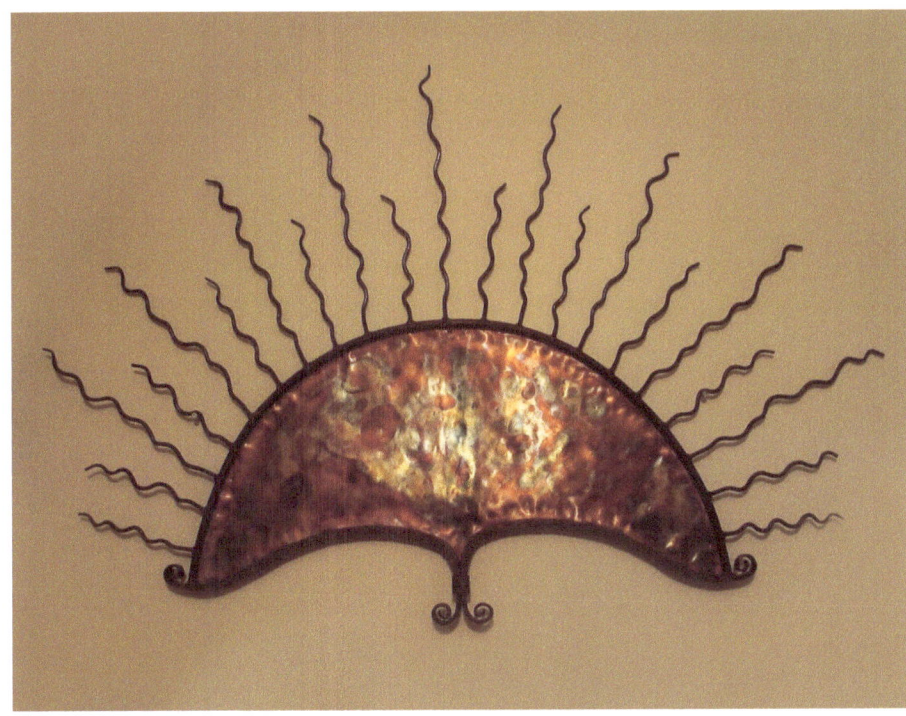

1 **Energy** 60x36" Forged steel & copper.

2 **A Passionate Moment** 12x60" Forged steel.

1

GRAEME SHEFFIELD

LOCATION: Guelph
WEB: ironwoodanvil.com
EMAIL: info@ironwoodanvil.com

Graeme hand forges original art pieces out of steel, manipulating positive and negative space to showcase the strengths and delicacies of the medium. To forge heirloom-quality pieces, he uses a combination of traditional and contemporary techniques with tools that have been used over the centuries. Sheffield notes "It's a pleasure to take an otherwise cold lifeless medium as steel and transform it into an object that allows people to appreciate its flexibility, strength and limitations at the same time." Graeme's work is displayed in commercial and private collections across Canada.

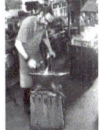

2

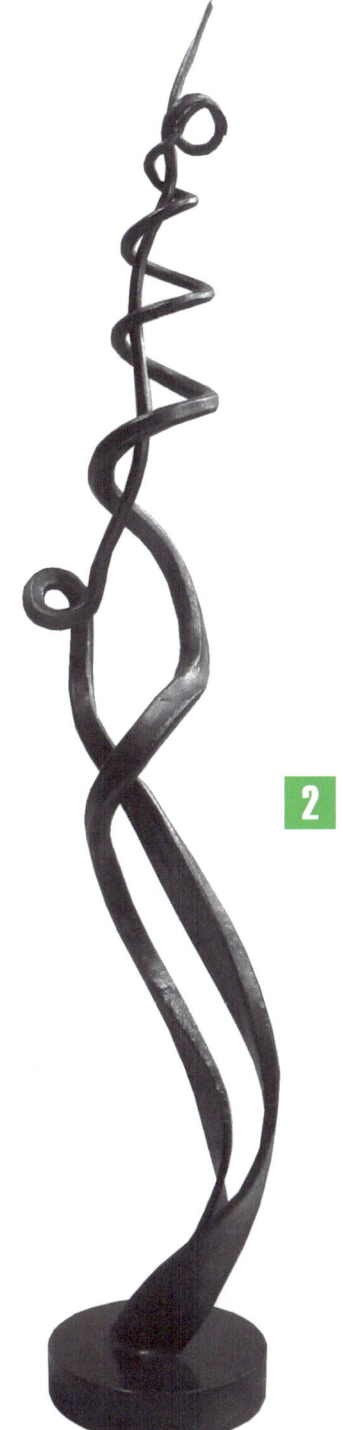

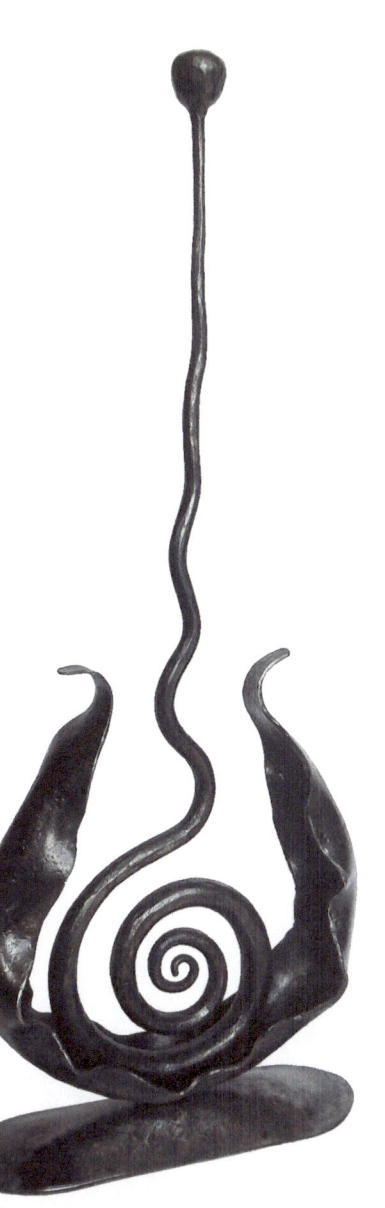

3

3 **Germination** 12x28" Forged steel.

1 Journey 5x5" Drypoint on Somerset paper, one of an edition of 4.

2 Rebirth 12x12" Drypoint & Etching on Somerset paper. Artist proof.

3 Interior Self-Portrait 12x12" Aquatint on Somerset paper. Artist proof.

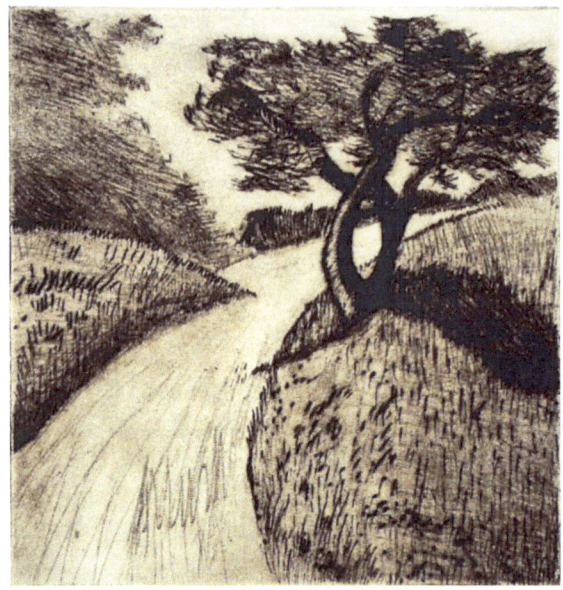

1

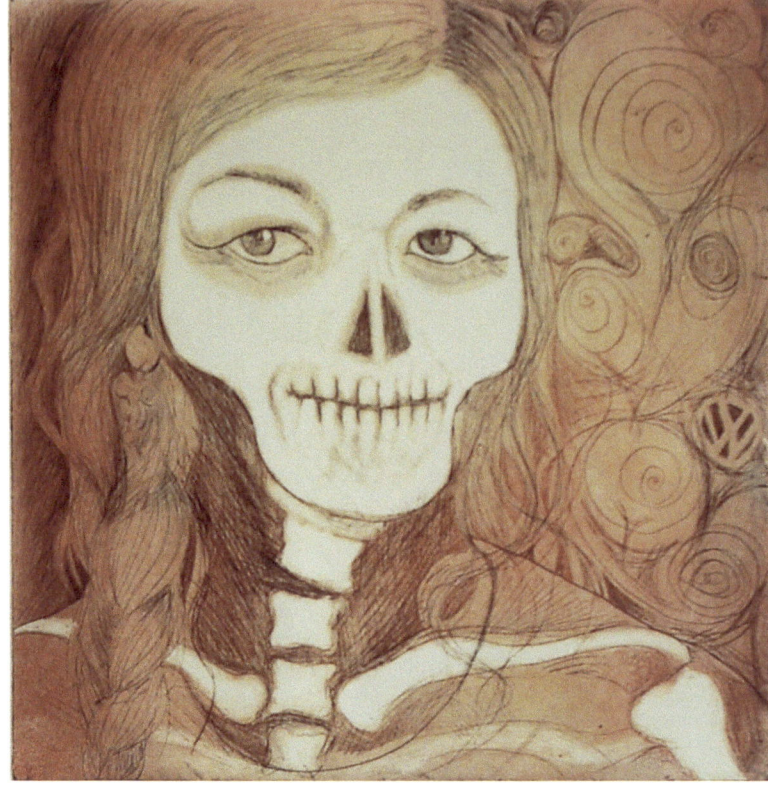

2

HEATHER FRANKLIN

LOCATION: Cambridge
WEB: riversideprintgroup.com:
EMAIL: ed@buttonfactoryarts.ca

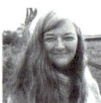

Heather Franklin is a visual artist living and working in the Region. After graduating from the Ontario College of Art, she has spent over 20 years working as an artist, instructor, curator, gallery technician and arts administrator. Heather has been involved in organizations such as; Waterloo Regional Arts Council, Kitchener Waterloo Society of Artists, Cambridge Sculpture Garden, Mayor's Celebration of the Arts, Arts Advisory Committee of Cambridge and the Waterloo Community Arts Centre. Recipient of Bernice Adams Award, Y.W.C.A. Women of Distinction Award, Citizen of the Year Award. Heather is currently a member of the collective, the Riverside Print Group. All of these images relate to a car accident I had last year and the pain and the healing process I went through, to become a new me!

3

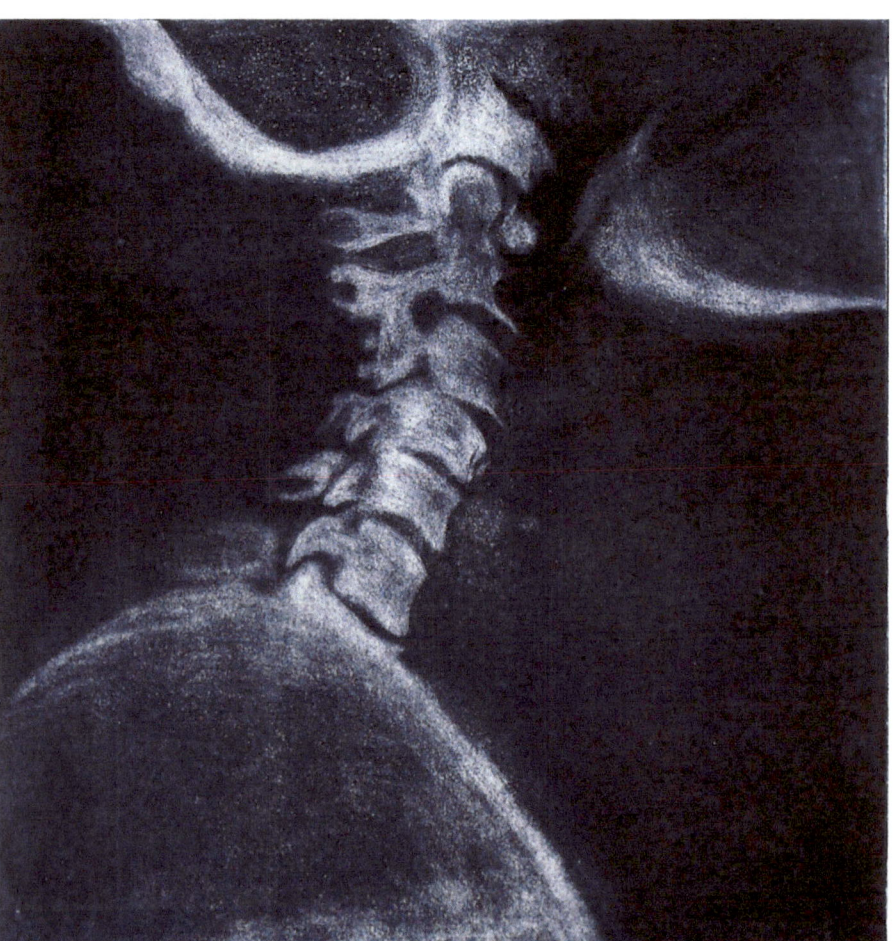

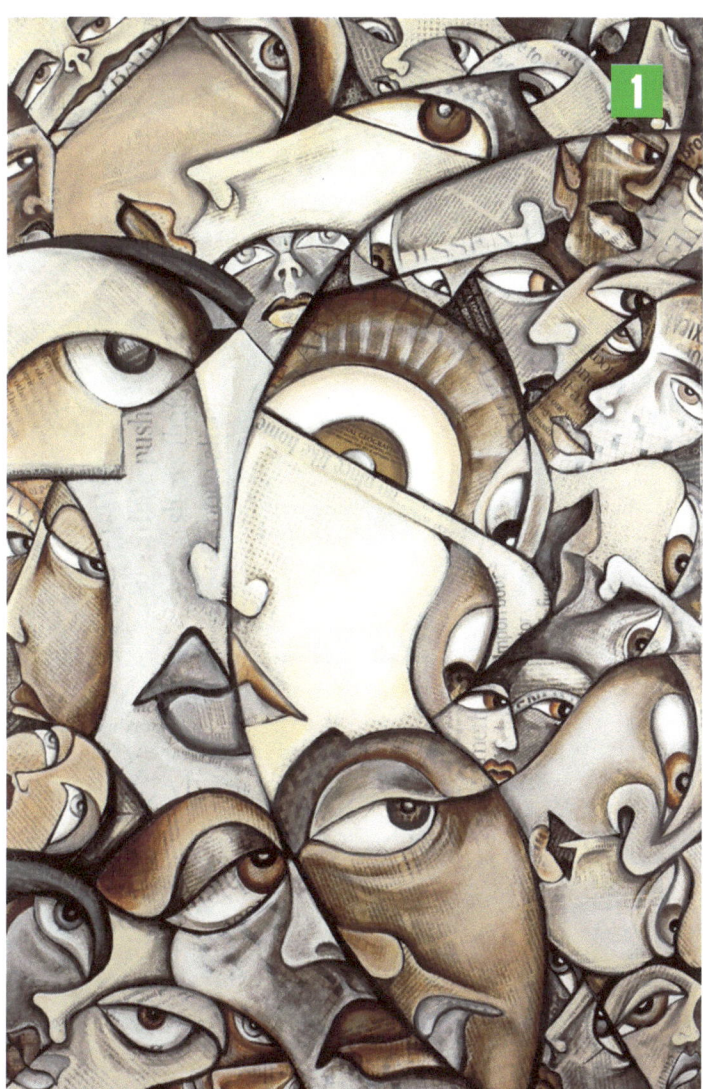

BARBARA YOUNG

LOCATION: Hespeler, Cambridge
WEB: (N/A)
EMAIL: ryoungq@rogers.com

Barbara started her creative career as a graphic artist in Toronto then Guelph. After a brief move to California, she decided to pursue an even more creative career as an artist. Her imagination has always supplied her with an unlimited amount of drawings and ideas which she transforms into paintings or collage. She is always curious about people's reaction to her unique, sometimes unusual artwork, but is most interested in the dialogue that is created by her work. Whether it is positive or negative, any reaction is what is most important.

1 The Desperate Crowd 24x36" Mixed media. From a pen & ink drawing in my sketchbook. Inspired by the events of Hurricane Katrina. The images of desperate people in the news had a profound impact on me, thus its use in my piece.

2 Noninvasive Species 9x12" Acrylic & pen. My whimsical imagination at work. Everything came off of the pen without much thought, but I soon realized most of these creatures are at risk of possible extinction and if things don't improve for them soon we will only have images left.

3 Bon Ton #4 12x16" Mixed Media. One in a series of lovely looking women wearing extravagant hats and outlandish prints that may or may not be very fashionable. Inspired by a late 19th century French fashion illustration.

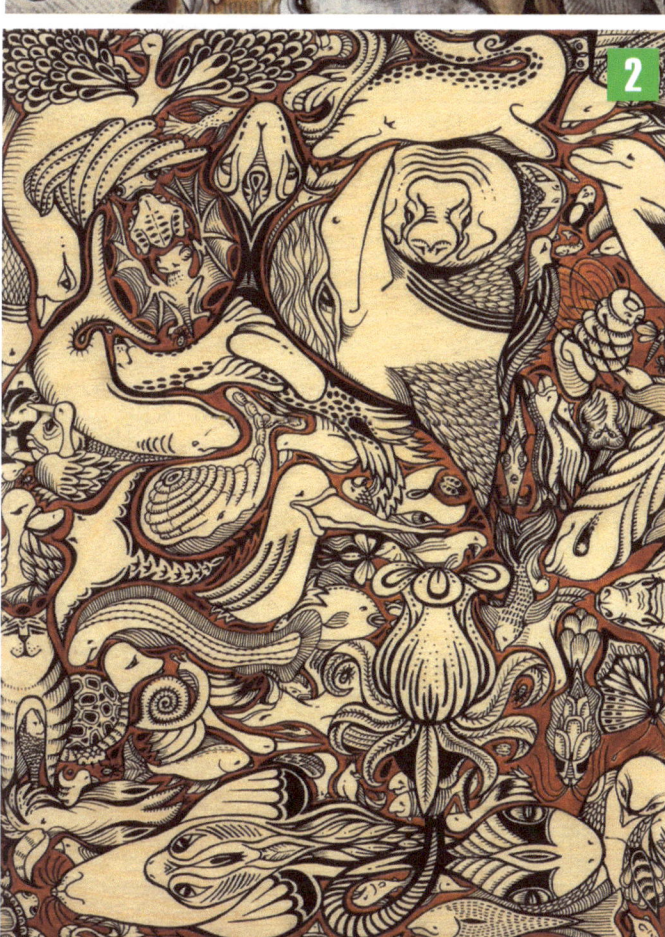

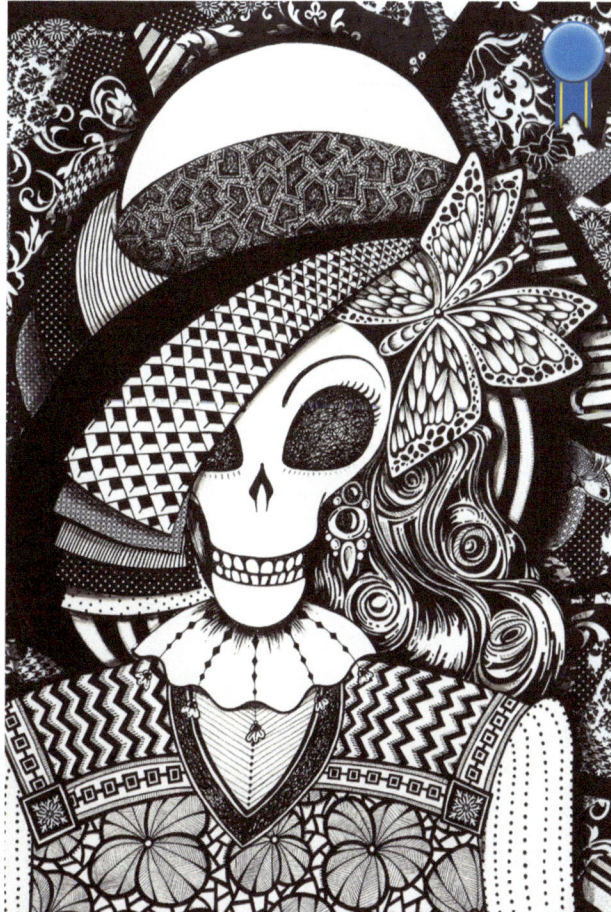

1

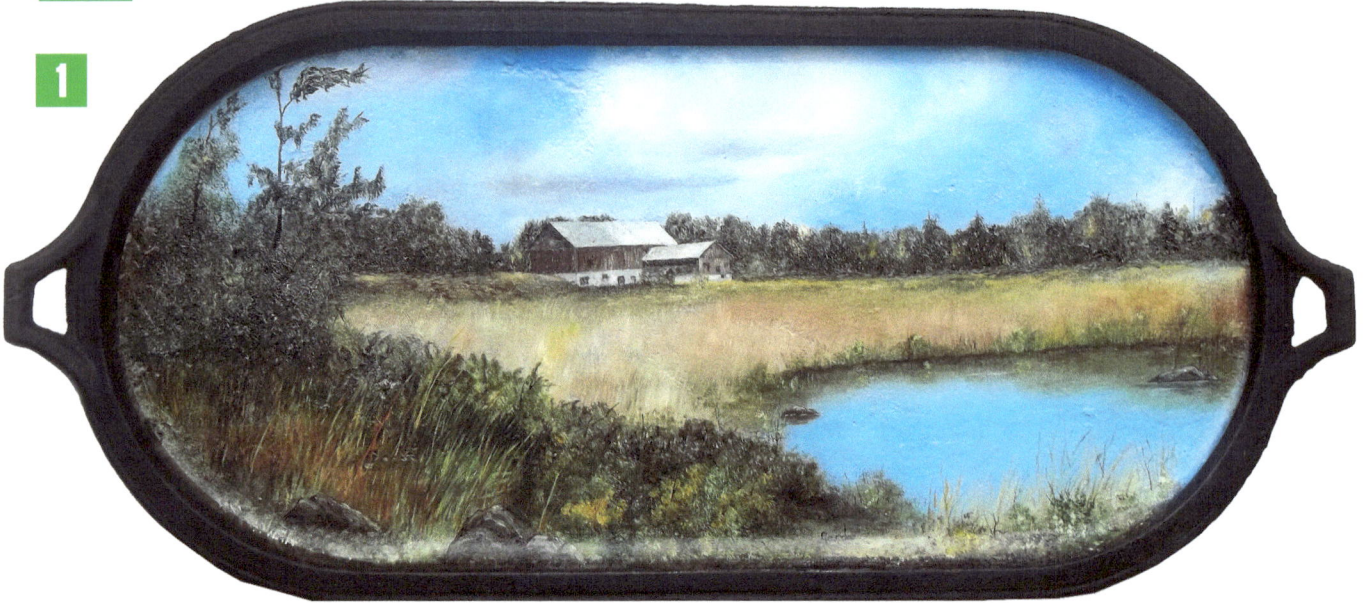

GERDA THIBODEAU

LOCATION: Guelph
WEB: (N/A)
EMAIL: (C/O) siouxtk@yahoo.ca

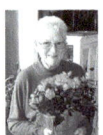
Gerda is a woman full of life, fun laughter and family dedication. She enjoys Septembers on the beach, reading and friends. Gerda paints mostly scenery & wildlife with oils. Her specialty is miniatures (3"x3"or less) so it is best to see them in real life as photography can't caputre their stunning detail. She also paints on larger canvas, wood slabs, old saws/milk cans, walls etc.

1 Cast Iron Skillet Tray 9x15" Oil on skillet.

2

3

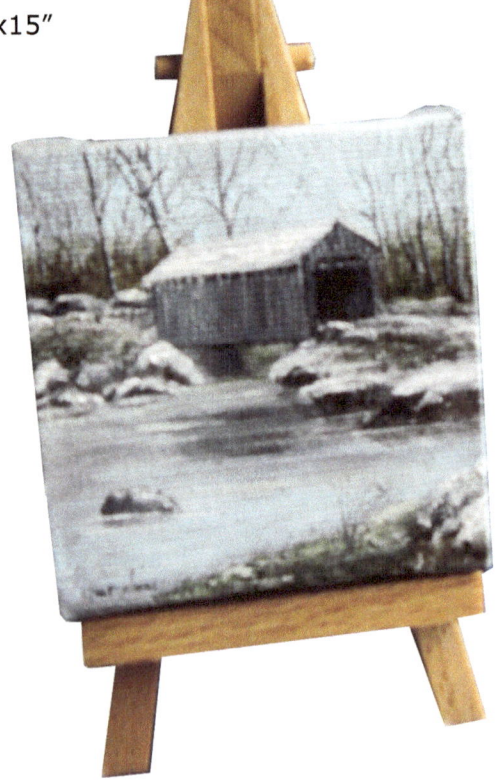

2 Covered in Winter 3×3" Oil on canvas.

3 Misty Serenity 12×13" Oil on canvas.

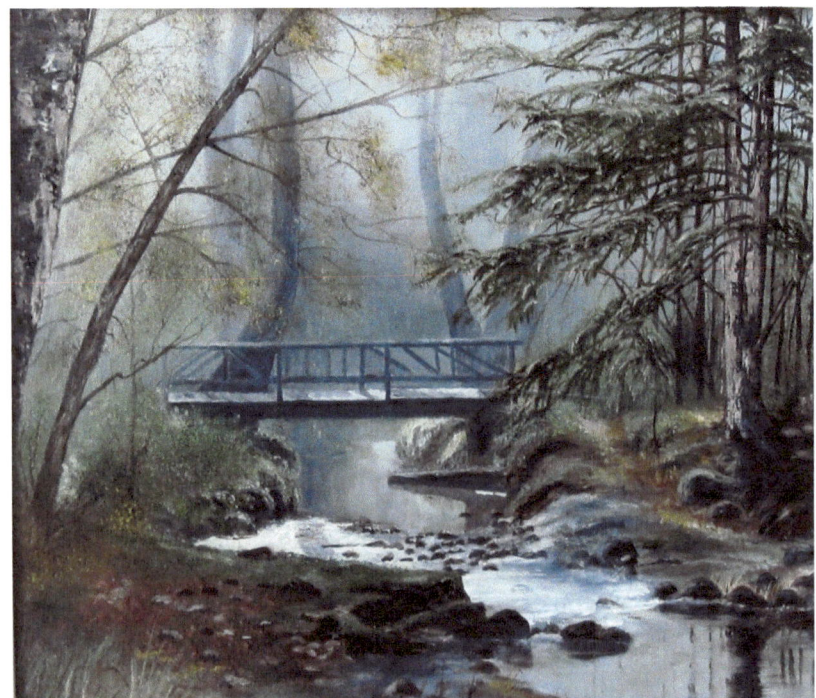

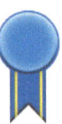

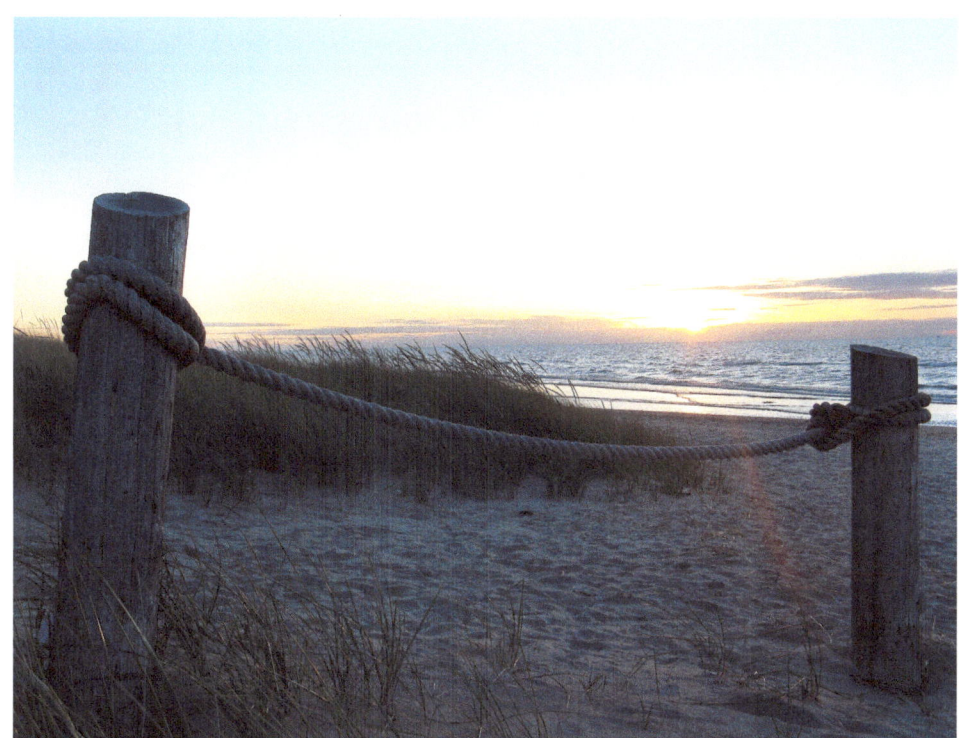

Sioux Thibodeau

LOCATION: Guelph
WEB: (N/A)
EMAIL: siouxtk@yahoo.ca

Sioux is an amateur photographer, mother and grandmother. Sioux takes photos of things that catch her eye and then her mother, Gerda, will sometimes paint them in oils. Fun loving, full of laughter, family and friends are Sioux's best attributes.

1 Tranquil Grass Photograph.

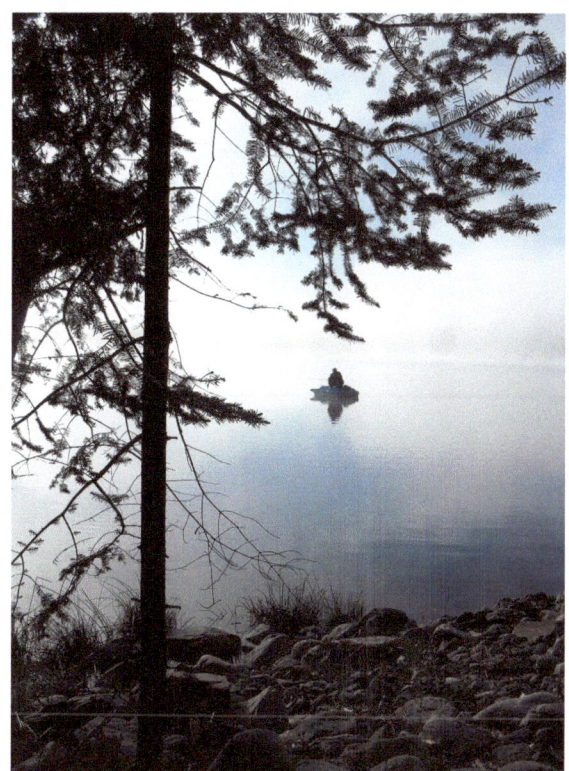

 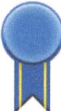

2 "Still" Fishing Photograph.

3 God's Artistry Photograph.

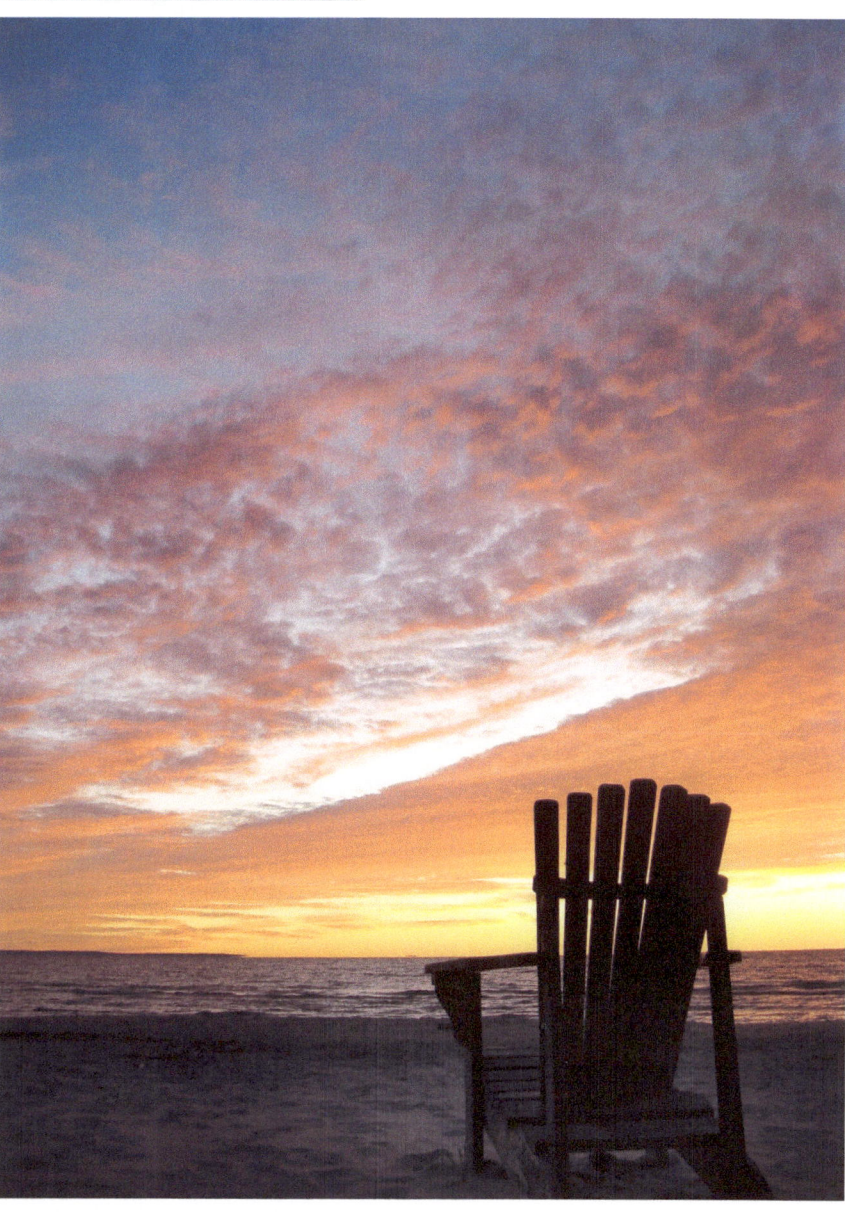

AGNES NIEWIADOMSKI

LOCATION: Ancaster
WEB: agnesmakes.com:
EMAIL: agnes.niewiadomski@gmail.com

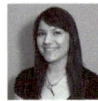

Agnes graduated with distinction from the Ontario College of Art & Design in 2008 from the Sculpture/Installation Program. She loves all things handmade. She works in a variety of media including, but not limited to wood, fibre and cake!

1 Brick Wall (detail)

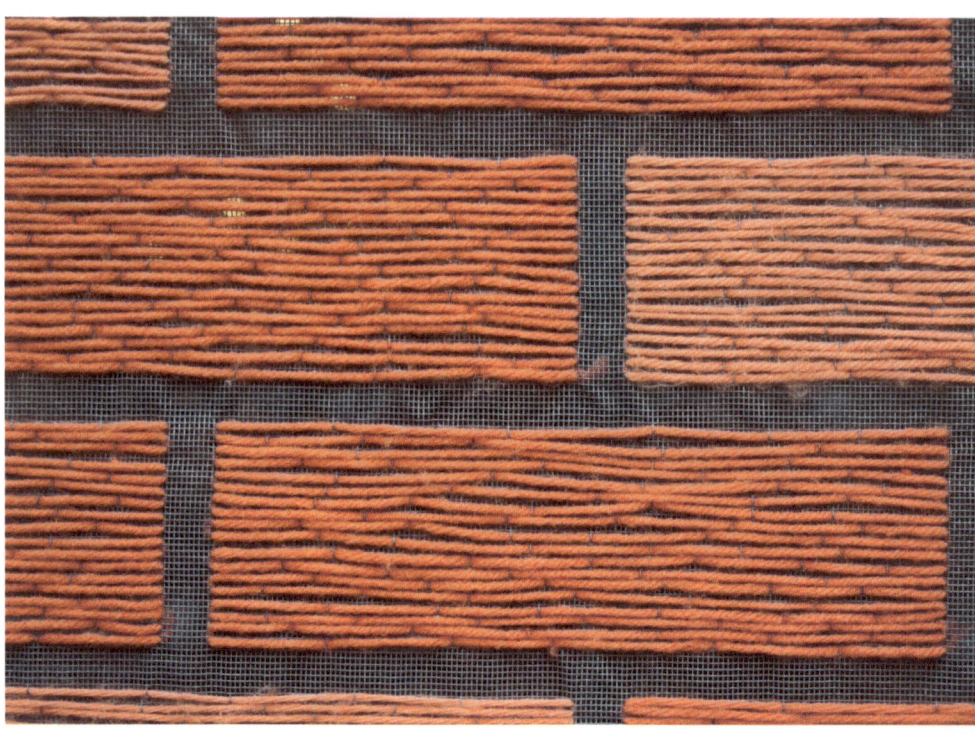

1

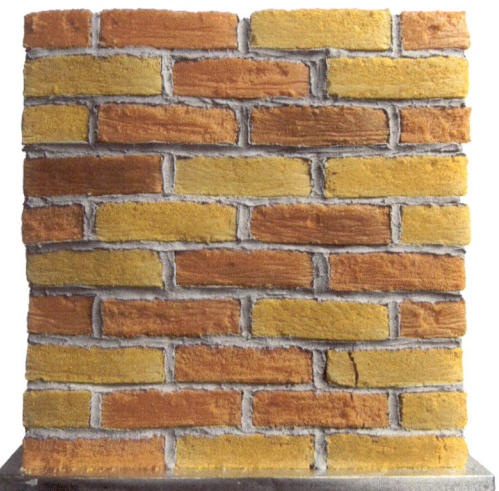

2

2 Cake Wall 2'x2'x4" 30 cake bricks baked in custom aluminum pans, assembled with butter cream 'mortar' icing. See video on my website.

3

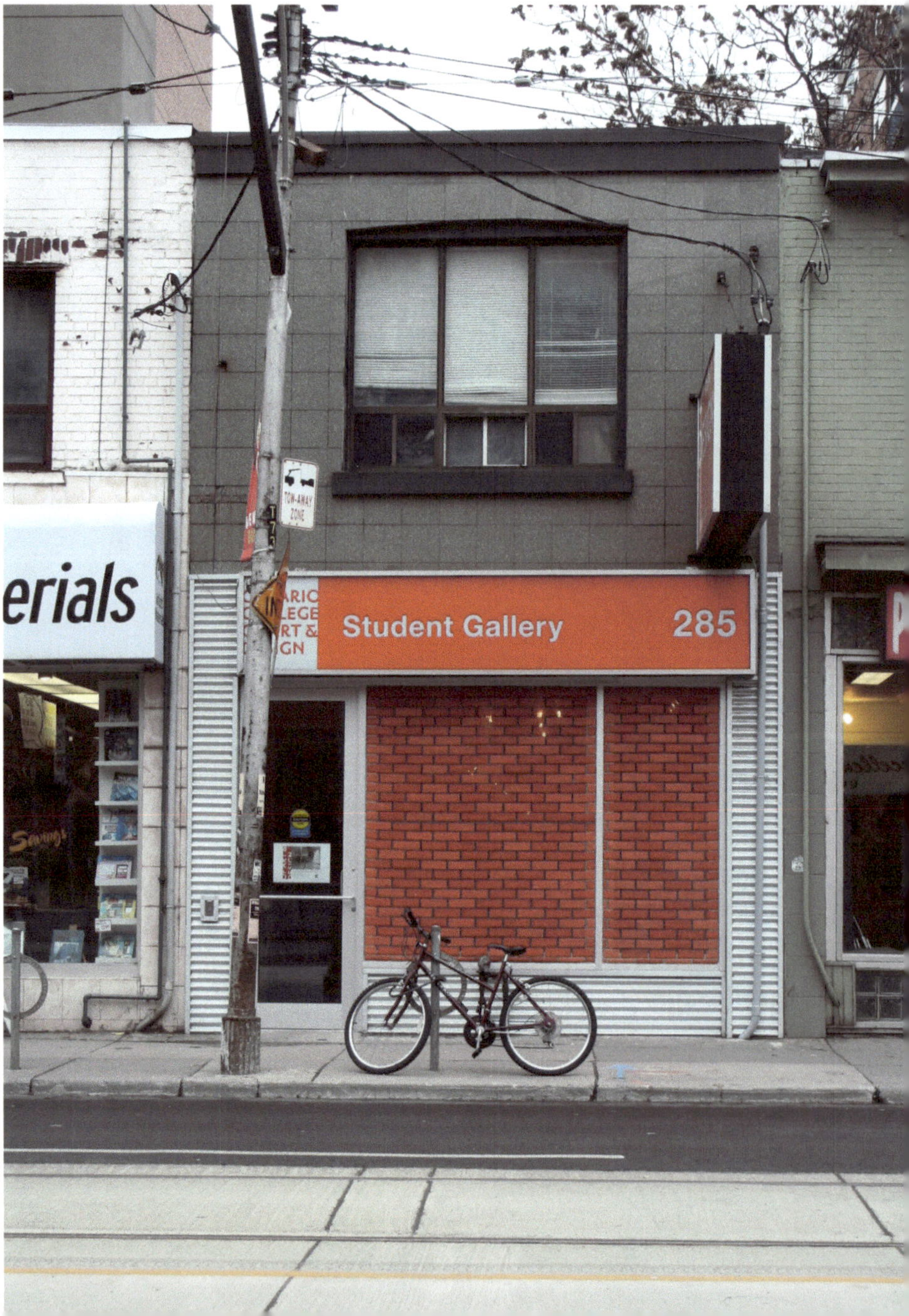

3 Brick Wall 6'x7' & 6'x3' panels. Hand embroidered acrylic yarn on fibreglass mesh screening.

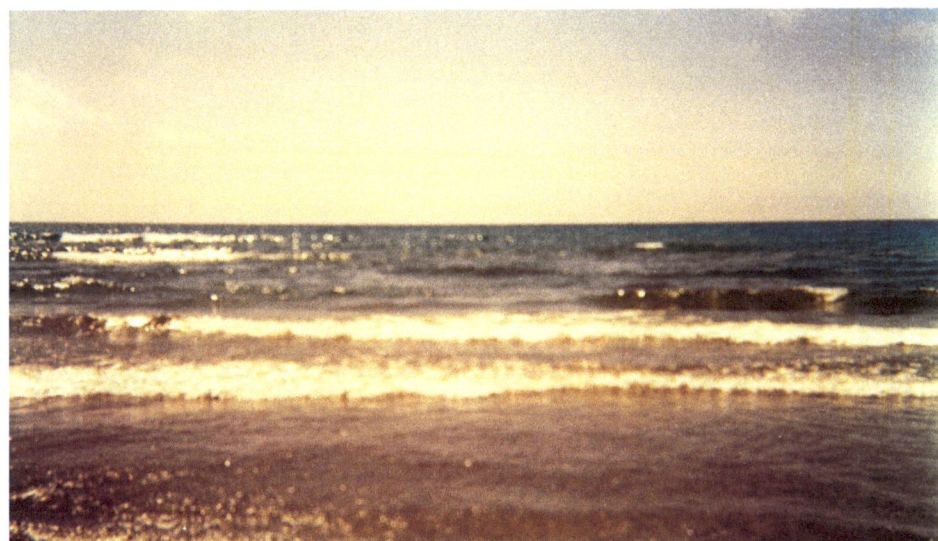

1

AINSLEY BOYD

LOCATION: Guelph
WEB: ainsleyboyd.com
EMAIL: ainsley.boyd@gmail.com

Ainsley's photographs are about seeing as we did when we were children; before we were taught how to see, essentially re-learning vision. It's about enjoying the transitory sensual pleasures of life, the small moments, and bringing whimsey and joy into our rushed routine. Her images are shot with film using vintage cameras and embrace the out of focus and grainy qualities, drawing attention to the object of the photograph while creating an unfamiliar image of the familiar world.

1 Lethargic Tide Photograph.

2 Sanctuary Photograph.

3 Urban Gossip Photograph.

2

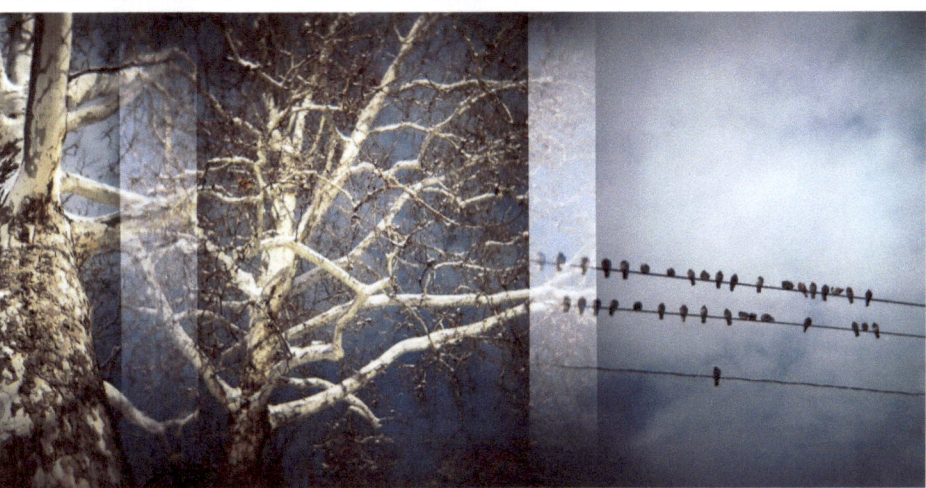

3

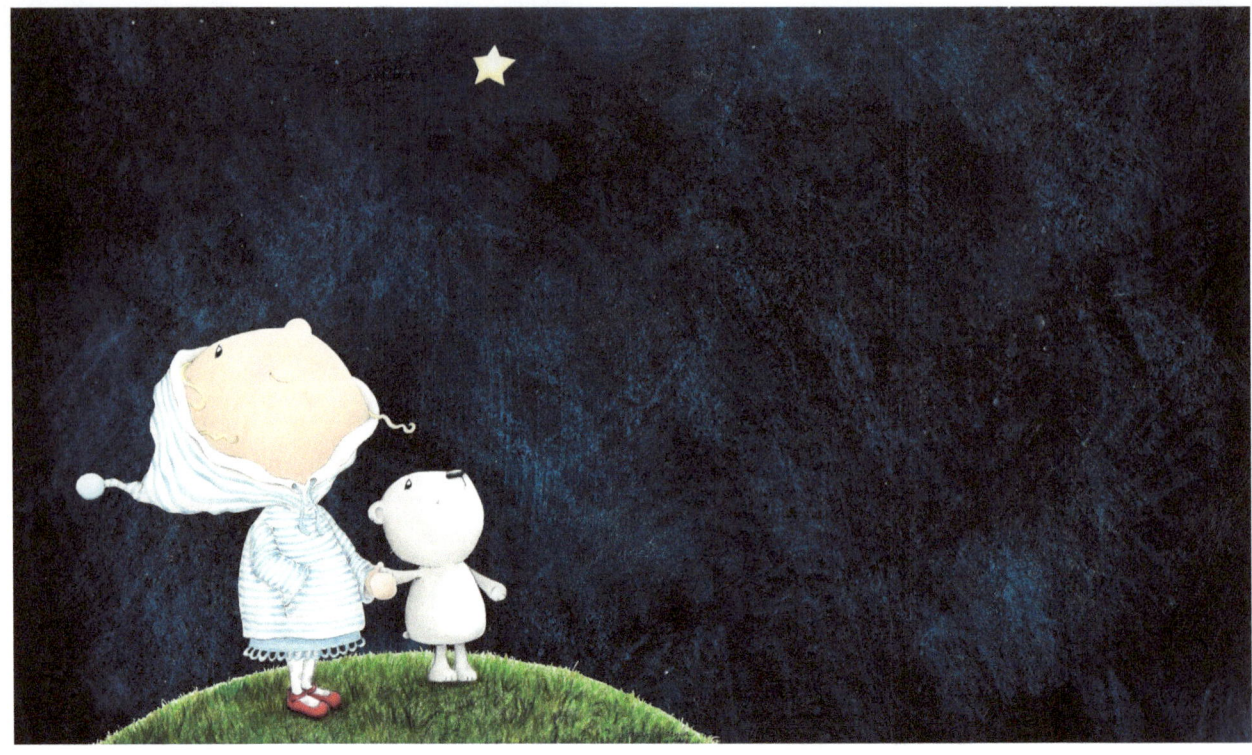

1 **Star Light** approximately 9½x7½" Mixed media.

2 **Owl by Moonlight** approximately 7½x7½" Mixed media.

3 **Jack & Peep** approx. 6x6½" Paper clay, wire & mixed media.

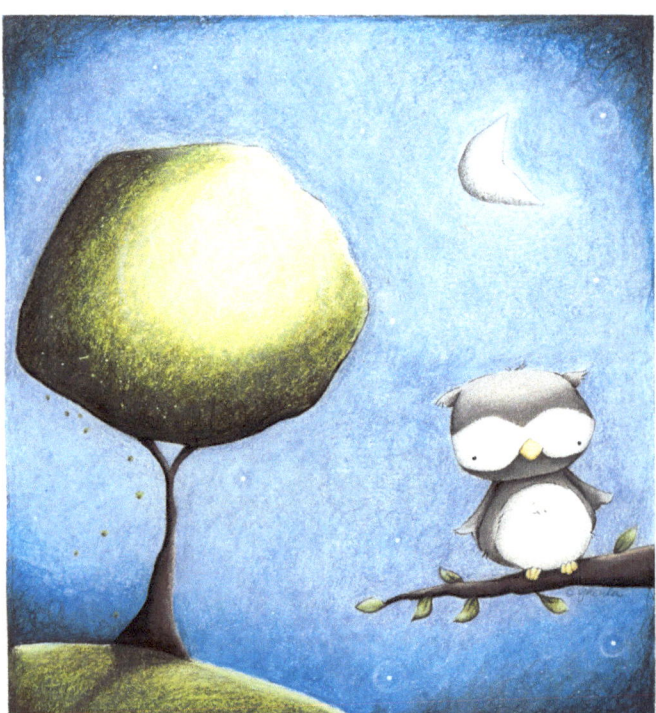

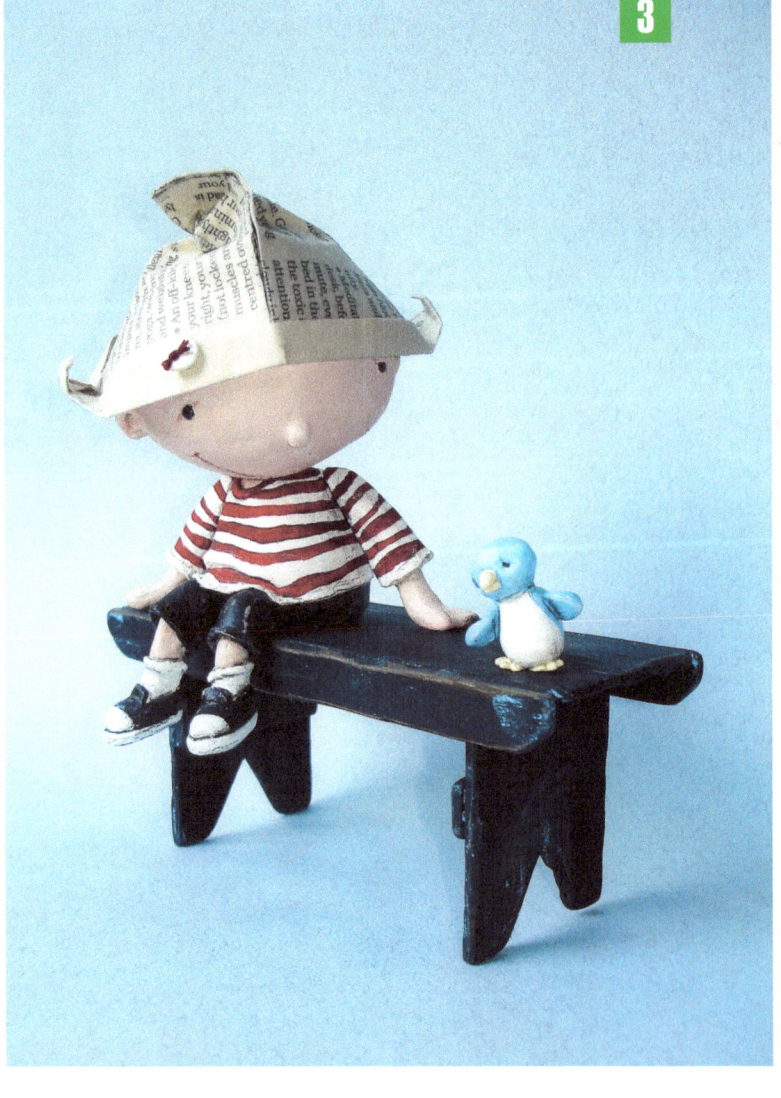

STACEY YACULA

LOCATION: Guelph
WEB: staceyyaculastudio.blogspot.com
EMAIL: systudio@rogers.com

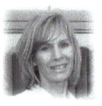

Stacey Yacula has been creating since she was a child. Her illustrations and sculptures are often inspired by nature and her family both in the past and the present. She is intrigued by a child's innocence and sense of discovery...they have this uncanny ability to take in our world with such a sense of purity.

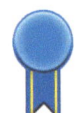

SONA MINCOFF

LOCATION: Guelph
WEB: sonamincoff.com
EMAIL: art@sonamincoff.com

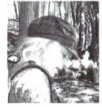

Life in the art world began for Sona as a portrait artist while still a teenager and then later moving to Guelph to study art at the University. The most experience came from experimenting with oil paint and dry pastel to grasp the fleeting dreams impressions, images that make up the semi-conscious human mind. Sona has lived in Guelph since 1981.

1

1 The Visit 15x15" framed. Pastel on Strathmore paper.

2 Lonely Forest 20x24" Oil on canvas.

3 Edge of Red Forest 20x24" Oil on canvas.

2

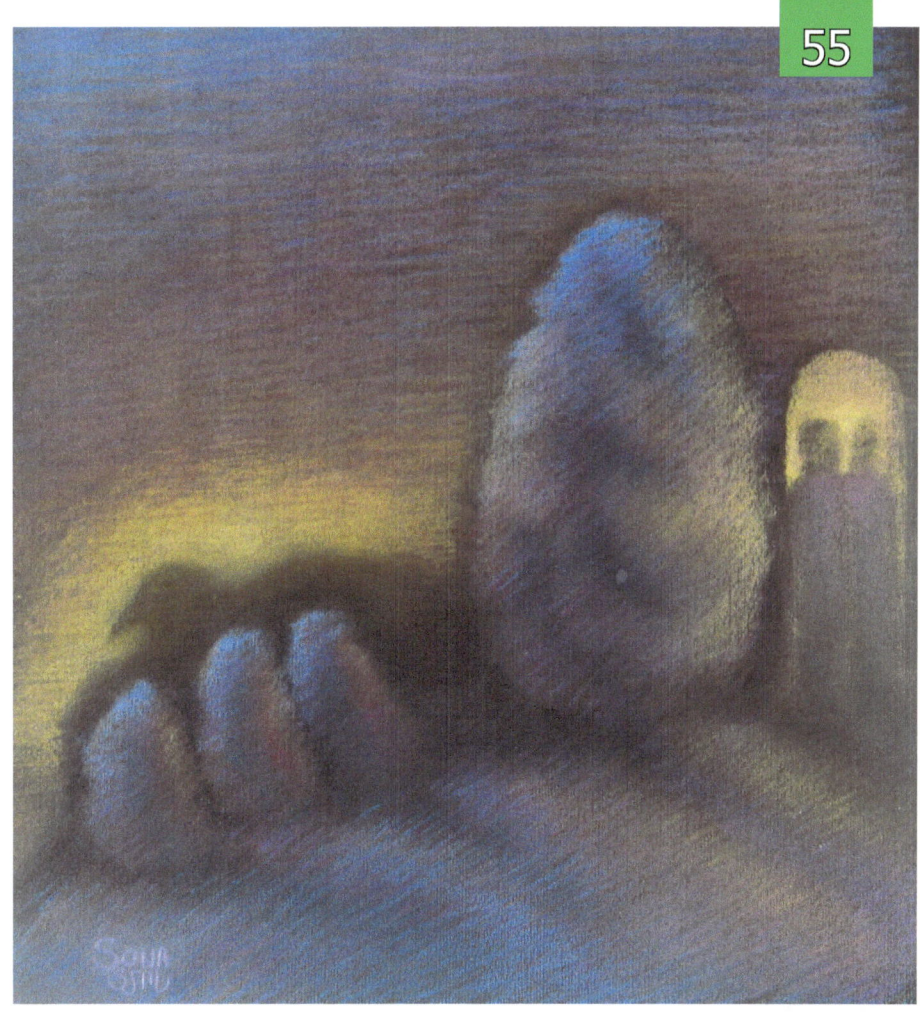

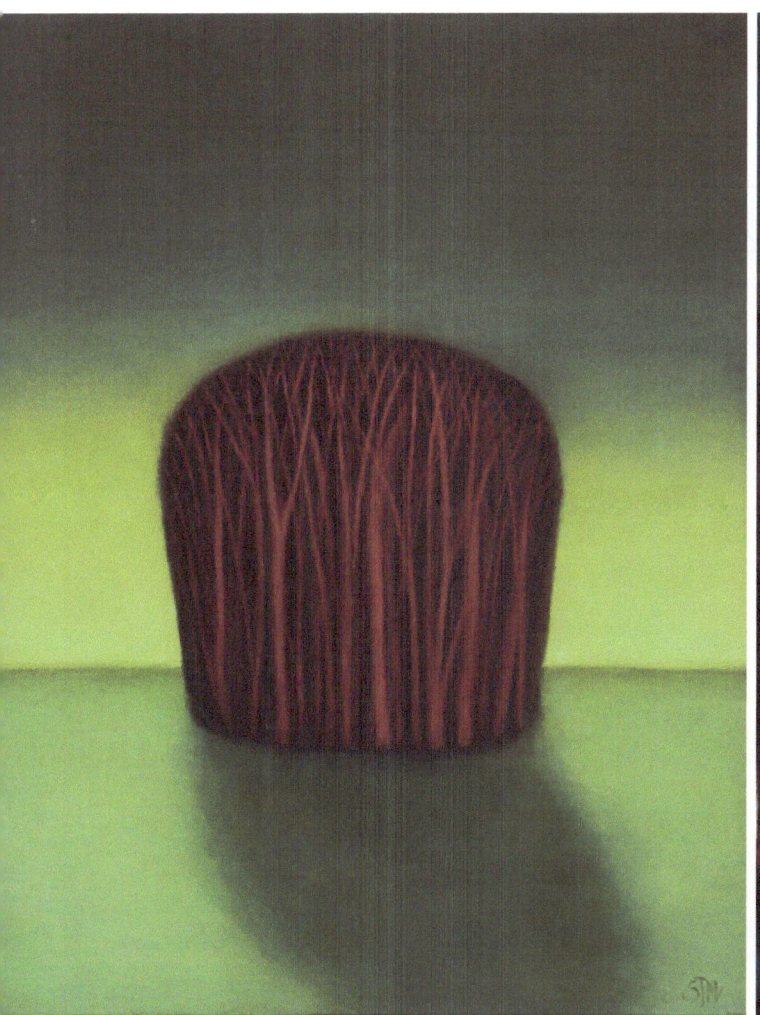

3

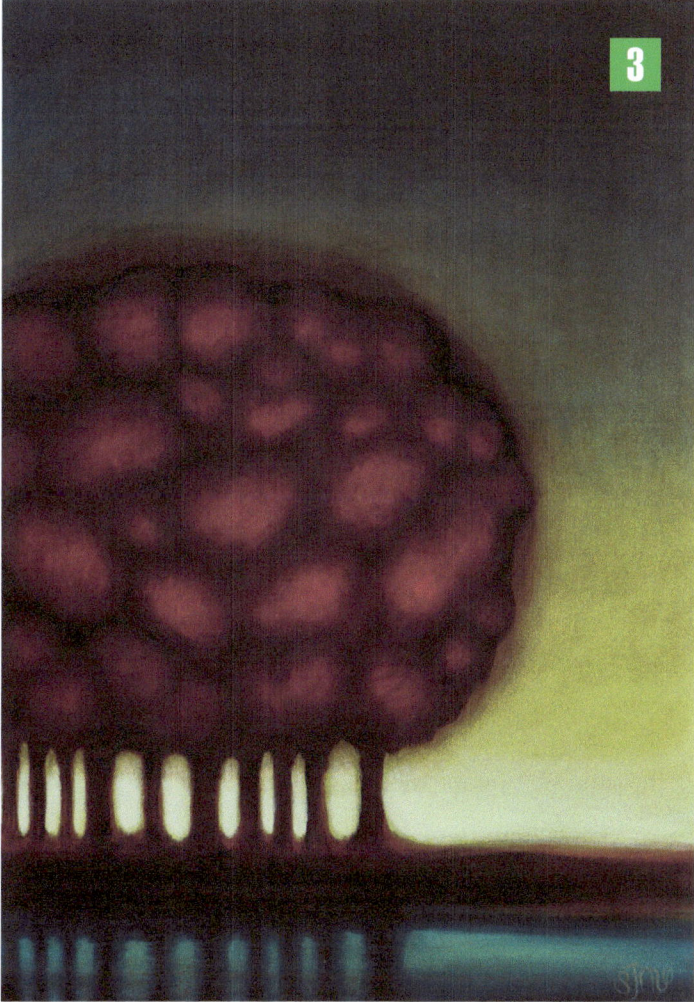

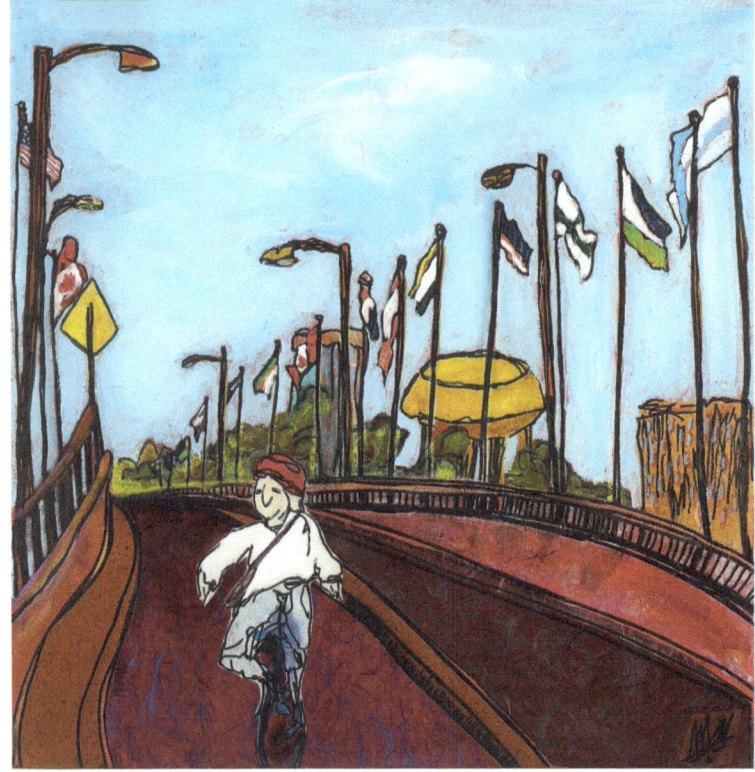

1

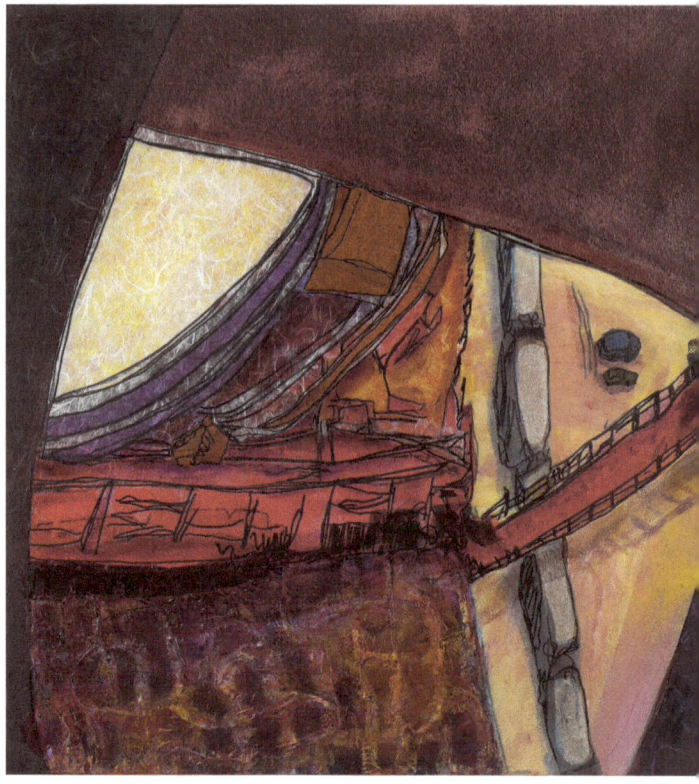

2

MICHELE BRANIFF

LOCATION: Cambridge
WEB: (N/A)
EMAIL: mbraniff@rogers.com

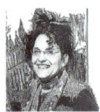

Michele's paintings are whimsical, boldly colourful—slightly mischievous; not married to reality but quite divorced and living happily ever after. Paintings are mixed media collage. Her paintings can be seen at Gallery M, Cambridge, JMR Gallery in Bayfield, art shows and in many private collections. Michele has had an eclectic working career: lawyer, mediator, adjunct lecturer at University of Waterloo, self-employment coach, program manager with Lutherwood.

3

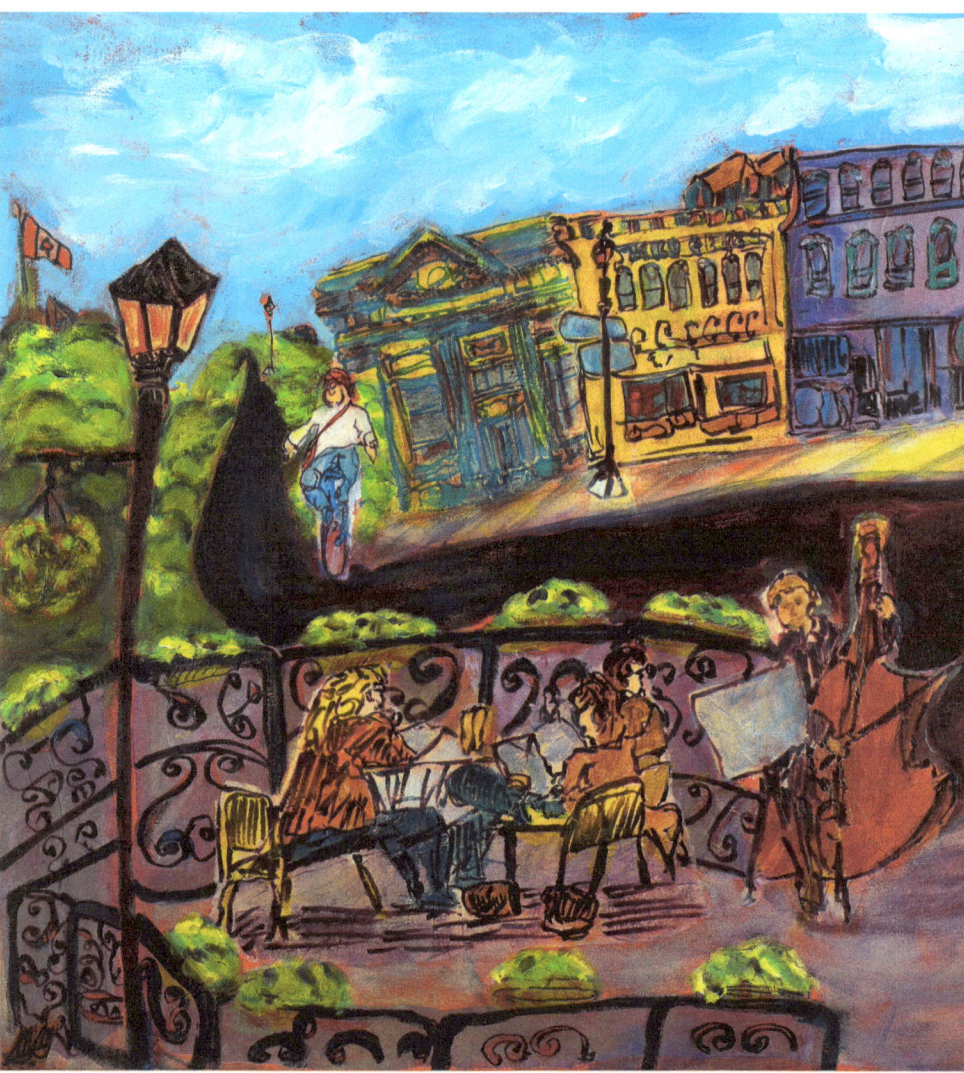

1 **Free Spirit on the Bridge of Flags** 24x24" Mixed media collage with acrylics and Japanese papers.

2 **See'n Tower Floor** 30x30" Mixed media collage with acrylics and Japanese papers.

3 **Celebration at Water & Main** 24x24" Mixed media collage with acrylics and Japanese papers.

BEV DE JONG

LOCATION: 15 Isabella Street, Terra Cotta

WEB: bevdejong.com

EMAIL: dejongbeverly@hotmail.com

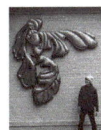

Bev de Jong is an internationally exhibited local artist. She studied and taught at the Alberta College of Art before catching wonder-lust which brought her to study at Cranbrook Academy of Arts and then settle in Terra Cotta where she produce art and a family. She has been fascinated with producing art in a variety of media for gobs and gobs of years and continues to do so.

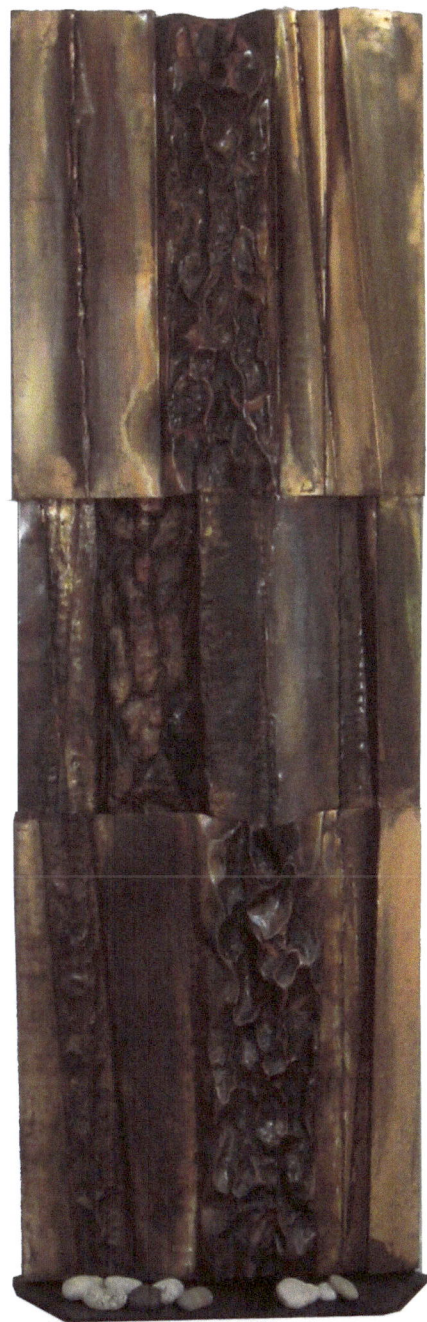

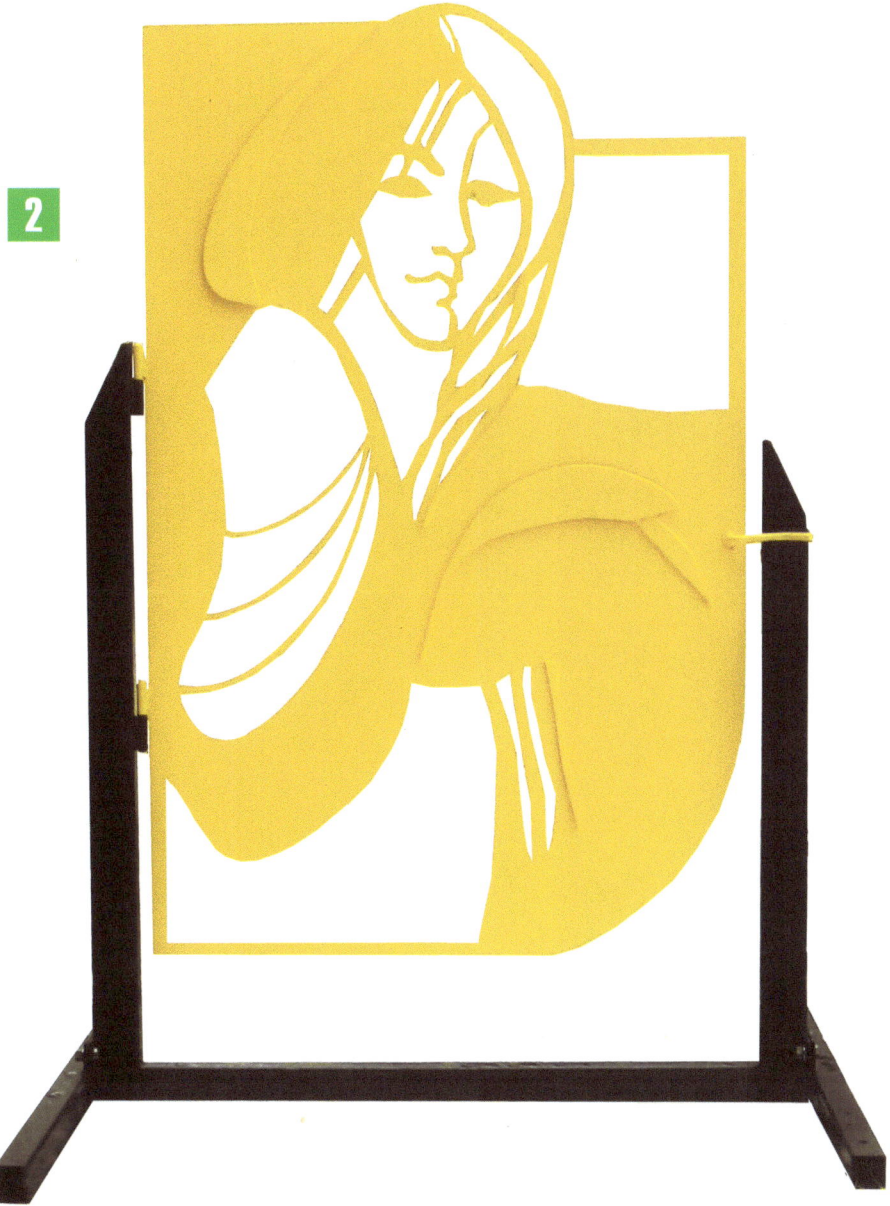

1 **Water Wall** 27x82x24" copper forged corner trickle fountain.

3 **Fire** 46x23" Carved from copper laminated on plywood.

2 **Paula Gate** 48x67" Industrial powder coated steel garden gate.

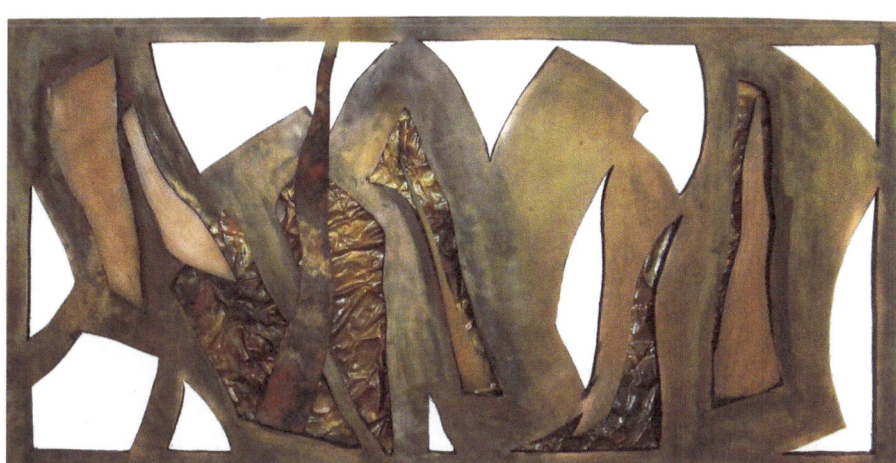

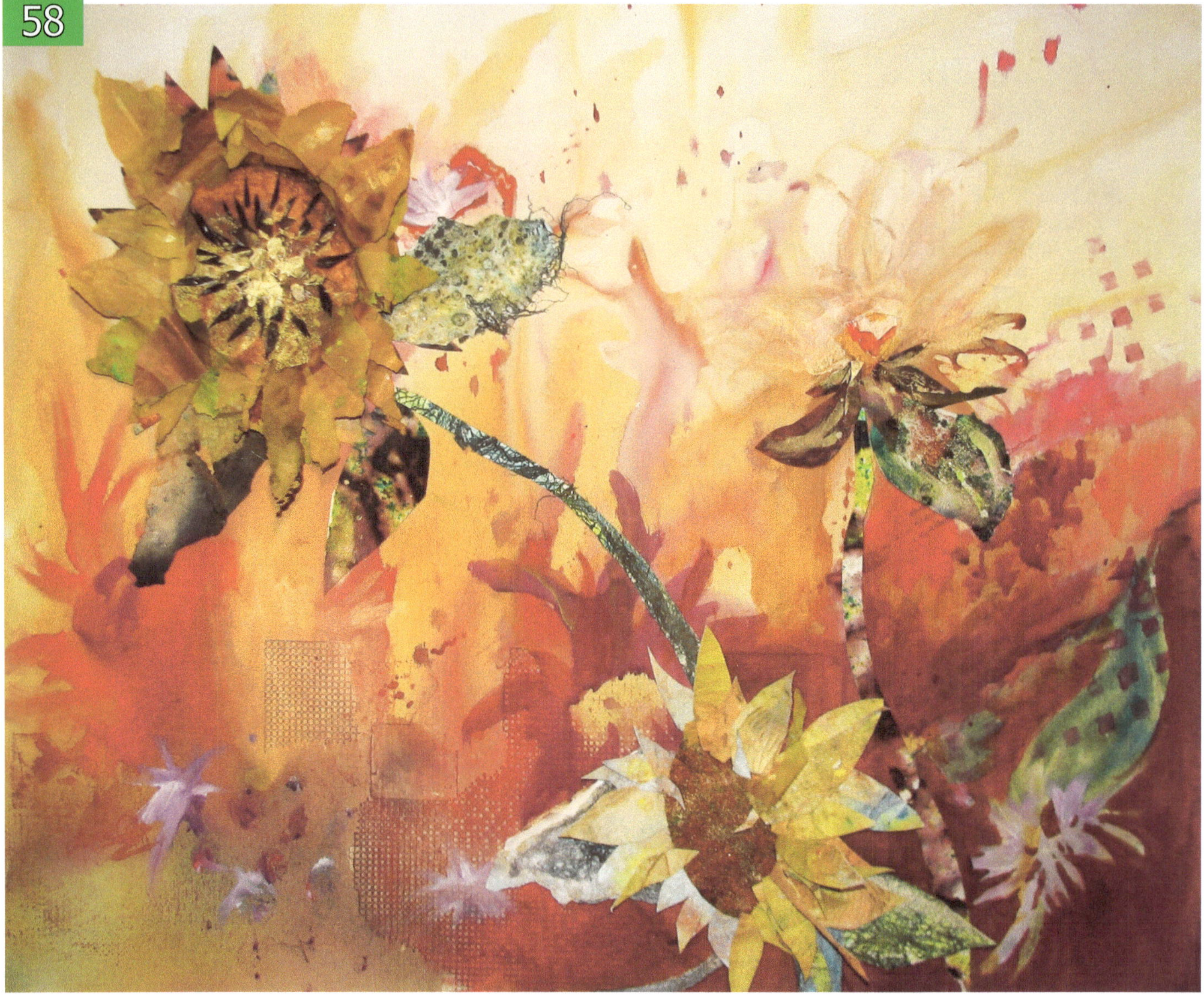

1 Sunflower Medley 22x30"
Three dimensional acrylic collage on canvas.

2 Night Club 22x30" Abstract acrylic on watercolor paper.

LORNA COLE

LOCATION: Guelph
WEB: (N/A)
EMAIL: lornapcole@hotmail.com

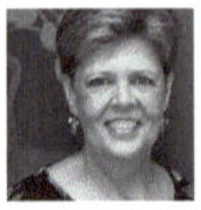

Lorna thoroughly enjoys the life-long process of learning to express herself through art. Her paintings are filled with light, bold color and interesting topics. Workshops and courses have given her not only the basics of art, but also the techniques and philosophies of recognized artists such as Zoltan Szabo, Peter Spataro, Nita Engle, Frank Francese and Taylor Ikin. Latey her focus has changed from realistic watercolors to acrylic abstracts, collages and/or multi media pieces. Her paintings currently reside in homes in Canada, the U.S. and Australia.

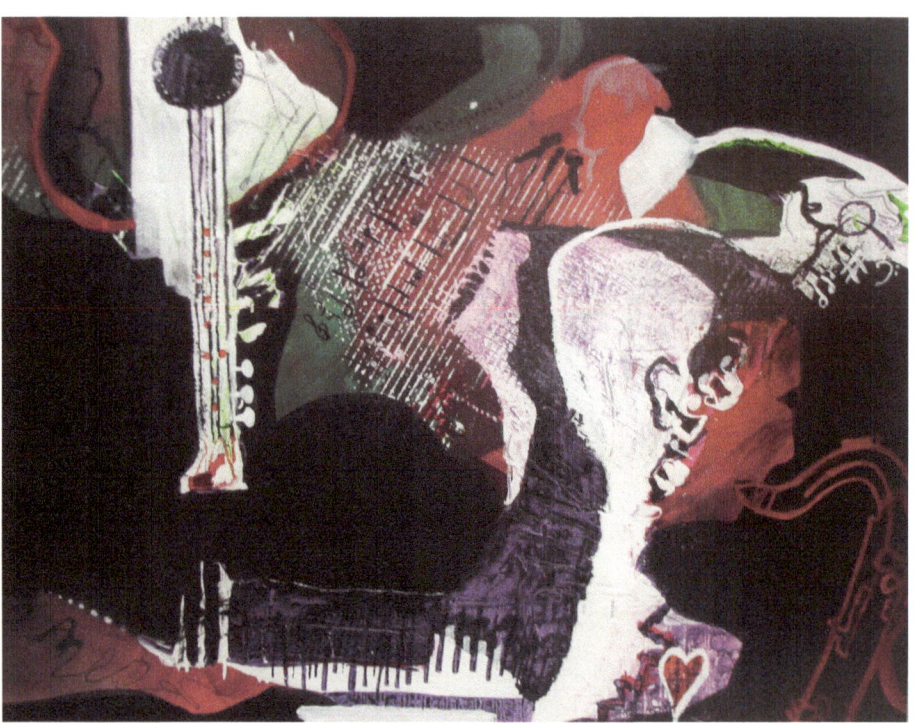

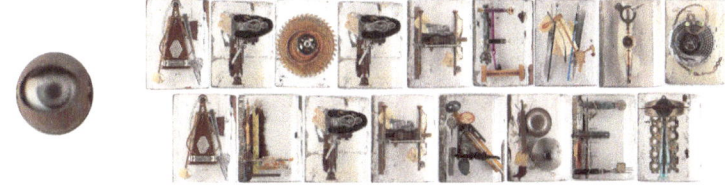

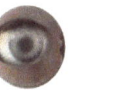

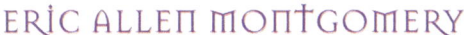

ERIC ALLEN MONTGOMERY

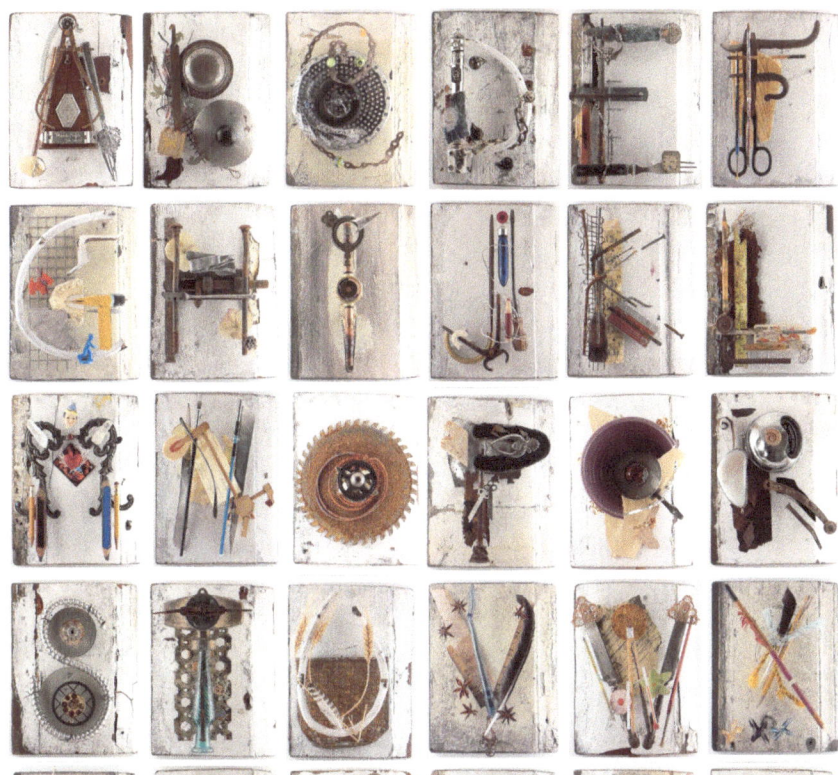

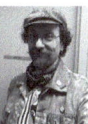

1

ERIC ALLEN MONTGOMERY

LOCATION: 152B Northumberland St Guelph ON, N1H 3A9 (by appointment)

WEB: http://www.facebook.com/media/set/?set=a.6695366188.20625.654211188&l=cea395037b

EMAIL: memoryboxer@yahoo.ca

I utilize a wide variety of found, altered, and created objects and materials to celebrate events, interpret themes, or simply to tell stories, both real or imagined. Form and Function combine with Reality and Myth, linking the technical expertise of a Craftsperson, the aesthetic and philosophical explorations of an Artist, and the wit and whimsy of a Story Teller. Come find me at the Guelph Farmers Market Saturdays, and we'll share stories and STUFF!

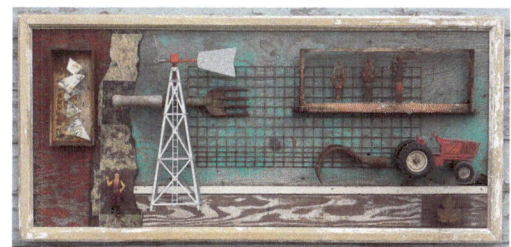

2

1 Apophenic Alphabet Each letter 5x9x3" mixed media assemblage: various found and altered materials on vintage baseboard. Original series photographed for digital based works: cards, prints etc.

2 Heritage 23x50x6" mixed media assemblage entirely "as found" including: vintage toys, garden implements, cast steel Centennial maple leaf, bee hive comb frame, seed box, mirror frame, found wood, linoleum.

3 I Haven't Laughed So Hard... 6x9x1.5" mixed media assemblage: vintage playing card, doll, plastic pig, hand marbled paper, Letraset, wood, glass.

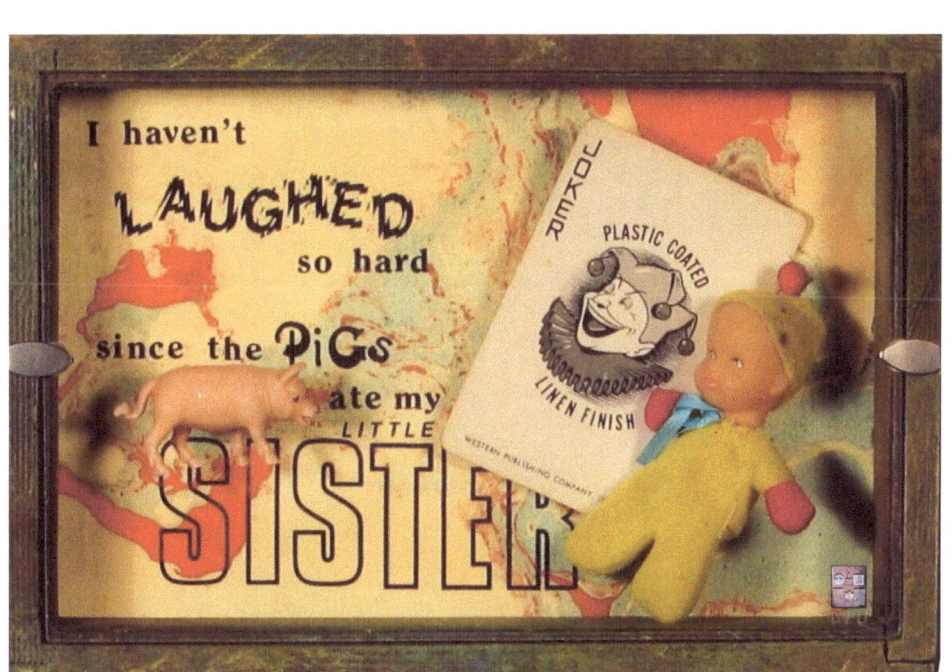

3

AMAR BHUEE

LOCATION: Cambridge
WEB: meltingartistdesigns.etsy.com
EMAIL: meltingartistdesigns@hotmail.ca
meltingartist182@hotmail.com

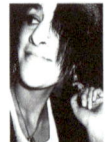

Amar's work is bright and playful. When it comes to her photography, she loves to capture everyday things and show people how beautiful it actually is. Amar also works with silk ink water colours, sketching with ink, book binding, makes home décor item and jewellery accessories with her own photographs and prints, such as pendants, earrings, rings, tile coasters, magnets, compacts, pocket mirrors and so much more. Some of her products can also be found at: Book Express (Cambridge Centre, Cambridge), Gallery M (63 Dickson St, Cambridge- Across from Cambridge City Hall) and The Relique Studio- located on 71 Dickson st Cambridge Ontario.

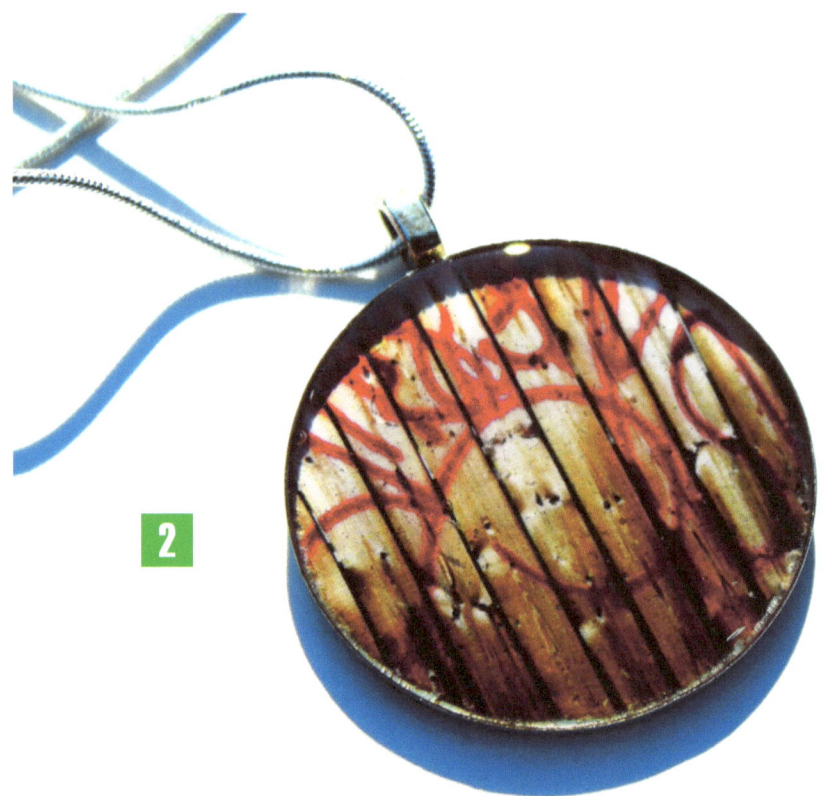

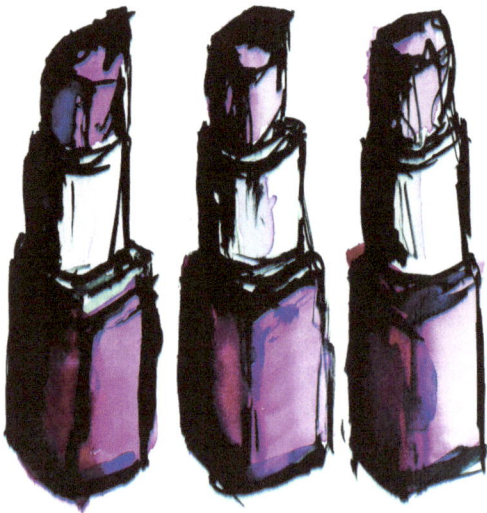

1 **Trip-Stick** Silk ink watercolors.

2 **Red Words Photo Pendant** Photograph in a hand made pendant.

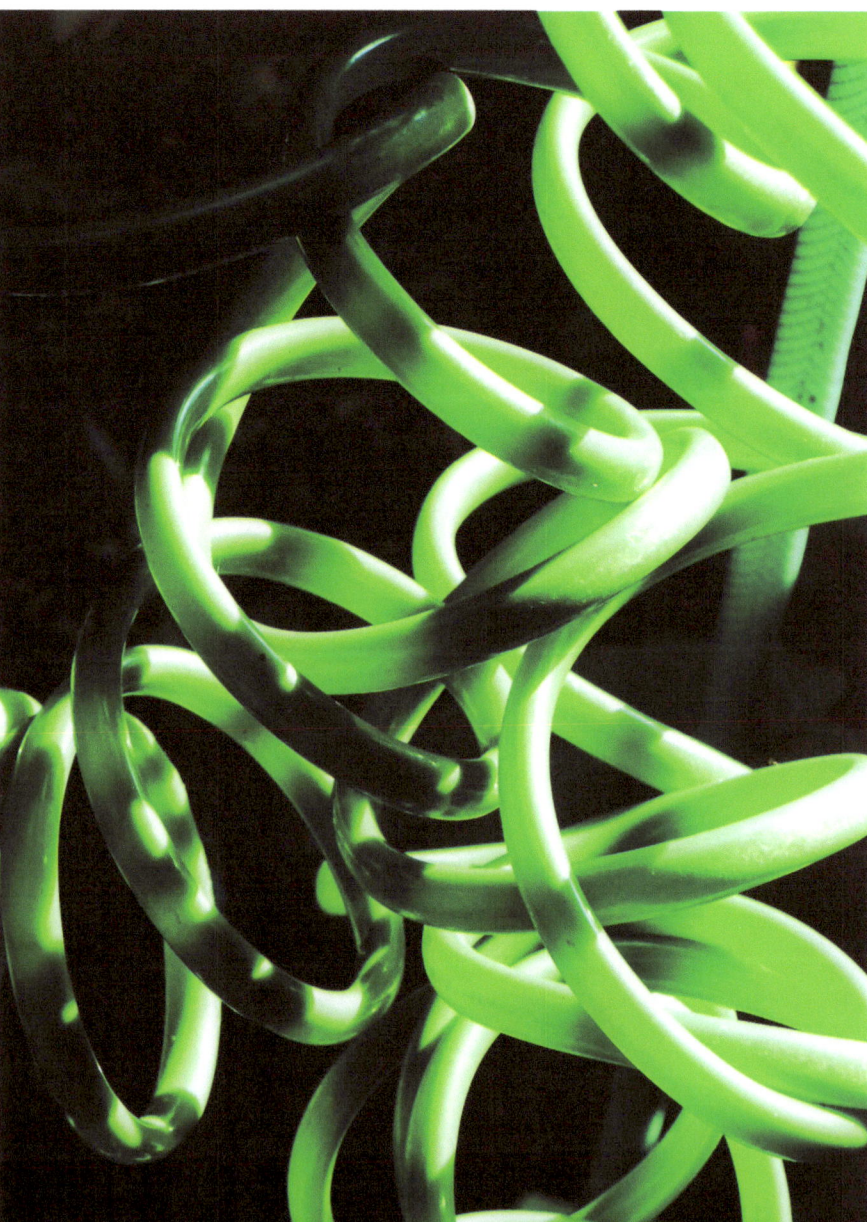

3 **Water Hose** Photograph.

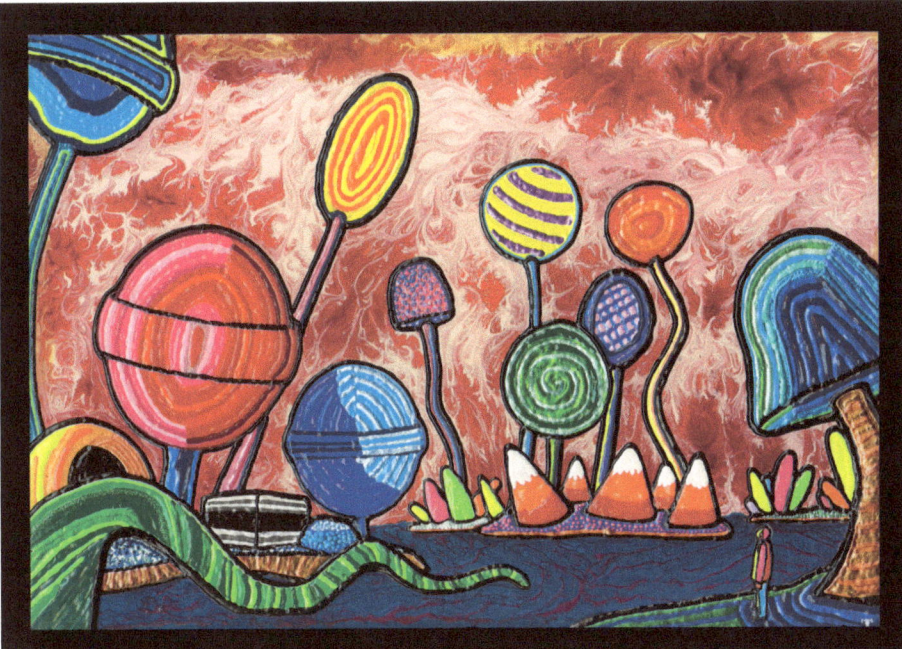

1 **Candy Land** 13x18" Fabric paint and enamel.

2 **Lung Tree** 14.5x9" Sandpaper cutout, paint pen, fabric paint, spray paint and acrylic gel medium on MDF board.

1   **2**

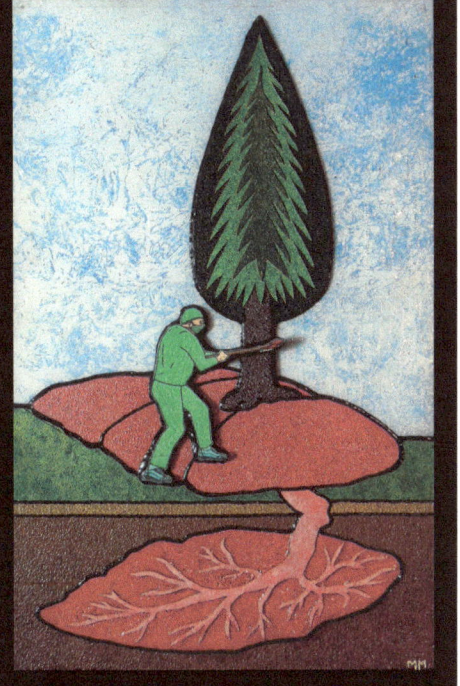

MATTHEW MUELLER

LOCATION: Cambridge
WEB: artofmattmueller.com
EMAIL: mattjm79@gmail.com

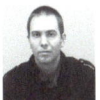

Born in 1979, I grew up in Cambridge. After high school, I took a job with my uncle working construction. Almost 3 years went by doing this job. I knew it wasn't what I wanted to do with the rest of my life but I wasn't sure how to make the change or even what it was that I wanted to pursue. In 2003, an injury while I was on the job, had decided for me. I fell and tore my knee. I had to have surgery and was out of commission for quite some time. During this time of limited mobility, I began to express myself through paint. I started doing abstract oil paintings on canvas with no definitive direction in art, except for knowing that I started to enjoy expressing feeling. I successfully completed the Art Fundamentals one-year program at Sheridan College in 2007, and gained acceptance into their BAA Illustration program. I am currently in the forth year of the program.

3 **A Half Truth** 10x13" Acrylic & transparent inks on illustration board.

3

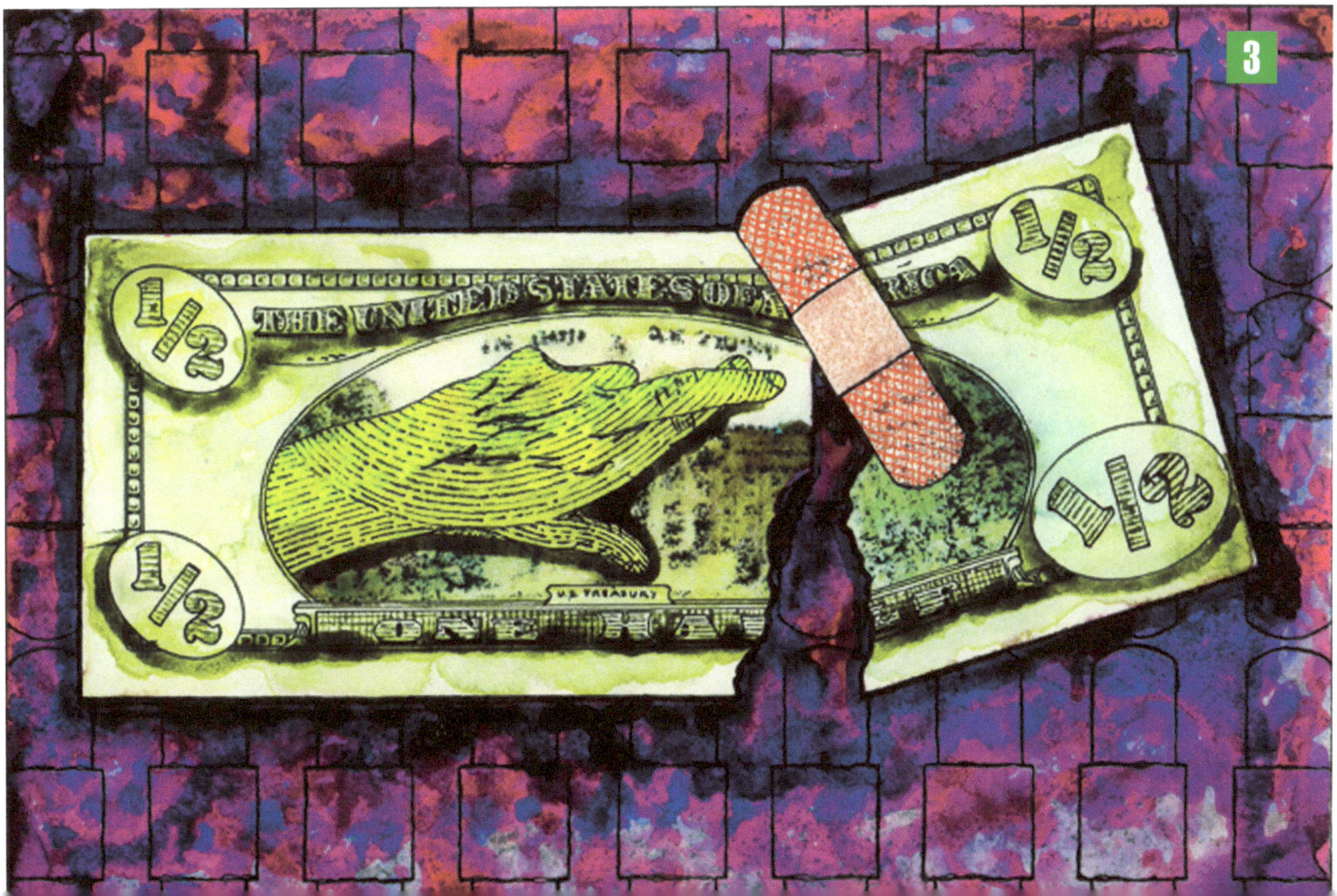

IRENE MACCRIMMOM

LOCATION: Guelph West Hills Art Group
WEB: (N/A)
EMAIL: (N/A)

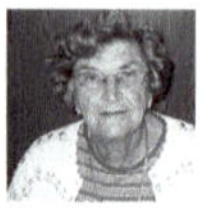

Member of the West Hills Art Group. I advanced from "T" shirts to watercolours captivating cats, trees and woods, seas and mountains. I paint enthusiastically three days a week with various Guelph watercolour clubs. I have studied at local workshops and in distant workshops in Scotland, France, Italy, Mexico and the United States, where I have sold many paintings. I am passionate about painting vivid watercolour paintings.

1 **Morning Light** 10x14" Watercolour.

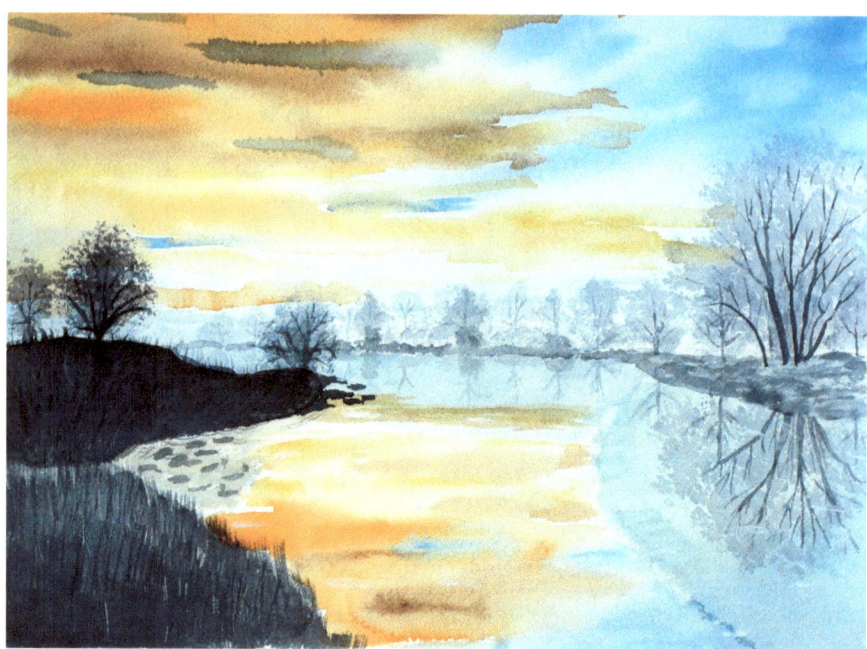

1

2 **Open Door** 10x14" Watercolour.

3 **Fuoco...Island of Fire** 10x14" Watercolour. 10x14".

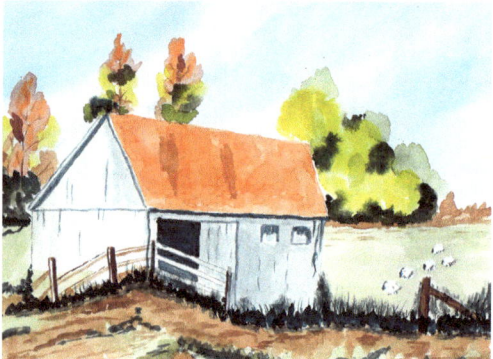

3

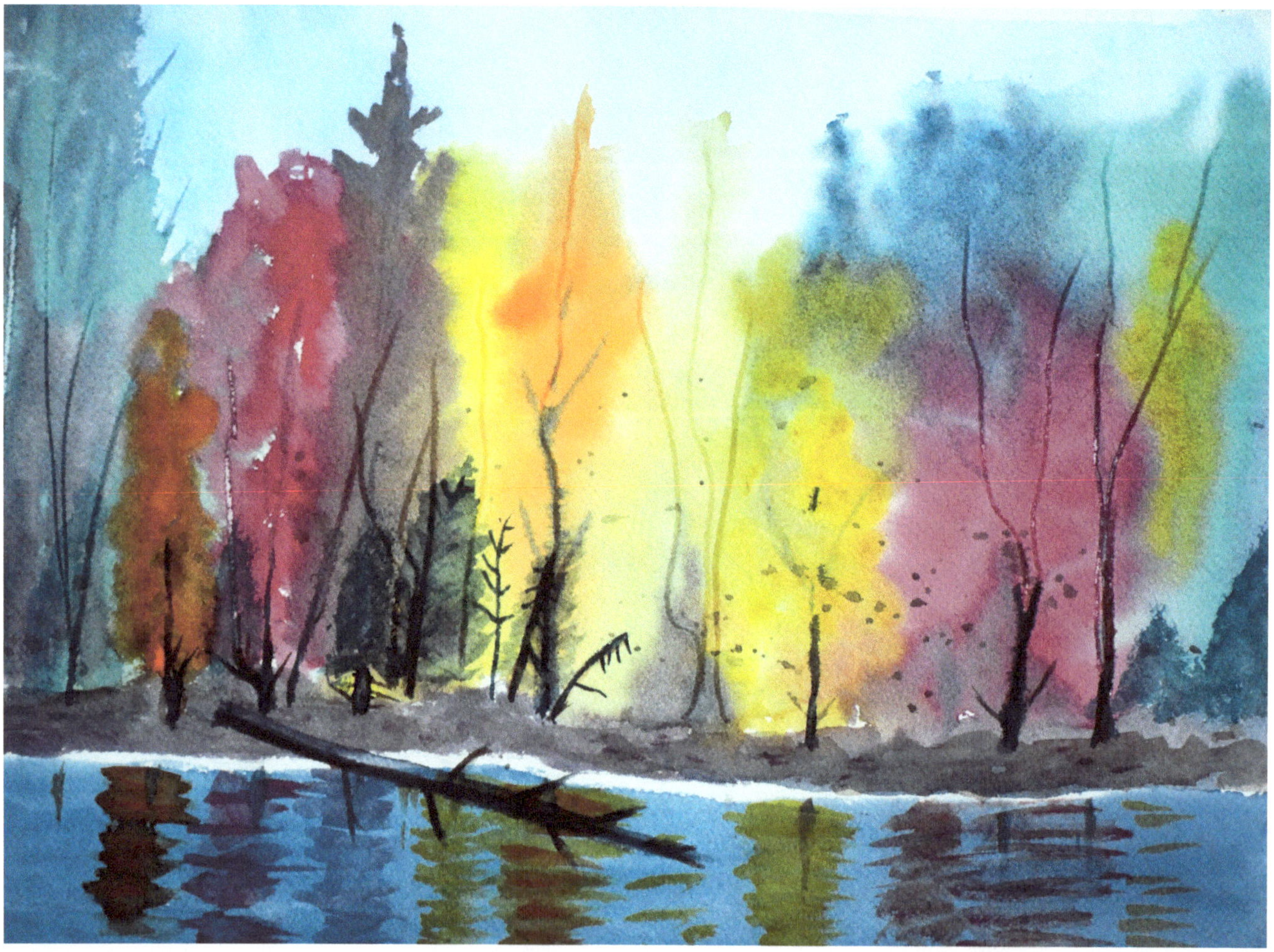

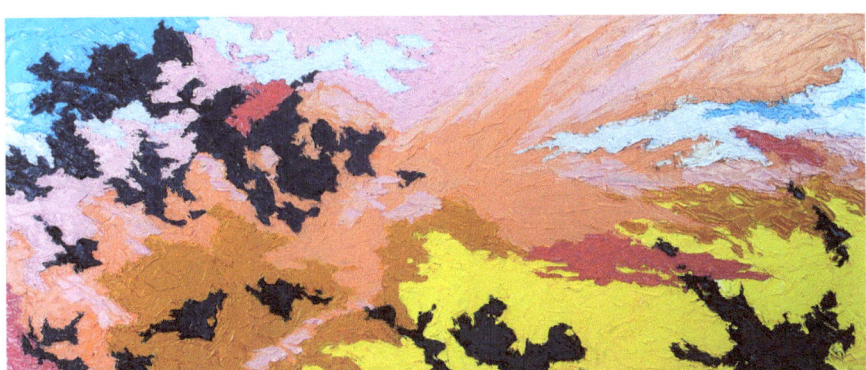

1

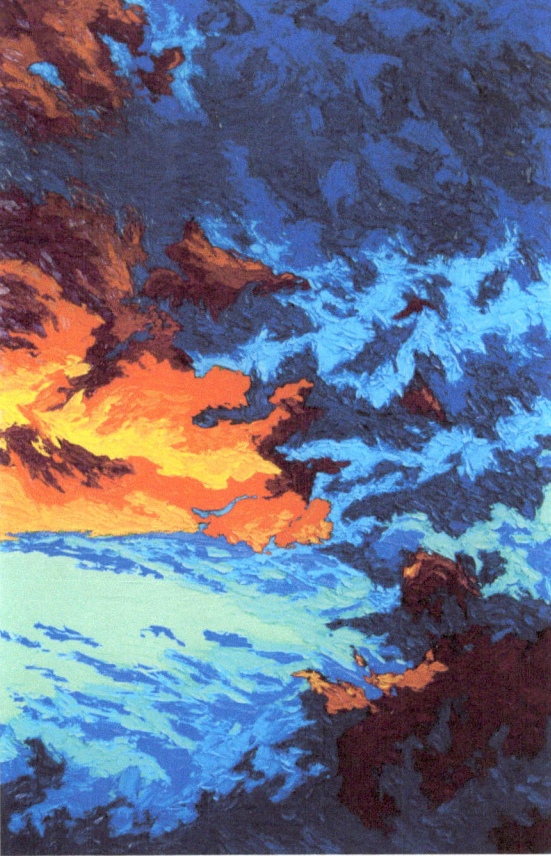

3

JEFF FERST

LOCATION: Cambridge
WEB: jeffferst.com
EMAIL: jeff@jeffferst.com

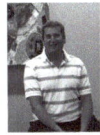

Jeff Ferst's abstract paintings have been called life-affirming, flagrantly flamboyant and juicy. Ferst was born in NYC and studied art at NYU. His work is that of a colourist and his geometric landscape paintings have been exhibited across the US and Canada. Lately Ferst has returned to his more "traditional landscape" roots composing vivid canvases of the Canadian countryside that are tactile and inviting.

1 Evening Sky 24x72" Oil on canvas 2011.

2 Dancing Clouds 48x72" Oil on canvas 2011.

3 Morning Sky 60x40" Oil on canvas 2011.

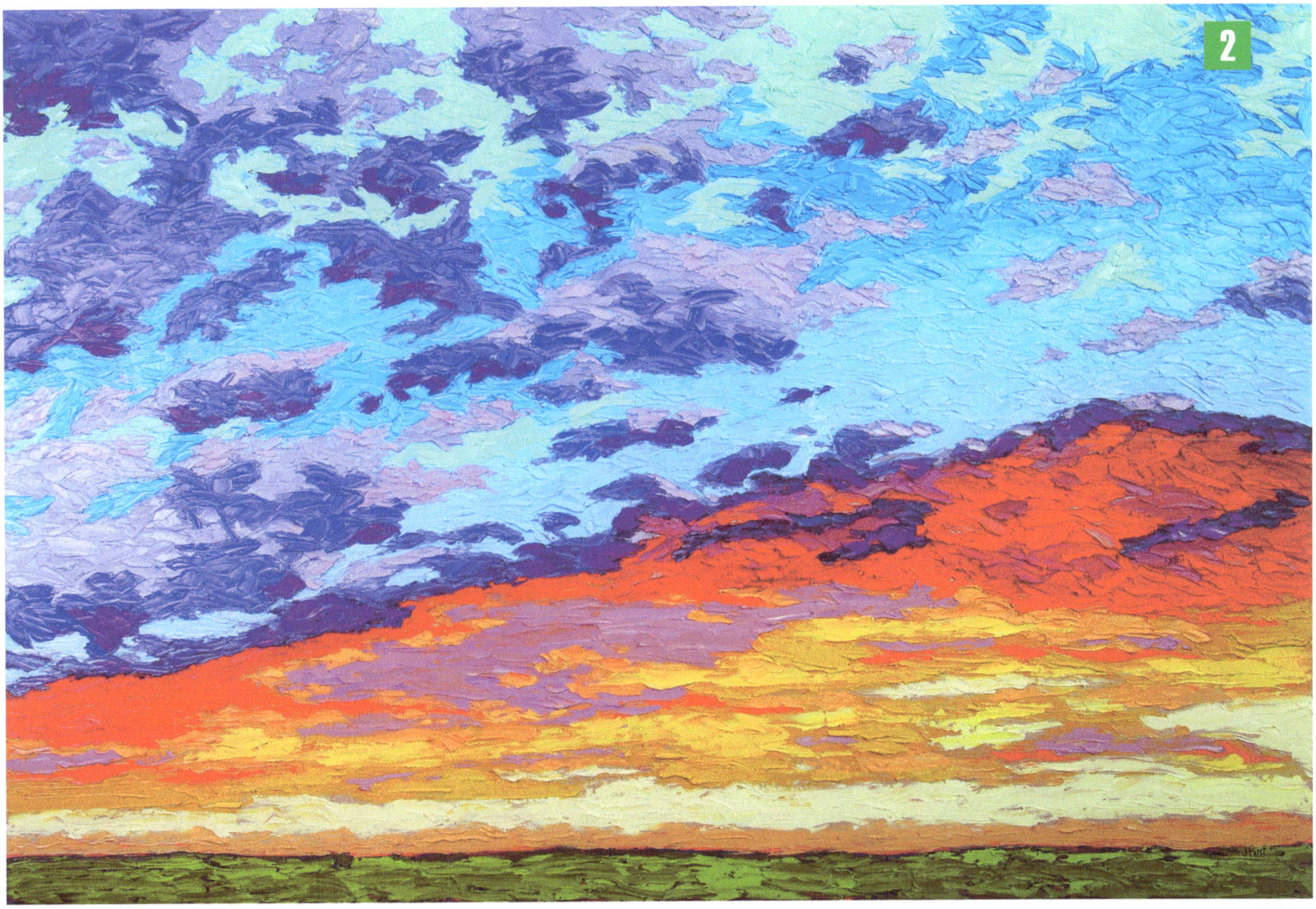

2

JESSICA HOFLICK

LOCATION: Guelph
WEB: jessicahoflick.com
EMAIL: jhoflick@gmail.com

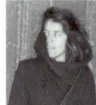

Raised in rural Ontario, Jessica's art reflects a relationship between her roots in the Kawarthas, and the urban setting of her now-home of Guelph. Jessica holds a B.A. Honours in Studio Arts from the University of Guelph, and a Graduate EXA certificate from Haliburton School of the Arts. Her art is inspired by the Canadian Landscapes that she encounters, both daily and while travelling the Country. Jessica Keeps a full time studio Practice, and teaches art within her community.

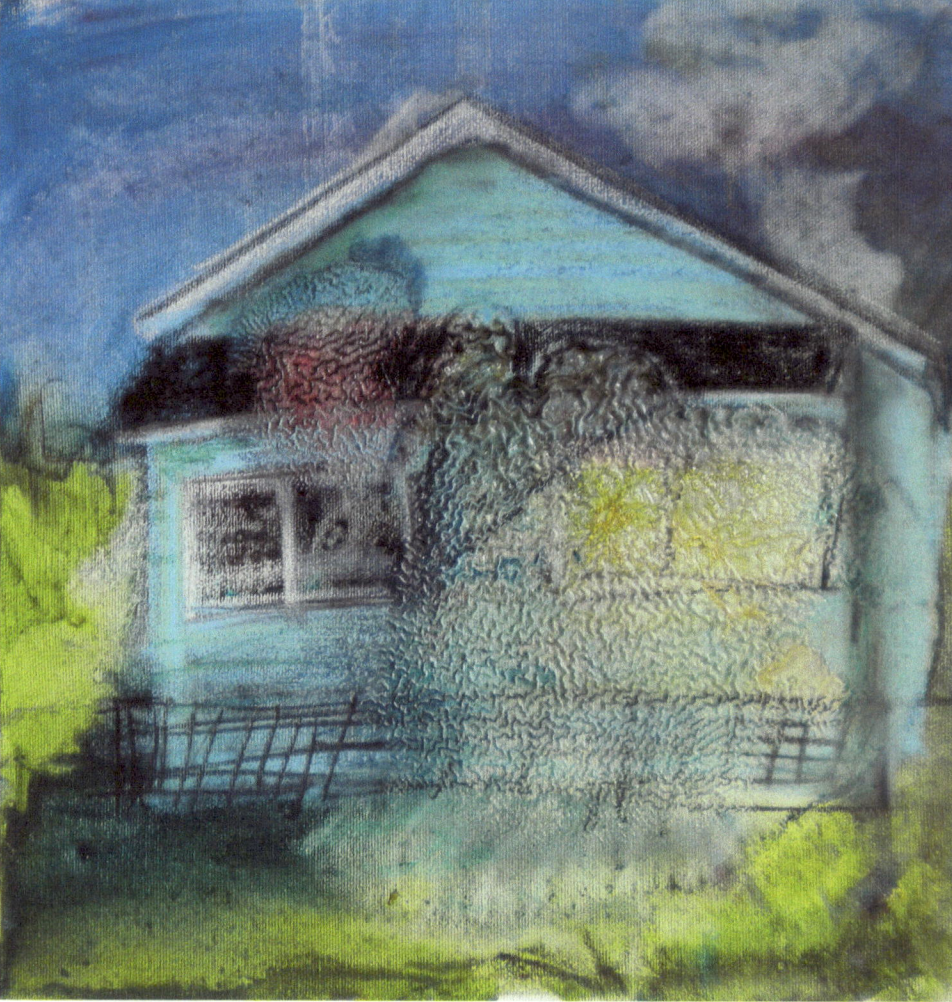

1

1 Untitled-Wasaga House 1
12x12" Oil on Canvas. Abandoned House Series – exploring rural Ontario.

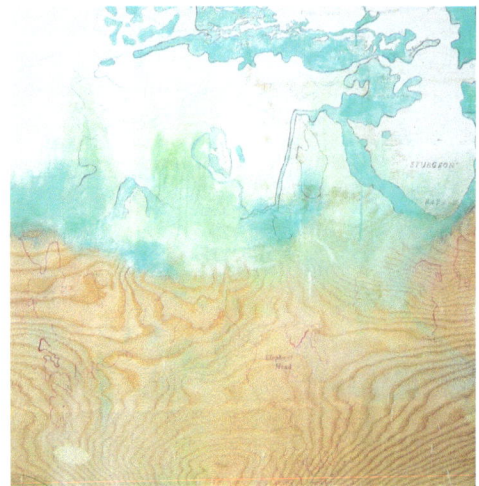
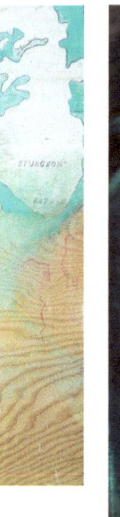

2

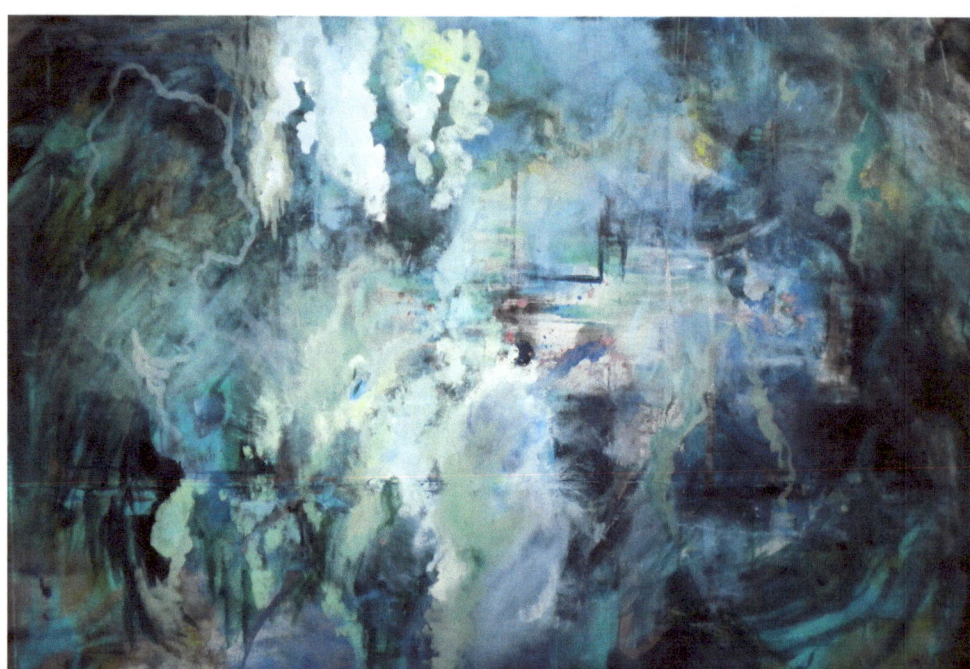

3 Sturgeon Bay Water Charts
4x4' Acrylic on fir plywood. Examining rural textures as mirrored by natural topographical land formations.

2 Untitled 4x6' Oil on Canvas. Exploring the relationship between man made structures and natural forces.

3

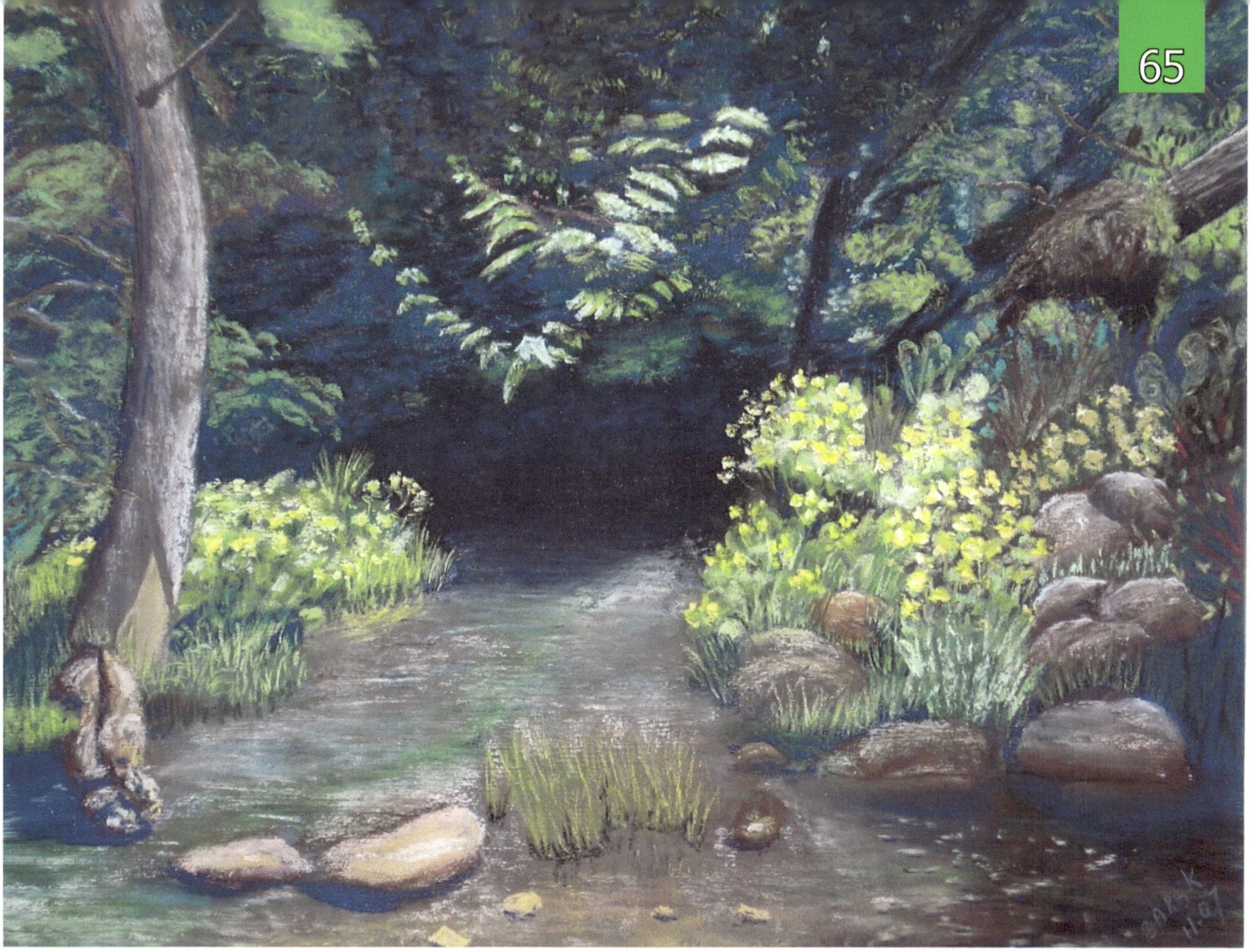

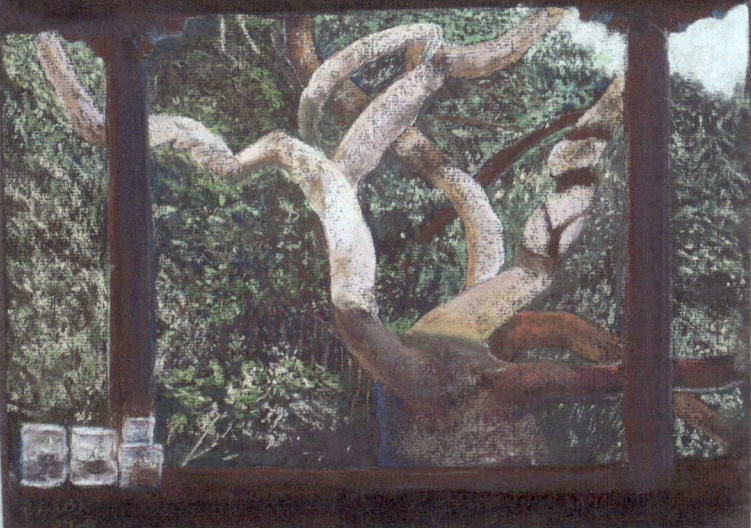

1 **Wellspring Pastel** 12x16"

2 **Terpentine Tree** Pastel 8x12"

3 **Algonquin Park Reflections** 8x12"

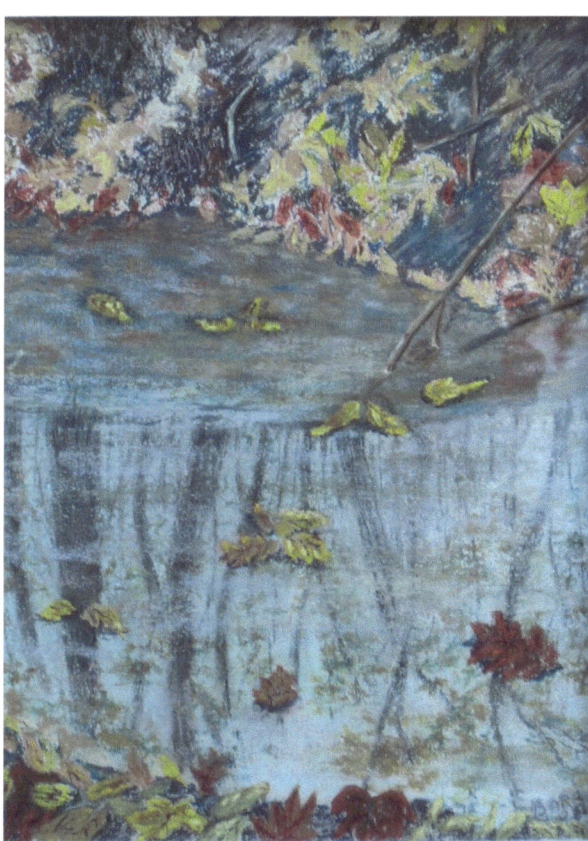

BARB KERKHOVEN

LOCATION: 213 Bristol St. Guelph
WEB: (N/A)
EMAIL: bkerkhoven@rogers.com

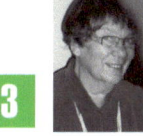

In my late teens I did some pastels but didn't stay with it. Then in my sixties I took up painting again, first water colour and then back to pastels. I love the directness of the chalk pastel medium and consider myself a rank amateur. The reason I like to paint is that I love light, in shadows or direct and indirect reflections and find I am not able to photograph what I see. So, I try painting. At the rate I am learning to catch what I see I may be over a hundred before I get it, but I do enjoy trying.

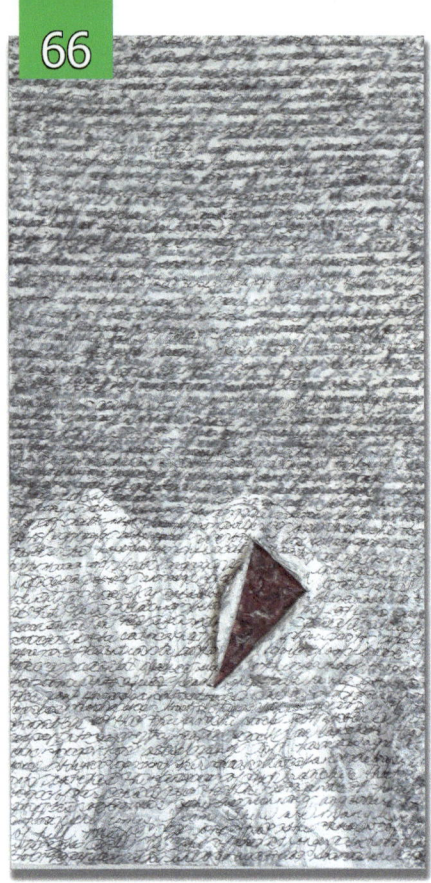
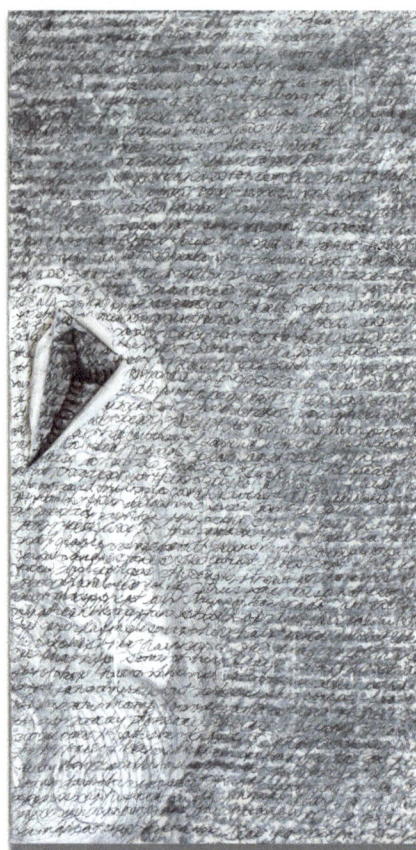
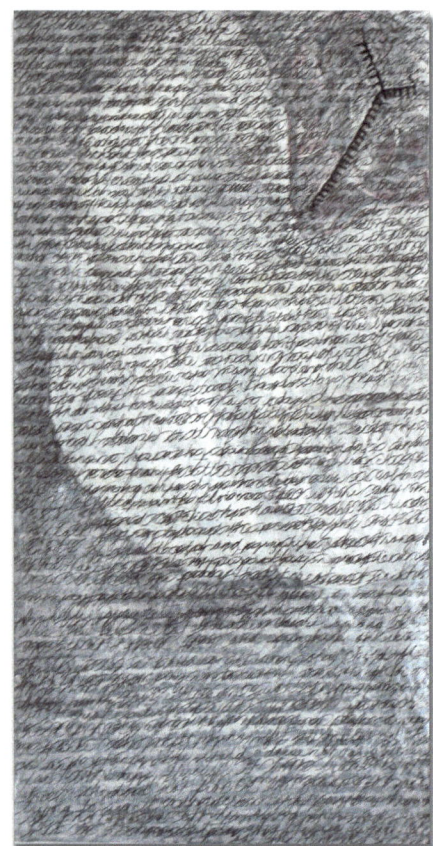

1

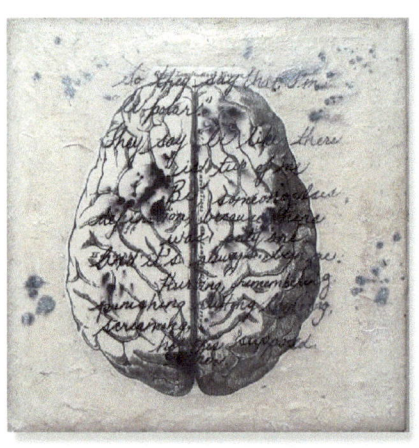
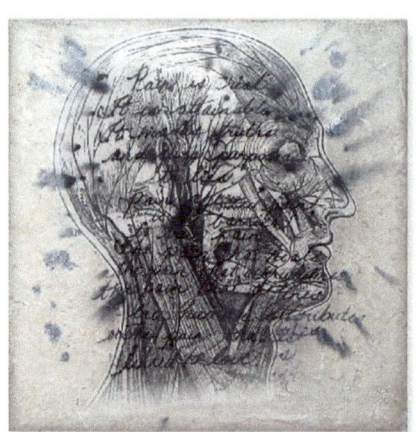
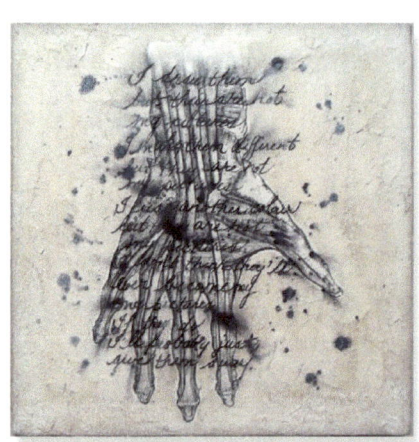

2

KIMBERLEY H DENNY

LOCATION: Galt East, Cambridge
WEB: kimberleydenny.ca
EMAIL: kimberleydenny@gmail.com

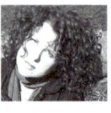

Kimberley has lived in Cambridge for the last 7 years with her husband, their two girls, and their dog (the breathing carpet), Maddie. Kimberley has been working as a mixed-media artist for over 5 years creating paintings that explore mental health issues, and attempt to create visual representations of mood disorders. Kimberley's primary goal is to create work that helps people understand what a mood disorder 'looks like', rather than what a mood disorder 'feels like'.

1 **OCD (Trauma/Therapy/Closure)** 10x18" each. Mixed media on linen. Each panel consists of seventeen layers of automatic writing. The tears are actual 'Y' incisions that a doctor would make in the correct part of the frontal lobe, with stitching holding layers of paper together. Brain mass created from moss and man made fibers.

2 **Anatomy of a Mood Disorder** 12x12" Mixed media on linen. About establishing the link between the body and mood disorders that affect it.

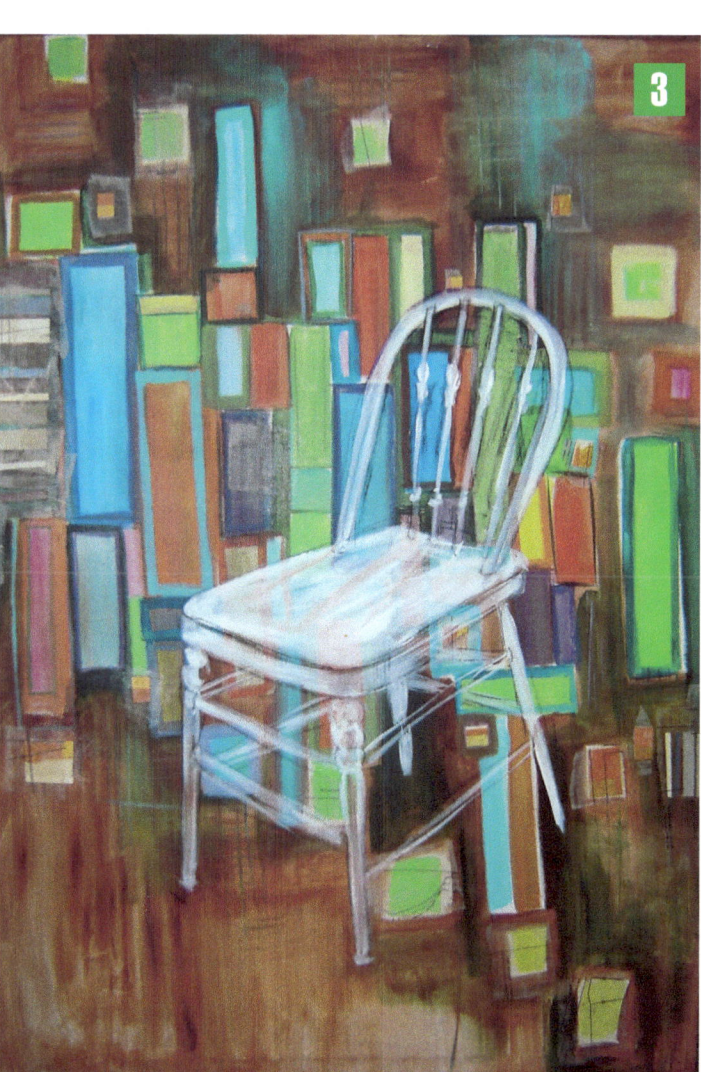

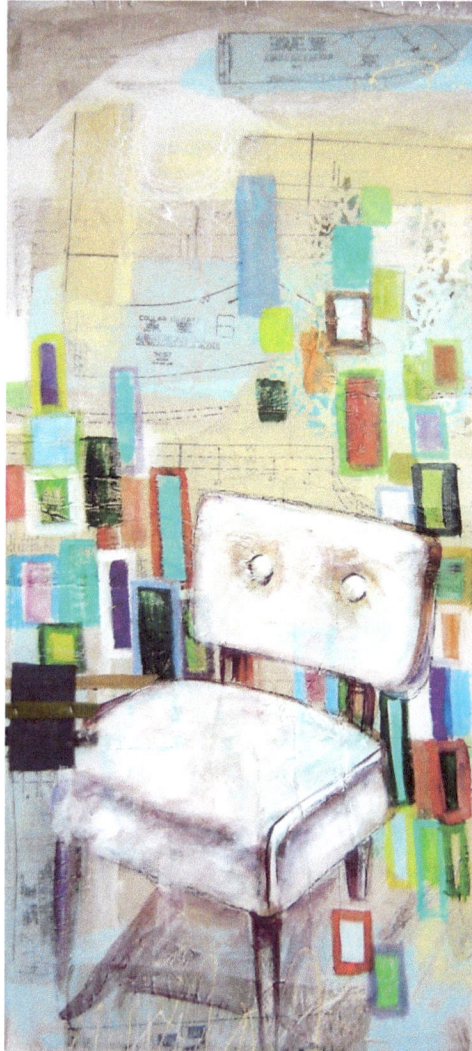

KIM TURNER
LOCATION: 12 Stonehaven Pl Cambridge
WEB: (N/A)
EMAIL: artfullsprouts@hotmail.com

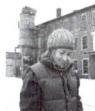

Kim Turner has spent 20 years in the graphic design industry working primarily in print. For the last 9 years, Kim has owned Artfull Sprout, a small business that produces one-of-a-kind handbags, totes, throws, painted murals and graphic design work. Kim's love of colour, texture and design are represented in her acrylic, mixed-media assemblages. Kim completed her Graphic Design and Advertising Diploma at Conestoga College with additional courses and associations at Laurier, Disney and CMG (Colour Marketing Group).

1 Nest 55x93" Acrylic & Mixed-Media on canvas.

2 Throne 2 33x47" Acrylic & Mixed-Media on canvas.

3 Throne 1 34x47" Acrylic & Mixed-Media on canvas.

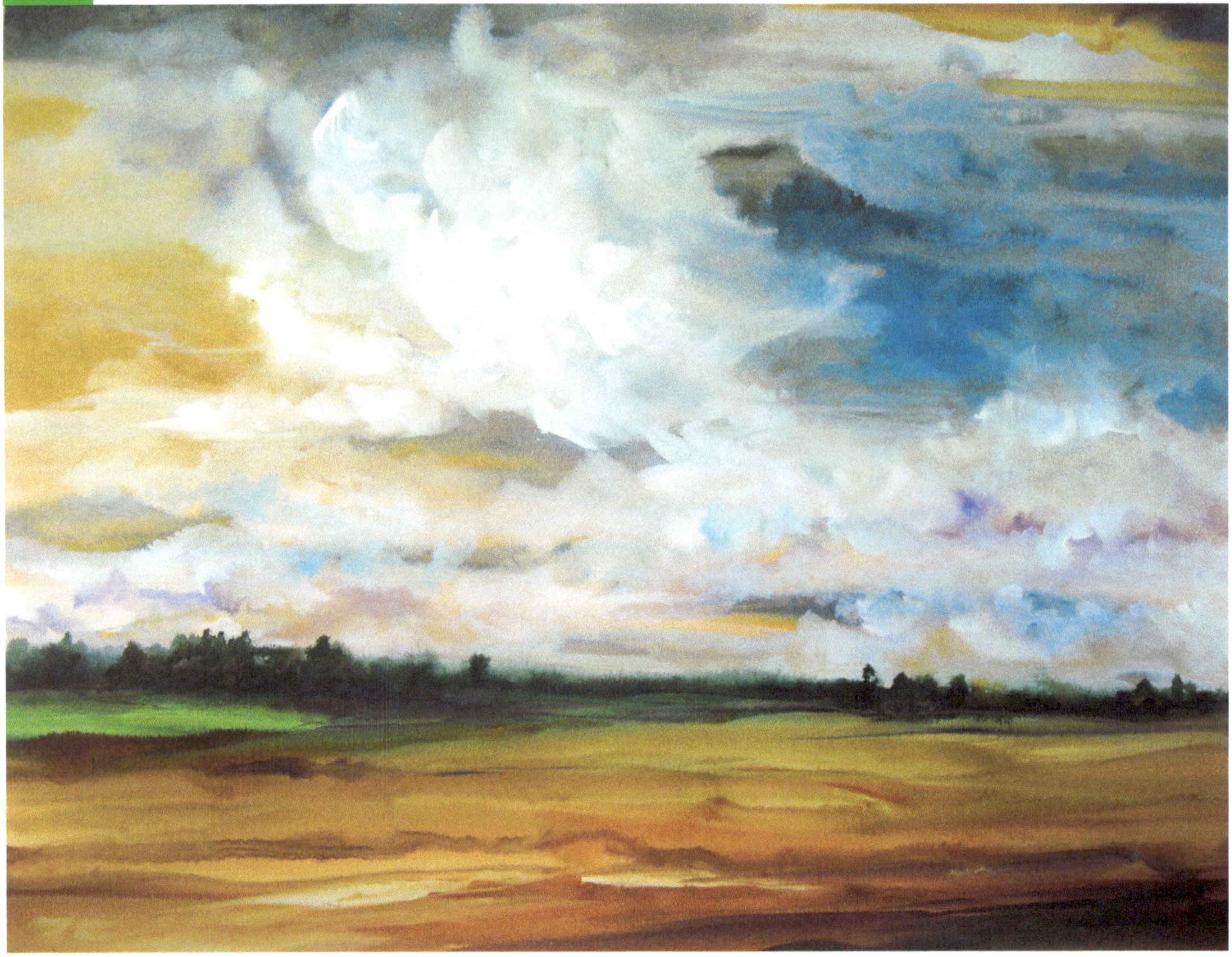

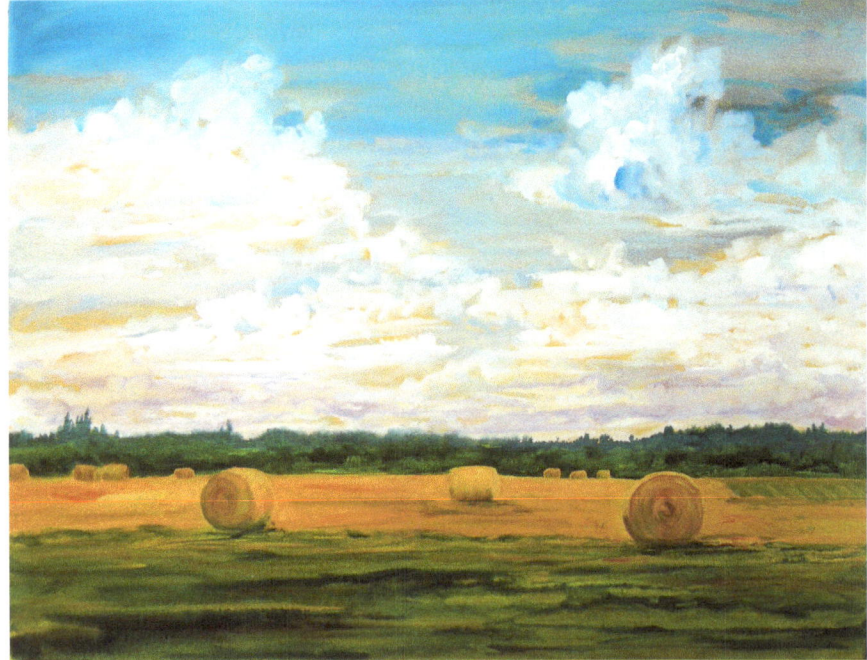

1

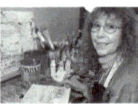

2

MARGARET A PETER

LOCATION: Guelph
WEB: margpeterprints.com
EMAIL: margpeterprints@sentex.net

Margaret is a printmaker and painter whose interest in texture is reflected in her floral, landscape and fossil images. She is a graduate of Windsor Teachers' College and the University of Guelph. She has taught in the school system and was the printmaking instructor at Wilfrid Laurier University from 1988-2006. Workshops in printmaking and acrylic painting have been taught across Ontario. She rejoices in the beauty of nature and the joy and inspiration it brings her. Marg loves creating interesting skies in her landscape paintings and has had her work reproduced in International Artists Magazine and Guelph Life magazine. Her work is in collections world wide. Her painting studio is at the Williams Mill in Glen Williams near Georgetown while her printmaking studio is in her home in Guelph.

1 Coming Storm Acrylic on 22x30" aquarius watercolour paper is typical of my exciting skies.

2 Bountiful Harvest 3x4' Acrylic on canvas reflects my love of the Ontario harvest.

DAISY FRESH

LOCATION: 36 Pollock Ave Cambridge
WEB: (N/A)
EMAIL: Dfresh@rogers.com

I have a strong passion for the history of the human experience. The media of choice is oils or acrylic. The paintings make a consistent reference to history, people and may include decorative symbols. Currently I am growing towards creating more emotion in my work. The figures in the paintings are not portraits of the people around me. They are my "figures of speech" that tell a human story. My goal is to stir emotion and connect with the viewer.

1 Insomnia.

2 I'm Here 36x48" Acrylic on canvas. I have shown the house as important as the figure because it is the surviving witness.

3 Powerless 36x48" Acrylic on canvas. The second completed painting in the series, "my life as a house".

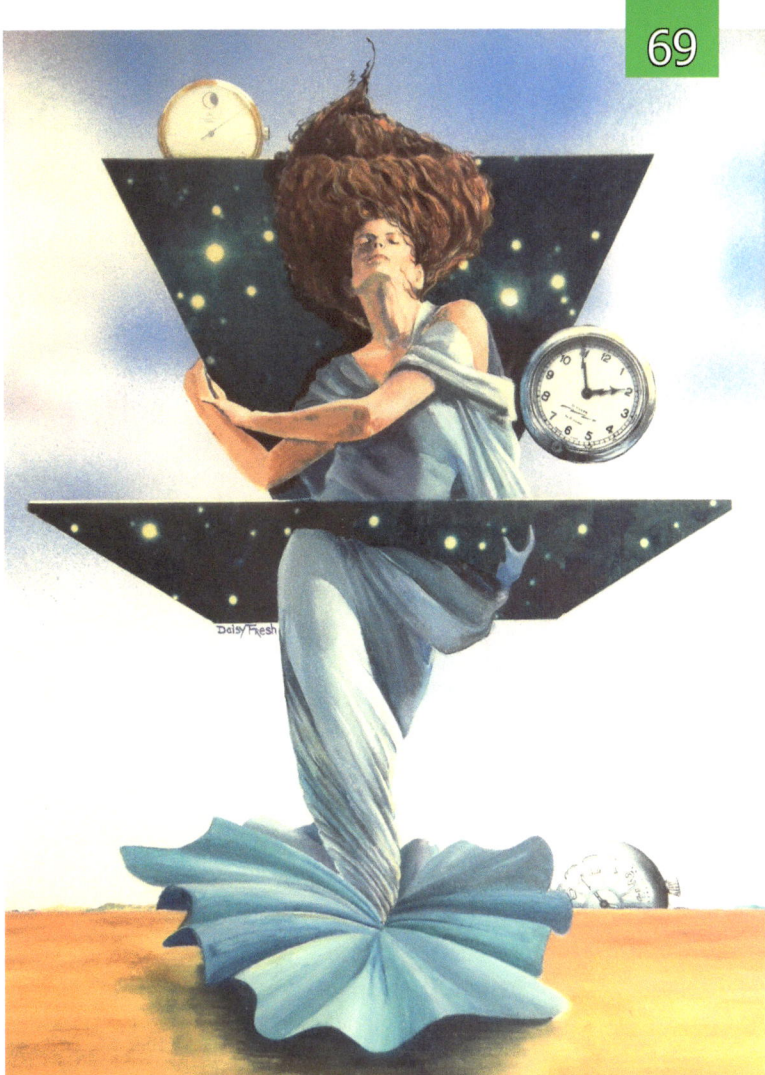

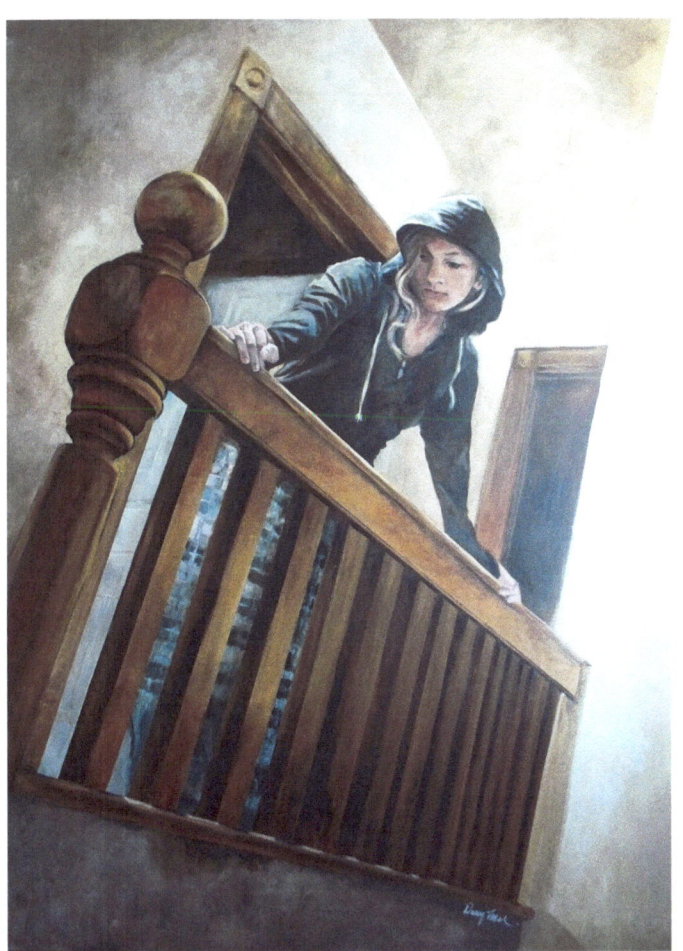

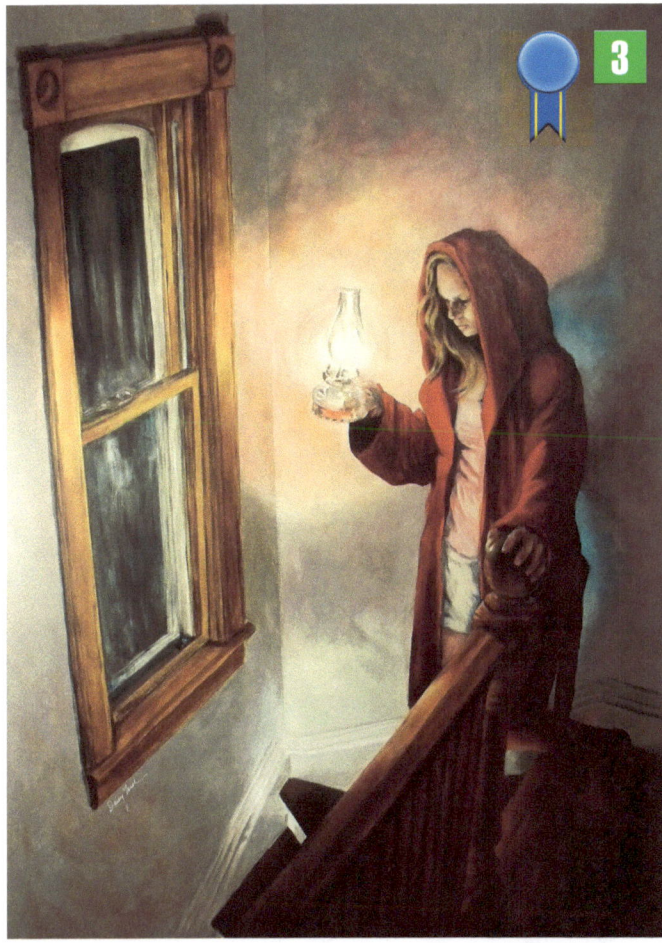

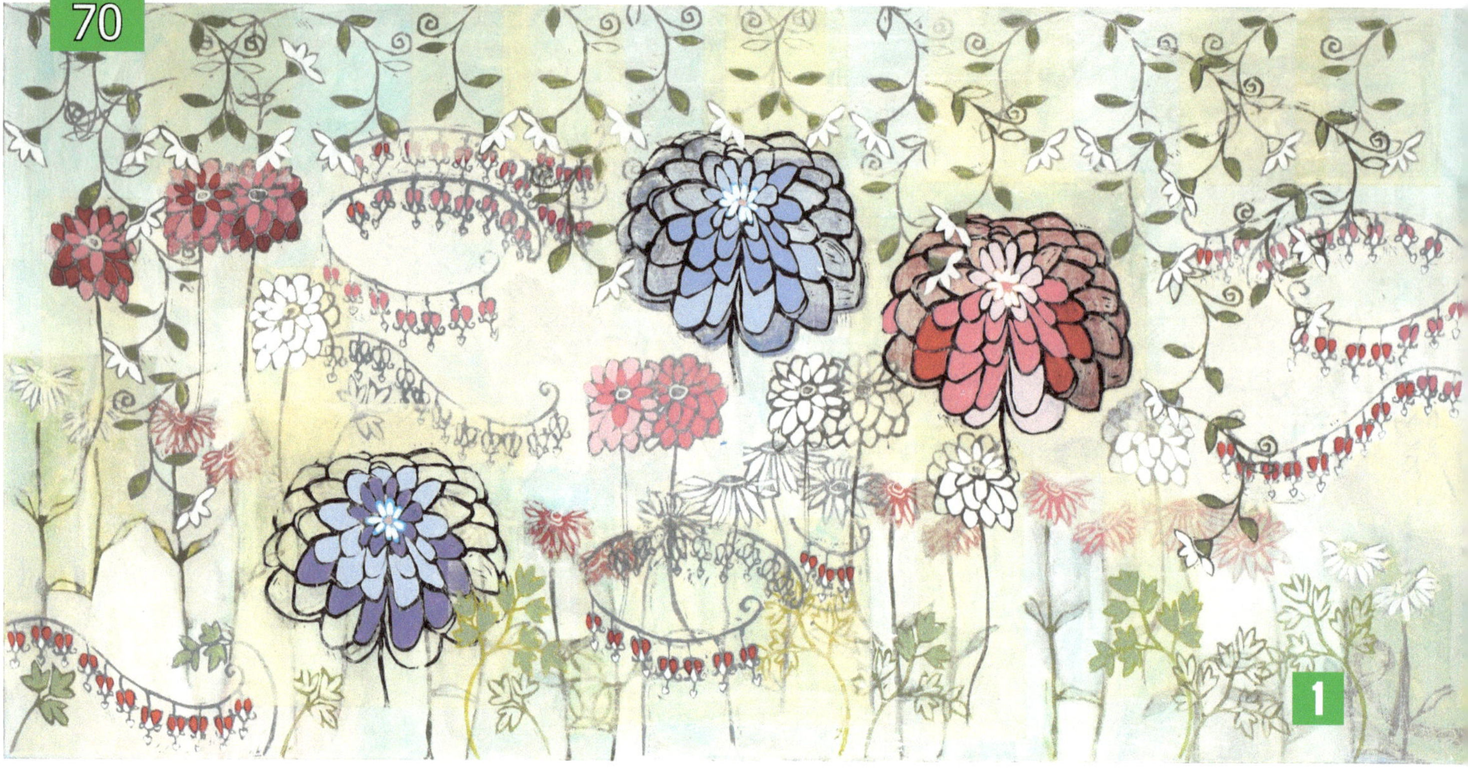

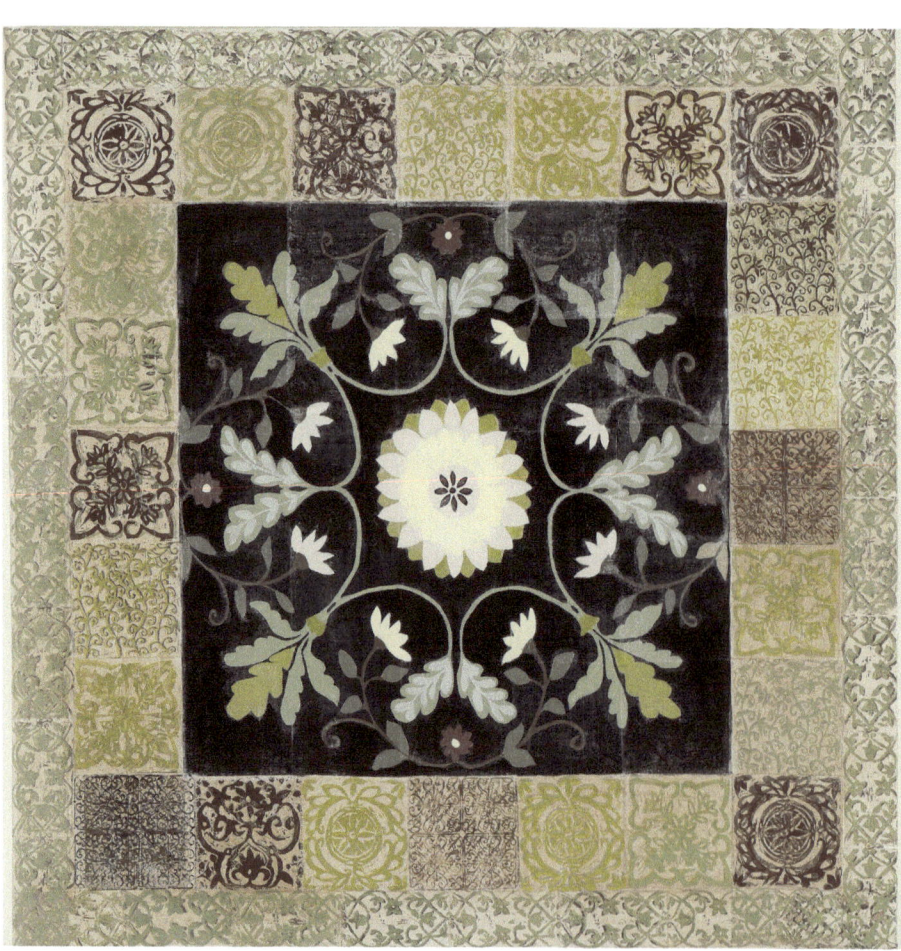

1 **Zinnia and Bleeding Hearts** 30x60" Block print, acrylic and mixed medium, washi on canvas.

2 **Brown Chrysanthemum** 48x48" Block print, acrylic, mixed medium and papers on canvas.

3 **Snaps with Bleeding Hearts and Zinnia** 24x24" Block print, acrylic and mixed medium, washi on canvas.

MARIA PEZZANO

LOCATION: Guelph
WEB: mariapezzano.com
EMAIL: mariapezzano@gmail.com

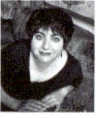

Maria Pezzano's use of print-making and painting has gained her great recognition, locally and regionally. Her fascination with botanicals, combined with repetition of patterns, and colours create a style uniquely her own. These process pieces, incorporate block printing, acrylic paint and mediums, washi and other papers which in turn allows Maria's work to reveal elements of transparency and depth while holding true to her lighthearted style.

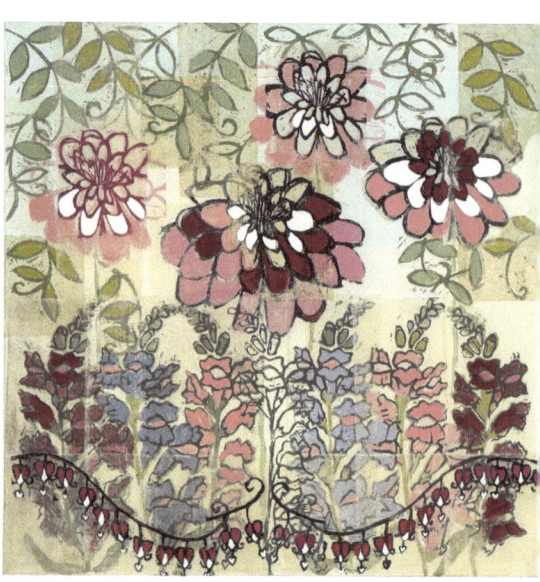

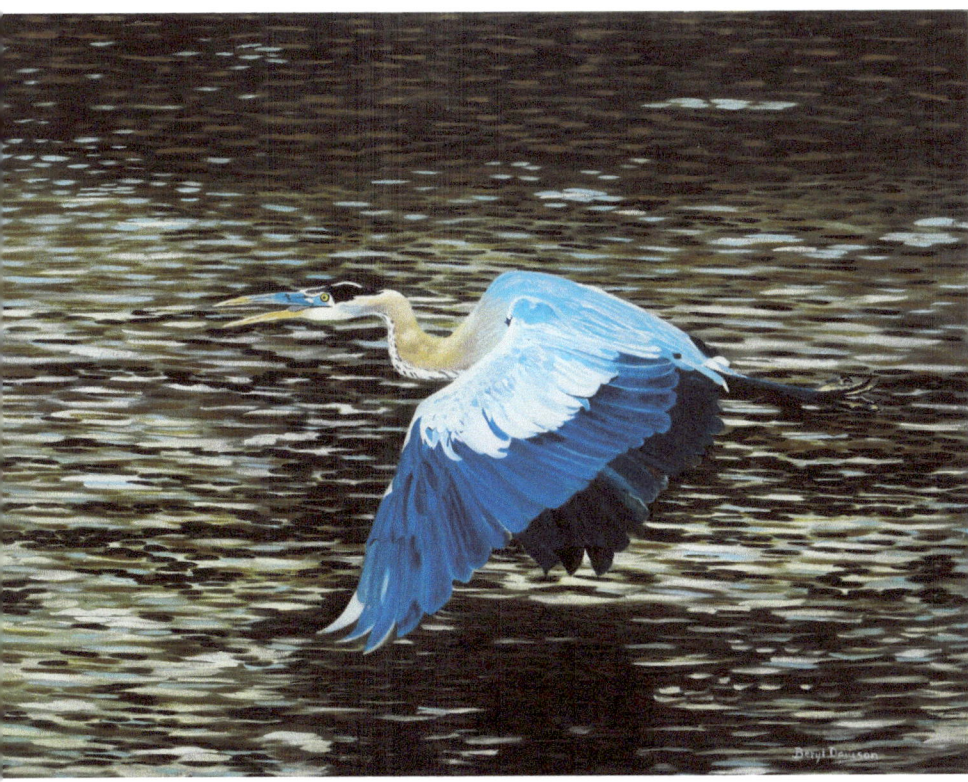

1 **Blue Heron in Flight** 30x40"
Oil on Canvas.

2 **Wild Algonquin Iris** 10x13"
framed to 16x20" mixed media
watercolour and acrylic.

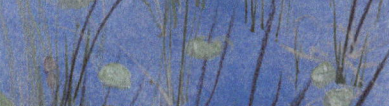

BERYL DAWSON

LOCATION: 6154 Wellington Rd 29,
RR4 Fergus N1M 2W5

WEB: beryldawson.ca
www.wellingtonartistsgallery.ca

EMAIL: emberyl@hotmail.com
wellingtonartistsgallery@hotmail.com

I am basically self taught, being a painter of photo realism working in oils and watercolour. My work records buildings and sites of historical importance as well as flora and fauna of the Canadian landscape. Wellington Artists' Gallery and Art Centre has consumed my time for the last four years. Located at 6142 Wellington Rd 29, this co-op Gallery boasts a Membership of 45 highly qualified artists.

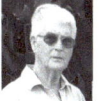

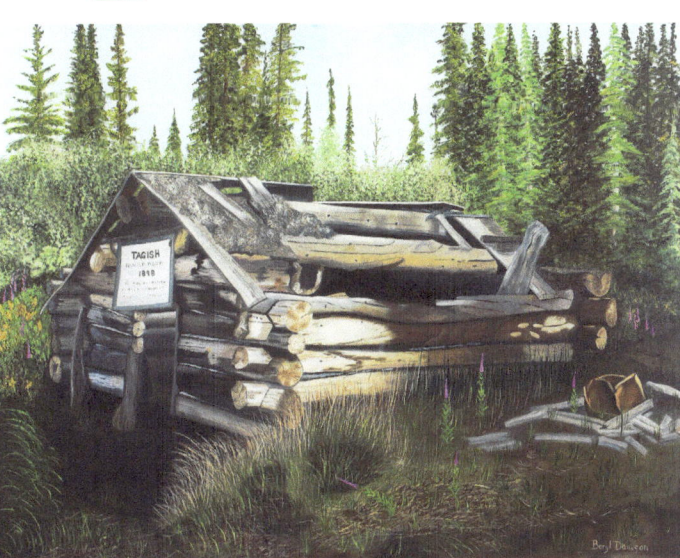

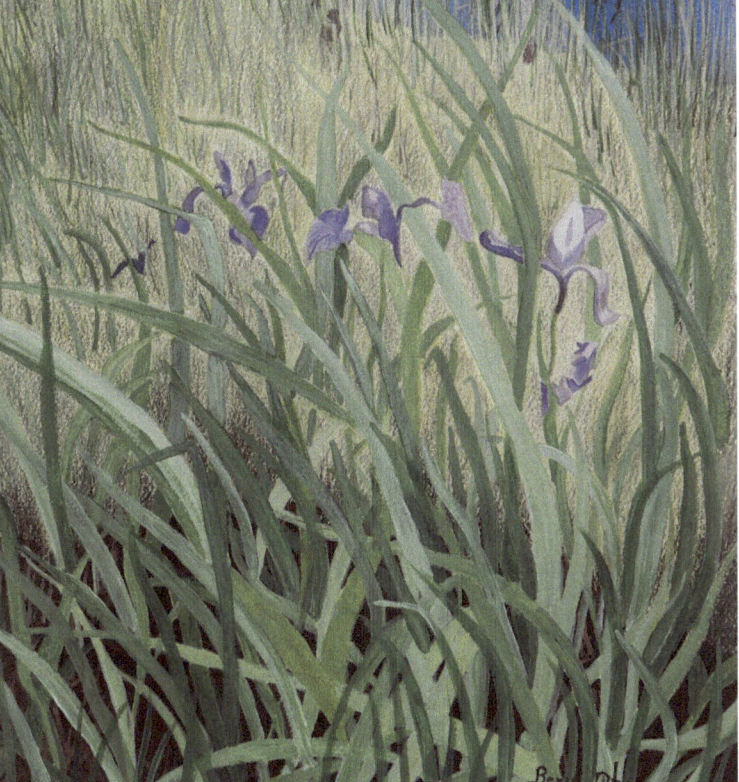

3 **North West Mounted Police
Post 1898 - Tagish - Yukon**

BHUPI RAJPUT

LOCATION: Cambridge
WEB: henna4you.com
EMAIL: Bhupi@henna4you.com

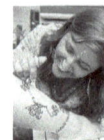

Bhupi is an incredibly talented Mehendhi (Henna) artist who combines a rare blend of old school tradition with modern trend-setting design. Bhupi is a traveller, she was born in Kenya, raised in England where she graduated with a BSc (Hons). She now lives in Canada with her husband, Sanjeev & two kids. Photographs from her backpacking days were memories of a wonderful adventure but today, they are her inspiration. Bhupi loves the art and the traditions that go with henna, so when she got the opportunity of taking her artistry a step further, it was a dream come true. She started painting glassware and porcelain. Each piece is signed and dated thus bringing a unique ethnic art into peoples homes and this is something she can smile about. The best part the paints are food and dishwasher safe.

1 **Wine Decanter With Four Red Wine Glasses** Simla design

2 **Porcelain Teapot & Mugs** Simla design.

3 **Wine Glasses** Stiletto, Taj, Simla, Katumba, Swirly Grape designs.

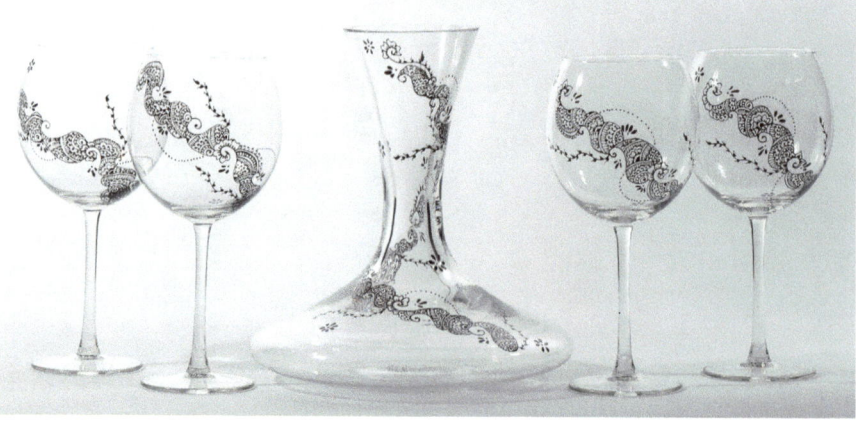

1

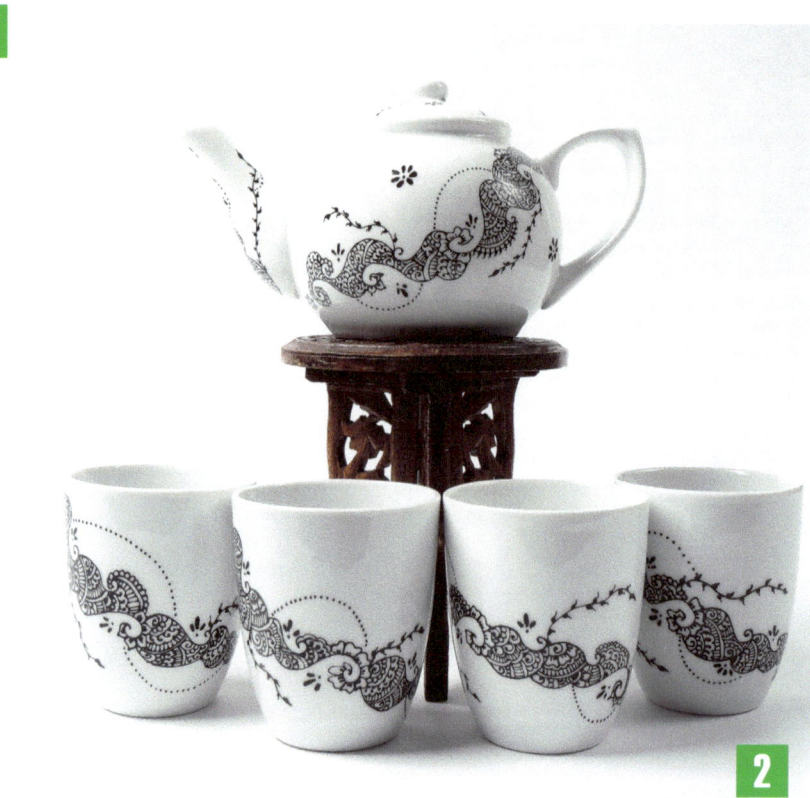

2

3

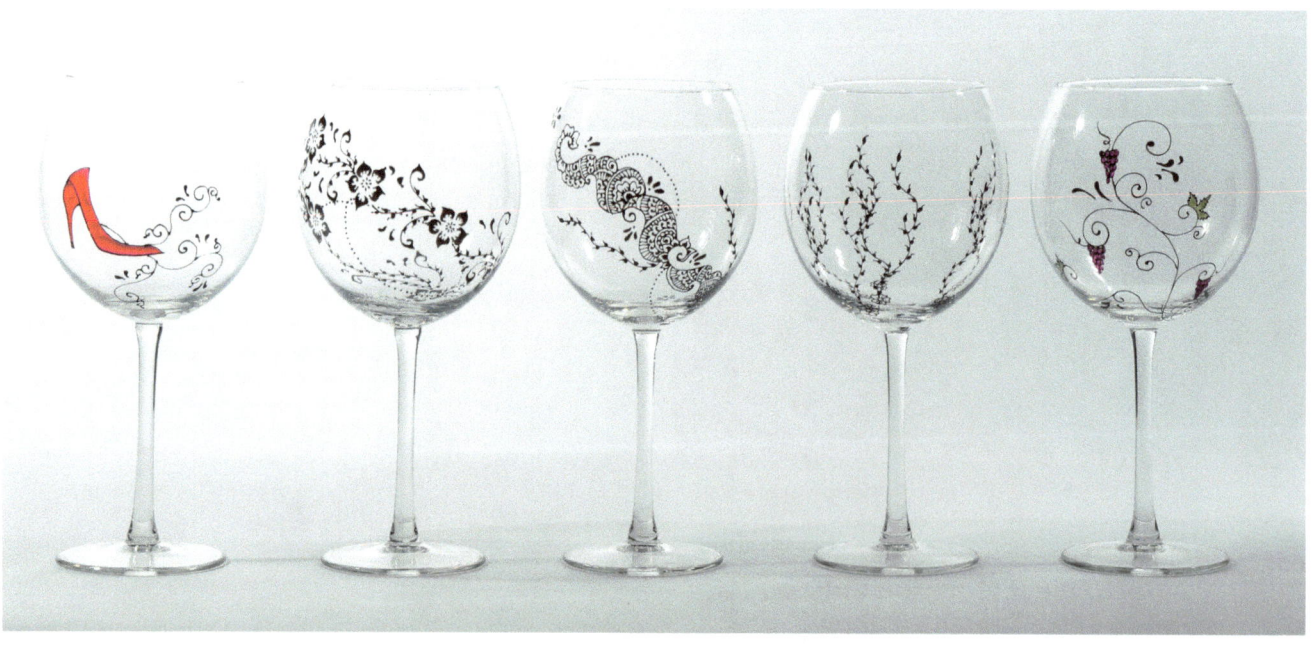

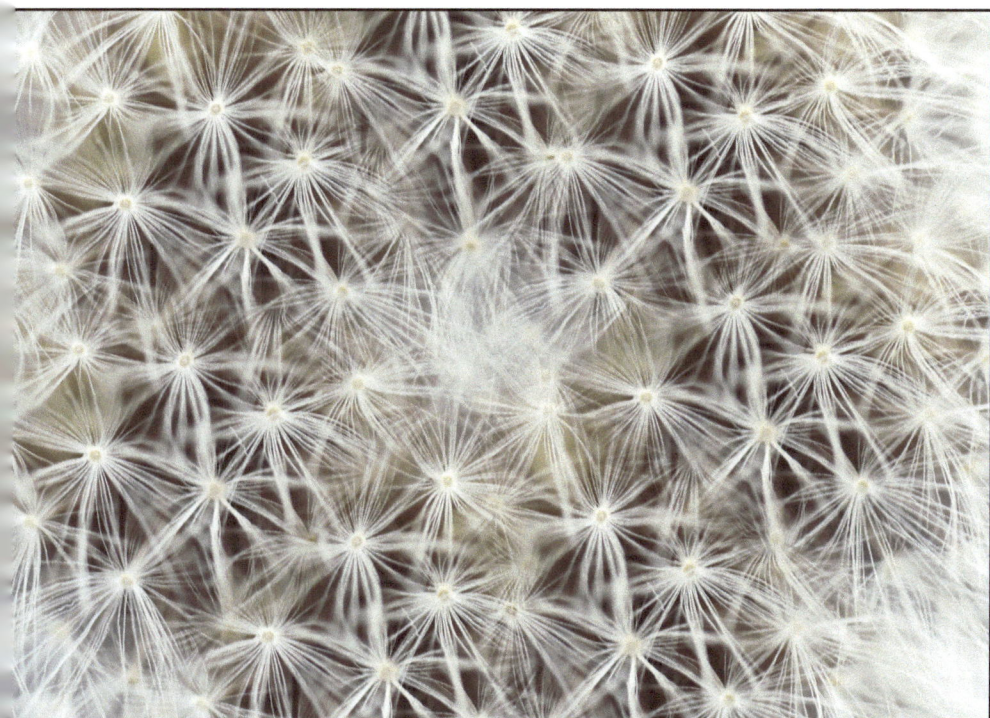

TRACI COTTINGHAM

LOCATION: Cambridge
WEB:
http://traci-cottingham.artistwebsites.com
EMAIL: catcottingham@rogers.com

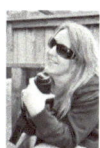
I have had a camera in my hand as far back as I can remember. I have a huge passion for Photography and Fine Art. I love to shoot but I also love the creativity that can occur upon editing. My work evolves like I do. One thing will always stay the same and that's how much fun I am having!

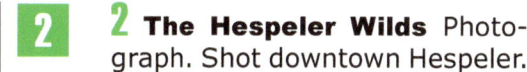
1 **Seeds Of Wishes** Photograph. Plenty of wishes to go around!

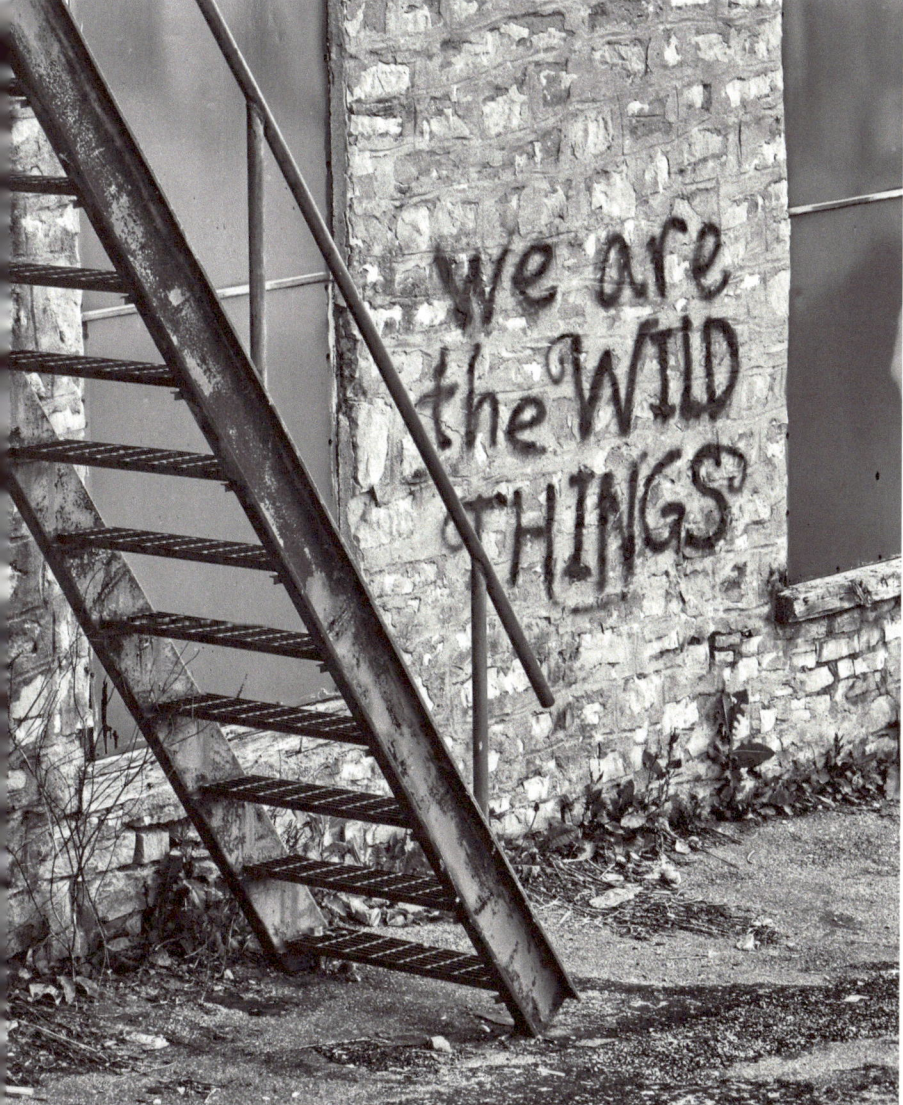

2 **The Hespeler Wilds** Photograph. Shot downtown Hespeler.

3 **Up** Photograph. Shot downtown Ottawa.

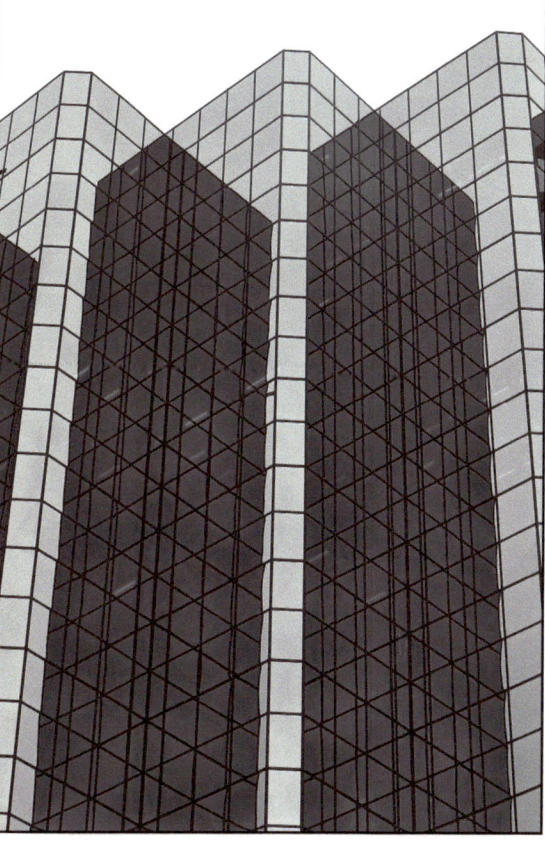

MAGGIE TILLEY

LOCATION: Guelph
WEB: (N/A)
EMAIL: Maggie.tilley@gmail.com

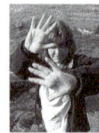

Maggie found her way to Guelph from an idyllic childhood on the Welsh border. There she spoke Welsh in school; picked wild mushrooms and was companion to gnomes, hedgehogs and fairies. Her father, Derek Tilley, was her art teacher and mentor and Maggie followed in his footsteps, completing a degree in Fine Arts and Sociology at University of Guelph. As you might surmise from her egg tempura, she has been most keenly influenced by the classics, her favorite artist is Caravaggio. Since graduating, Maggie has been most strongly represented by her portraiture and murals where she successfully experiments in Trompe L'Oeil. You may have seen her leprechauns and elves at the Guelph Mental Health or her oil landscape in Queens Park – presented to Bob Rae whilst leader of the NDP Party. The once owner of BeaDazzled Bead Shop she now paints and beads in her overstocked studio on Egdehill Drive.

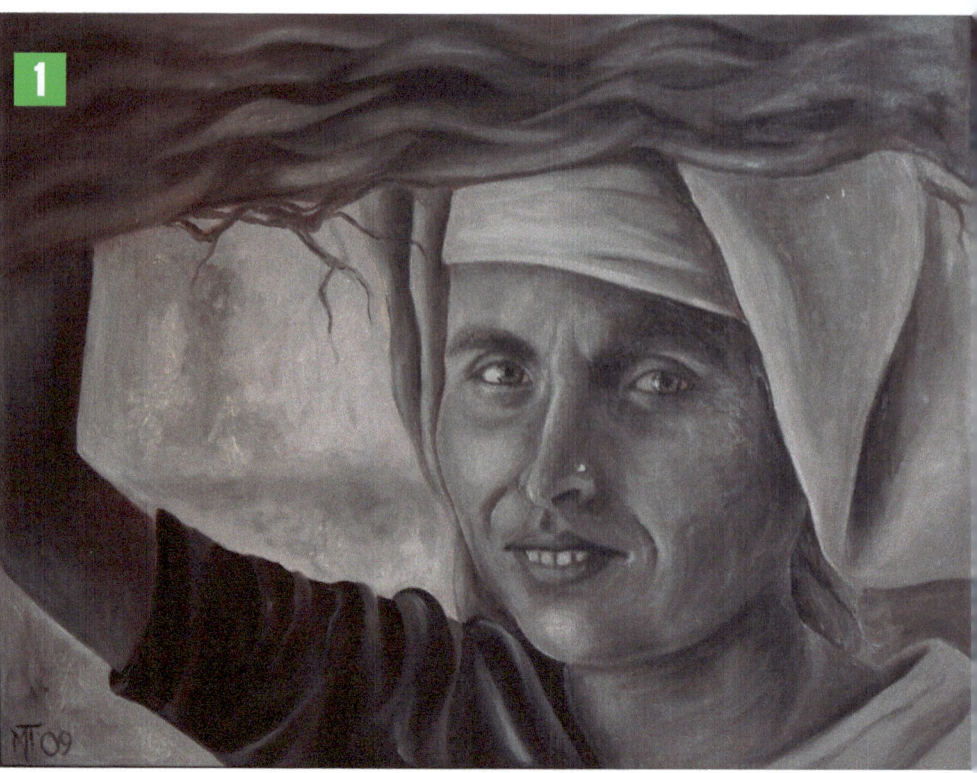

1

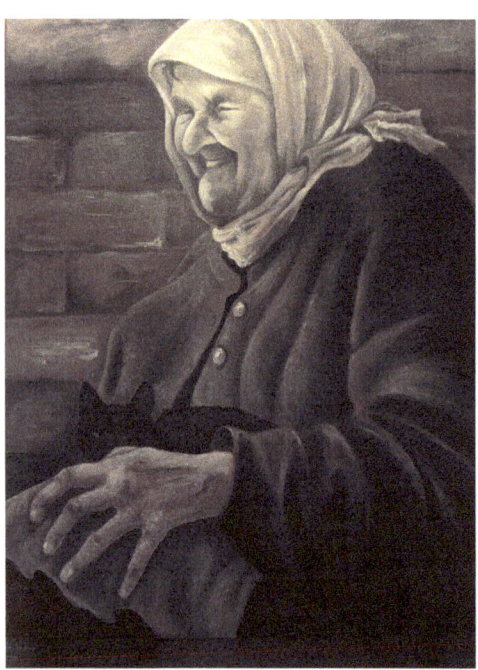

2

3

1 Rajasthan 30x40" Oil on canvas.

2 Babushka 33x42" Oil on canvas.

3 Egg Tempera 10x12" Egg tempera on masonite.

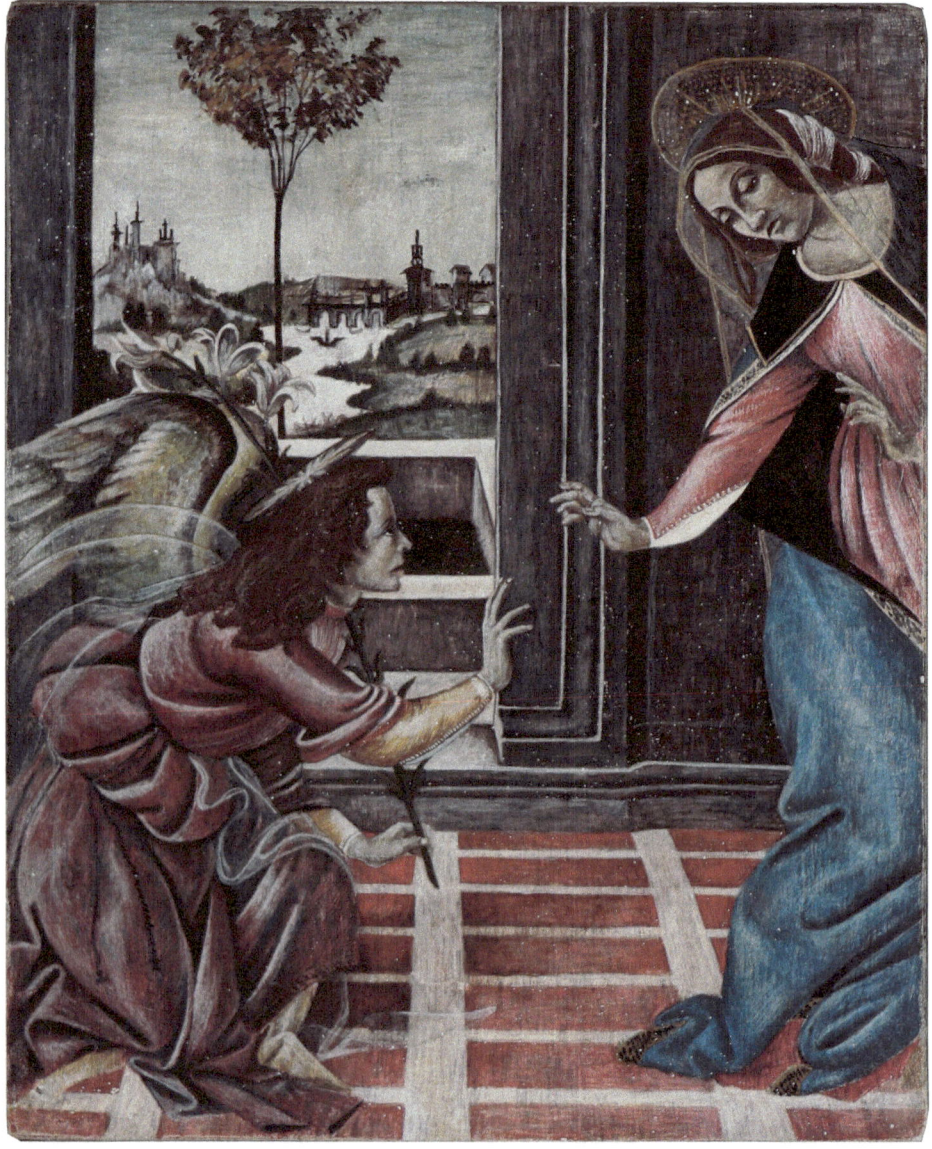

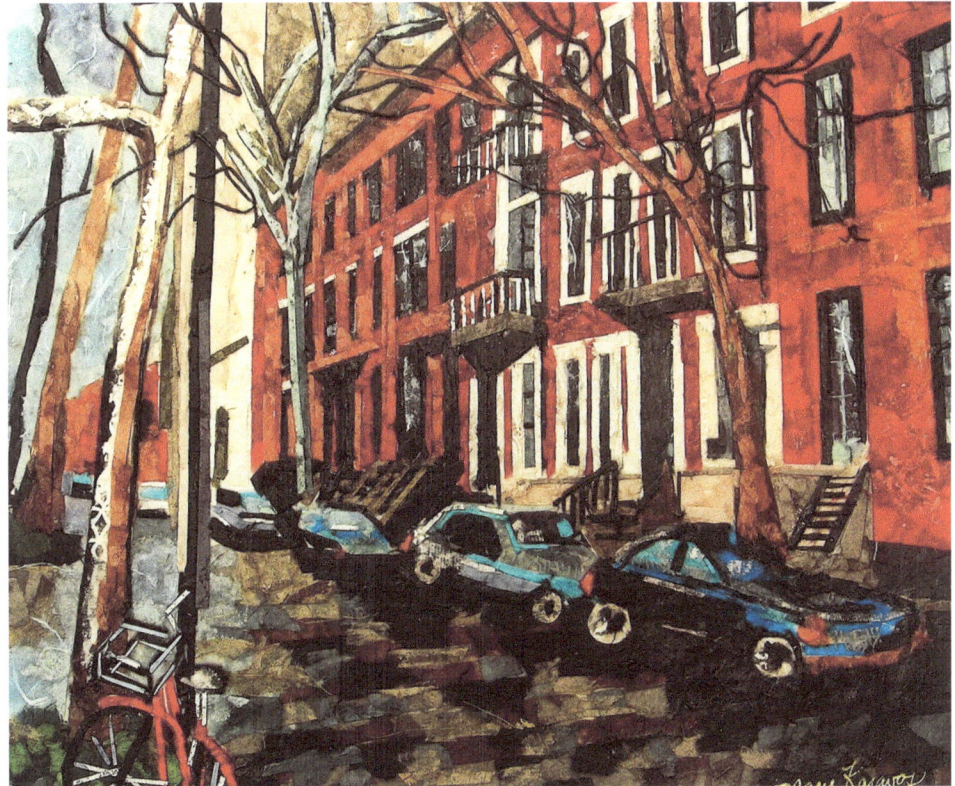

MARY KARAVOS

LOCATION: Guelph
WEB: karavosart.com
EMAIL: info@karavosart

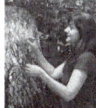 Mary graduated in Fine Arts from the Ontario College of Art and Design. In her final year, she was selected for a year of advanced studies in Florence, Italy. Combining her Florentine influences with her sense of the remarkable qualities of paper, Mary established her distinctive style of collage. She creates spontaneous abstracts and representational images from a colorful palette of paper fragments. Only the finest Japanese , Thai and Nepalese papers are selected for her work. No paint is used in her art.

1

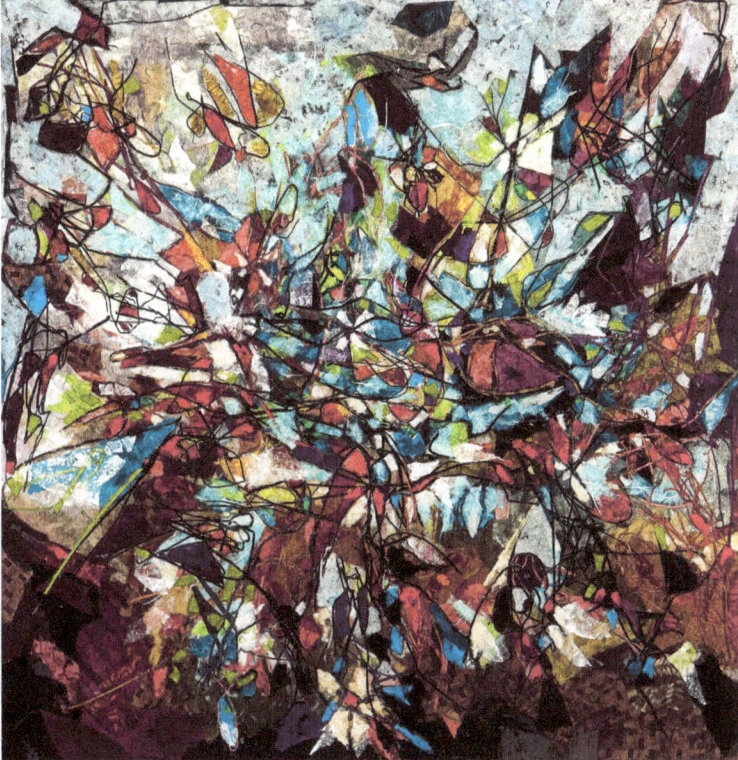

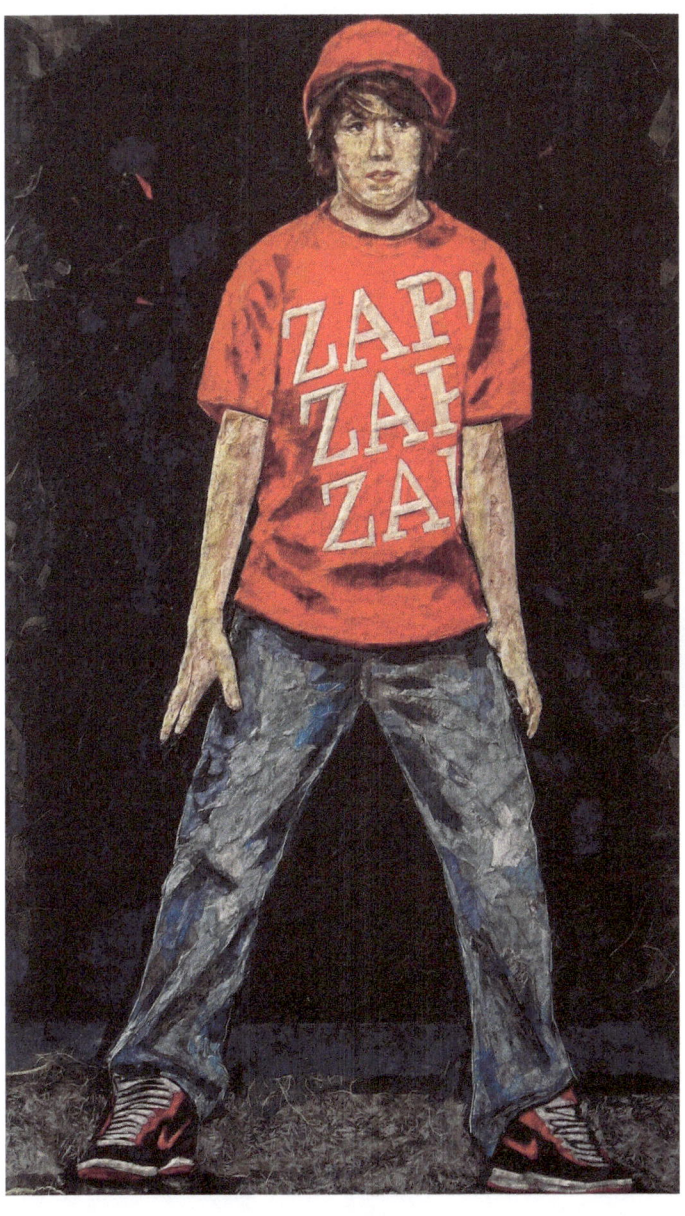

3

2

1 **City In Red** 10x12" Japanese, Thai and Nepalese papers on watercolor paper.

2 **Zap** 18×30" Japanese, Thai and Nepalese papers on canvas.

3 **Calligraphy of Color** 36×36" Japanese, Thai and Nepalese papers on canvas.

1 **Smolder** Photograph.

2 **Joy** Photograph.

3 **Harmonious Sea** Photograph.

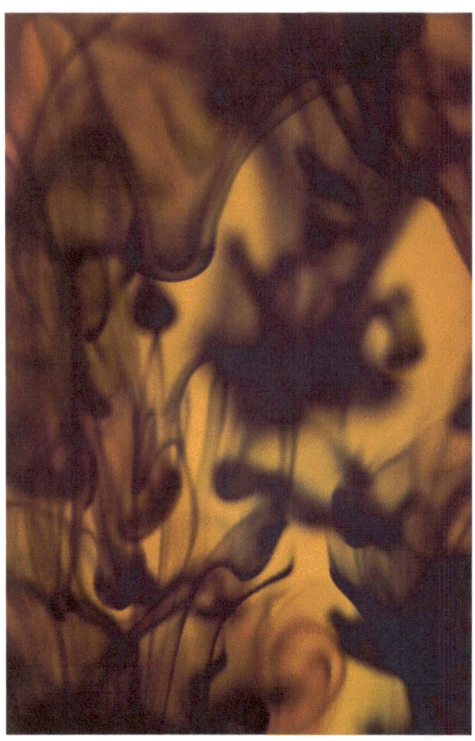

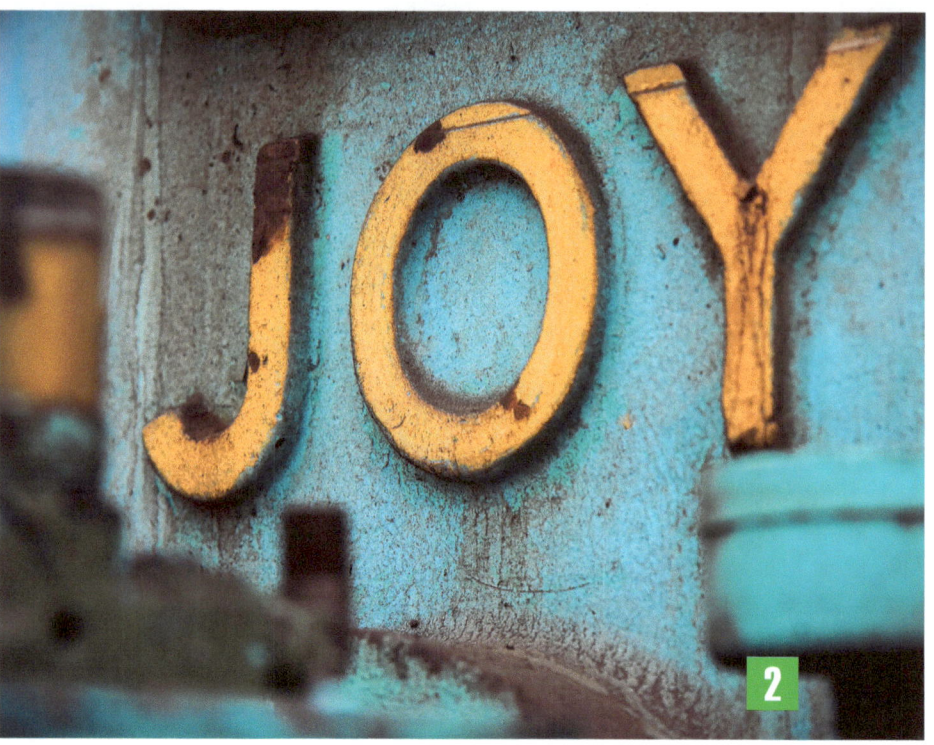

LAURA COOK

LOCATION: Cambridge
WEB: vision-photography.ca
EMAIL: laura@vision-photography.ca

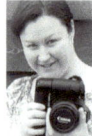

The true art of my photography lies not in the camera but in my mind's eye. Appreciating and capturing what is before me, presenting it's everlasting beauty brings me great joy. I draw my inspiration from the world around us, which often is over looked or taken for granted. I have valued the importance of preserving memories for as long as I can remember. I present these images with anticipation of sharing an emotional response with my audience. I continually strive for growth and push the boundaries with my creativity. I step outside my comfort zone by exploring avenues to improve my artistic endeavours. I am honoured sharing this vision with you.

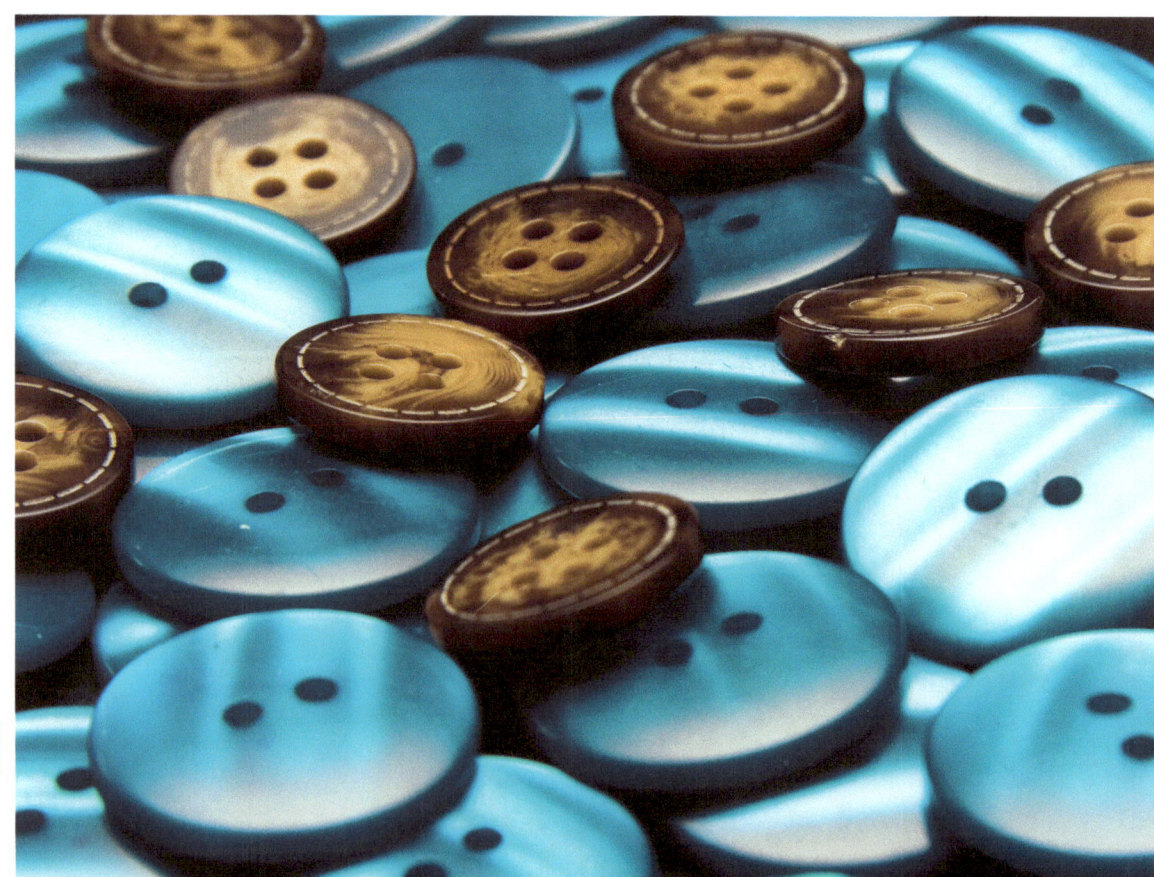

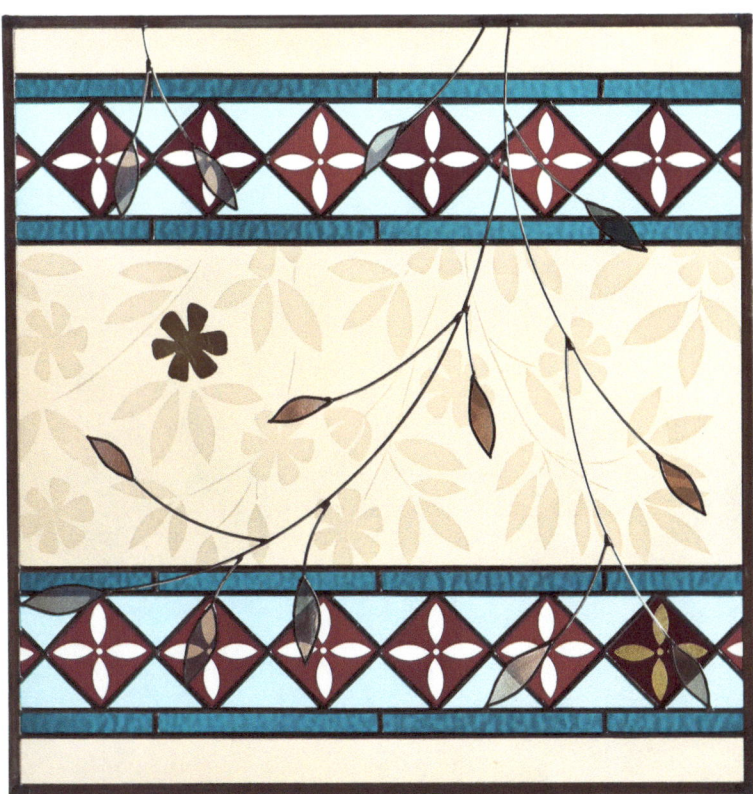

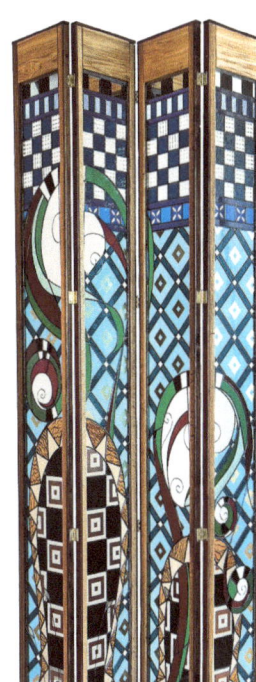

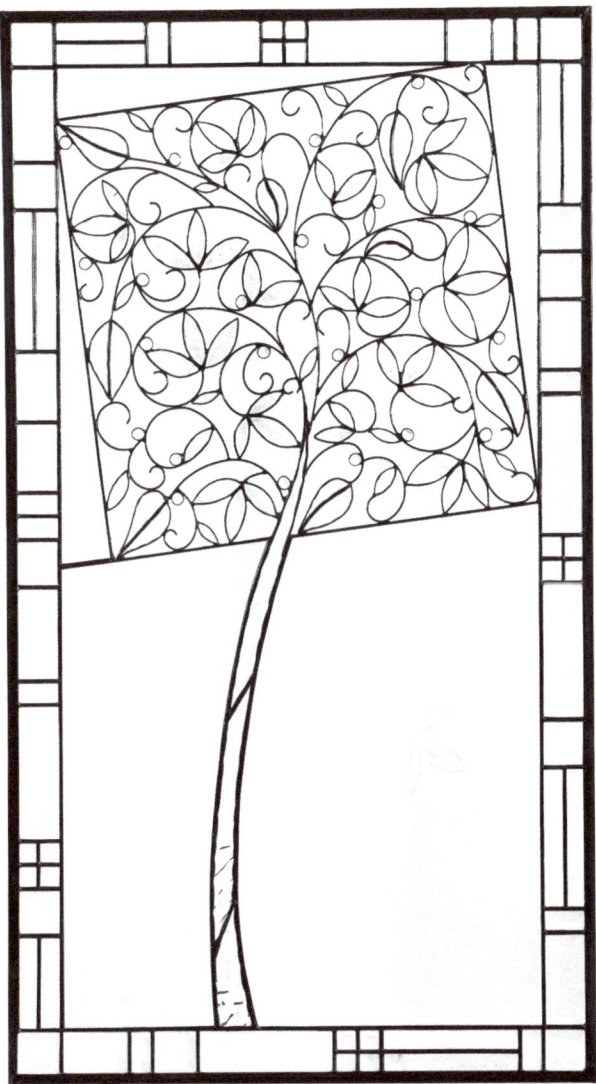

1 Vine 18x18" Stained, etched, dichroic glass with gold leaf, 2009

2 Gaudi-esque Fiddlehead Screen 1 48x94" Stained and leaded glass, dichroic glass, gold and copper leaf paint, copper wire, walnut, oak and ash wood frames, 2009.

3 Tree of Hope 22x43" Etched and beveled glass, copper wire, 2010.

LYNN CHIDWICK

LOCATION: 123 Woolwich Street, 3rd floor, Guelph ON N1H 3V1
WEB: chidwick.ca/stainedglass
EMAIL: lynn@chidwick.ca

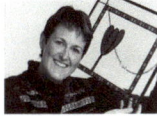

Born in Kenya, Lynn obtained a Masters of Environmental Studies from York University in Toronto. After working in that field for a number of years, she realized her passion for art. Lynn worked in several stained glass studios before she established her own stained glass studio in Guelph in 2000. The predominant aspect of Lynn's work is influenced by her study of the Arts and Crafts Movement. Currently, there is particular emphasis in the eras of Art Deco and Art Nouveau. Using a variety of methods including fusing, gold leafing, etching, sandblasting, painting, layering, and leading, Lynn integrates the various elements of such artists as Morris, Mackintosh, Gaudi, Guimard, and Klimt in an attempt to capture both the quality of their work and understand the influences that resulted in their masterpieces.

BARRY SCUTT

LOCATION: Guelph
WEB: (N/A)
EMAIL: barryscutt05@gmail.com

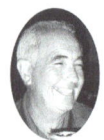

Barry emigrated from England in 1967. He always enjoyed cartooning and was on the staff of the Soccer America out of California, editorial cartoonist for Guelph Life and a regular contributor to Playboar Magazine. In the early 70's started Triangle Sports where he was responsible for most of the writing, photography and cartoons. Started Scutt Signs in 1979 when both lettering and artwork was done with a brush. Retired in 2007. Began working with watercolours 15 years ago painting from photographs taken of old cottaes and pubs around Sussex during trips visiting family back home. Did illustrations for book of golf games called "Let's Play Wolf" and is currently working on illustrations for children's stories about "Freddee the Friendly Fish".

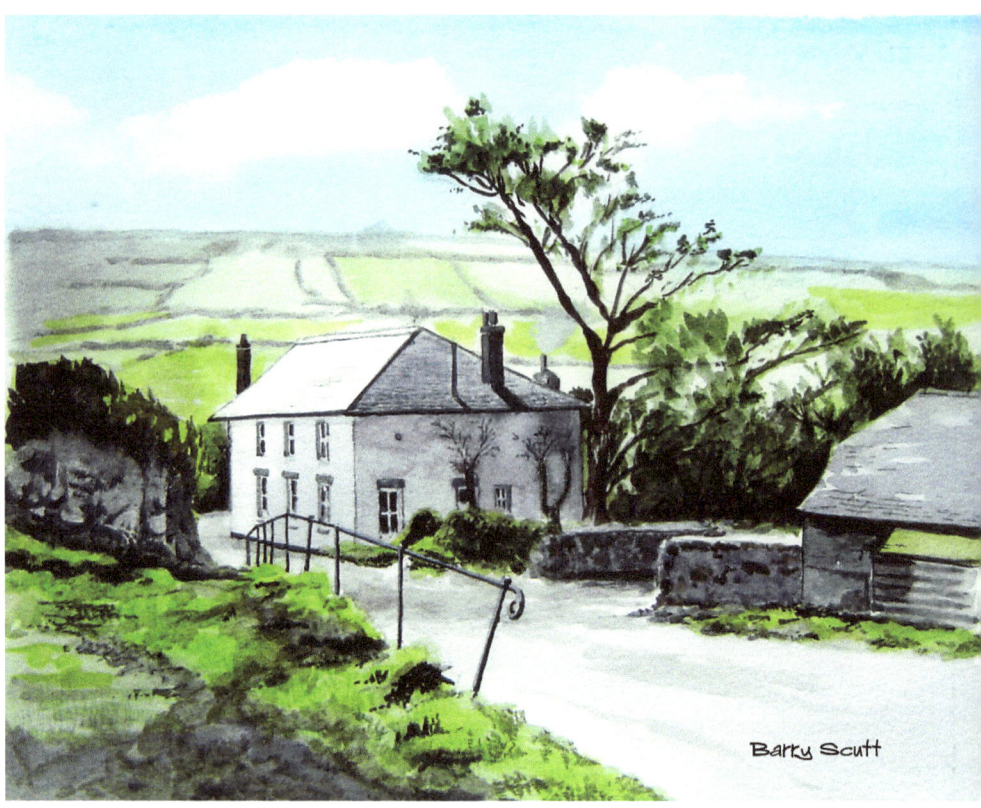

1 Zennor 12x9" Watercolour village in North Devon, England.

3 Lady in Spain 14x11" Acrylic.

2 Tulip 14x11" Acrylic.

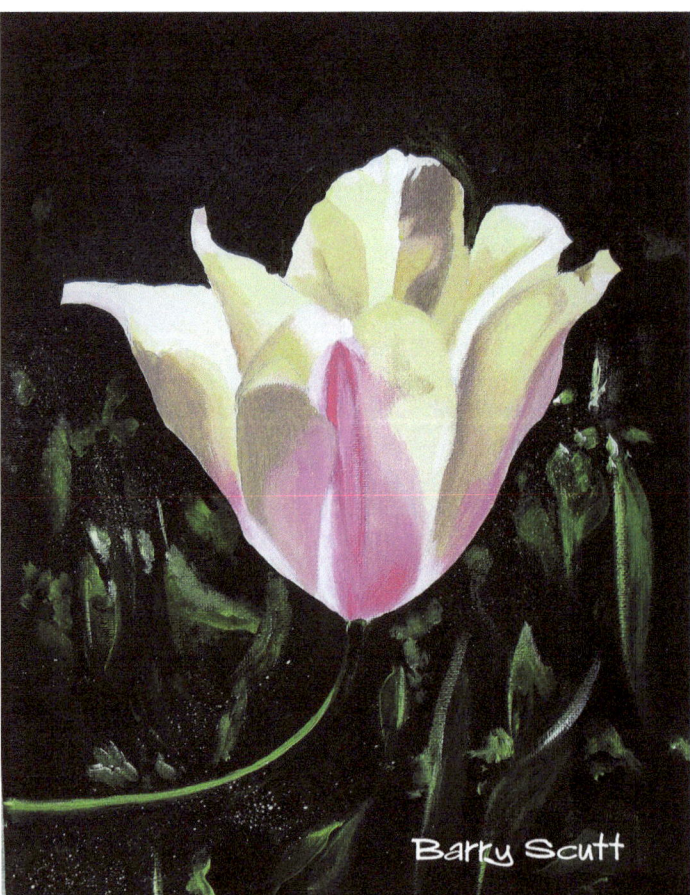

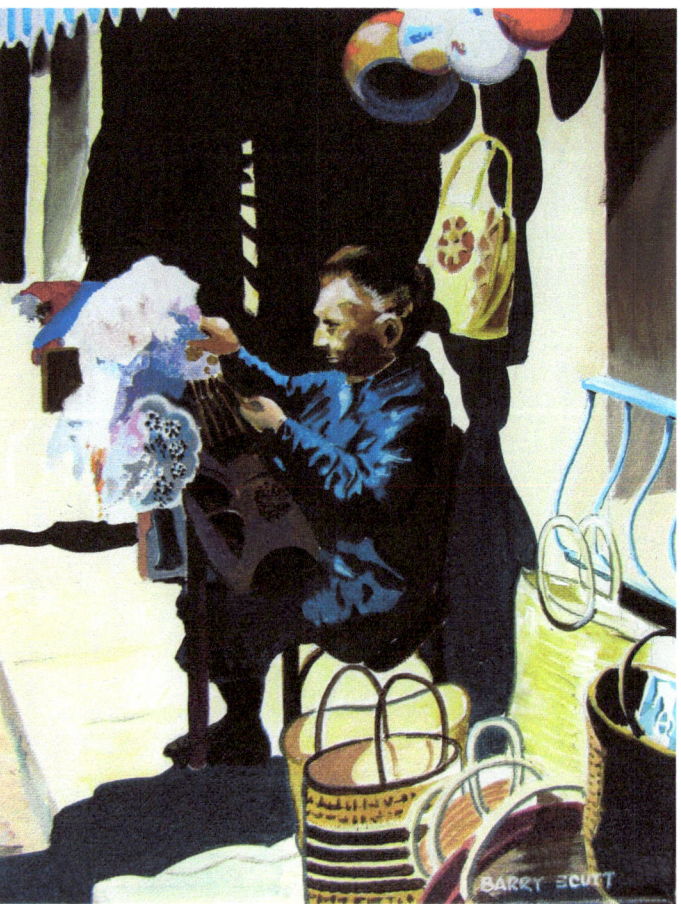

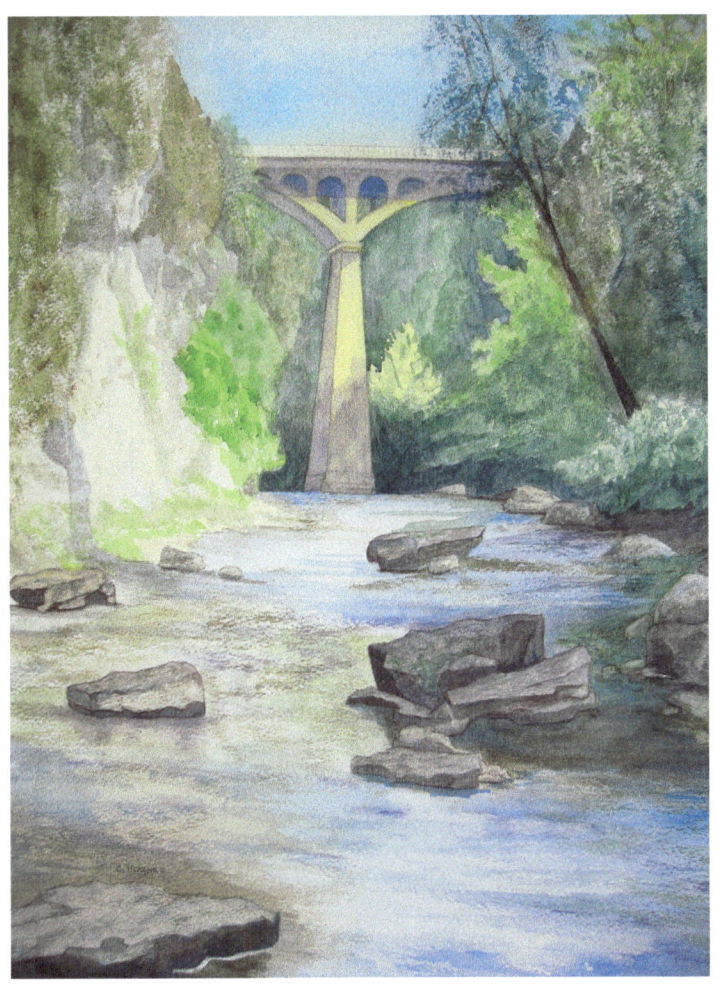

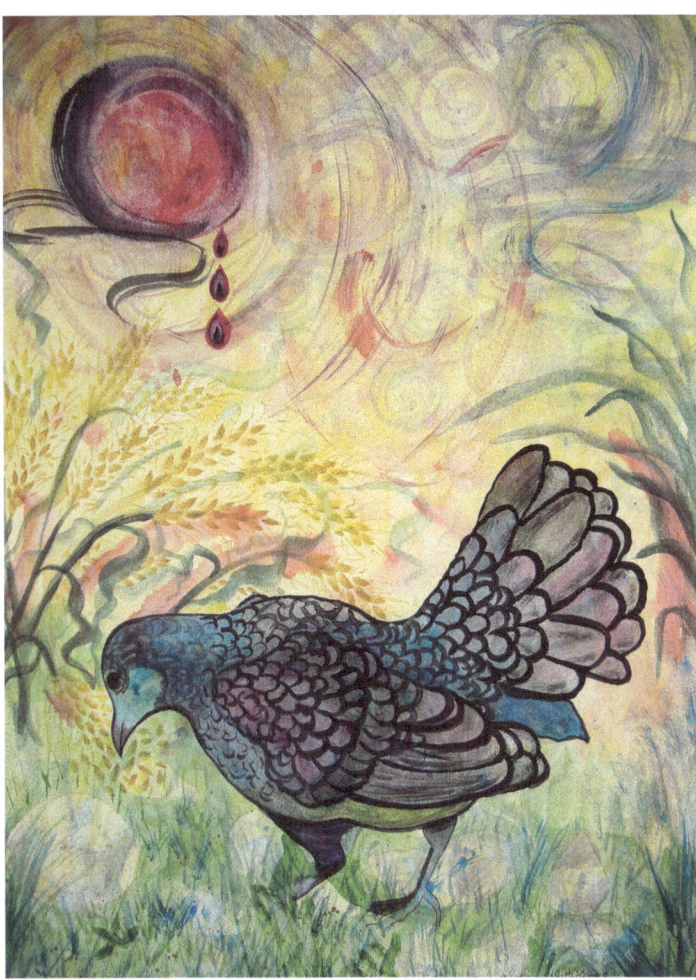

1 **Elora Gorge** 21x14″ Watercolour on paper.

1 **2**

2 **The Legend of Cerridwen** 19x14″ Watercolour & ink on paper.

CAROL HUGHES

LOCATION: Rockwood
WEB: carolhughesart.wordpress.com
EMAIL: chughesstudio@bell.net

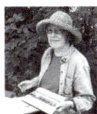

Carol Hughes did basic studies in art at university but completed her degree in English. After working for many years in communications and public relations, she began painting in watercolour in 2003. While continuing to exhibit her vibrant, nature-inspired watercolours, she has also been exploring sumi-e and mixed media works.

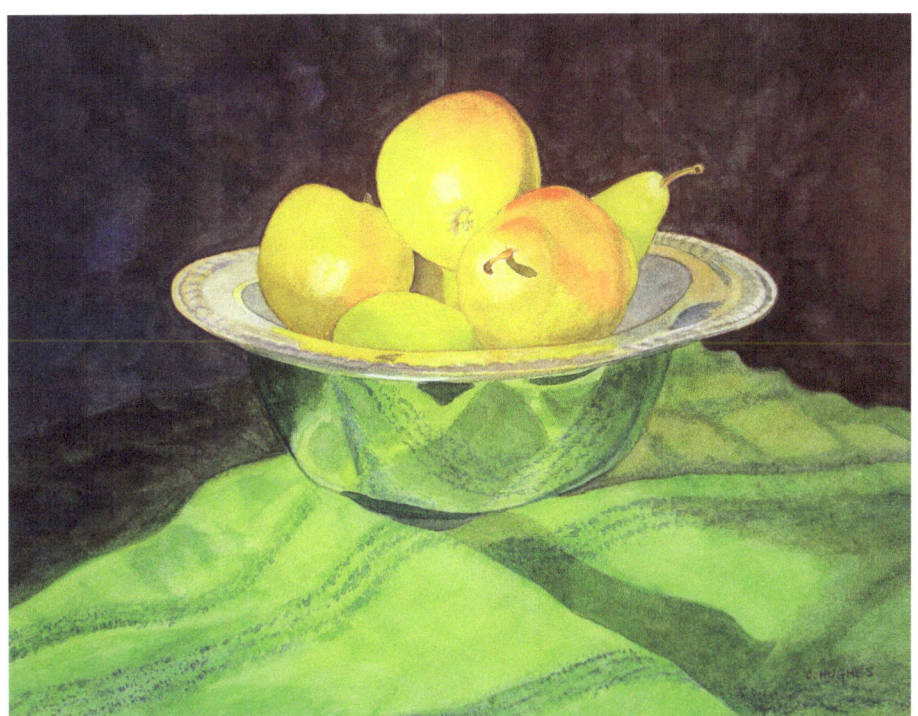

3 **Gold and Silver** 10x14″ Watercolour on paper.

3

CHARLOTTE TIMMINS

LOCATION: Timmins Tileworks
410 Westminster Dr. S., Cambridge.
WEB: timminstileworks.ca:
EMAIL: charlottetea@bell.net

Charlotte has never been to art school. She started doodling in College out of severe boredom and never stopped. She paints on floor tile designed to hang on walls. The big ones are the most fun to do. In recent days she has taken to gleefully smashing raw tile into sharp shapes and painting that.

1

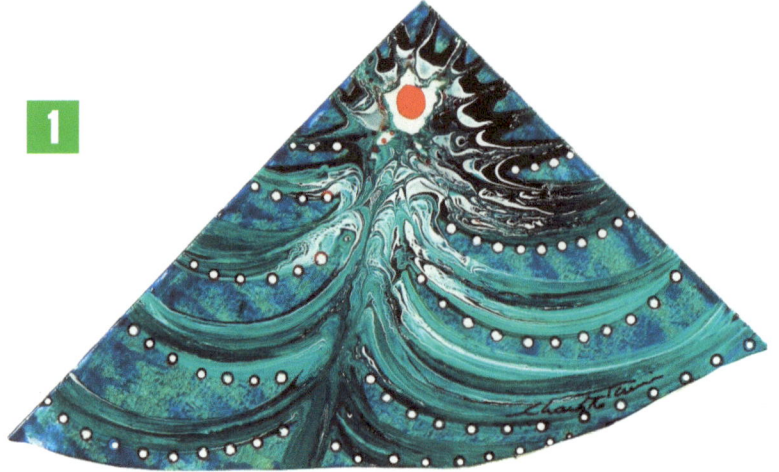

1 Painted Tiles

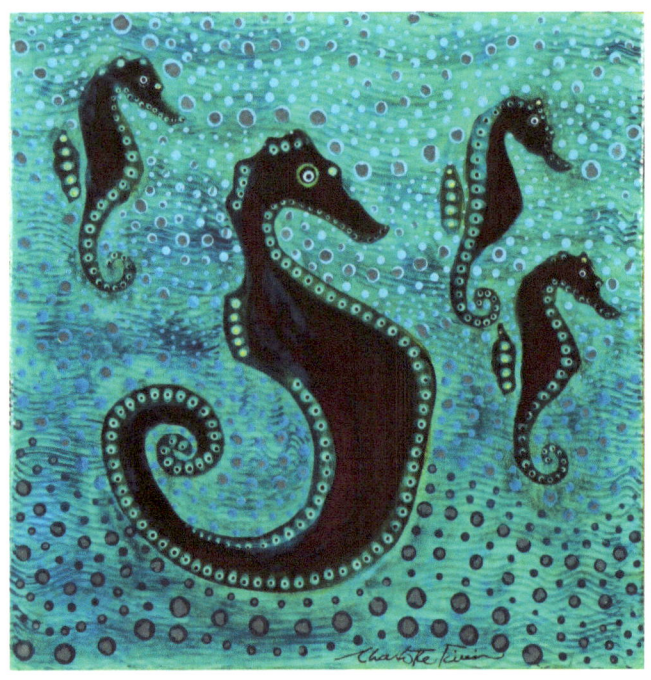

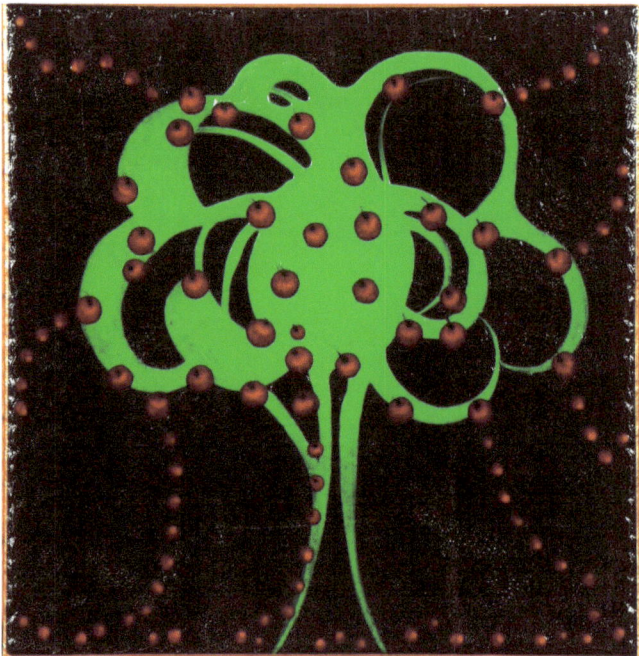

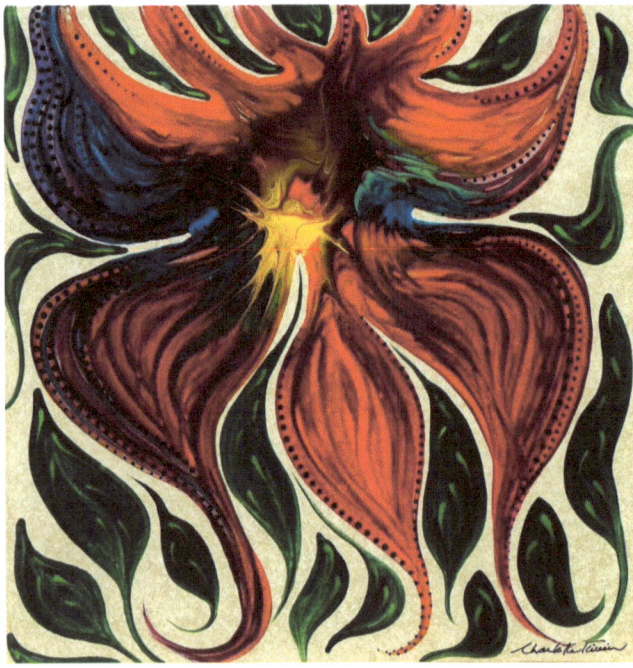

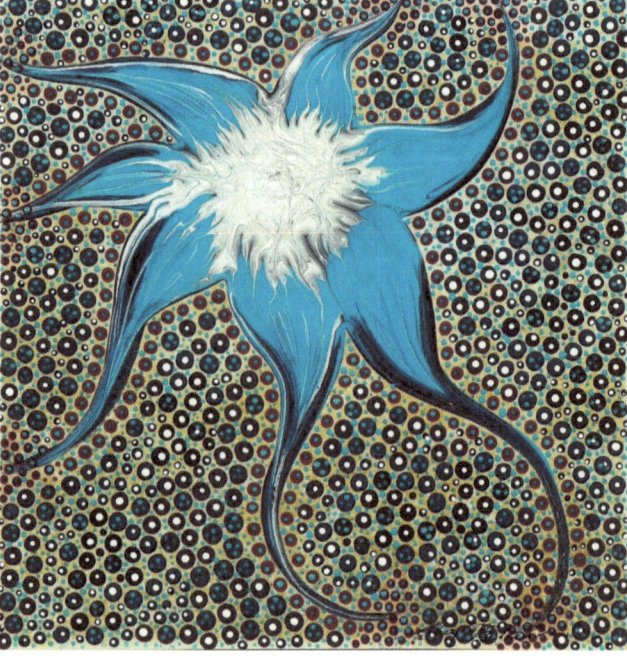

ANN HARVEY

LOCATION: Cambridge
WEB: aaharveyartist.com
EMAIL: adria.ann@sympatico.ca

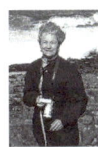

Ann Harvey SCA, CFS who has been painting in the Waterloo Region for many years, has won awards for her innovative paintings. Her media of choice are watercolour, acrylic, and encaustics painted on paper, canvas and board and the resulting paintings feature great texture and unusual colour. Ann is an elected member of the Society of Canadian Artists, the Colour and Form Society and a Signature member of the Toronto Watercolour Society. She belongs to Kitchener Waterloo Society of Artists and Studio 30 in Cambridge.

1

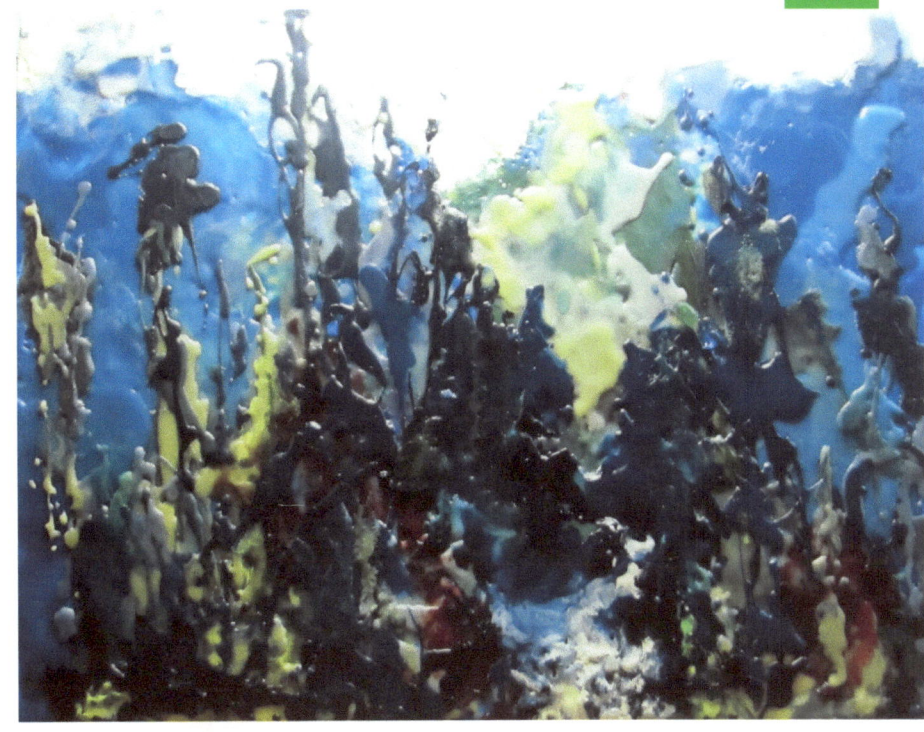

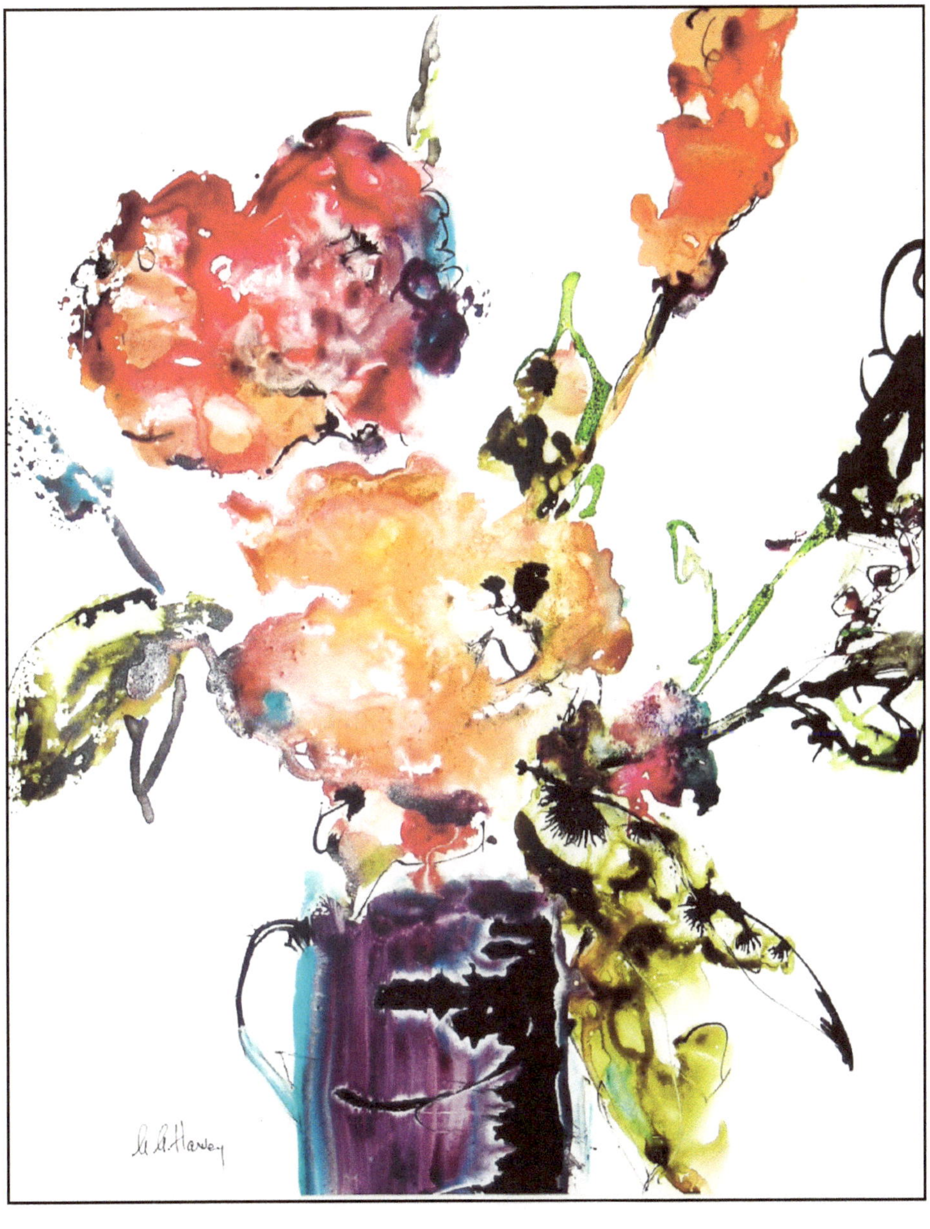

2

1 **Mountain Panorama** 24x30" Encaustic on board.

2 **Hydrangeas** 26x20" Watercolour on paper.

3 **Swift Water** 30x30" Acrylic on canvas.

3

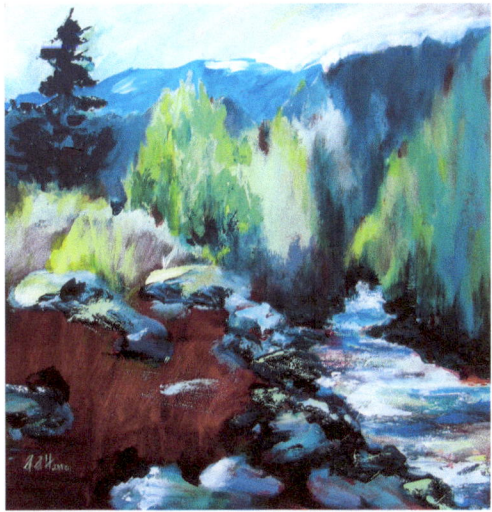

JOAN VANDERKAMP

LOCATION: Guelph
WEB: (N/A)
EMAIL: (C/O) maddog14@rogers.com

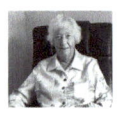

Joan Rosemary Vanderkamp was born in St. Andrews, Scotland into a family of artists. She grew up during Workd War II and was strongly affected by the dark winter evenings, when the lights were turned off and blackout imposed. She longed to be able to travel and enjoy the sunsets, the glowing colours of the Fife countryside and the mountains further north. She still loves to paint landscapes. After studying at the Universities of St. Andrews and London, she emigrated to Canada where she met her husband. It was only after his death, her children were grown and she retired from a career in publishing that she had time to develop her interest in art. She studied with such outstanding artists as Soltan Zabo, Brian Ateo, Doug Mays etc. She has served on the executive of the Guelph Creative Arts Association and as President of the Evergreen Watercolour Painters Group. Her work has been displayed at many juried shows and her paintings hang in many private collections in Europe, the US and Canada.

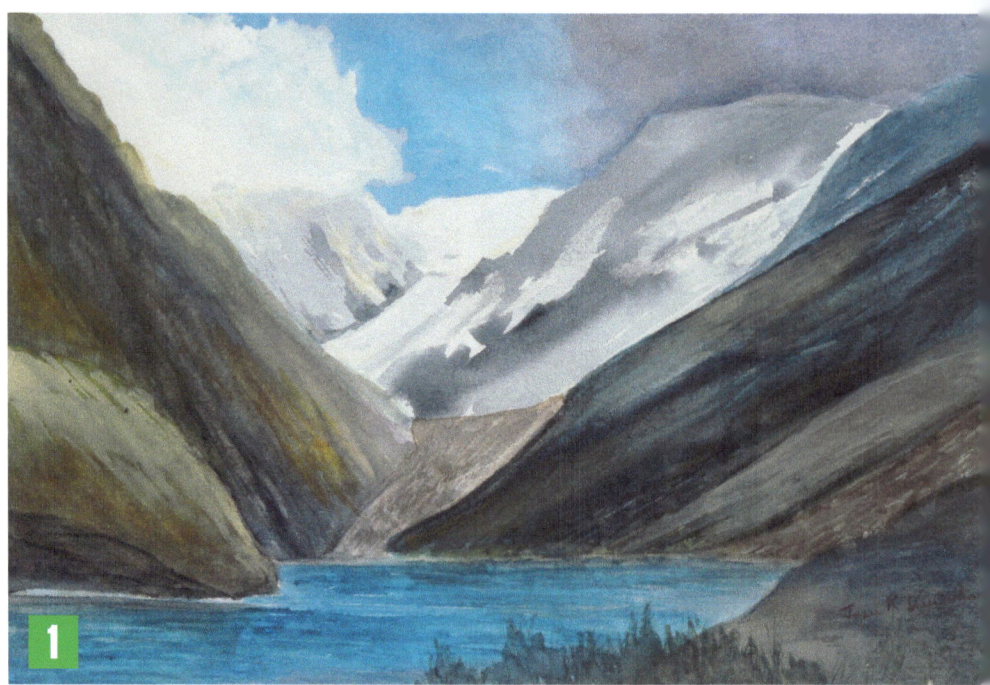

1 New Zealand Fiord
14.5x10.5" Watercolour.

2 Dance of the Sunflowers
15x10.5" Watercolour.

3 Mississippi Magic 12x9"
Watercolour.

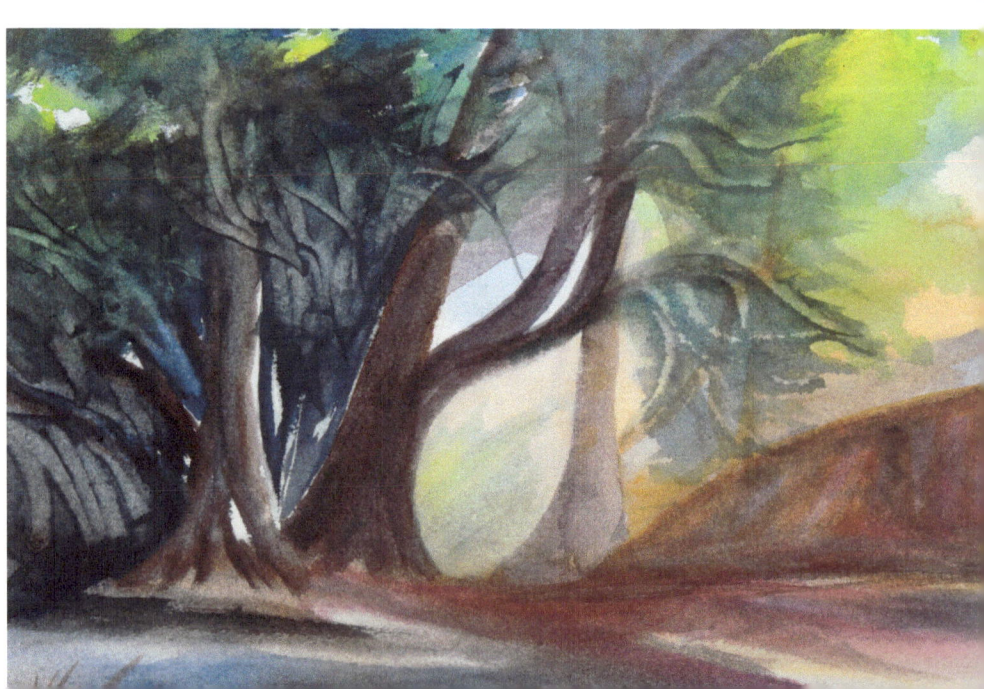

1 **Comox Waterfall** 9½x12½" Watercolour on paper. Beautiful Vancouver Island, BC, is an artist's paradise.

2 **Three Sisters** 9½x13½" Watercolour on paper. Inspiration was from the garden in springtime.

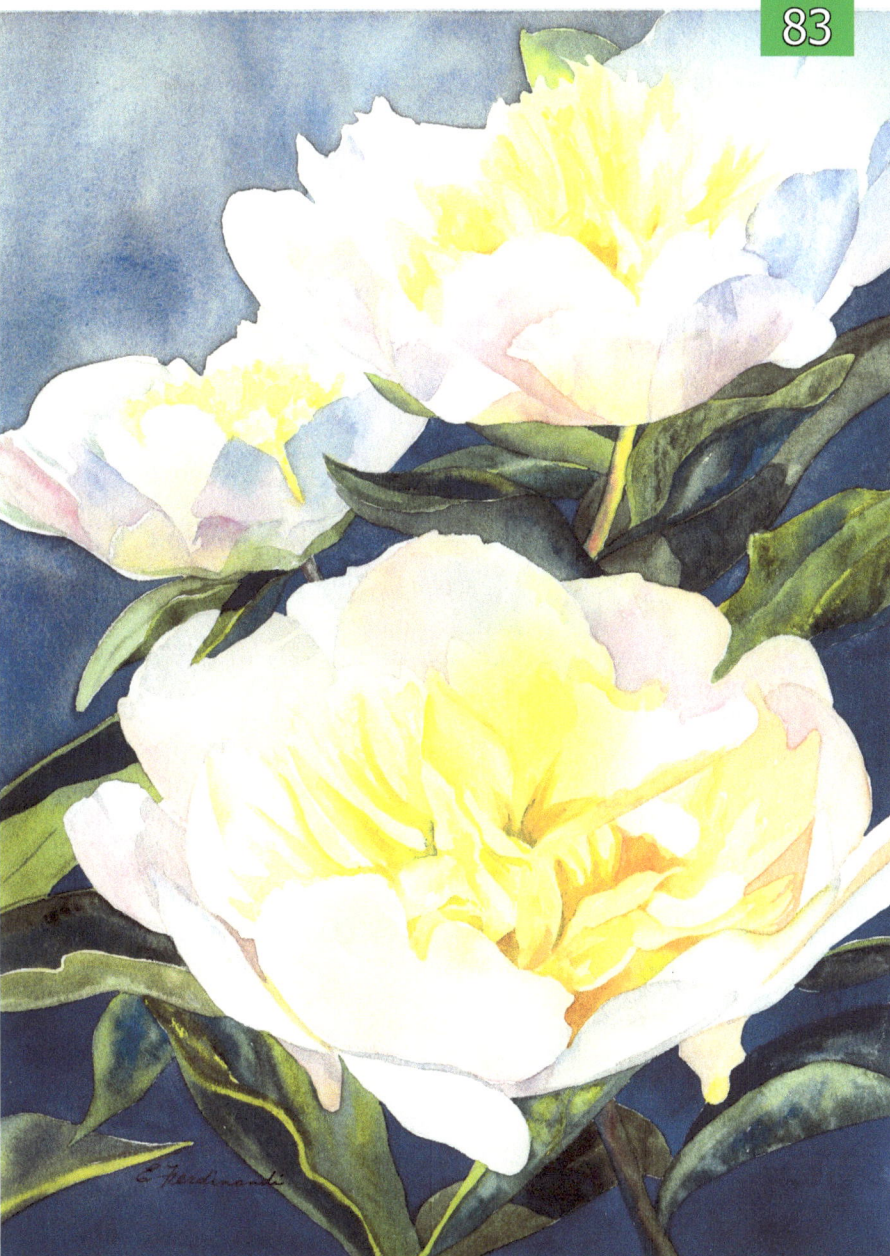

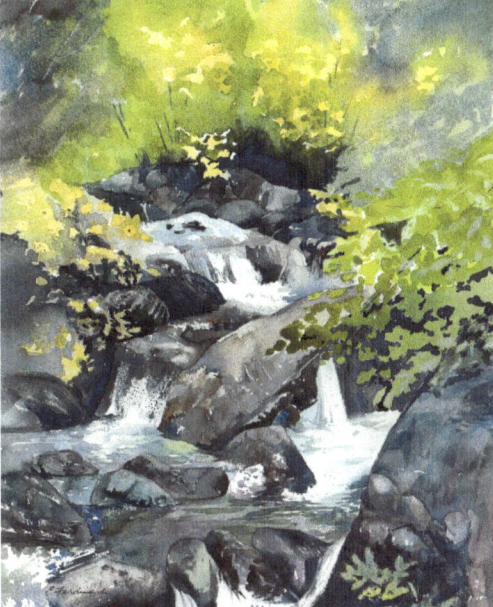

ELAINE FERDINANDI

LOCATION: Guelph
WEB: (N/A)
EMAIL: elaineferdinandi@gmail.com

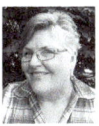
Elaine is a Guelph artist who has combined her love for watercolour painting and her desire to be a life-long learner by studying her craft with many talented artists over the past 10 years. Passion and practice enable her to achieve successful landscape, still life and floral paintings which capture light with bold colour. She is a member of the Guelph Creative Arts Association and the West Hills Art Group. She has participated in local Art Shows and has completed many commissioned works.

3 **Coastal Experience** 10x14" Watercolour on paper. Oregon coastline has a painting waiting at every turn.

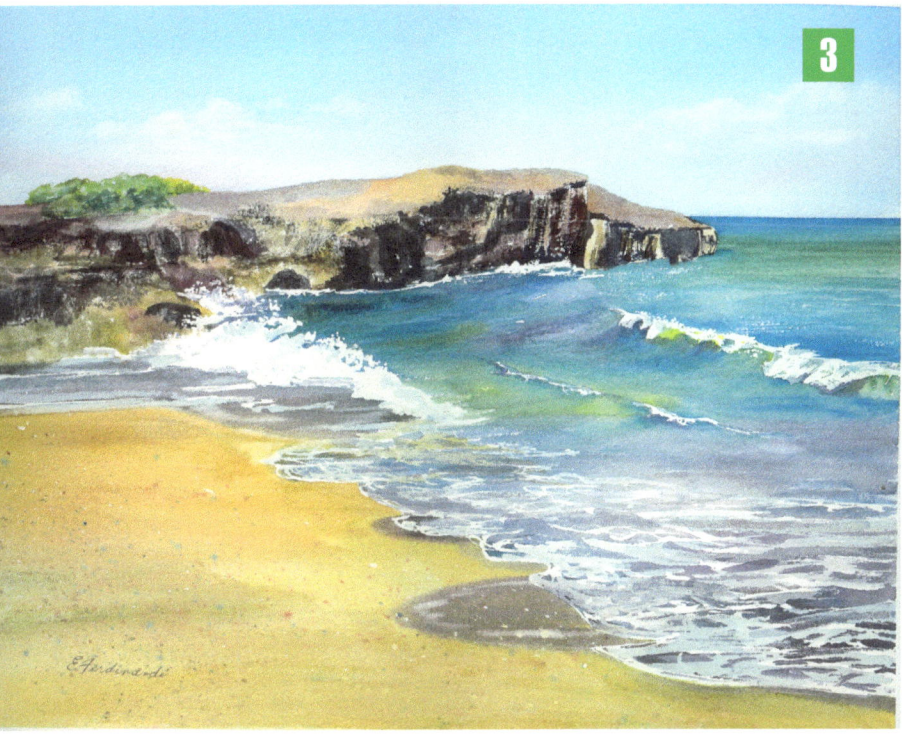

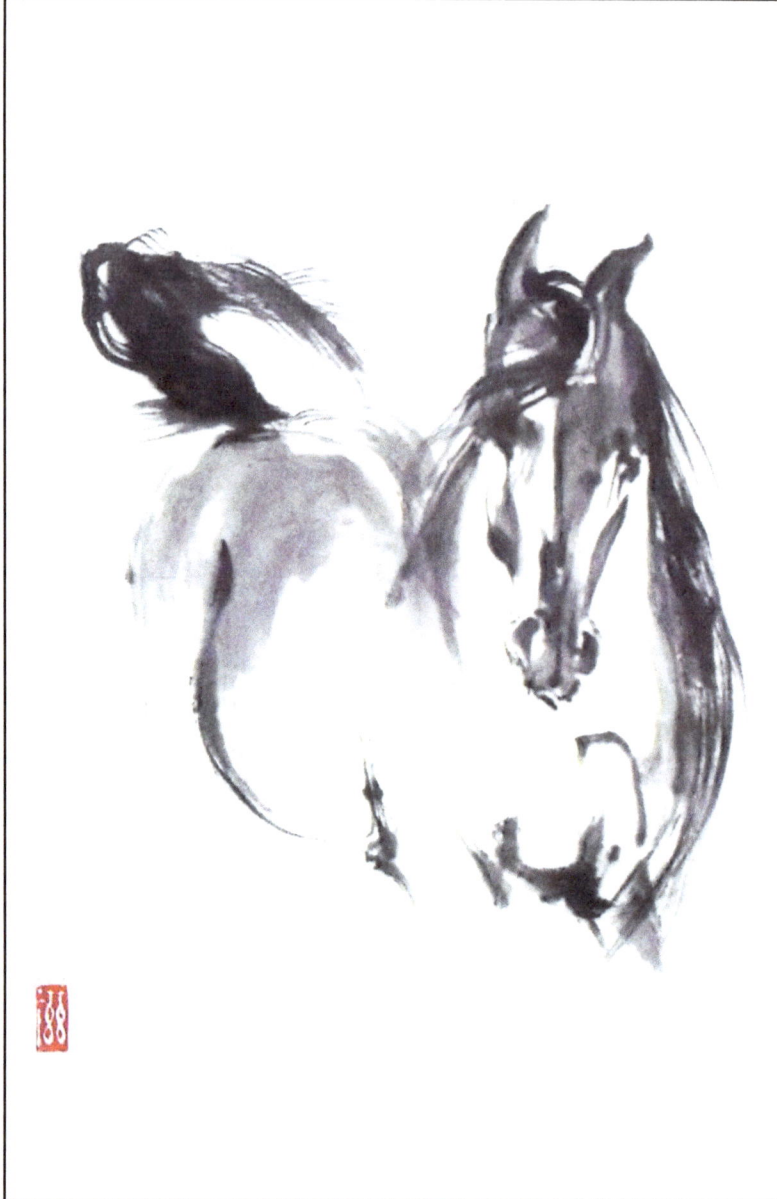

ROSLYN LEVIN

LOCATION: Shelburne
WEB: artbyroslyn.on.ca
EMAIL: roslyn@artbyroslyn.on.ca

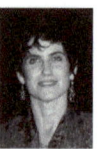

Roslyn Levin, award-winning Ki/sumi-e Painter, moves & breathes with the brush as she paints her Zen-like creations. With sensitive brushwork, using black, white, an infinity of grays, and at times, colours, Roslyn creates paintings with simplicity, elegance, beauty, & serenity at their heart. In recent months one jury stated they "applaud your work for its energy, quality of line, and composition" while another awarded her for "an innovative and personal approach" to sumi-e.

1 Windy Meadow 12x18" Ki/Sumi-e Painting on rice paper mounted on canvas.

2 To Flow as Water 9x18" Ki/Sumi-e Painting on rice paper mounted on canvas.

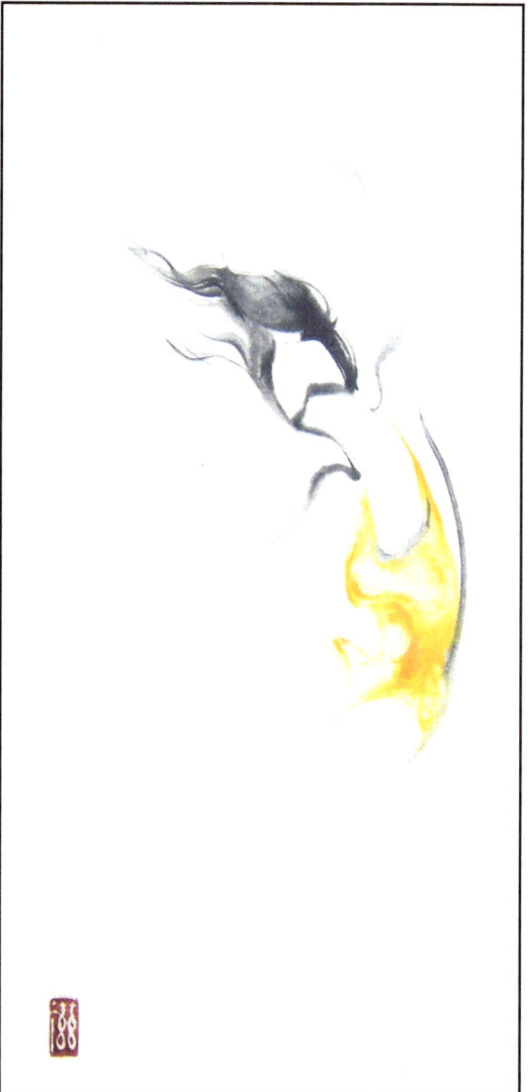

3 Tiger Nap 18x14" Ki/Sumi-e Painting on rice paper mounted on canvas.

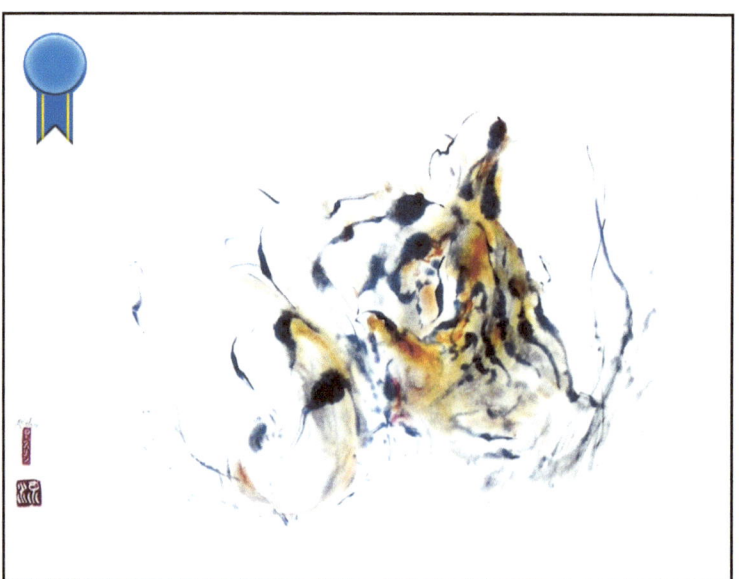

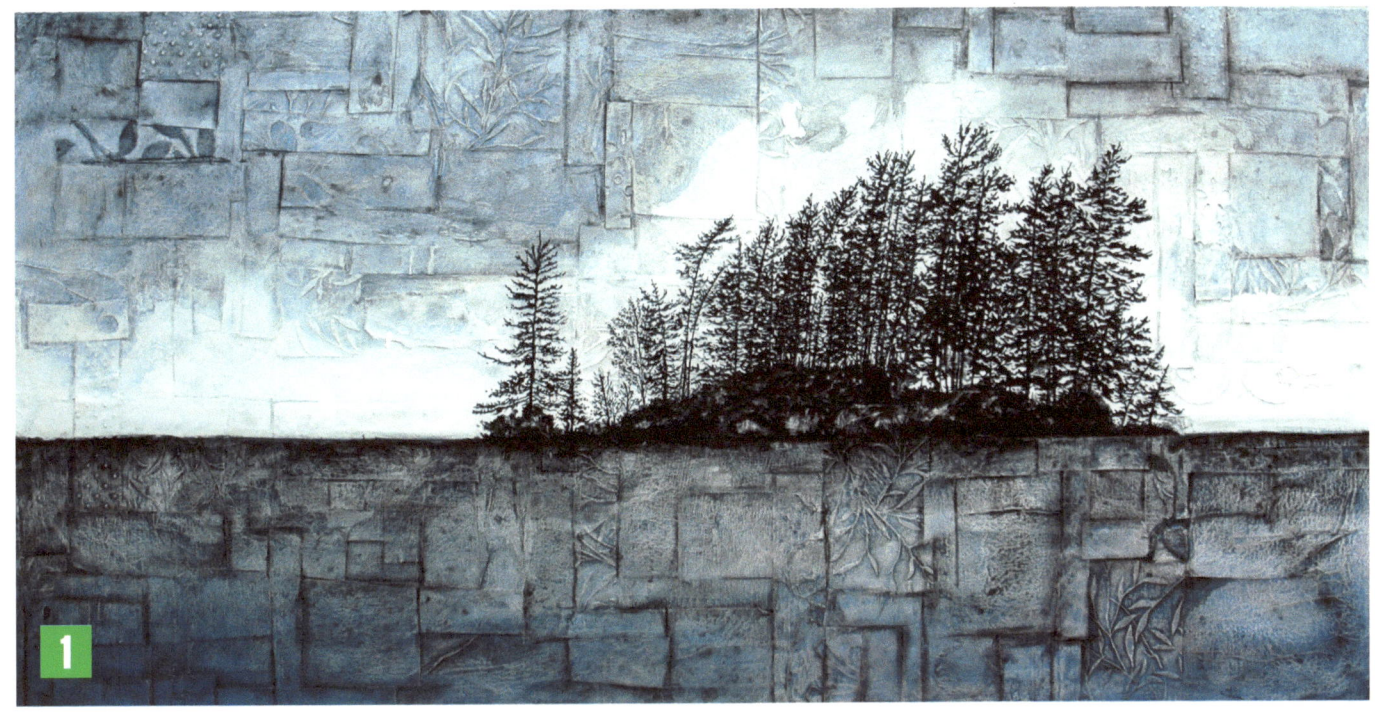

1

Karin Silverstone

LOCATION: Guelph
WEB: karinsilverstone.com
EMAIL: kmacleod2497@rogers.com

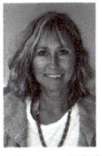

Silverstone is a graduate of the University of Guelph, with an Honours BA specializing in Fine Art. She is a part-time visual arts teacher at John F Ross and has been teaching since 1995. Her work is inspired by the pattern and decoration movement of the 70s and reflects themes of nature, exploring concepts of longevity and harmony. Her textural mixed media artworks are based on photos of Canadian landscapes that she has been fortunate to explore.

1 Off Wilson 36x20" Acrylic mixed media.

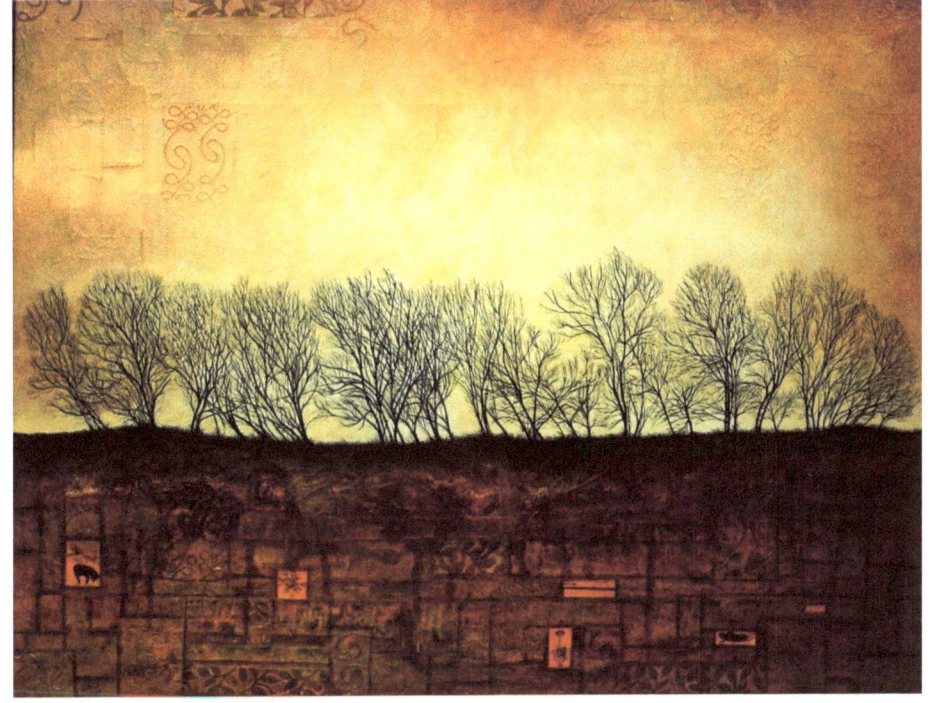

2 **2 Shadows** 36x48" Acrylic mixed media.

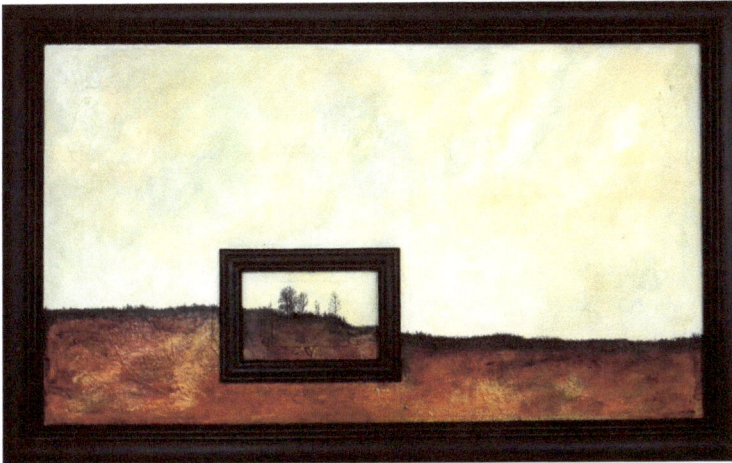

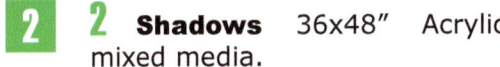

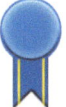

3 3 Framed Trees 28x18" Acrylic mixed media.

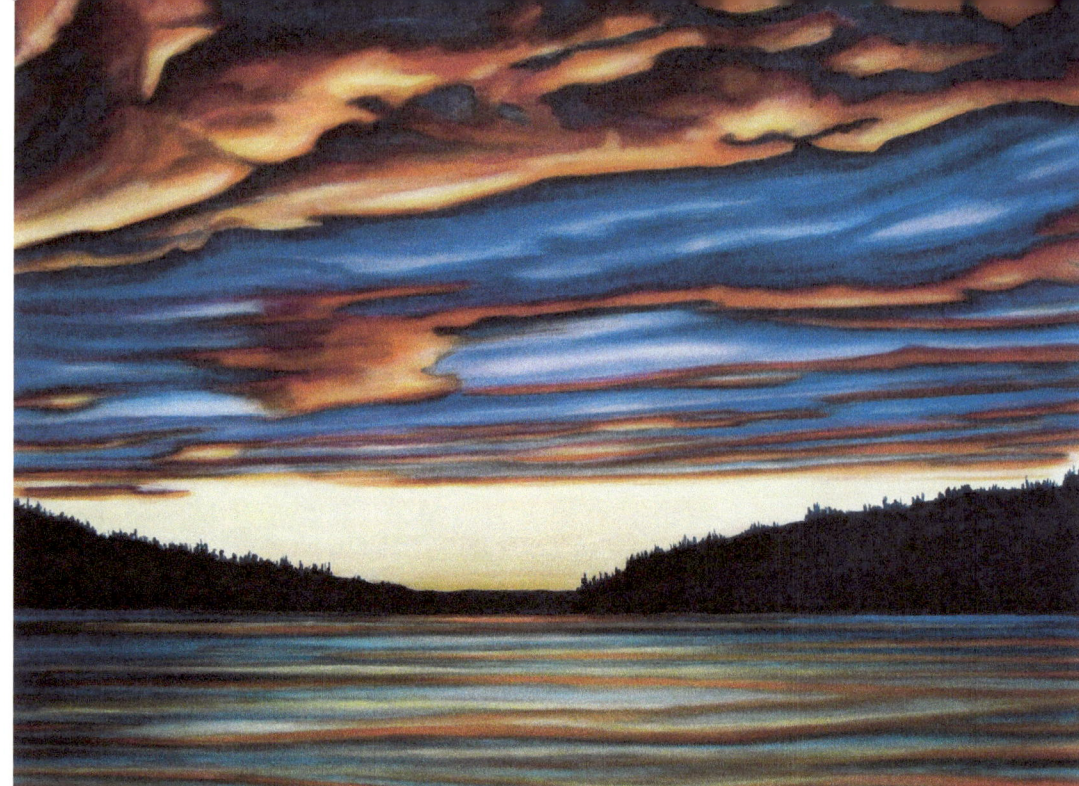

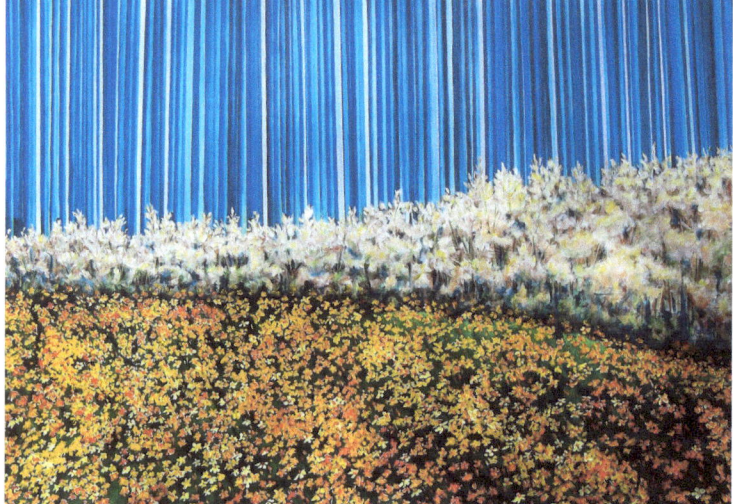

KATHLEEN MORIN

LOCATION: Guelph
WEB: kathleenmorin.com
EMAIL: kath@kathleenmorin.com

Kathleen is a Guelph artist with strong Northern Quebec roots. She has a love of the outdoors and her art depicts nature's very own masterpieces. She is now a member of the Whitestone Gallery in downtown Guelph and is looking forward to a productive year. She paints mostly in acrylic on canvas and her artwork has been described as "vibrant", "fresh" and "Group of Seven on Acid" to name a few. She is presently working on an art project to raise self-worth and confidence in girls while promoting awareness to the "Because I am a Girl" campaign.

1 Last Cast On The Moisie River 24x36"
Acrylic on canvas.

2 Blue Sticks In The Garden 48x60" Acrylic on canvas.

3 Across the St. Lawrence River 15x30"
Acrylic on canvas.

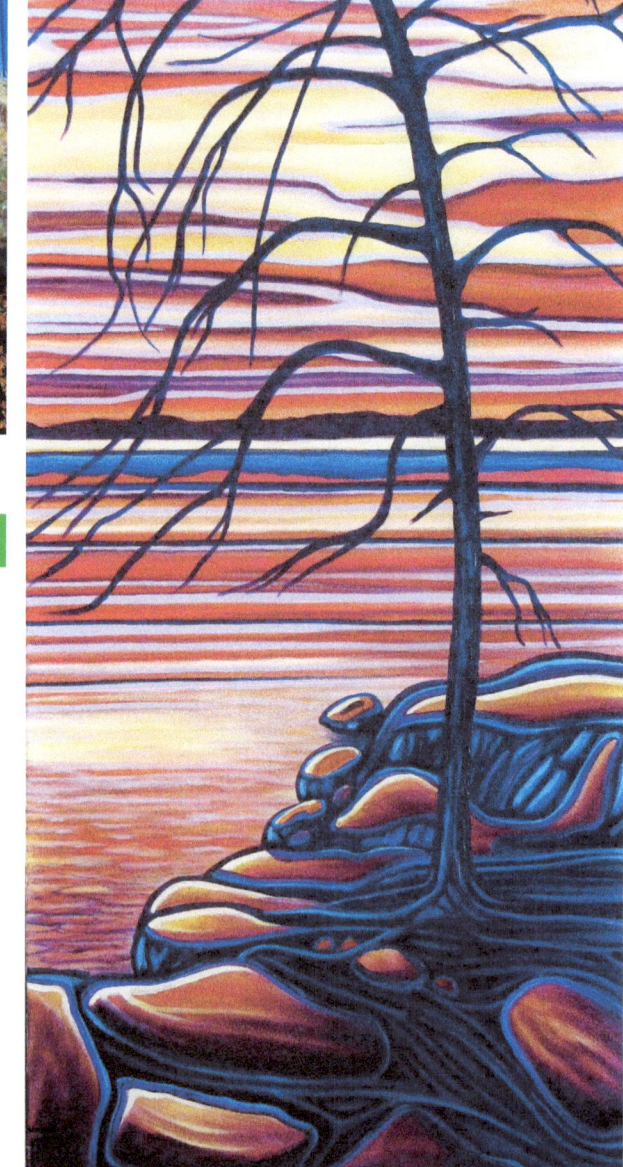

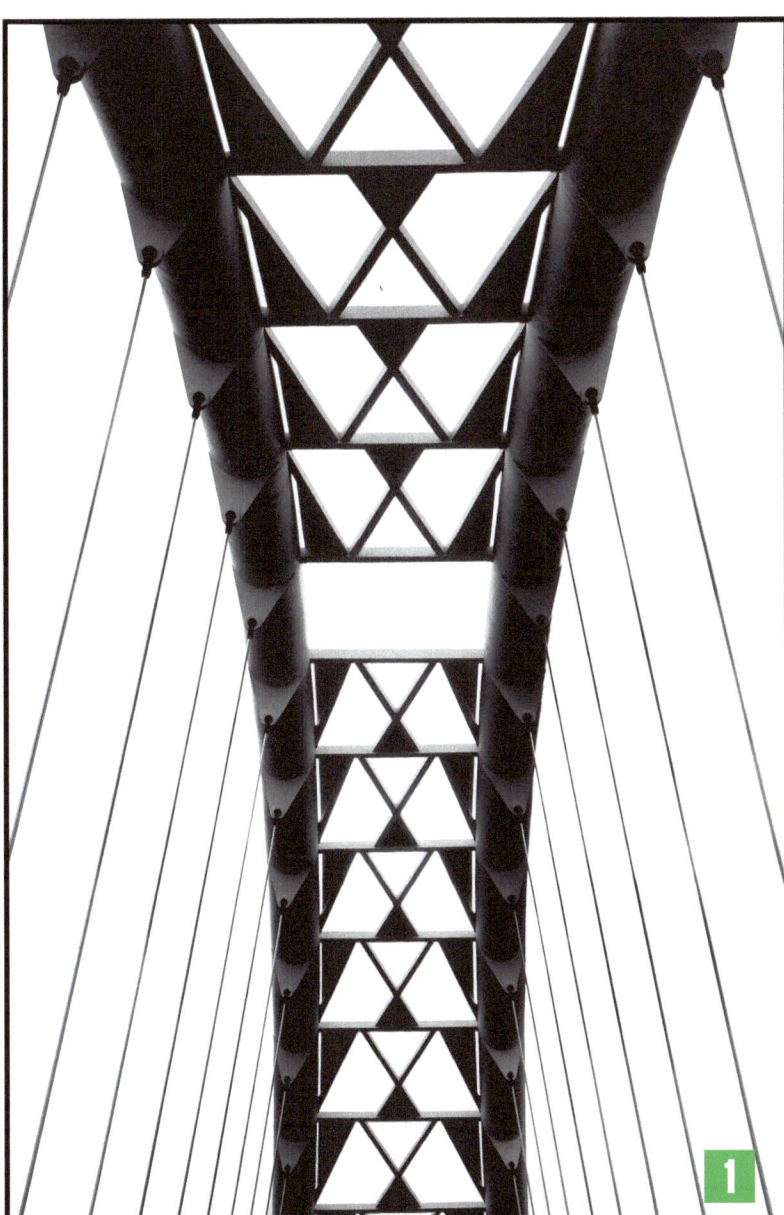

1

EMA SUVAJAC

LOCATION: Guelph
WEB: emasuvajac.com
EMAIL: info@emasuvajac.com

While completing a degree in the sciences, Ema began to pursue photography as a part time hobby. Her first photographs were of landscapes, gardens, and insects, though she later delved into portraiture and now spends much of her time photographing fashion and beauty for various publications. Despite this, she still enjoys capturing the essence of the natural and manmade world, and often makes her travel decisions based on what kinds of photographs she can capture while there. As her photography business flourishes, Ema is ecstatic that this hobby has turned into a career.

1 **Untitled** Photograph.

2 **Untitled** Photograph.

3 **Calgary Ablaze At Morning** Photograph.

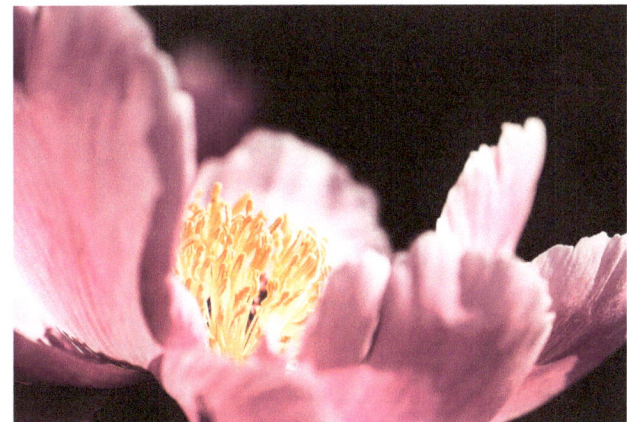

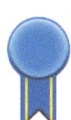 2

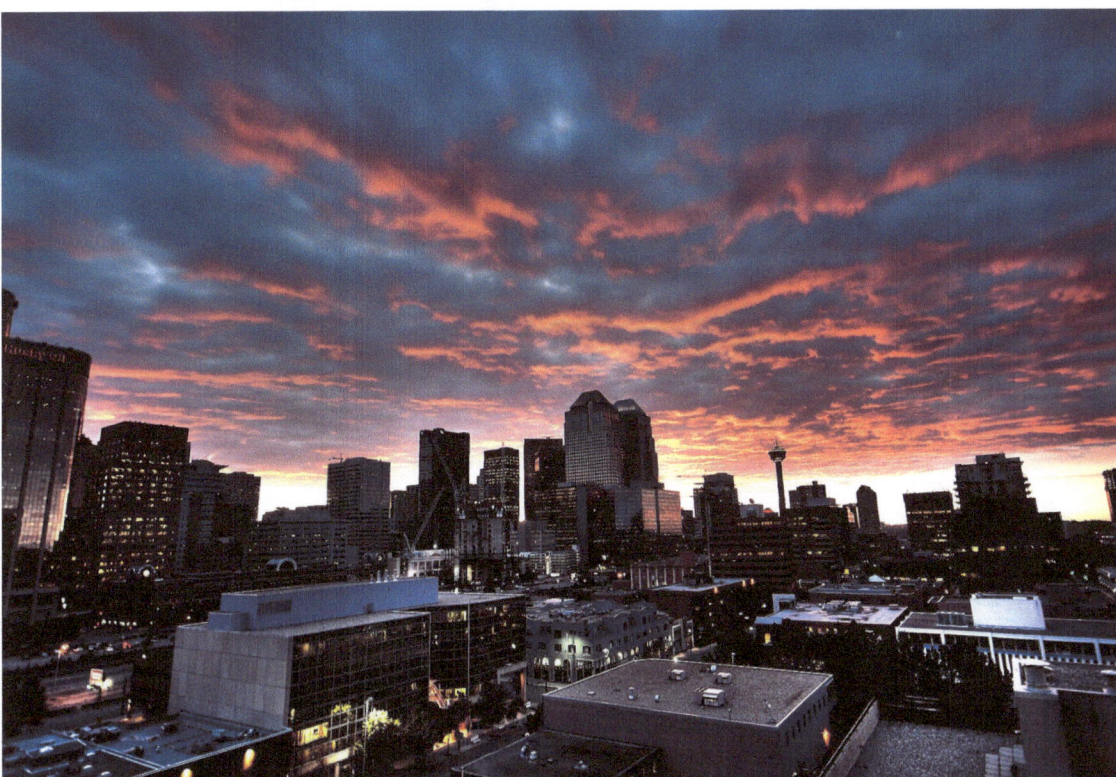

3

BETTY ANNE DOUGHTY

LOCATION: Cambridge Guelph
WEB: (N/A)
EMAIL: (N/A)

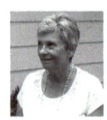

Betty Anne Doughty is an artist from the Rockwood area close to Guelph. After retiring from teaching she decided to pursue her long time desire to paint with watercolour. In the past few years she has taken lessons, studying under several well known watercolour and drawing artists. Betty Anne enjoys the many challenges of this medium and has come to realize that her attention to detail is most obvious in her favourite subjects which are landscapes and the architecture of interesting and unusual structures including buildings and houses. At the present time she belongs to two watercolour artist groups including the West Hills Watercolour Club and theWatercolour Painters Club, both in Guelph. She continues to study under successful artists whenever she gets the opportunity.

1 Heaven on Seven 15.5x19.5" Watercolour.

2 Waiting for Winter 8x14" Watercolour.

3 Autumn`s Gold 8x14" Watercolour.

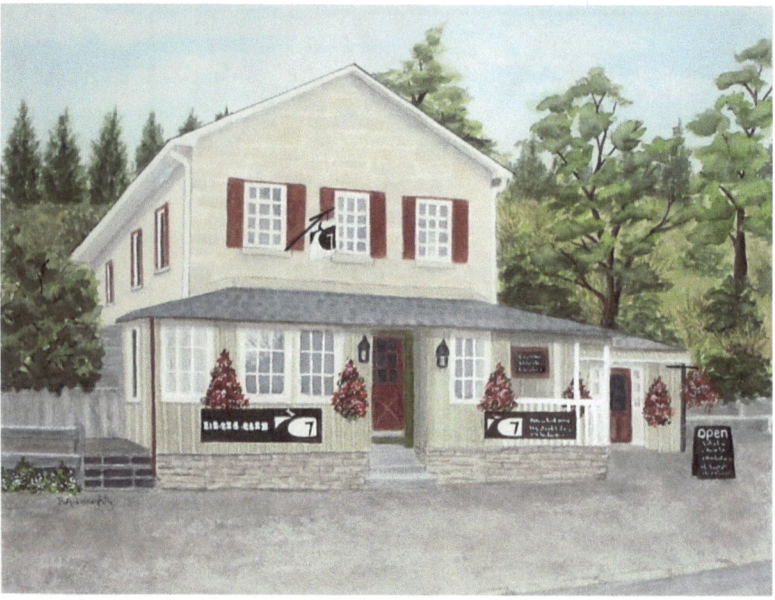

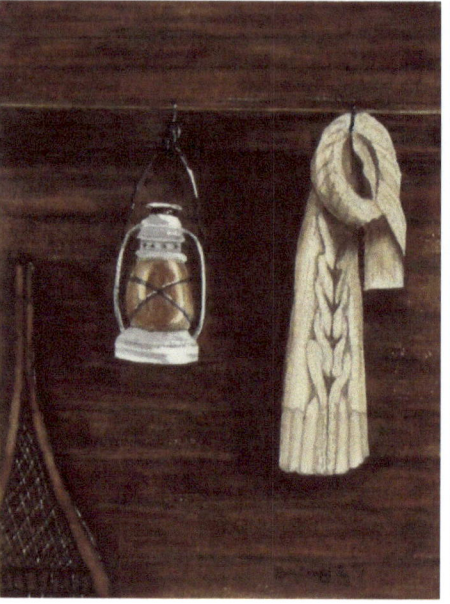

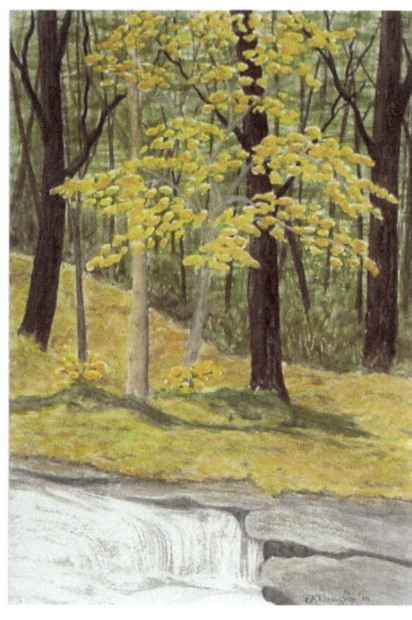

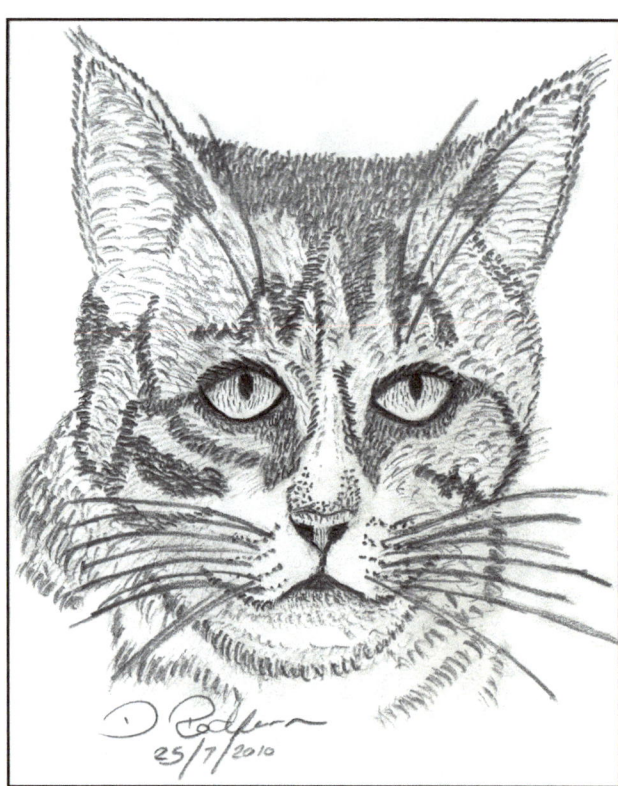

DARRYL REDFERN

LOCATION: Cambridge
WEB: darryl-redfern.fineartamerica.com
EMAIL: nwalesdaz@yahoo.ca

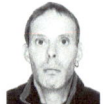

Darryl was born in the United Kingdom in 1973 and moved to Canada in July of 2009. Darryl had never drawn much till a neighbour persuaded him to give it a try, this was in july 2010. Since then Darryl has become popular in the artworld and has even had his drawings appear on the front of an online art magazine, not bad for a beginner.

1 Cat Portrait Pencil.

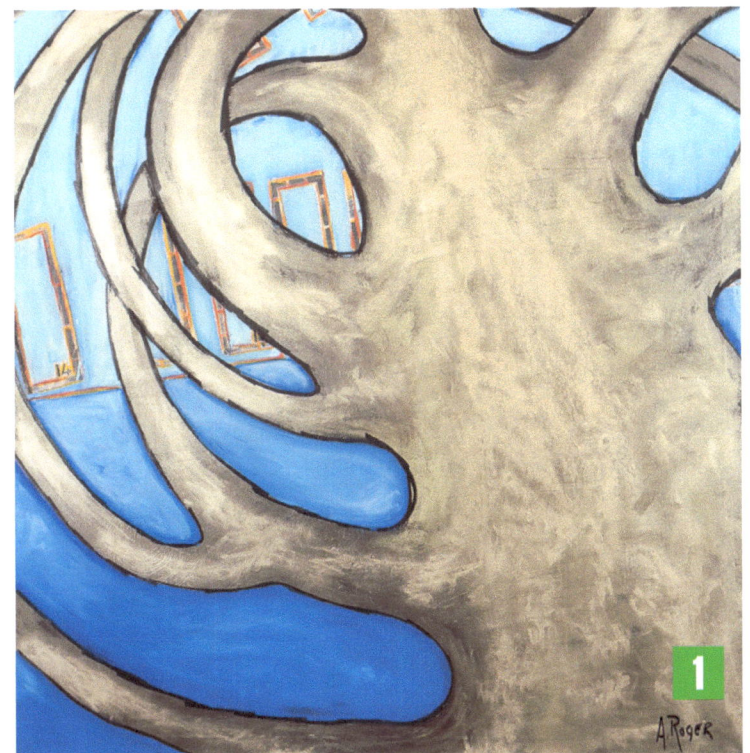

AMY ROGER

LOCATION: Cambridge/Kitchener
WEB: amyroger.com
EMAIL: amyroger@rogers.com

Amy Roger was born in Boston in 1966, raised in rural Minnesota, and moved to Ontario, Canada as a teen. She is formally educated in Fine Arts at Syracuse University in New York and San Francisco State University in California. She has worked for zoos and aquariums designing and fabricating Natural History exhibits. Roger has experience working for and exhibiting in several commercial galleries including Whistler, Toronto, Los Angeles and New York City, and as a docent and exhibit preparator in public museums and galleries from San Francisco to Kitchener. Amy Roger is inspired by country, city and everything in between - & all the personal and social issues associated with being human.

1 Tree of Life - Blue 48x48" Acrylic on canvas from SubRbanity series.

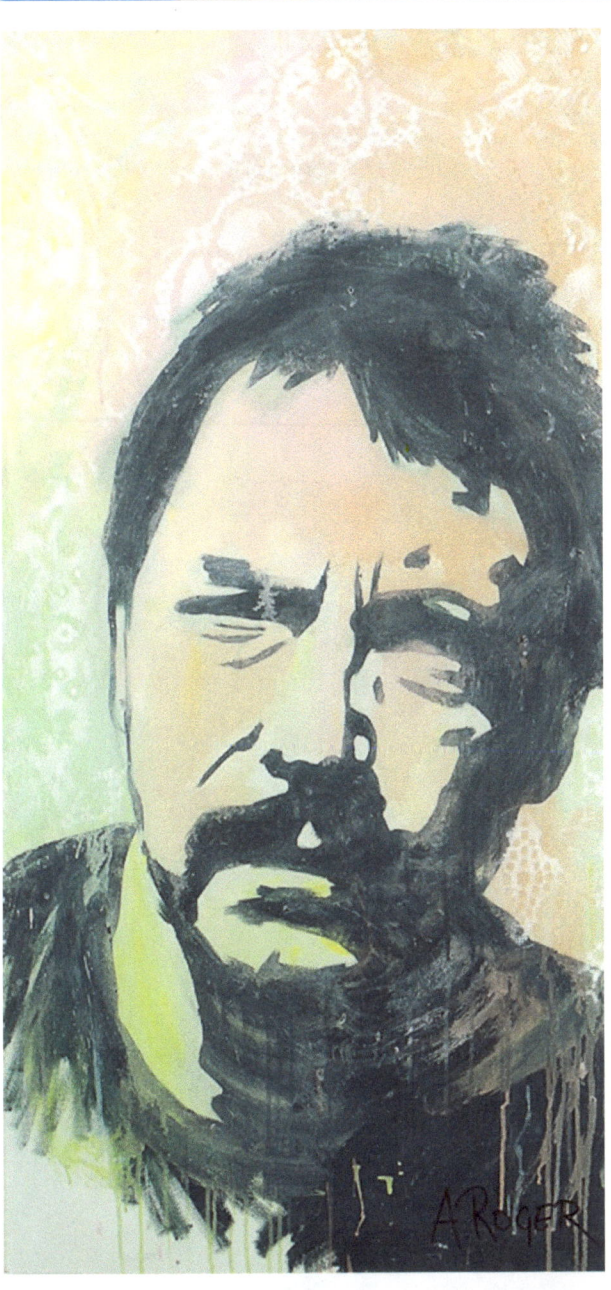

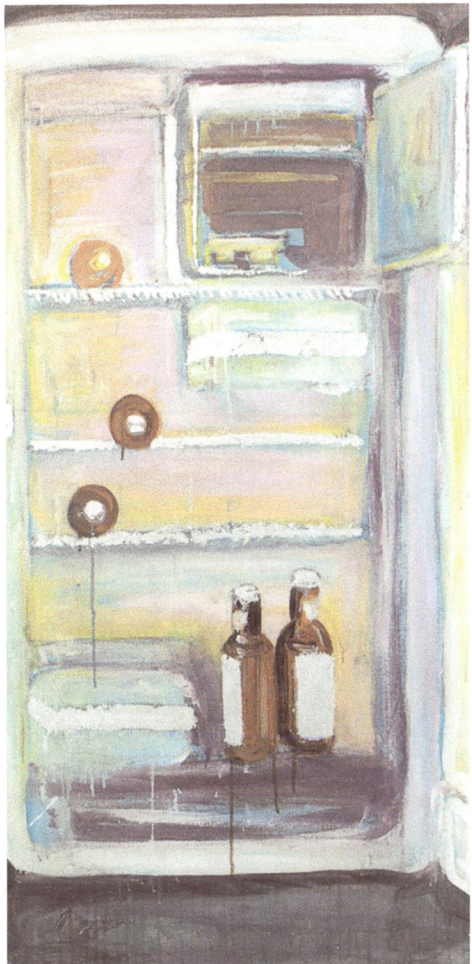

2 Lee 24x48" Acrylic on canvas from Domestication series.

3 Beer Fridge 24x48" Acrylic on canvas from Domestication series.

DONNA STARES

LOCATION: Wellington Art Gallery Fergus
WEB: (N/A)
EMAIL: donnastares@sympatico.ca

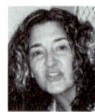

I was born in Waterloo Ontario. I learned at an early age that I love working with my hands. This desire translated into loomed bead work, mosaics, knitting, tapestry quilt work and finally water color and Chinese brush. I believe that the creative process comes from a deeply Divine place. I was recently reminded that paint is paint; it is what your Spirit brings to the canvas that creates the wonder.

1 Bird In Tree 16x20" Watercolour.

2 Turtle Speaks 16x20" Watercolour.

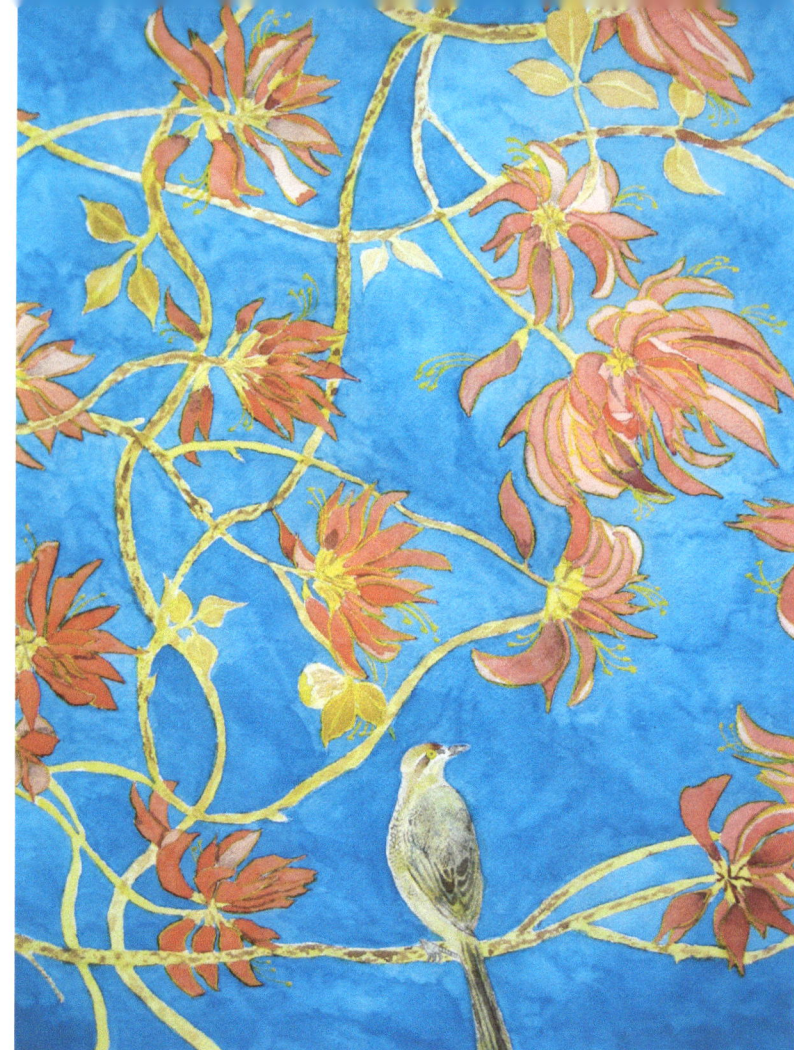

1

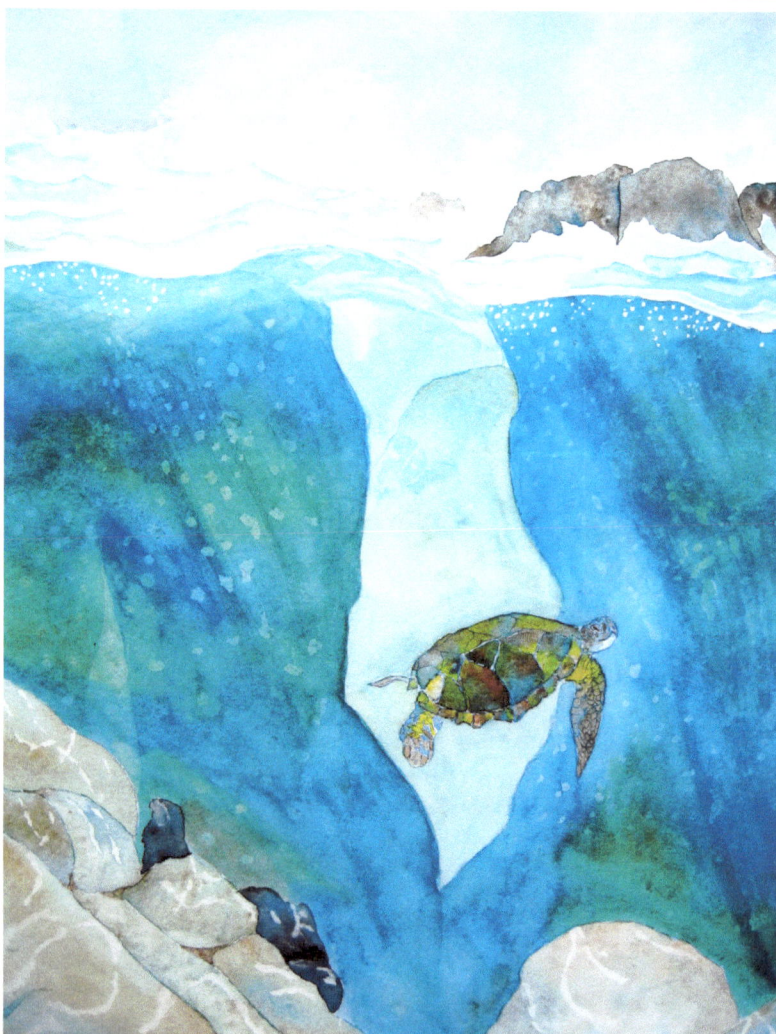

2

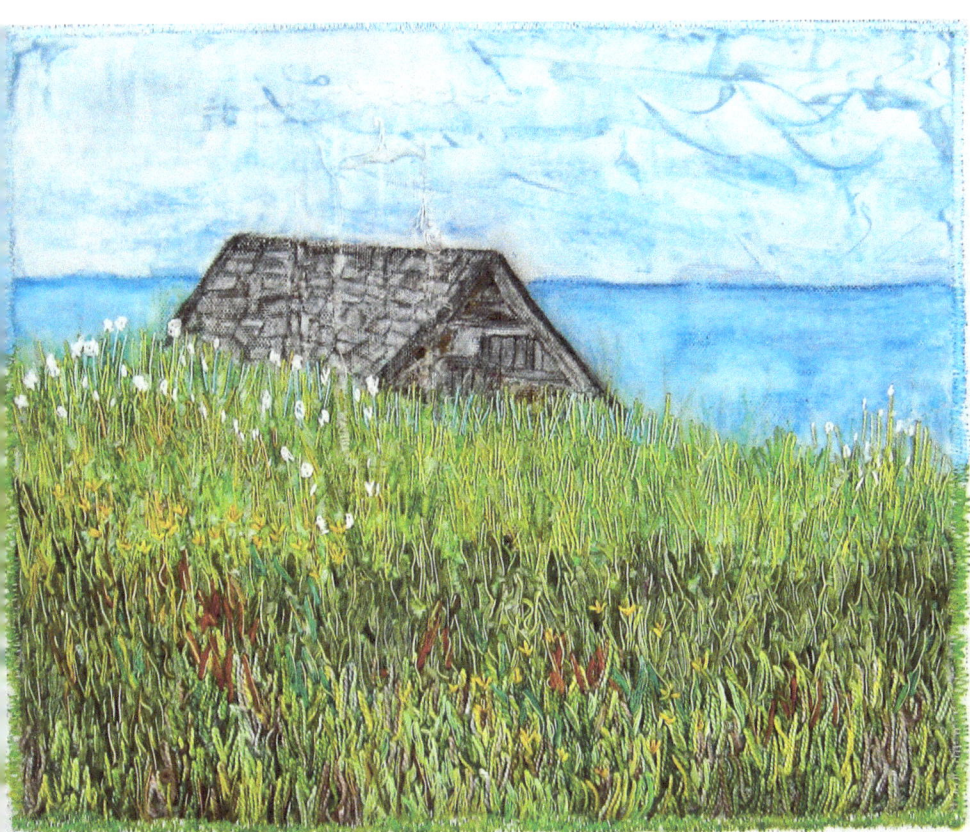

MAGGIE VANDERWEIT

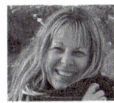

LOCATION: Fergus
WEB: stonethreads.ca
EMAIL: maggie@stonethreads.ca

Maggie creates her contemporary textile art using quilting, painting, dense and complex machine stitching, hand embellishment, found objects, collage, beads, mono-printing, silk fusion, faux encaustic and felting. She teaches, shows and lectures nationally and sells her work through her studio, galleries, Fair November and One of a Kind.

1 **Abandoned** 16x15" Textile Collage, mono-print, hand and machine stitching.

3 **XI** 16x20" Textile Collage, acrylic, machine stitching.

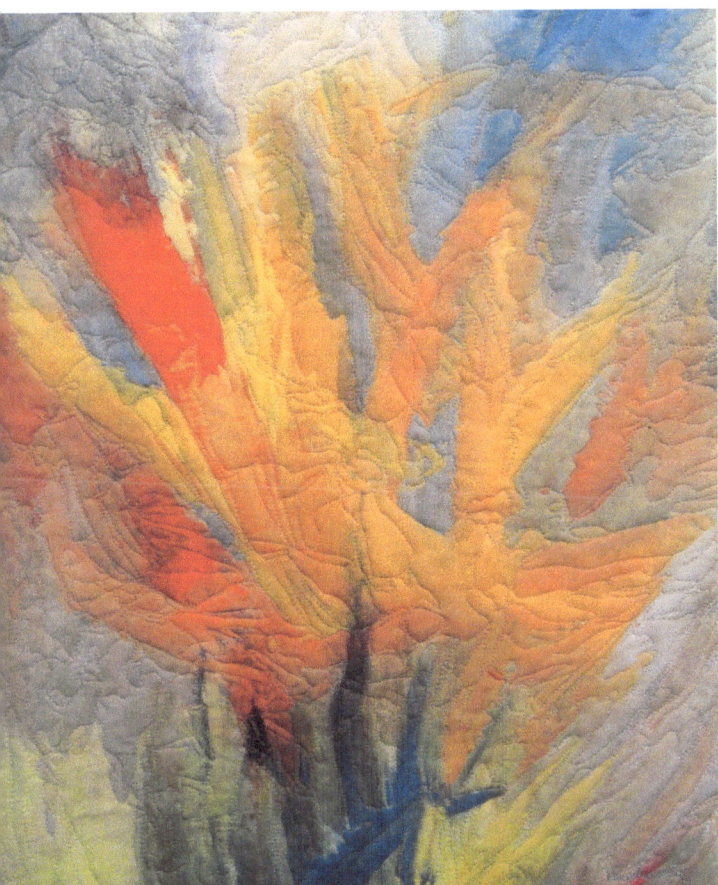

2 **Into Your Garden** Textile paint, machine stitching.

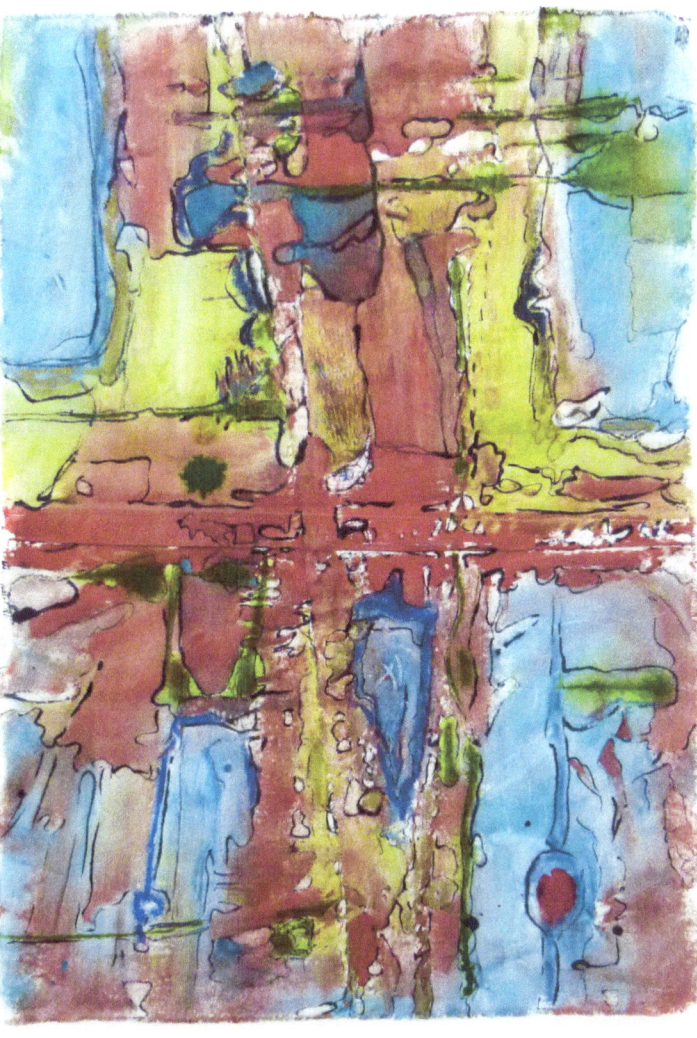

ELLE HOW

LOCATION: Ancaster,
WEB: http://ellehow.com
EMAIL: ellehow@bell.blackberry.net

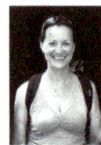

Elle has journeyed across Canada in search of the treasures left behind by the forces of Nature. Relying on her own interpretation of how to manipulate the oil/acrylic mediums to recreate her visions of what her canvas wants, allows Elle the freedom of expression few are brave enough match. A native Ontarian that loves to explore other parts of the world, with her family.

1 **Parry Sound at Night** 24x36" Acrylic.

2 **Solar Flares** 26x32" Acrylic on canvas. The Sun and its bursts of energy.

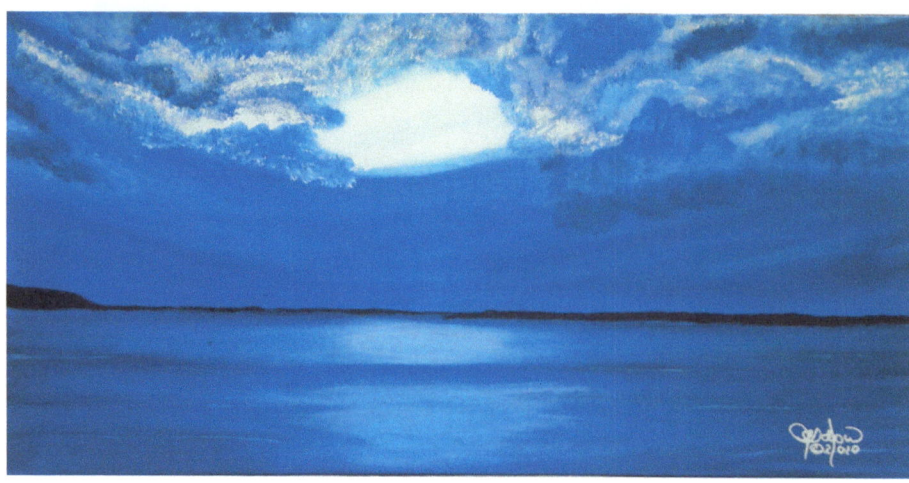

1

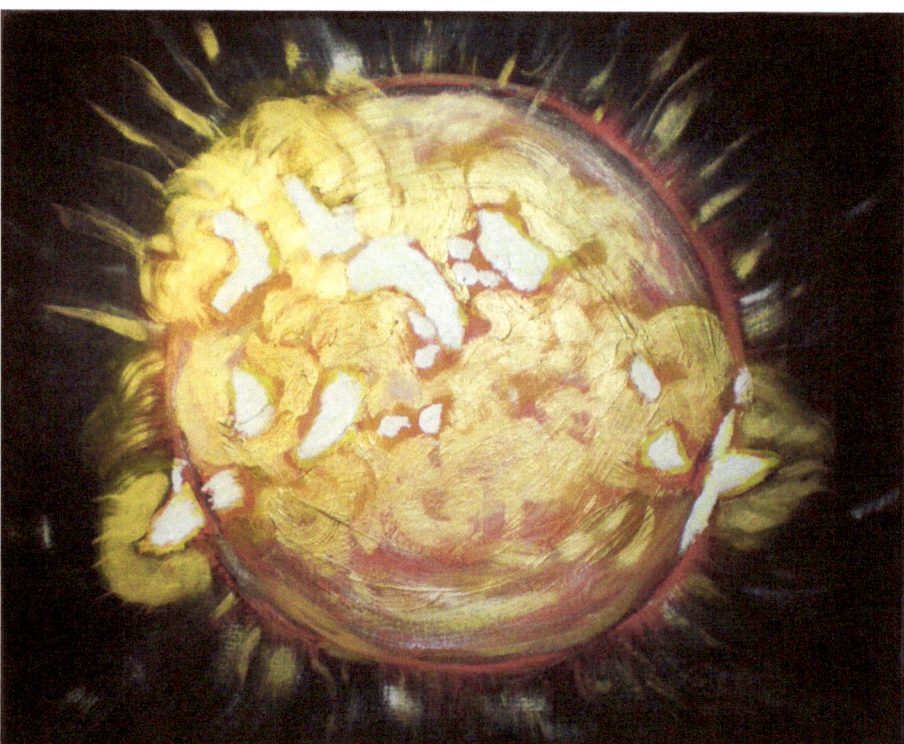

2

3 **Crowfoot & Bow Glaciers** 24x60" Oil on canvas. Jasper National Park, Alta.

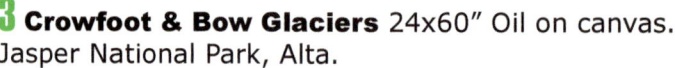

3

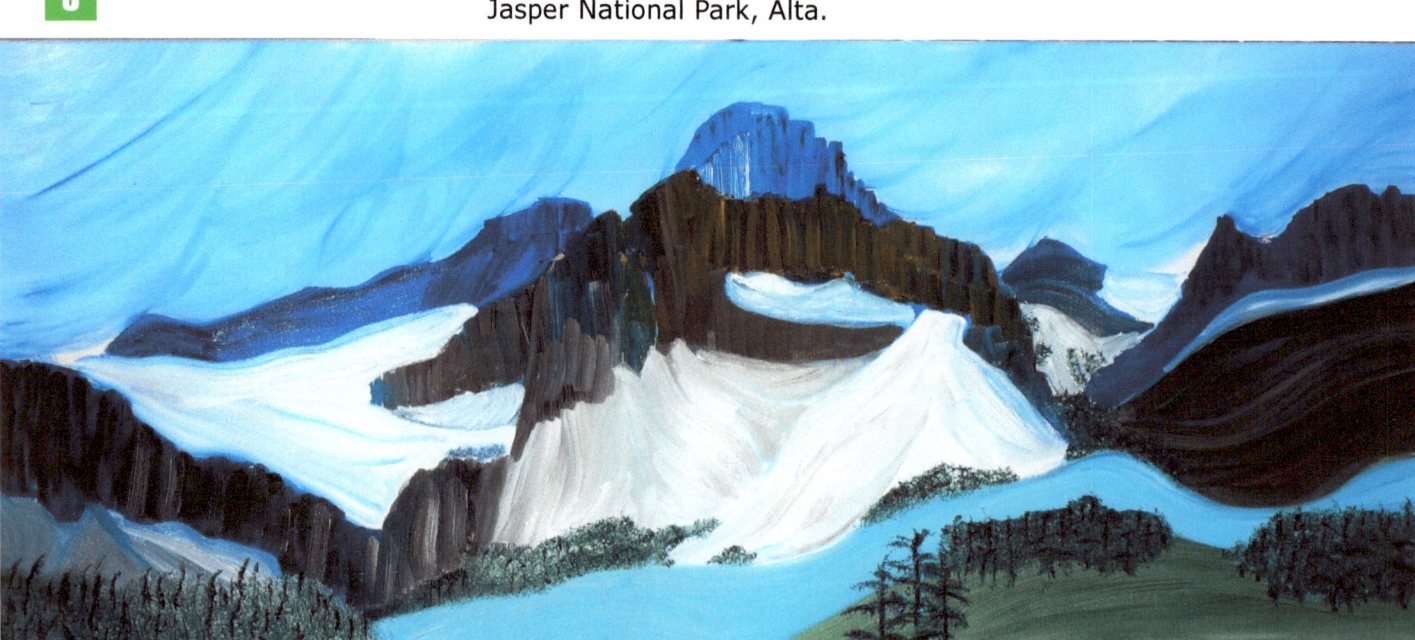

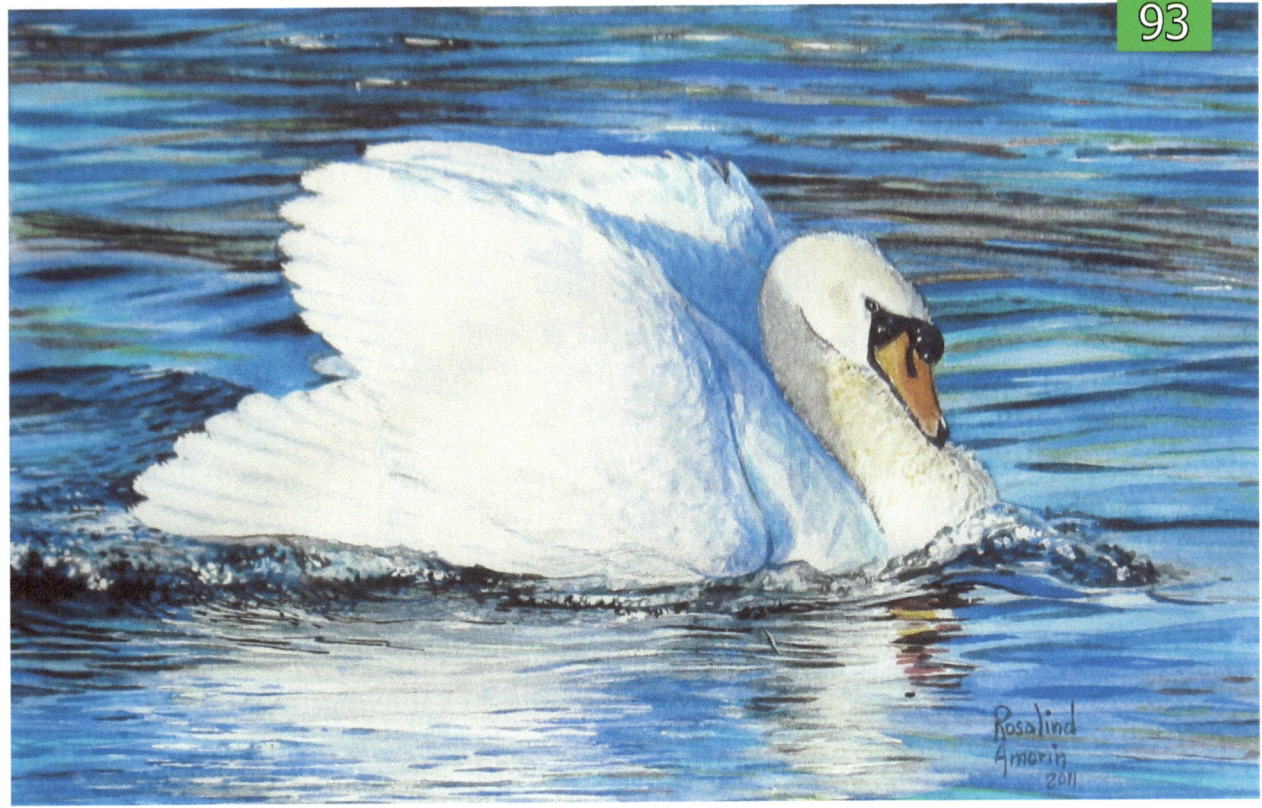

ROSALIND
SMURTHWAITE-AMORIN

LOCATION: Cambridge Guelph
WEB: (N/A)
EMAIL: iramorin@rogers.com

2 **Sunday Best** 8x10" Watercolour on paper.

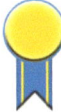

Rosalind was born in Worthing, England and travelled extensively throughout her younger years spending most of her childhood in North Africa. She immigrated to Canada as a teenager & completed High School at A.Y. Jackson where she won a scholarship to the Art Gallery of Ontario School. She then studied at Ontario College of Art. Rosalind moved to Cambridge in 1977 & worked for Lawson and Falle designing their first line of Imagecraft greeting cards. She lived in Ottawa for ten years & joined the Cumberland Arts Guild. As her work gained recognition & juried show awards, she launched her own business painting from clients favourite photographs. Over the past 25 years she has completed hundreds of commissions for a growing list of satisfied customers. Rosalind has recently moved back to Cambridge where she is setting up shop again and continues to do what she loves. Painting pictures that capture special moments.

1 **Swan** 7x10" Watercolour on paper.

3 **New Trucks** 7x7" Watercolour on paper.

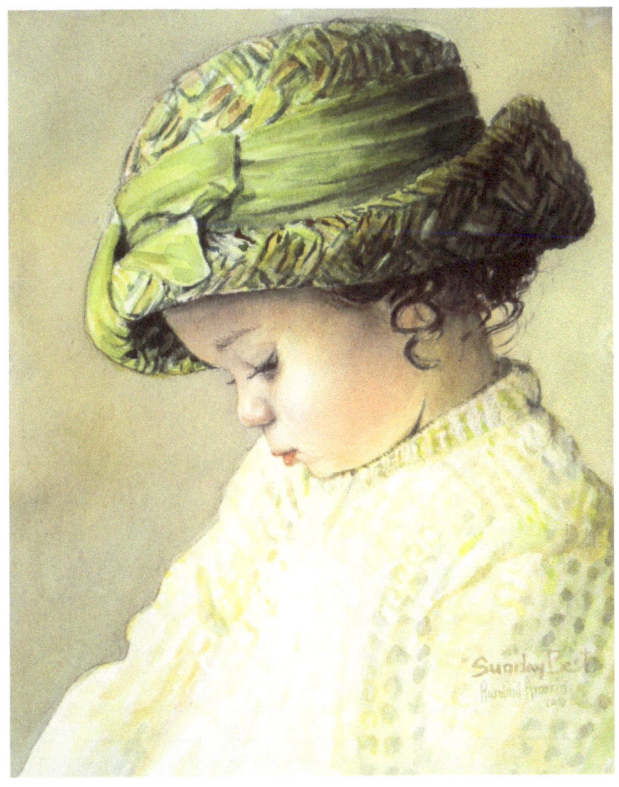

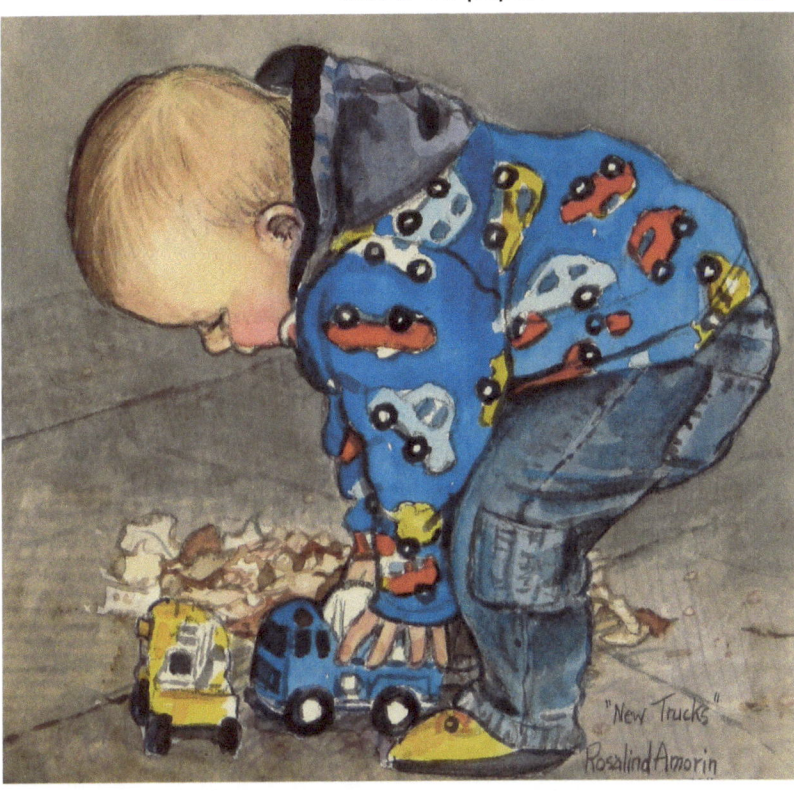

1 My Little Chickadee 9"x5.5"
Acrylic aquatint, ferric chloride etch and drypoint.

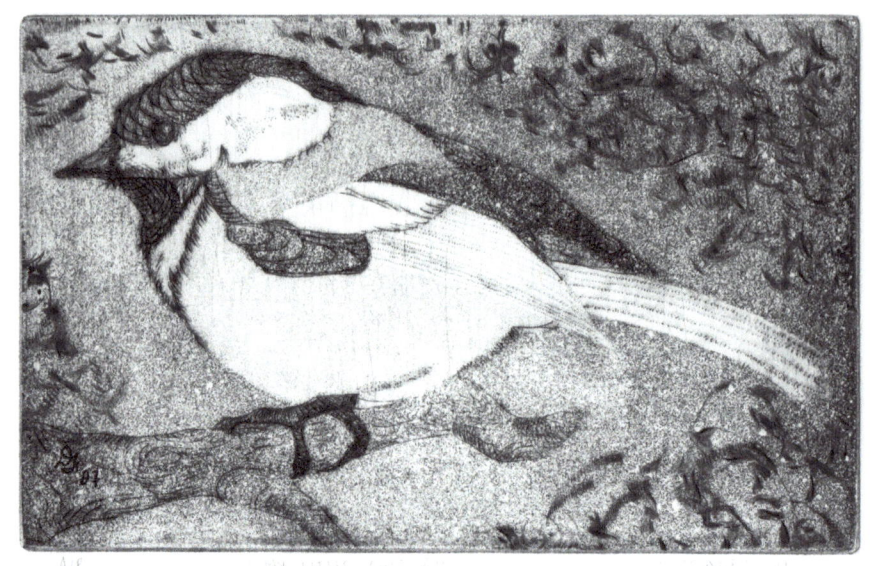

1

DONNA STEWART

LOCATION: Cambridge
WEB: riversideprintgroup.com
EMAIL: donna@riversideprintgroup.com

Donna is a founding member of the Riverside Print Group. In the studio, she is experimenting with the non-toxic intaglio techniques popularized by printmaker Keith Howard, including acrylic floor polish as a substitute for asphaltum hard ground, washing soda instead of Varsol, and corrosive salts in place of acids. Donna and her family reside in Hespeler.

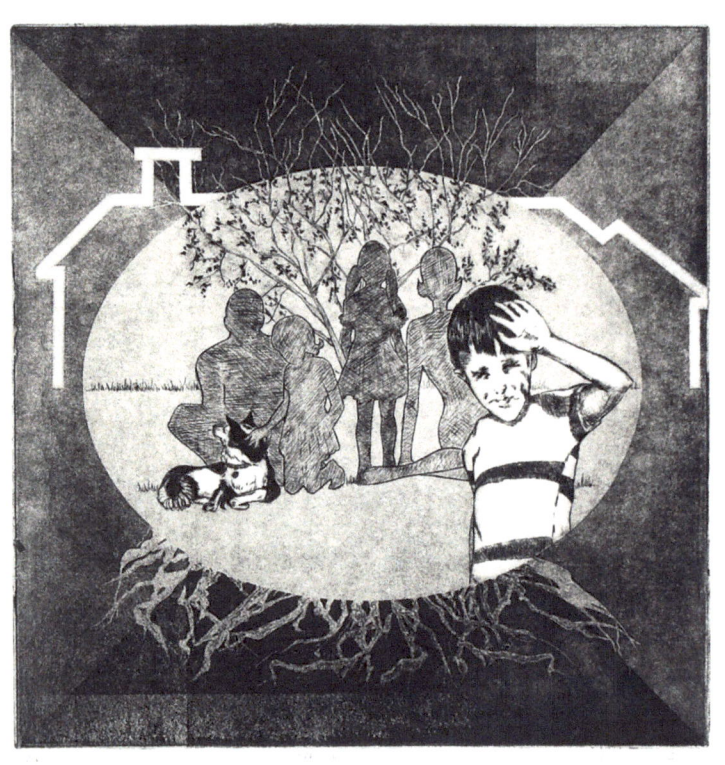

2

2 Safe as Houses 12x12" Sandpaper aquatint, sodium sulfate etch and drypoint.

3 Bea 1918, "non omnis moriar" 12x12" Screen filler destruction ground, sodium sulfate etch and drypoint with chine collé.

3

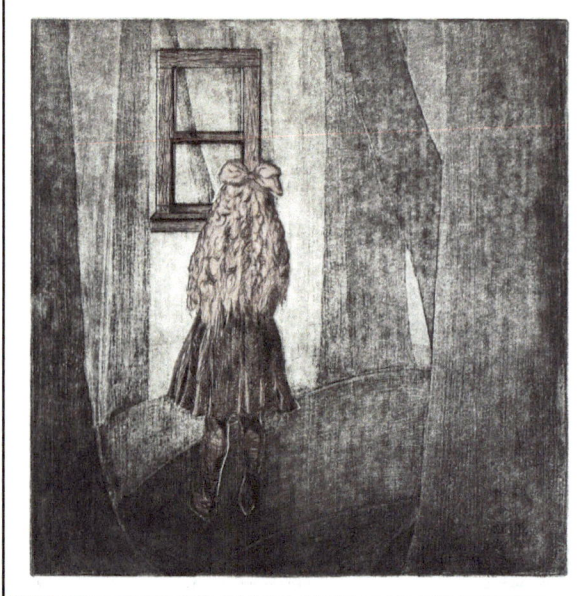

DAVID J. KNIGHT

LOCATION: Guelph
WEB: (N/A)
EMAIL: asinglevoice@yahoo.com

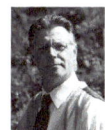

David is an archaeologist and visual and auditory artist who was born and raised in Guelph. He studied Fine Art at the University of Guelph (1987) and was elected Vice President of ED Video Media Arts Centre for 1988. David has recently researched the architecture and acoustics of San Vitale at Ravenna, Italy for his MPhil in Archaeology at the University of Southampton, UK (2010) and engages in the creativity between field/academic archaeology and art making. He has exhibited in Canada at Guelph, Toronto, Halifax, Ottawa and in the UK at Brighton, Southampton and Edinburgh.

1 **Rachel** 8×10" Graphite, conte, pastel and charcoal on archaeological planning vellum. Created in Colchester, Essex, UK 2001

2 **Lunar Pasts I** 31.56×23.67" Photography, digital painting. Created in Barcelona, Spain and Southampton, UK 2010.

3 **Solar Pasts II** 31.56×23.67" Photography, digital painting. Created in Barcelona, Spain and Southampton, UK 2010.

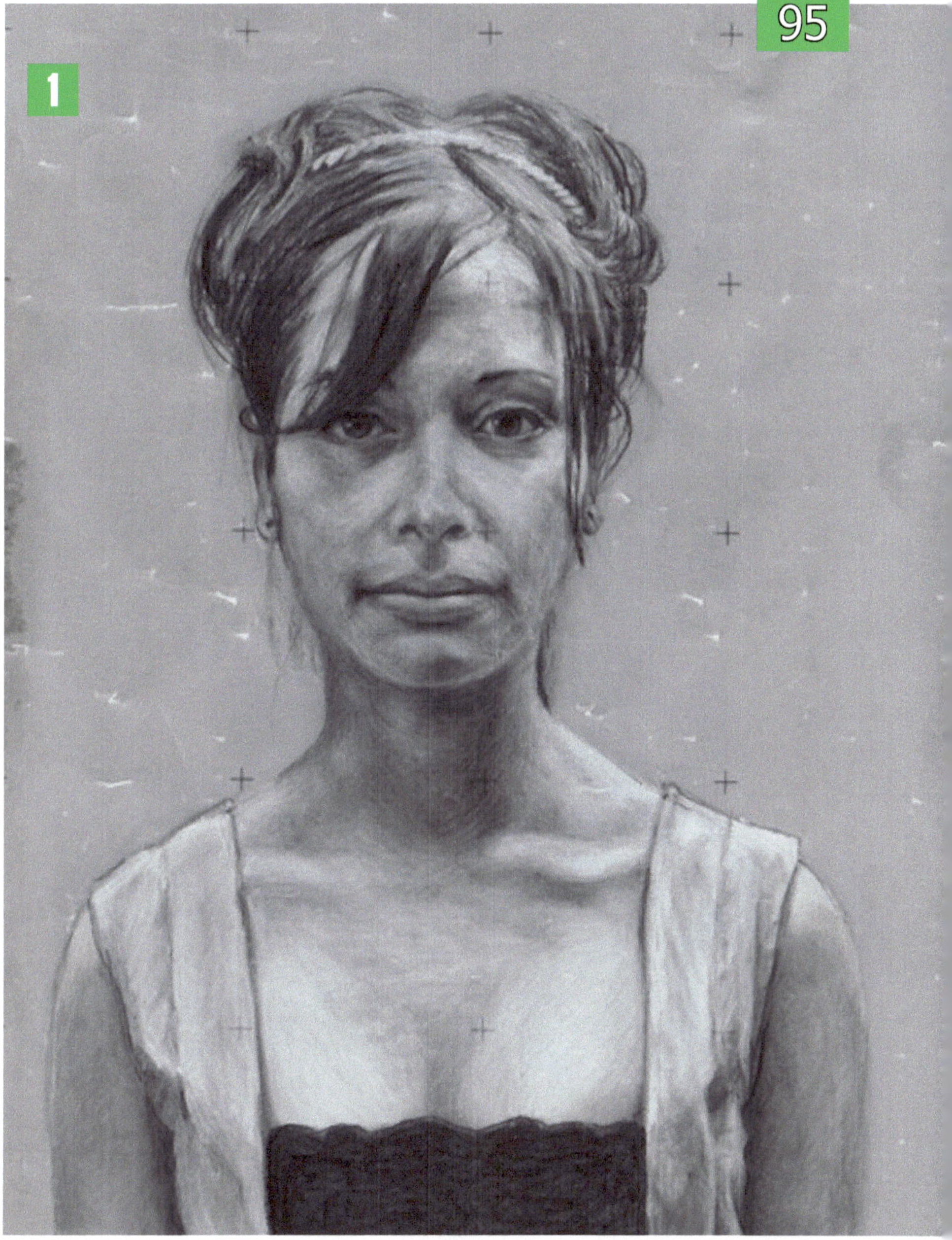

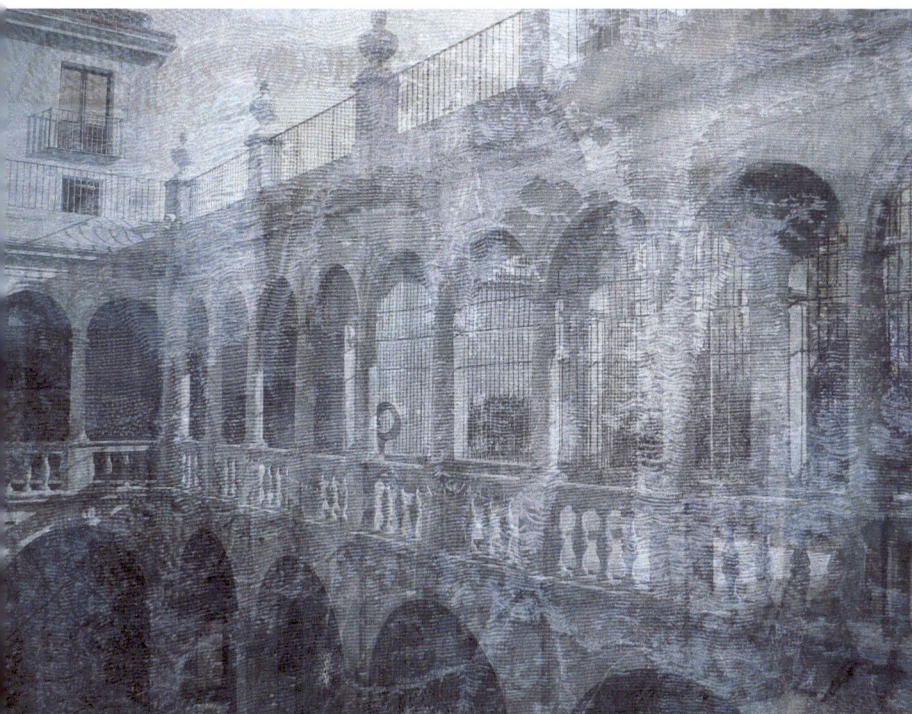

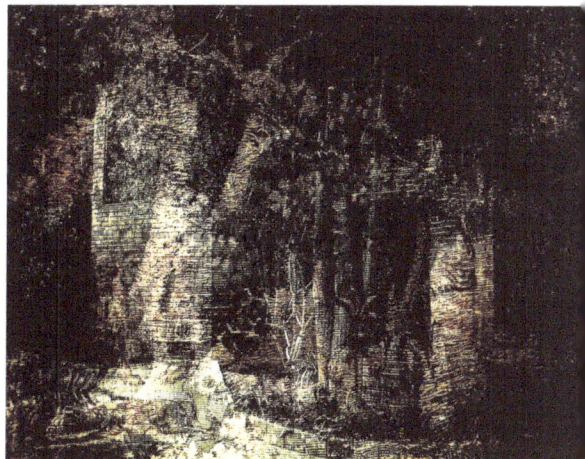

DAISY KURP

LOCATION: Guelph
WEB: (N/A)
EMAIL: daisyart@rogers.com

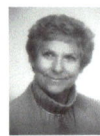

I paint in watercolor and acrylic and am just as excited painting realistic as I am abstract. I paint on paper, on canvas and on plexiglass. Have won many awards, and studied with the best of teachers throughout Canada and United States. In 1997 I was elected into the CSPWC, and I work with Guelph Creative Arts Association helping other artists to get exposure.

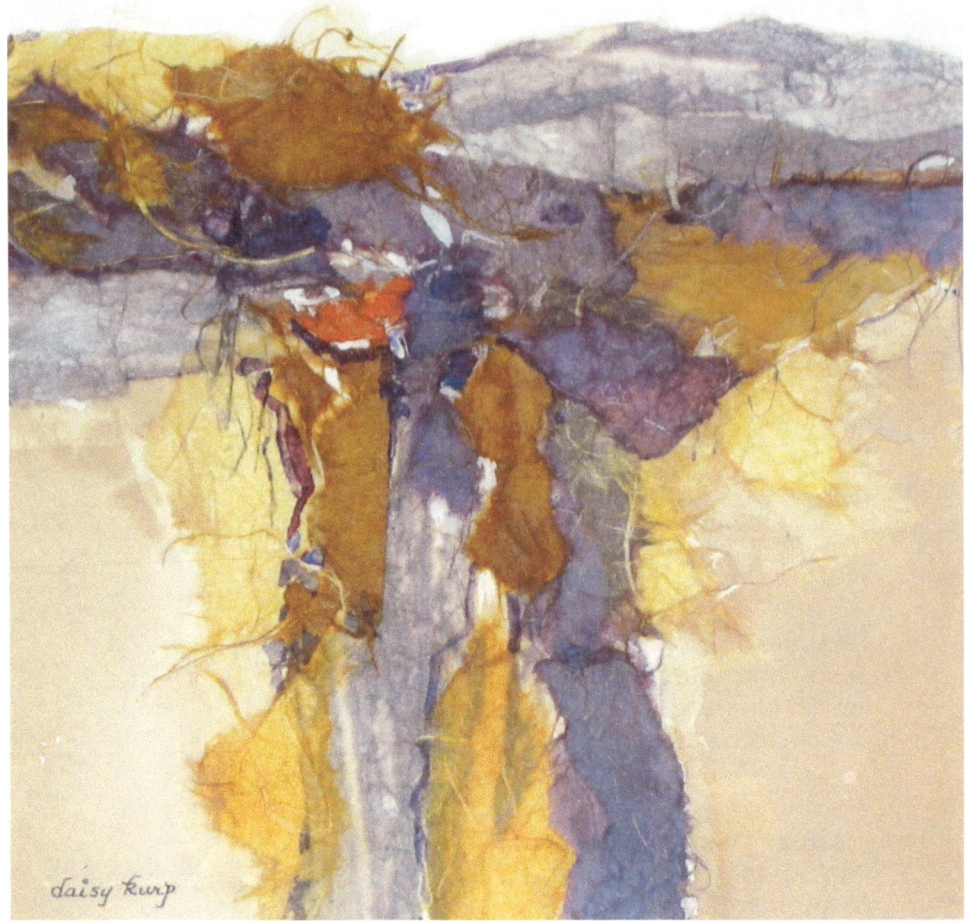

1 The West 17x17" Watercolor collage.

2 Hydrangea 22x30" Watercolor.

3 Autumn 22x30" Watercolor.

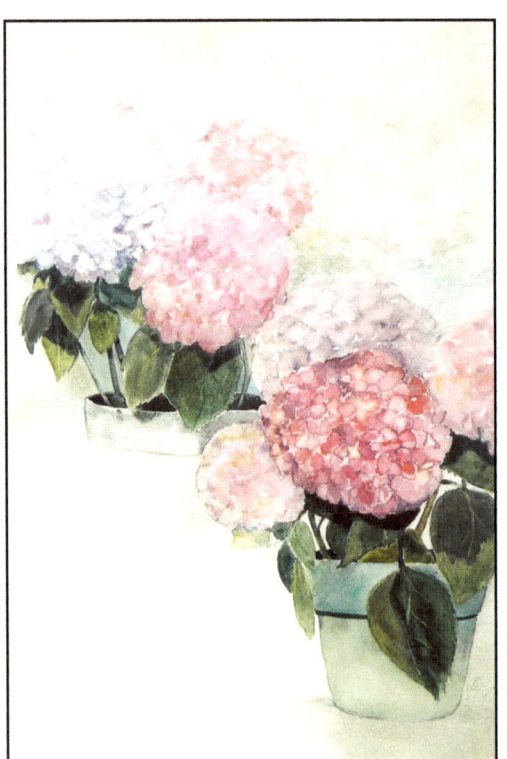

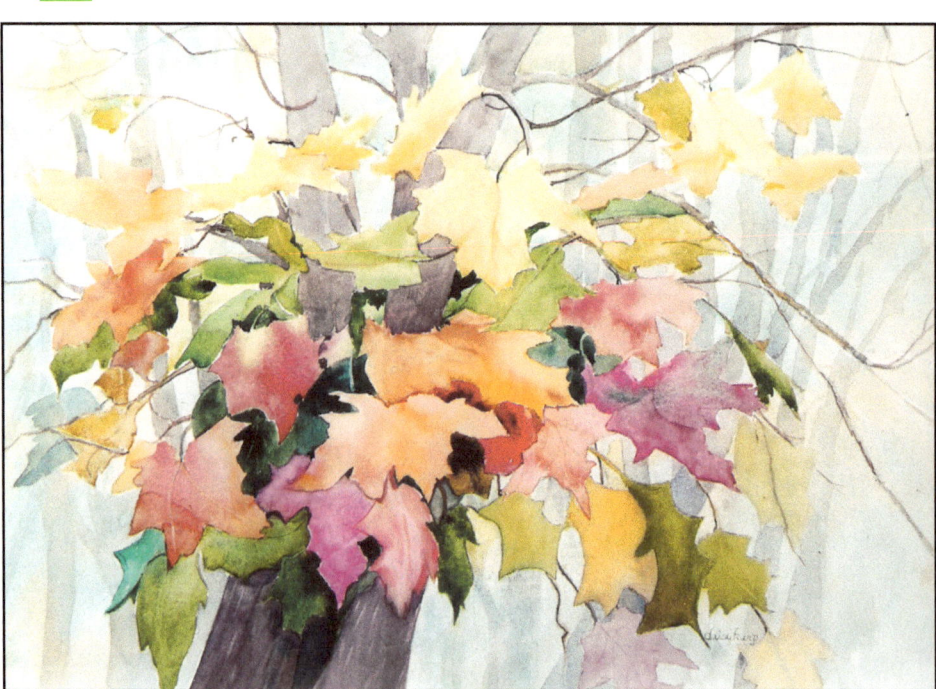

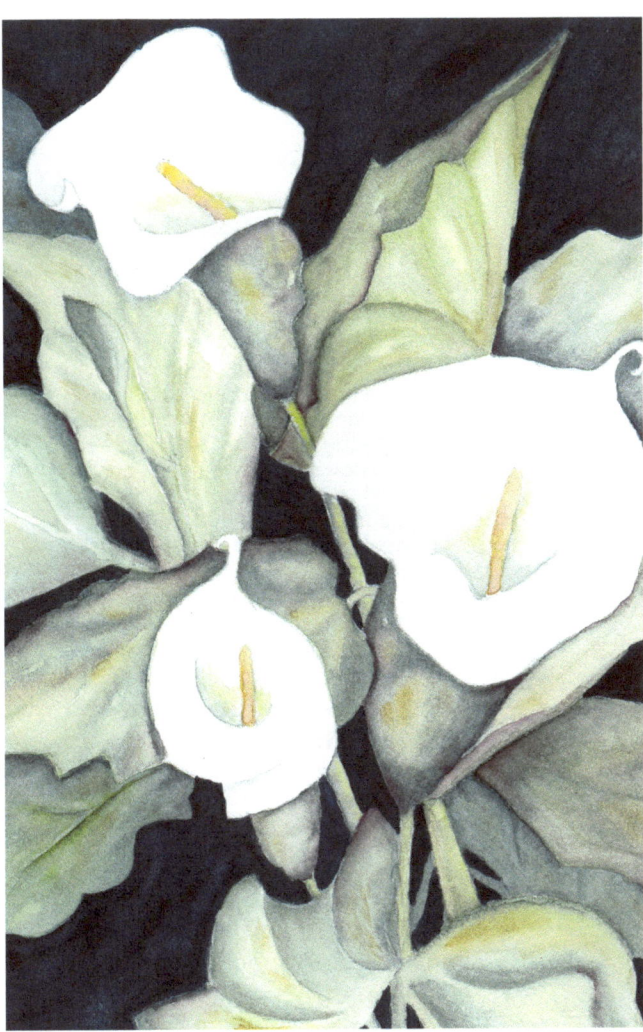

1

DALE VARDY

LOCATION: West Hills Art Group Guelph
WEB: (N/A)
EMAIL: bdvardy@rogers.com

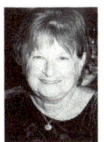

Dale Vardy is a retired elementary school teacher, mother of two and grandmother of two granddaughters. She began watercolour painting after retirement in 2002. She is treasurer of the West Hills Art Group and belongs to the Evergreen Senior Centre's Watercolour club. Dale has displayed and sold her paintings at Painting on the Green and the Bruce Peninsula Art Show. She has pursued her art, taking workshops with such outstanding artists as Gordon MacKenzie, Jack Reid, Linda Kemp and Marianne Broome. Dale has enjoyed displaying and donating paintings to many art auctions in Guelph and Exeter, Ontario.

1 **Calla Lilies** 18x24" Watercolour.

2 **Daffodils** Watercolour.

3 **Lynda's Iris** 10x12" Watercolour.

3

2

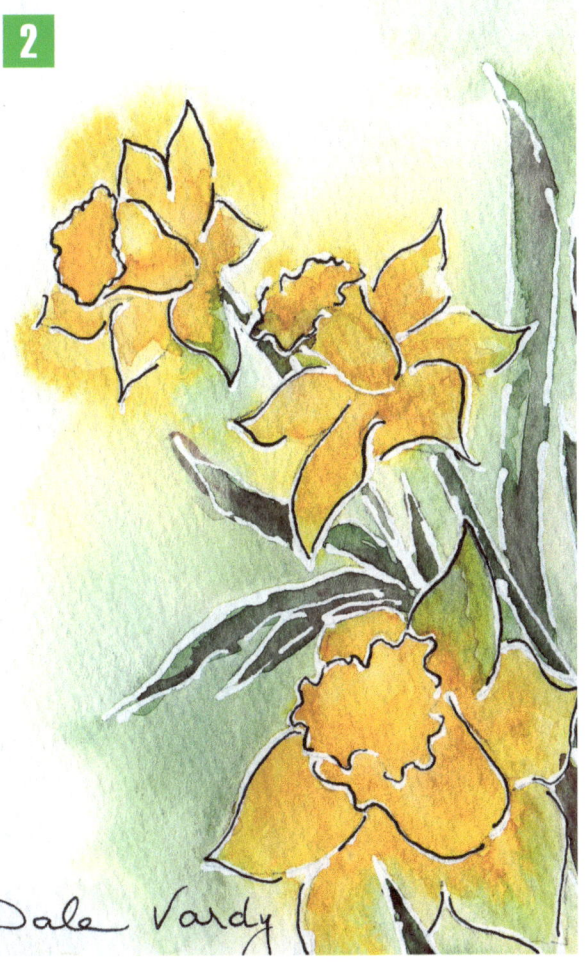

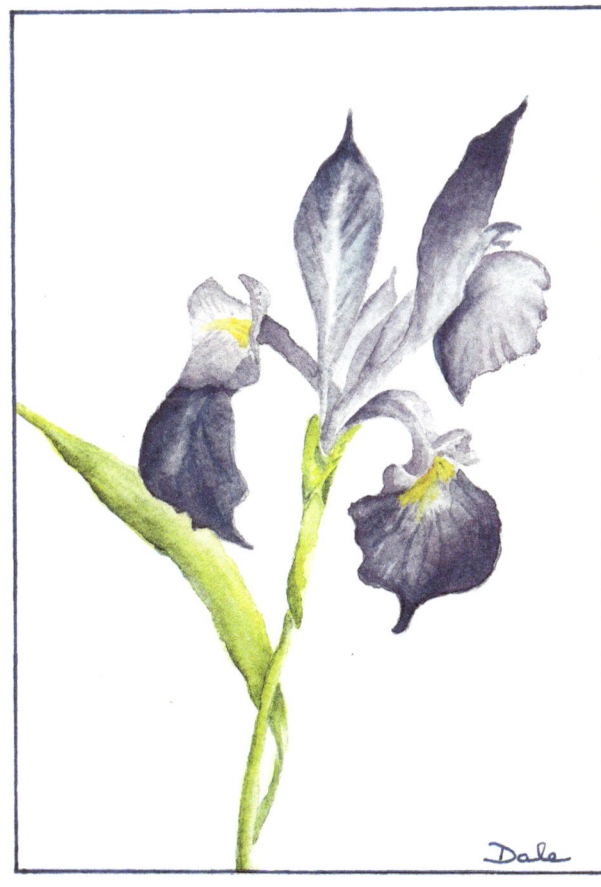

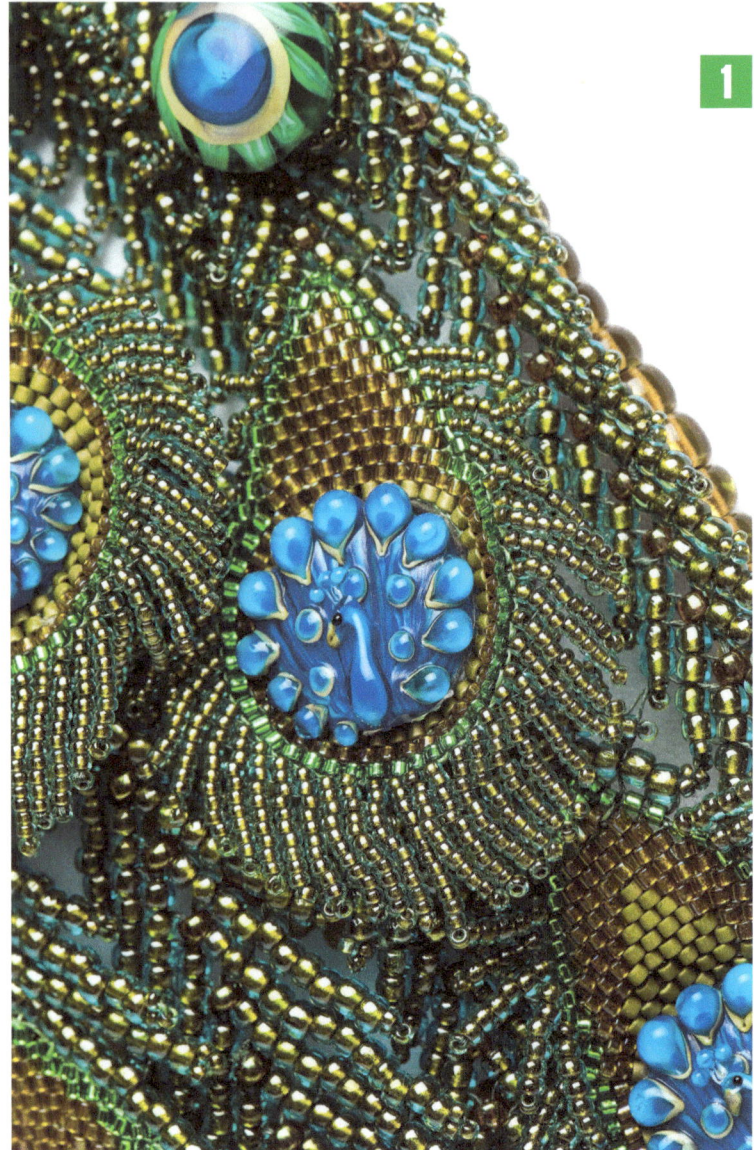

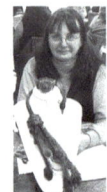

ROXANN BLAZETICH-OZOLS

LOCATION: Guelph

WEB: beadaddict.ca, mabeads.ca

EMAIL: beadaddict@sympatico.ca, mabeads@rogers.com

Roxann has worked with beads for over 10 year creating beaded jewellery kits and one of a kind pieces. She and Mary Ann Helmond collaborated on an Art Nouveau Peacock set of wearable art for the International Society of Glass Beadmakers annual Convergence III competition. Roxann created the original peacock sculpture with several beadwork stitches and a wire sculptural base using Mary Ann's lampwork beads as the focal points.

1 **Art Nouveau Peacock tail feather detail.** Japanese bead strands used to create fine feather details.

3 **Art Nouveau Peacock** entire set of wearable art. Lampwork beads and supporting beadwork sculpture designed to create a realistic peacock figure.

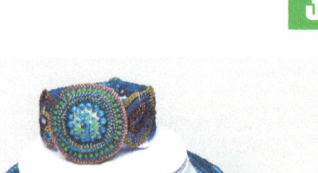

2 **Art Nouveau Peacock head and neck detail.** This original design used Japanese and Czech beads with a wire and mesh support.

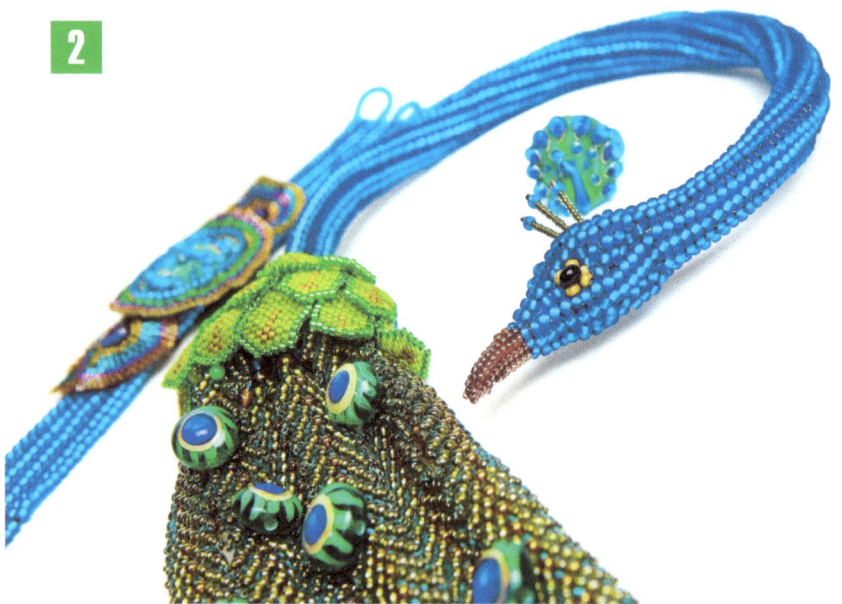

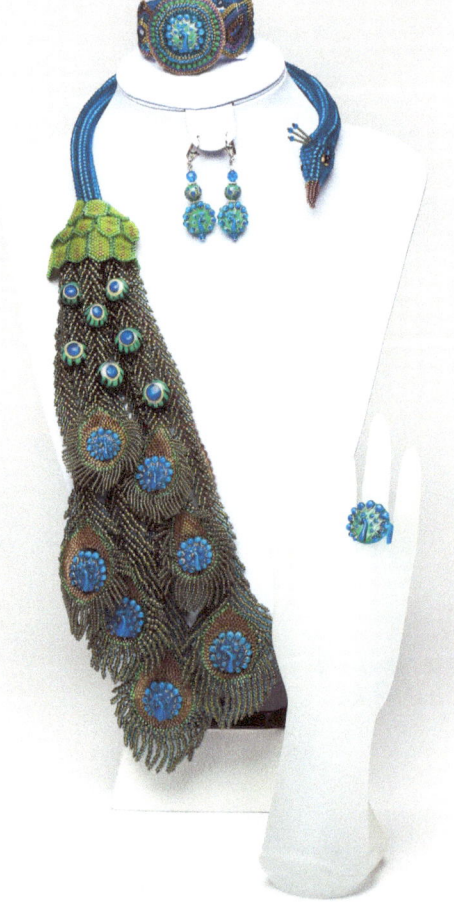

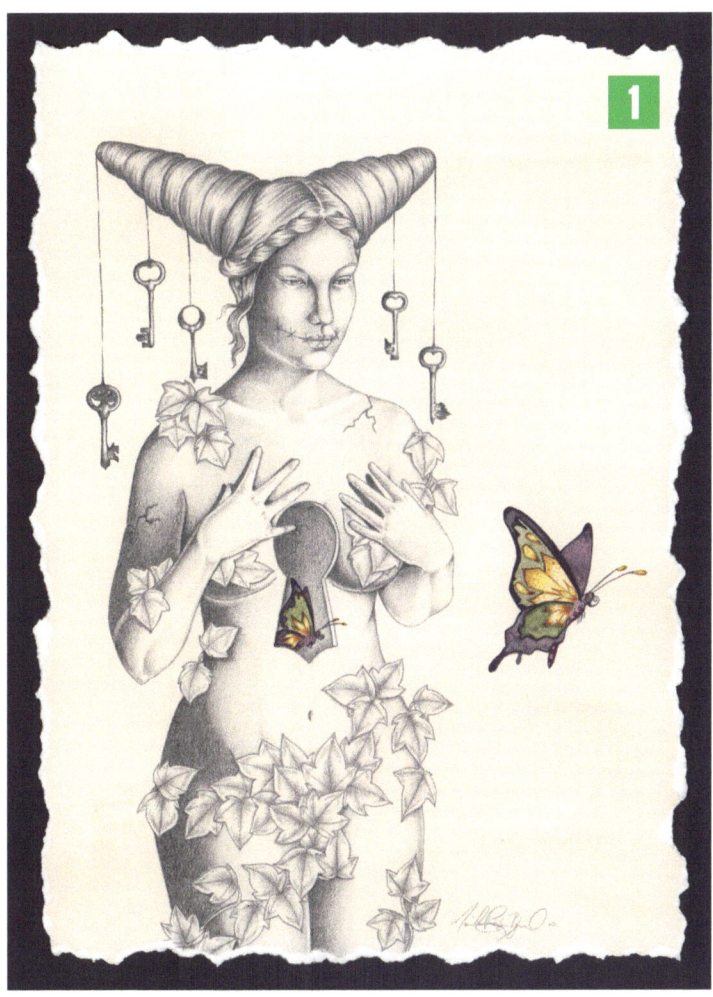

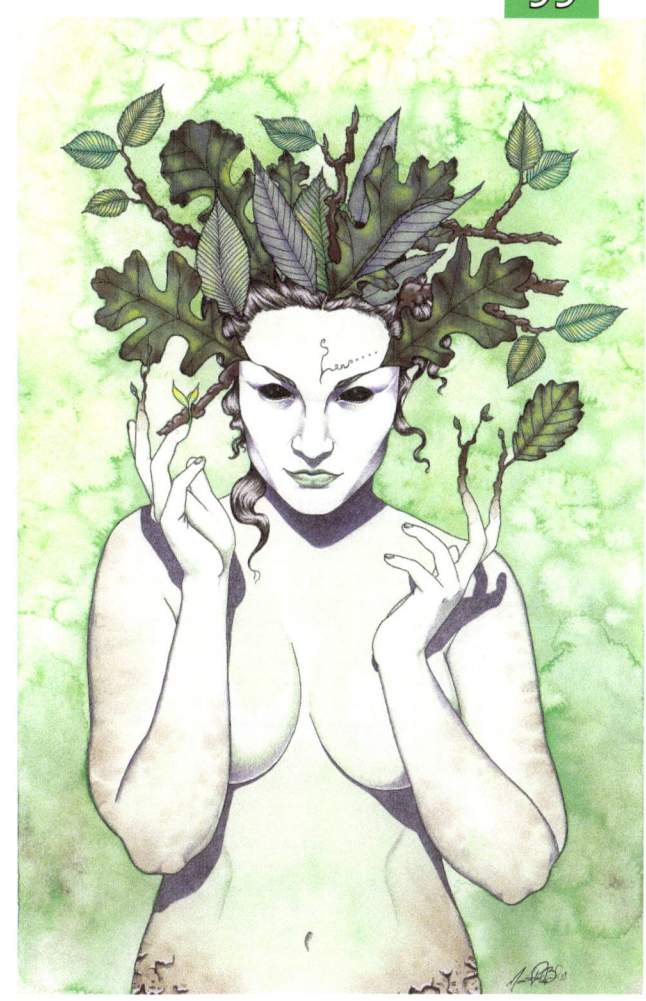

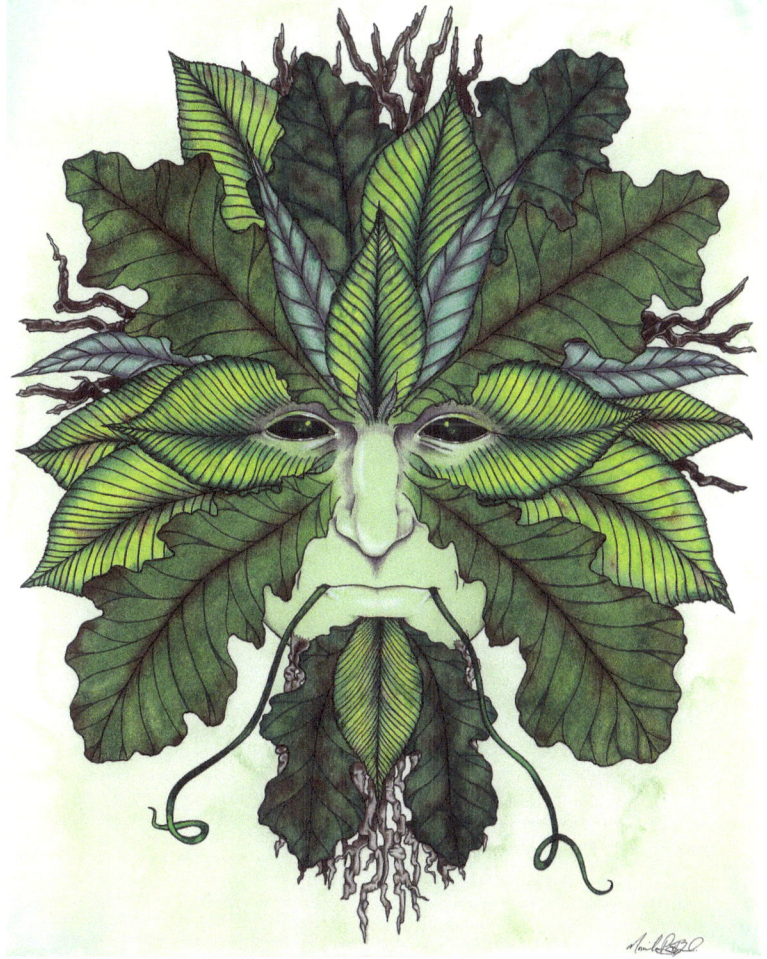

MONIKA PTOK-BYARD (FAEBYL ART)

LOCATION: Guelph
WEB: faebylart.com
EMAIL: Monika@faebylart.com

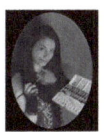 Born in Bangkok Thailand, Monika now resides and paints in Guelph. Fascinated by Myth and Folklore at an early age, Monika paints enchanting faeries and creatures enjoyed around the world by both children and adults alike. Monika's paintings are mostly done with watercolours, her favourites being Schmincke, Windsor and Newton and Daniel Smith on hot pressed watercolour paper. She also works with ink, coloured pencil, silverpoint and acrylics.

1 The Key 7.5x10" Graphite and watercolour.

2 The Green Faery 10x15" Watercolour, ink, coloured pencil.

3 Green Man 10.5x13" Watercolour, ink, coloured pencil.

1 **January Thaw** 26×18" Kiln-formed glass - made of small granules of coloured glass and melted glass shapes. No paint is used.

2 **On the River** 16x12" Kiln-formed glass made of small granules of coloured glass and melted glass shapes. No paint is used.

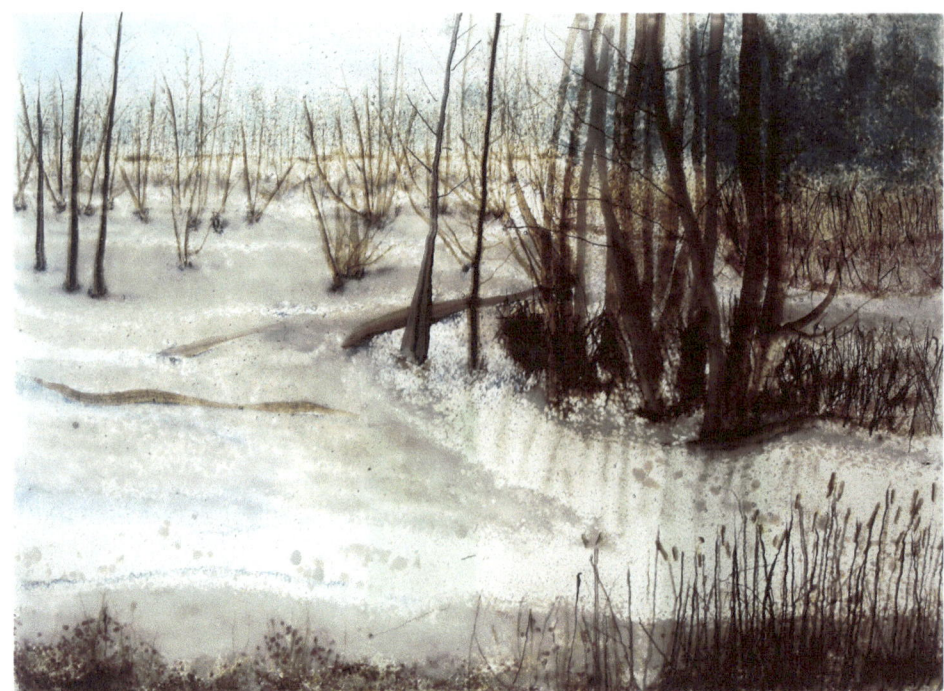

1

2

3 **Vanishing Glacier** 10×17" Kiln-formed glass manipulated in the kiln while hot.

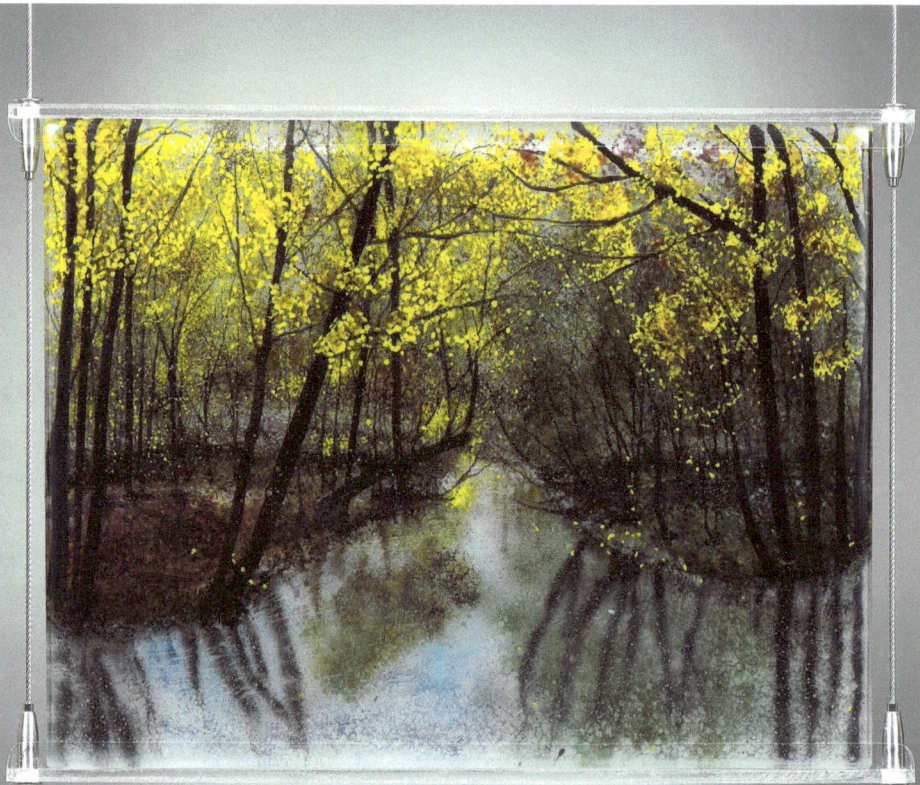

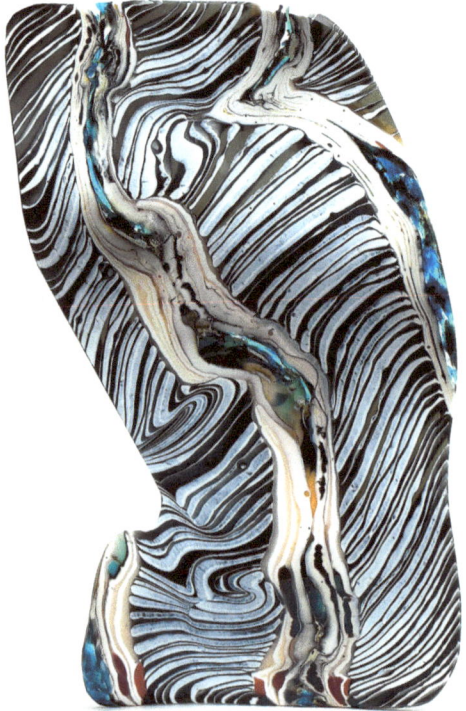

3

JERRE DAVIDSON

LOCATION: Alma
WEB: jerredavidsonglass.com
EMAIL: jerredavidson@gmail.com

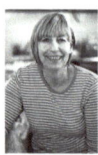

Born in Scotland, and currently living in Ontario, Jerre creates both realistic landscapes in glass and also more abstract representations of rock formations and strata. She works by melting and manipulating hot glass in a kiln. She has studied in many centers of excellence in the United States and has also travelled to the north of Scotland to further her education.

IRENE SMEDLEY

LOCATION: 131 Paisley St. Guelph
WEB: (N/A)
EMAIL: (N/A)

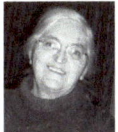

A lifelong art enthusiast, Irene was originally a painter in oils. During the past ten years she has become interested in other media, and is now working in watercolour, acrylic, and mixed media. Irene has progressed from painting mainly landscapes, buildings, and flowers, and is now also producing paintings of a wide range of subjects, including abstract and non-objective art. Since moving to Guelph Irene has become a member of a number of local art organizations and clubs. Her goals are to continue to work and grow as an artist, to be open to new ideas, and to be interested and supportive of the work of other artists.

1 **Rock Reflections** Watercolour.

2 **Huron Shore** 16x12" Watercolour.

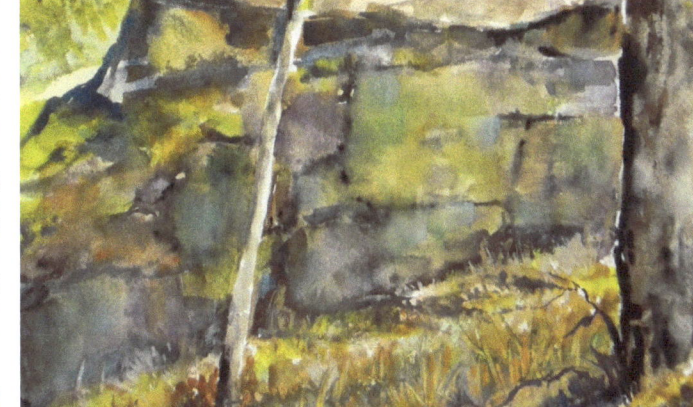

1

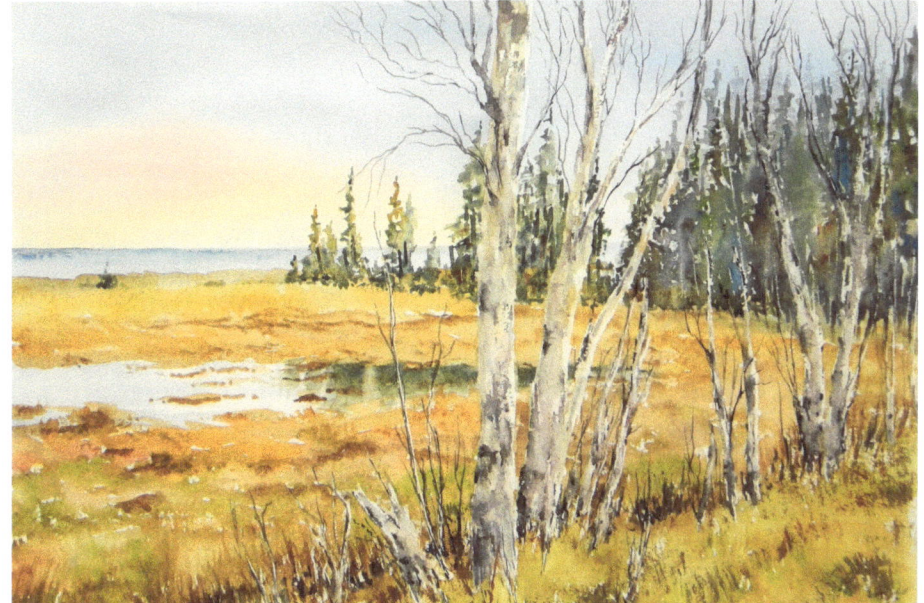

2

3

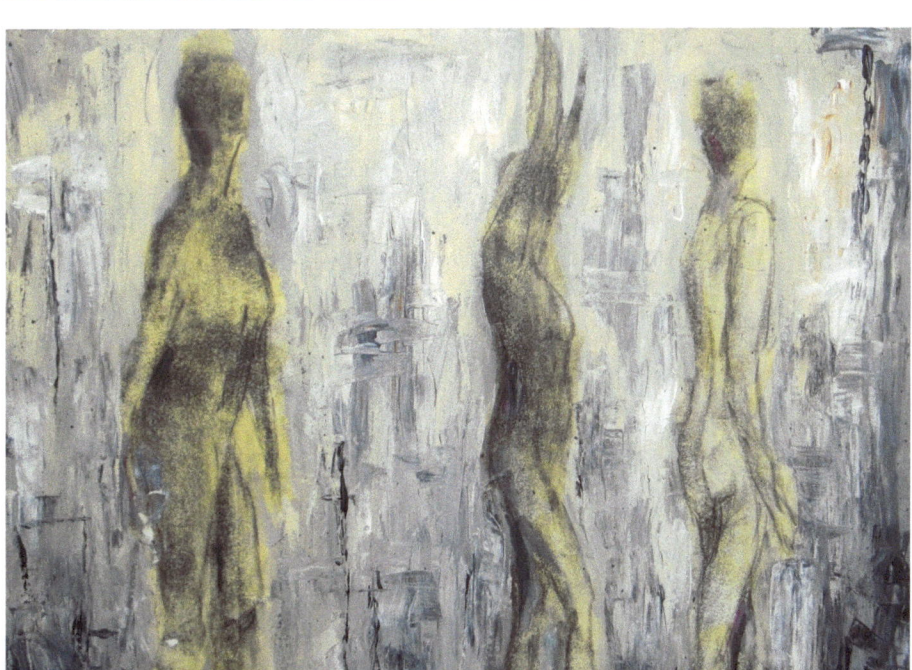

3 **Nudes** 24x20" Mixed media.

CHRIS ROWAN

LOCATION: Guelph
WEB: (N/A)
EMAIL: chris.rowan@hotmail.coml

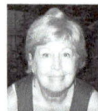 About 10 years ago I took a watercolour class, continued my artistic journey with workshops, weeklong instructions at Loyalist College Belleville, Elora & Arizona. Three years ago I began acrylic instructions, now enjoy producing large contemporary abstract art.

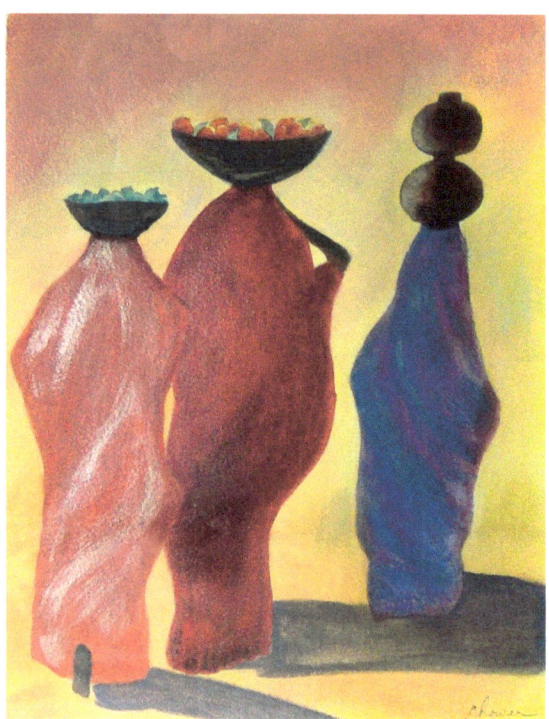

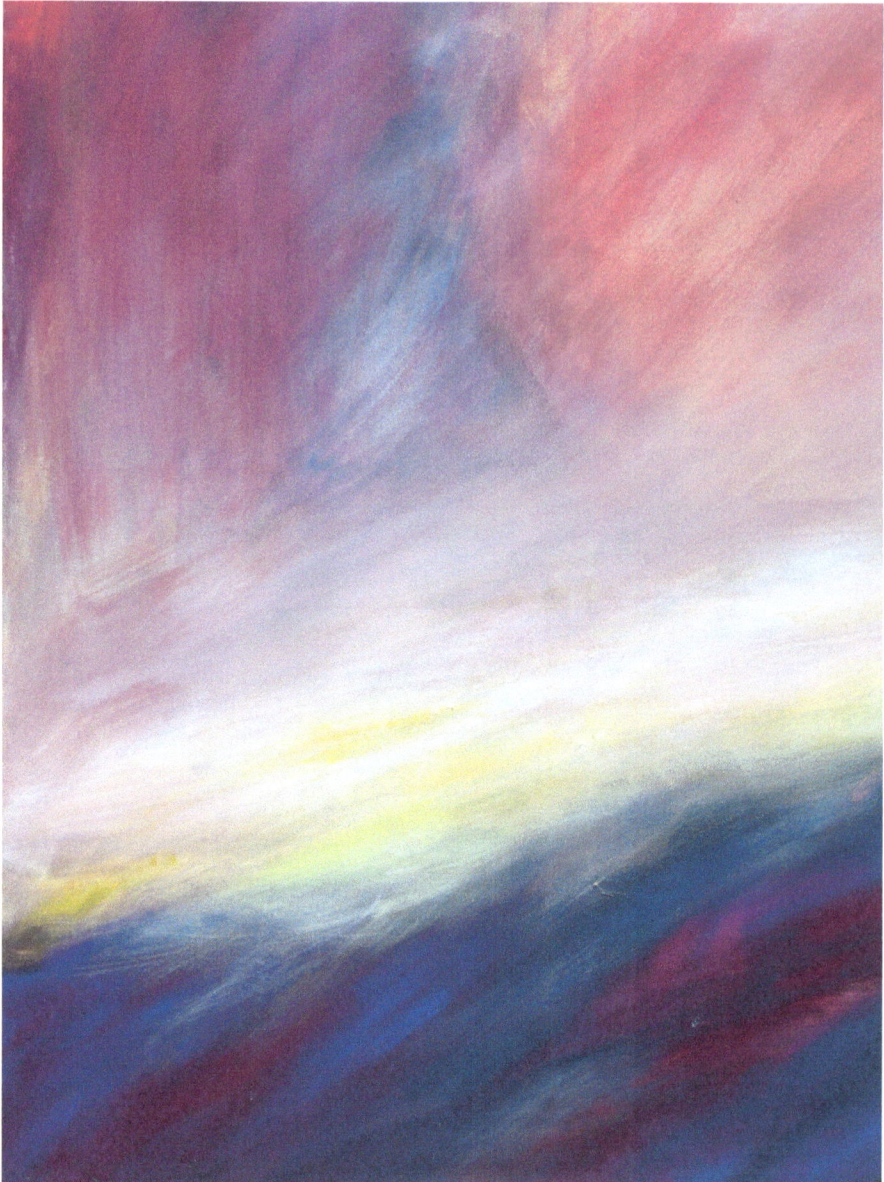

1 Perfect Balance 11x15" Watercolour.

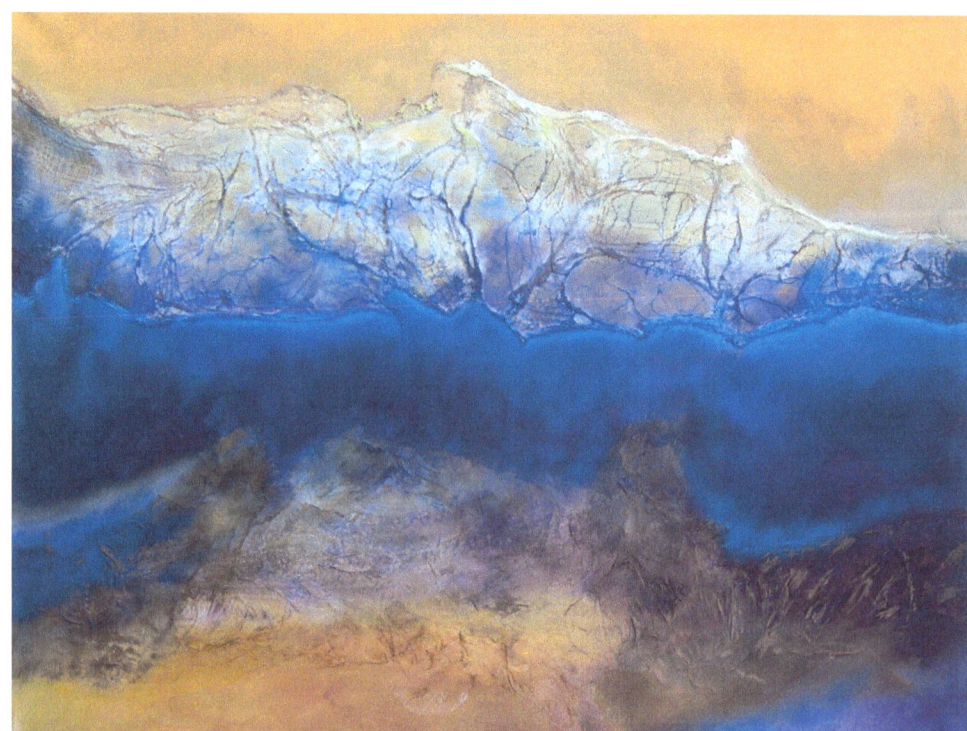

2 Colour Slide 31x39" Acrylic.

3 Mystic Mountain 23x32" Mixed media.

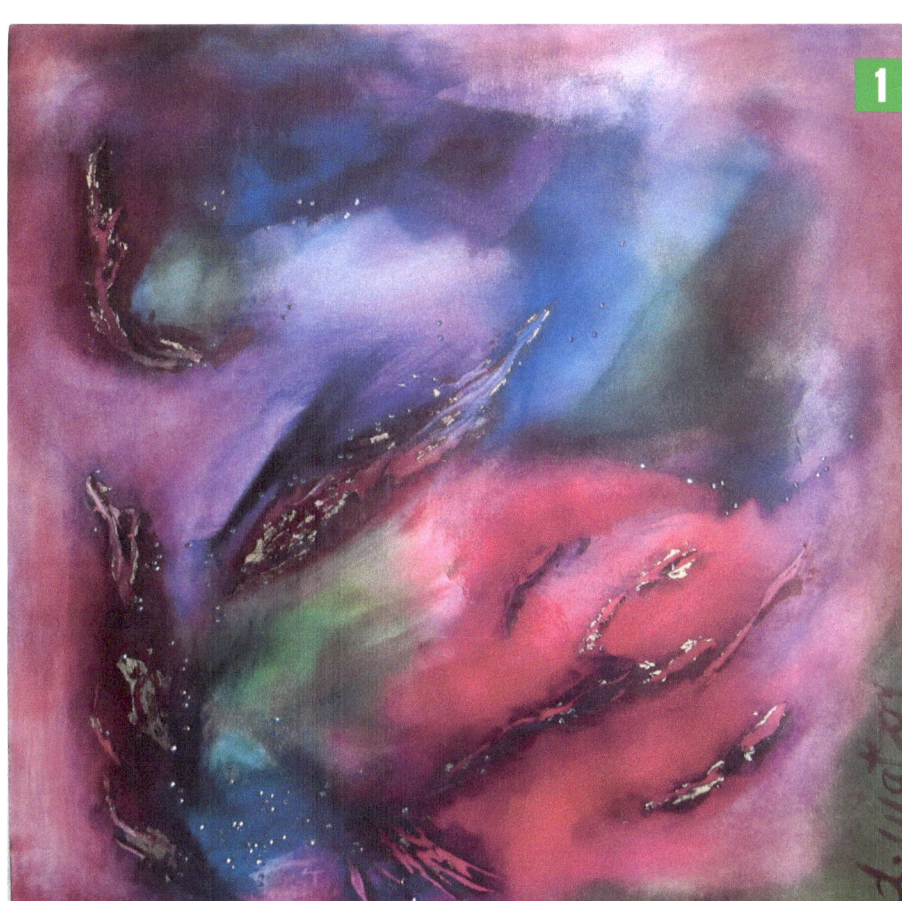

DARLENE WATSON

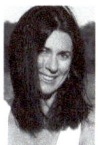

LOCATION: Guelph

WEB: artistdwatson.com

EMAIL: Darlene_watson@rogers.com

Art brings space alive with color and style while transforming ordinary into extraordinary. Darlene's background in Decorating and Design allows the creation of mood, atmosphere and gives power to draw in the senses and stimulate the mind. Commission Art upon request. Swarovski Crystal adds light, romance and a bit of whimsy to each piece. Art showing in Ottawa Gallery, Sauble Beach, Owen Sound and Guelph. Studio 54 ~ Visits by appointment.

1 **Fairy Dust** 48x48" Acrylic- gold leaf, tanzanite colour Swarovski crystal.

2 **Descending Ribbons** 20x80" Acrylic, silver leaf, clear Swarovski crystal.

3 **Starburst: 30x36"** Acrylic gold and copper leaf, Silk coloured Swarovski crystal.

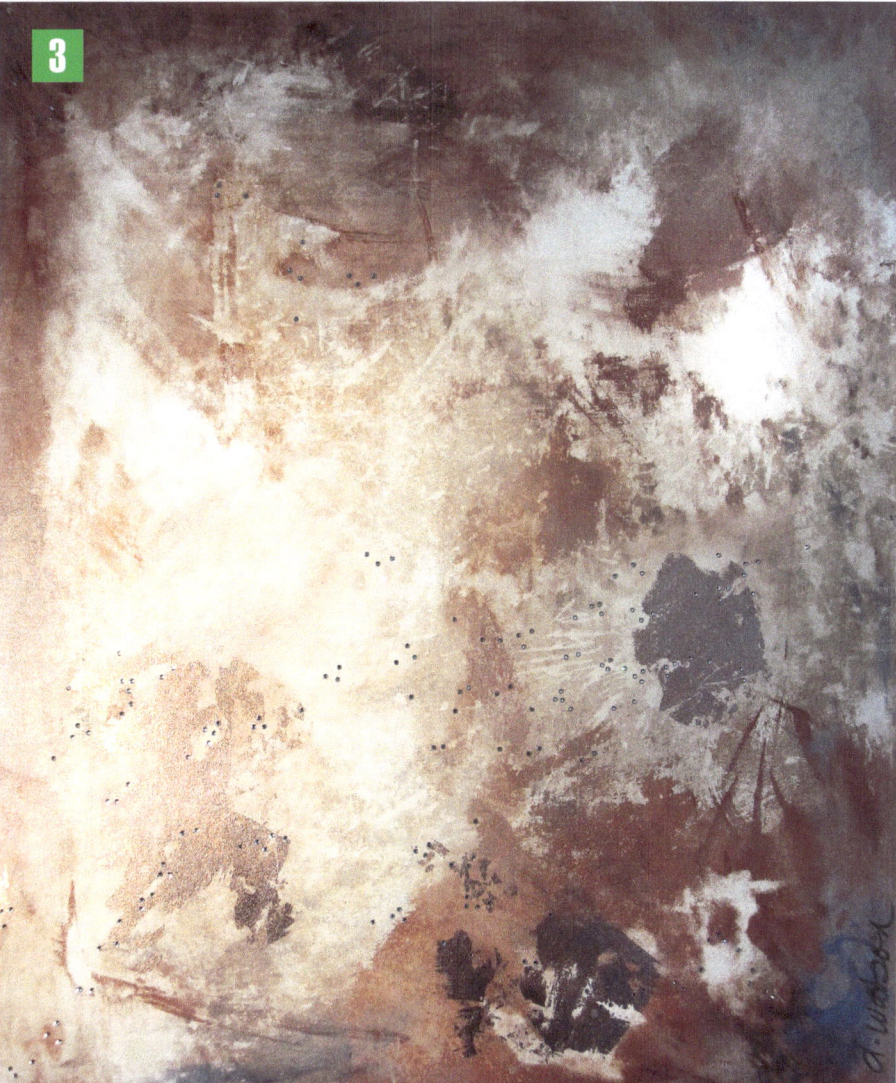

LISA CHANDLER

LOCATION: Guelph
WEB: lisachandler.villagecms.com
EMAIL: calmintheforest@gmail.com

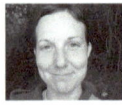

My name is Lisa Chandler. I grew up on the Niagara escarpment in Creemore, Ontario. I now live in Guelph, where I have found a similar love of the outdoors. The beauty that I find in nature inspires the energy in my work. I believe that nature has its own spirit and should be shown to everyone who isn't paying attention. I use acrylic paints to bring to life this hidden gem that is the flow of life.

1 Under The Apple Tree
12x36" Acrylic.

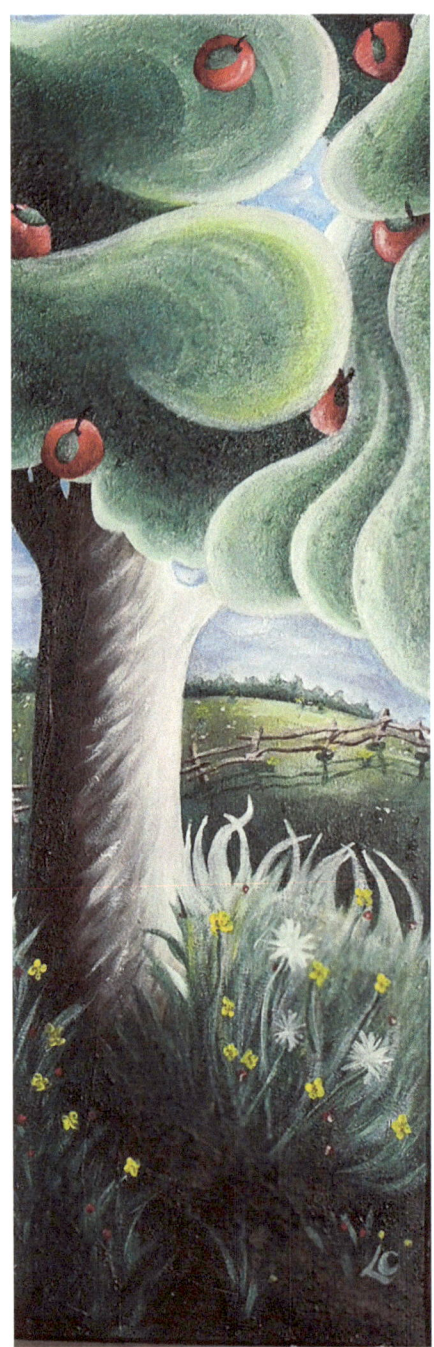

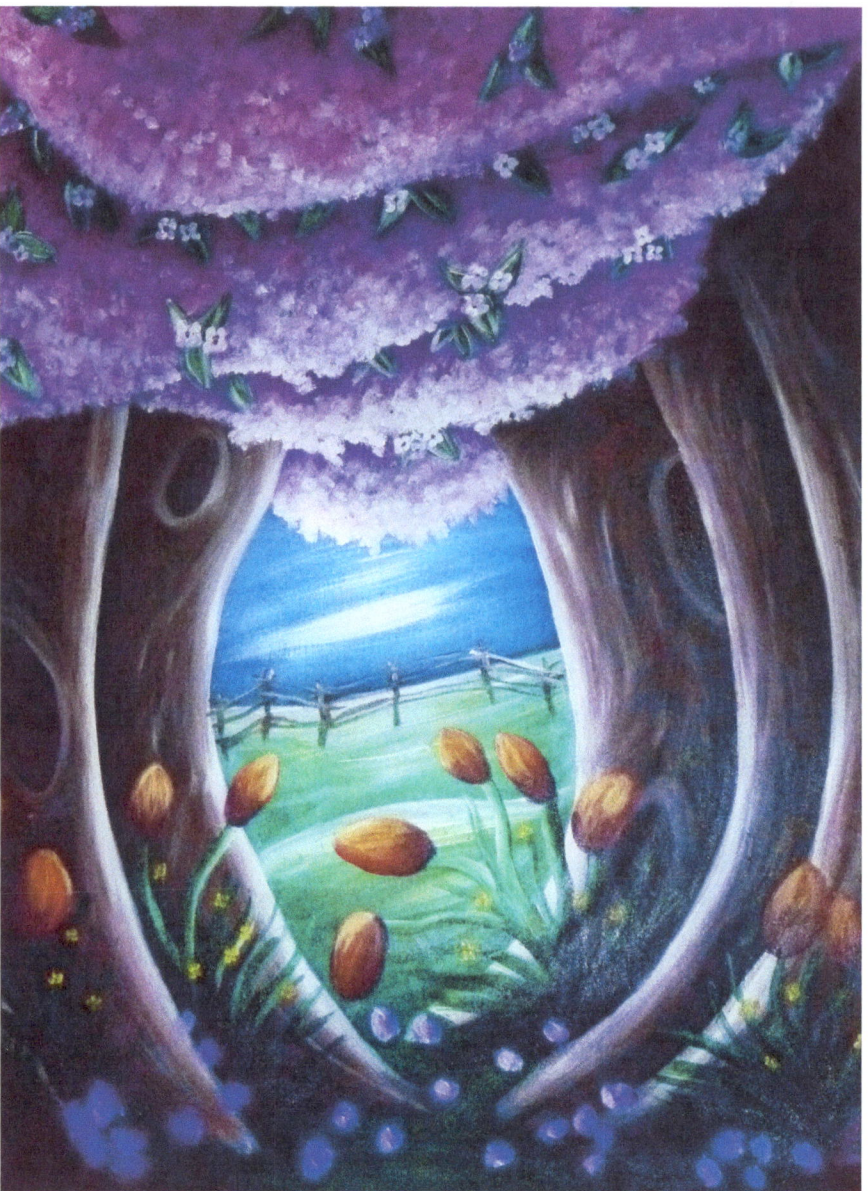

2 Spring In The Orchard
36x45" Acrylic on canvas

3 Phsycadelic Daydream
24x36" Acrylic on canvas.

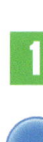

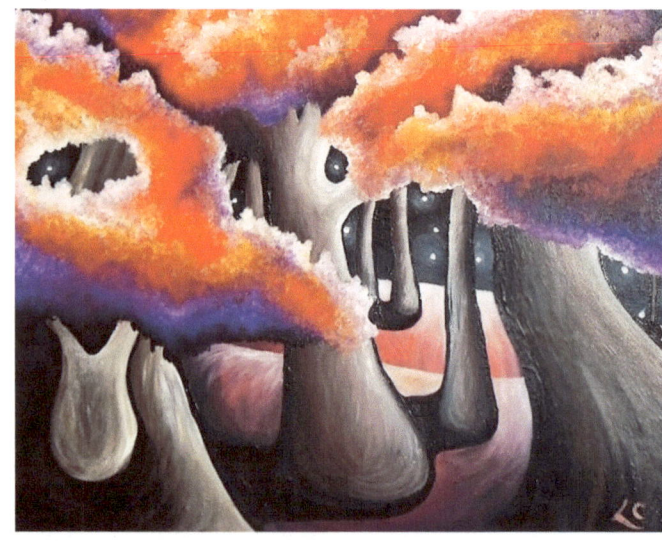

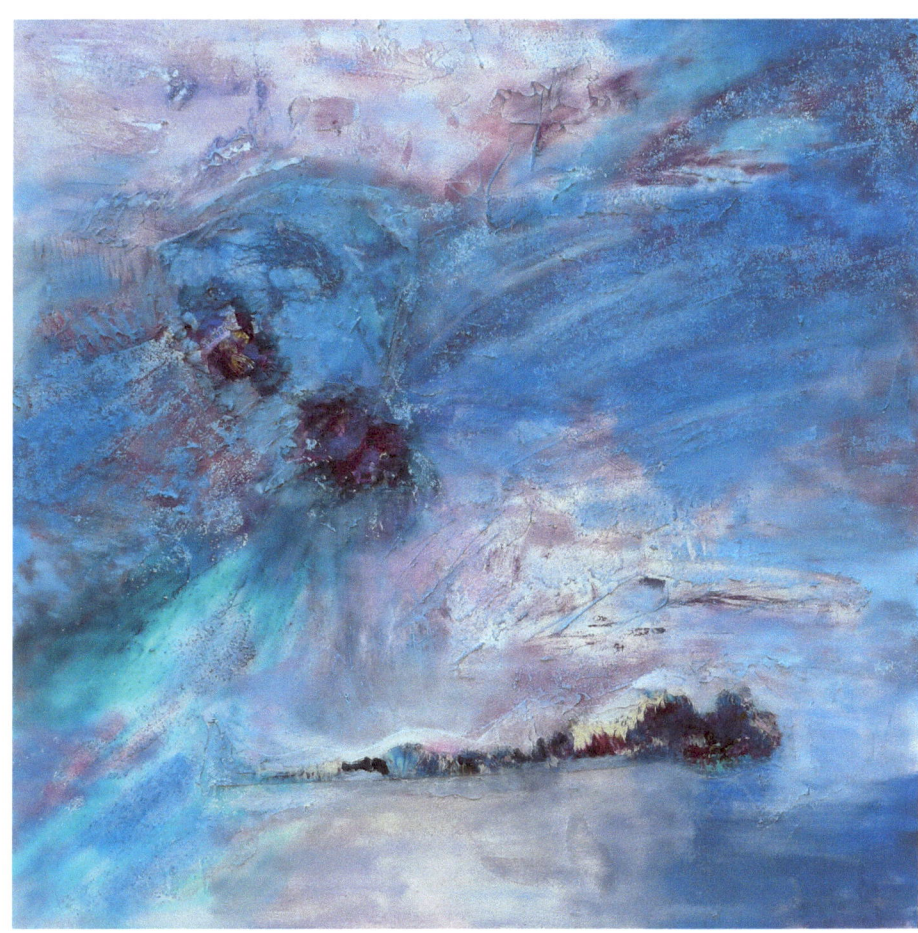

LOIS RYDER

LOCATION: Guelph
WEB: (N/A)
EMAIL: ryder.lois@gmail.com

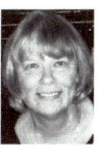

Lois is all about colour. The bolder the brighter the better. Lois displays her work in local galleries in Canada and the United States. She is a memeber of the central ontario arts Acc. Board member of the Guelph Creative Arts Acc. and president of the West Hills Art Group Guelph.

1

2 The Bridesmaids 12x20"
Mixed Media.

2

1 Aerial Perspective 36x36"
Mixed Media.

3 Looking Within 16x20"
Acrylics.

3

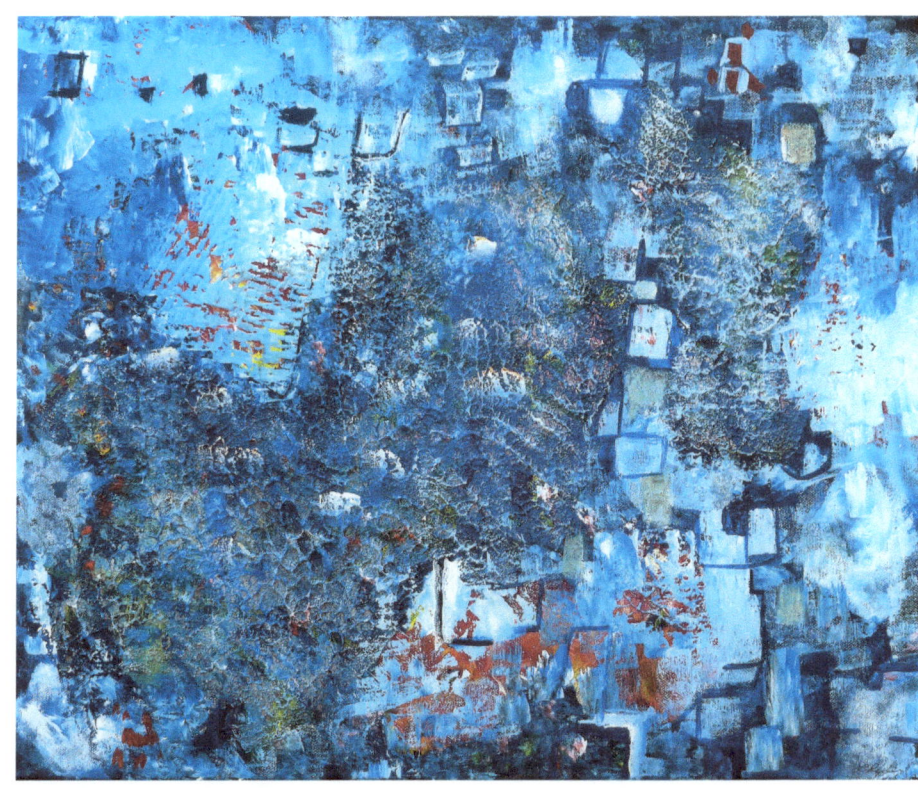

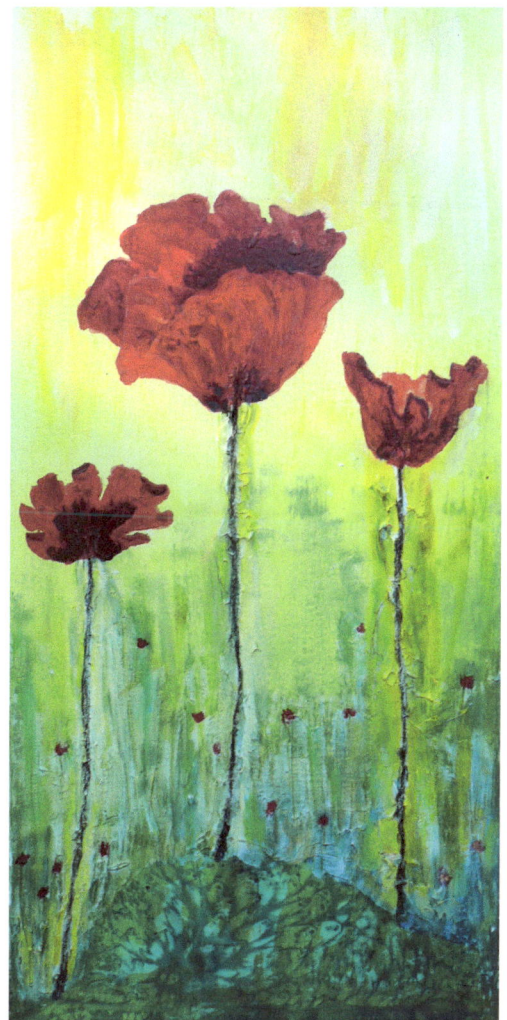

JESSICA BUCHANAN

LOCATION: Fergus
WEB: creativecanvaspaintings.webs.com:
EMAIL: jessie_buchanan98@hotmail.com

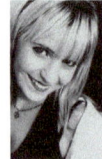

My name is Jessica Buchanan and I am a developing artist with a deep passion for painting. I have been artistic as long as I can remember, but over the last year I have been working hard on creating a collection of pieces. Once I had a starting collection of work I designed a portfolio to show my work to others and this started my business. I have done several customized peices of work for valued customers and am continually accepting new orders and challenges. I love what I do and my inspiration of painting is shown in the quality of my work.

1 **Vineyard Abstract** 16x20" Acrylic on canvas. Three piece abstract painting with use of gold leafing. (3 peice set)

2 **Salmon Sunset** 24x36" Acrlic on canvas. Use of shading and highlighting to create dimension.

3 **Italian Garden** 24×36" Acrylic on canvas. Night landscape with focal point.

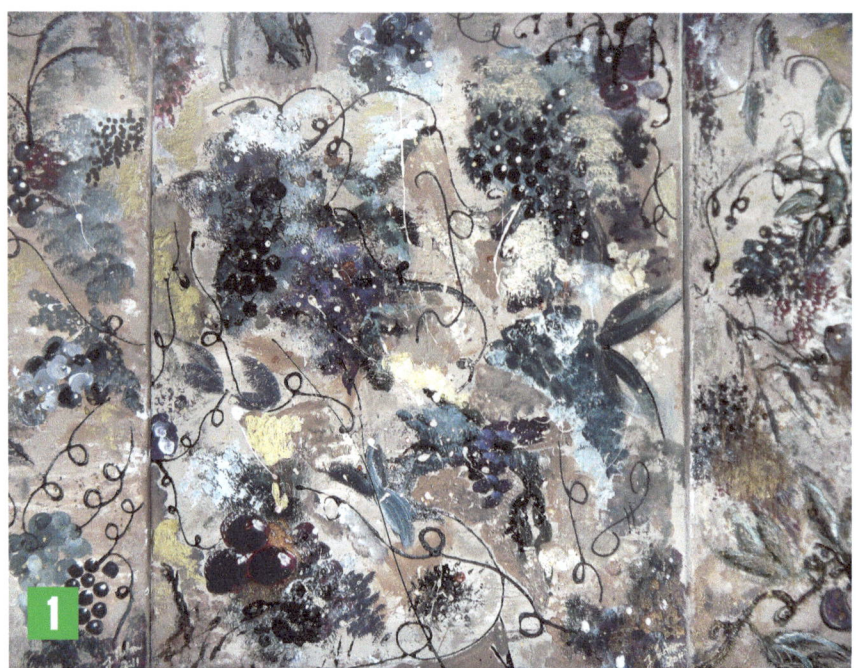

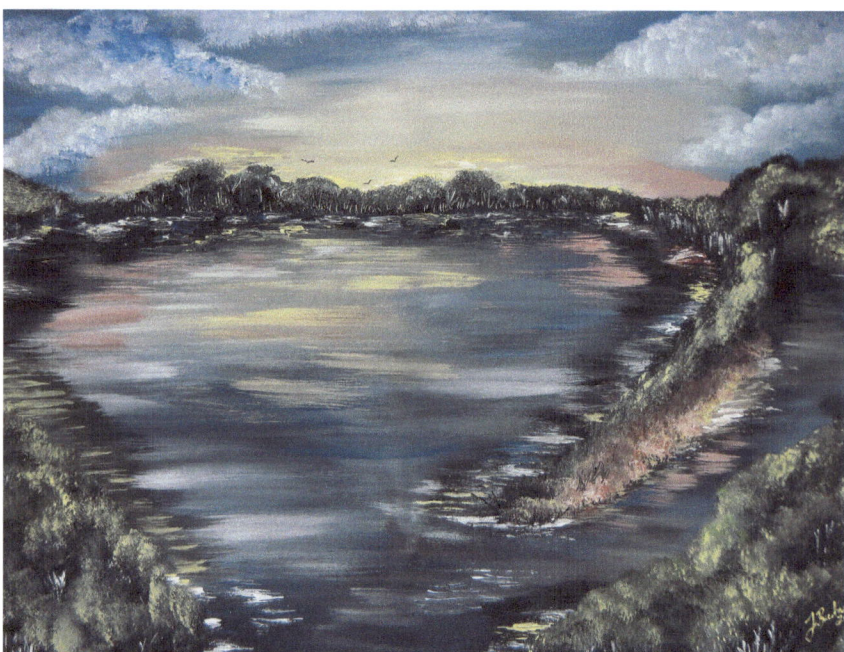

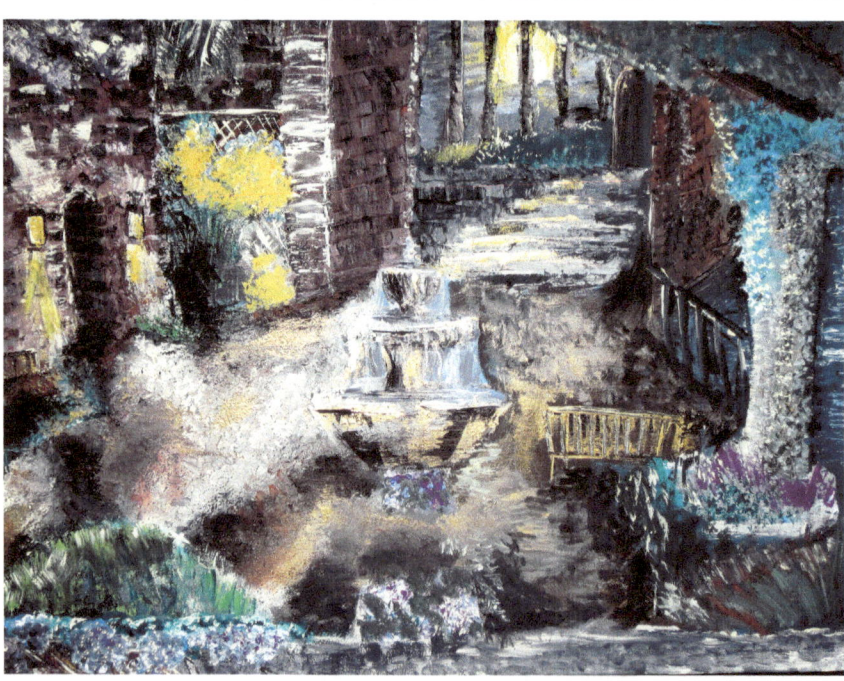

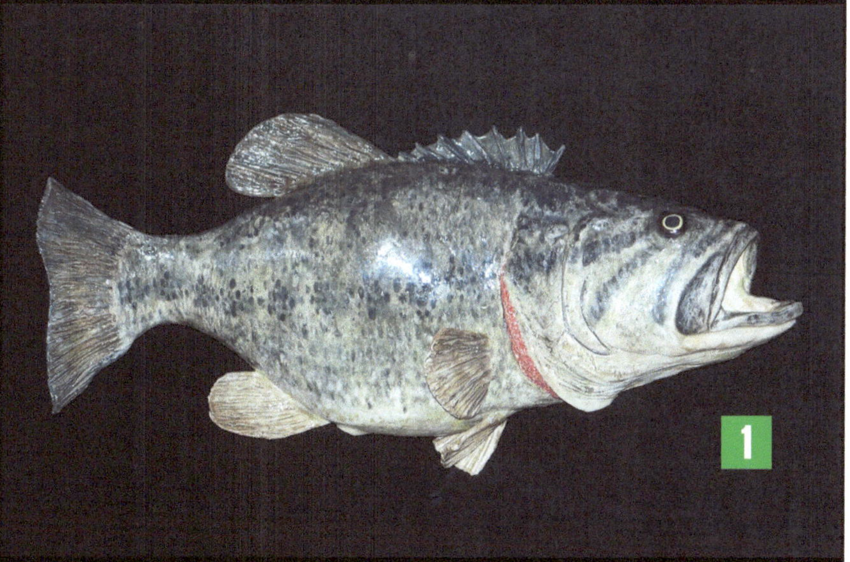

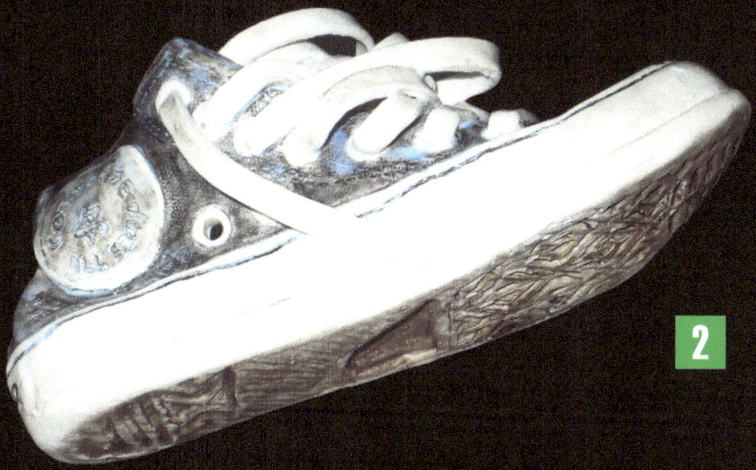

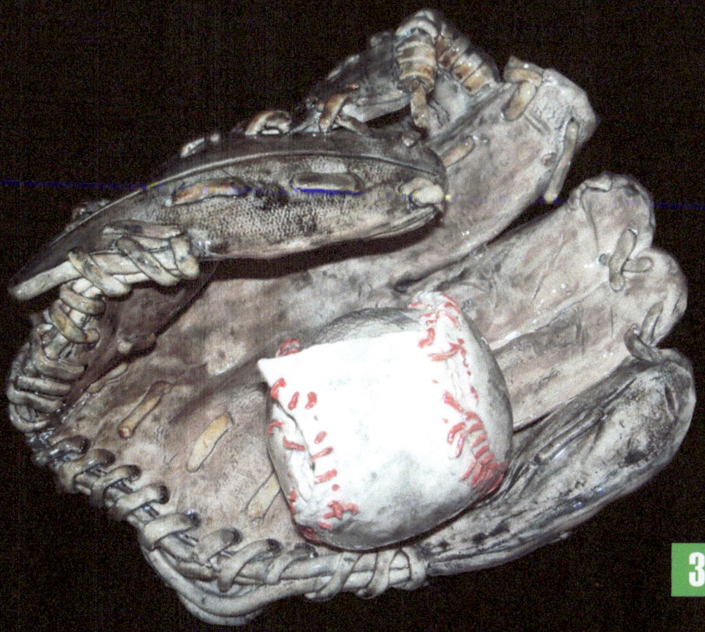

JEANNE YARDLEY

LOCATION: Village of Clyde
WEB: jeanneyardley.com
EMAIL: mjeanneyardley@gmail.com

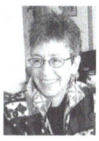

Jeanne Yardley creates 3-dimensional still-life art primarily out of earthenware and stoneware clay, celebrating the cultural narratives in everyday objects. She strives to represent scale and detail as realistically as possible in order to reveal the stories and memories embedded in the ordinary. In addition to self-teaching, she has studied pottery at Mohawk College (Brantford) and attended workshops and demonstrations through the Hamilton and Brantford Potters' Guilds. Ontario born, Jeanne has lived in Waterloo Region since 1973 and in Clyde since 1993.

1 Catch and Release 18x8x6" Stoneware. 2009. A wall-hanging piece showing the realistic detail and intense coloration of a trophy-sized local bass.

2 Sk8tr Girl 9x4x3.5" Stoneware. 2010. Emblematic for a generation, this life-sized and highly detailed Converse definitely has a few stories to tell.

3 Strike Three 10x10x6" Stoneware. 2010. A well-worn glove and ball that have been around the stadium a few times, this sculpture reflects many memories.

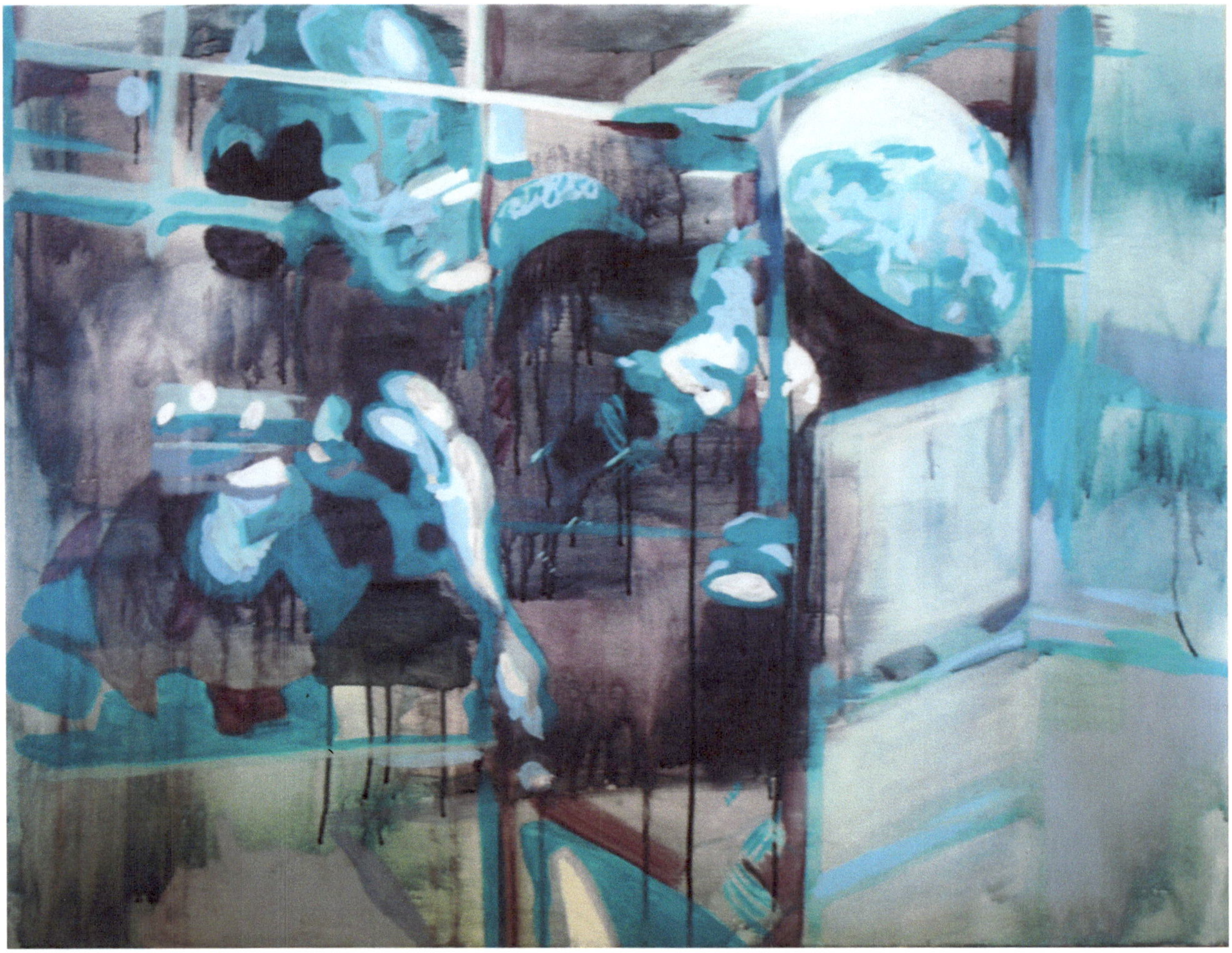

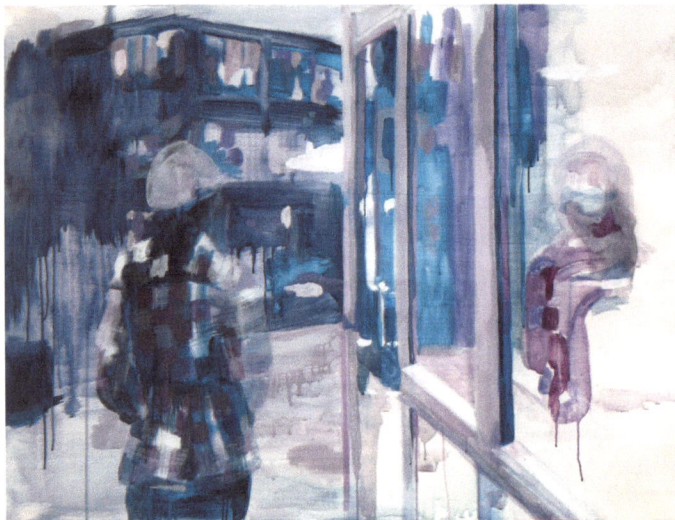

1

1 Reflection II 40×30″ Acrylic on canvas.

2 Reflection 48×36″ Acrylic on canvas.

3 DC 48×48″ Acrylic on canvas.

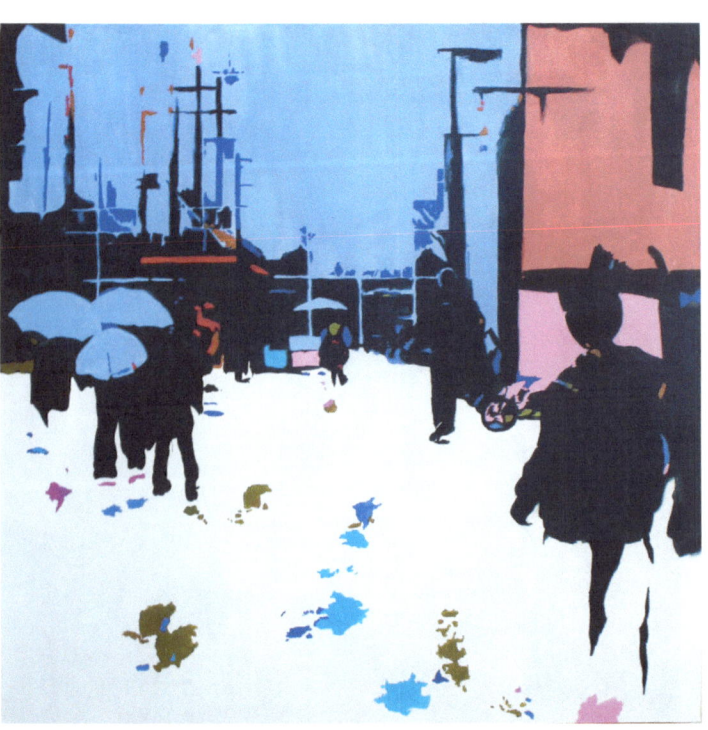

2

MONICA LIMA

LOCATION: Glen Morris
WEB: (N/A)
EMAIL: mslima9@gmail.com

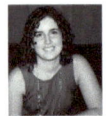 Monica is a recent graduate of the University of Waterloo. She graduated with a Bachelor of Arts Degree in Fine Arts and Business with a specialization in Drawing and Painting. Currently she is taking Digital Imaging at Conestoga College. She works with acrylic paint on canvas with images of reflections in architecture. She photographs her subject and uses photo editing software to manipulate images to simplified forms then paints in thin layers.

TINA NEWLOVE

LOCATION: Guelph
WEB: tinanewlove.com
EMAIL: tina@tinanewlove.com

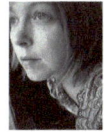

Tina Newlove continues to be recognized by curators and jurors as an artist who is making a significant contribution to the cultural life of Canada. The Arts & Letters Club of Toronto commissioned Tina to create their 1998/99 Executive List. Her painting "Organizing my Mind" is in the City of Toronto's permanent collection. Newlove received an Award of Merit from the Society of Canadian Artists for her painting "Step Lightly" at the Art Gallery of Hamilton. In 2008 Tina's sponsors for her exhibition 'PROTECTION' at the Latcham Gallery included Bruce Cockburn and the Ontario Arts Council. Most recently she was selected by the Art Gallery of Mississauga as one of the participating artists to be included in The Salmon Run Project, and has received the First Prize Award and an Honourable Mention in the Lakeshore Arts juried exhibition 'Through the Eyes of the Artist'.

1 Tornado Dreams 29x23" Watercolour. Tornado dreams often occur in response to tumultuous events or weather.

2 She Looked Away 8.5x5.5" Watercolour. She became silent after disagreements.

3 Woman in a Red Hat 3.5x2.5") Watercolour . Part of the artist's Trading Card series, this miniature painting is the size of a baseball card.

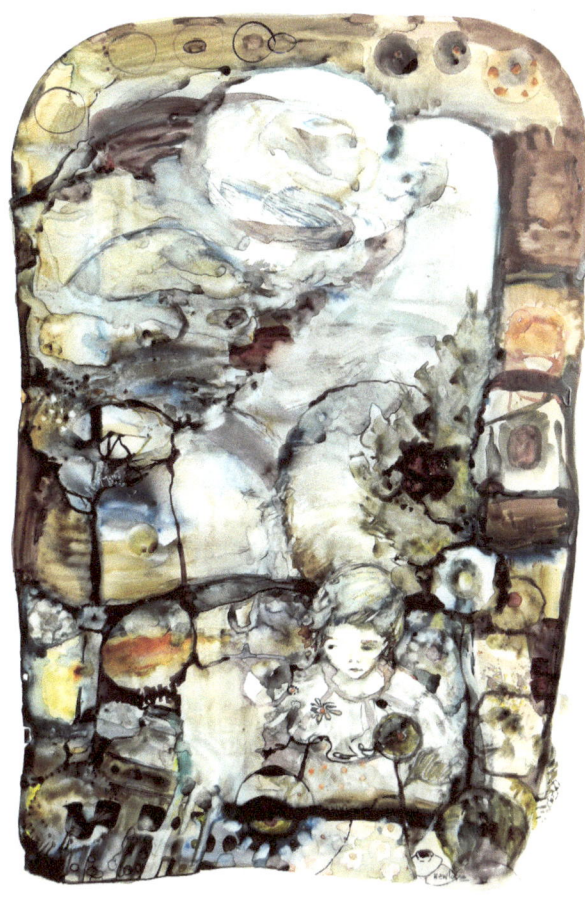

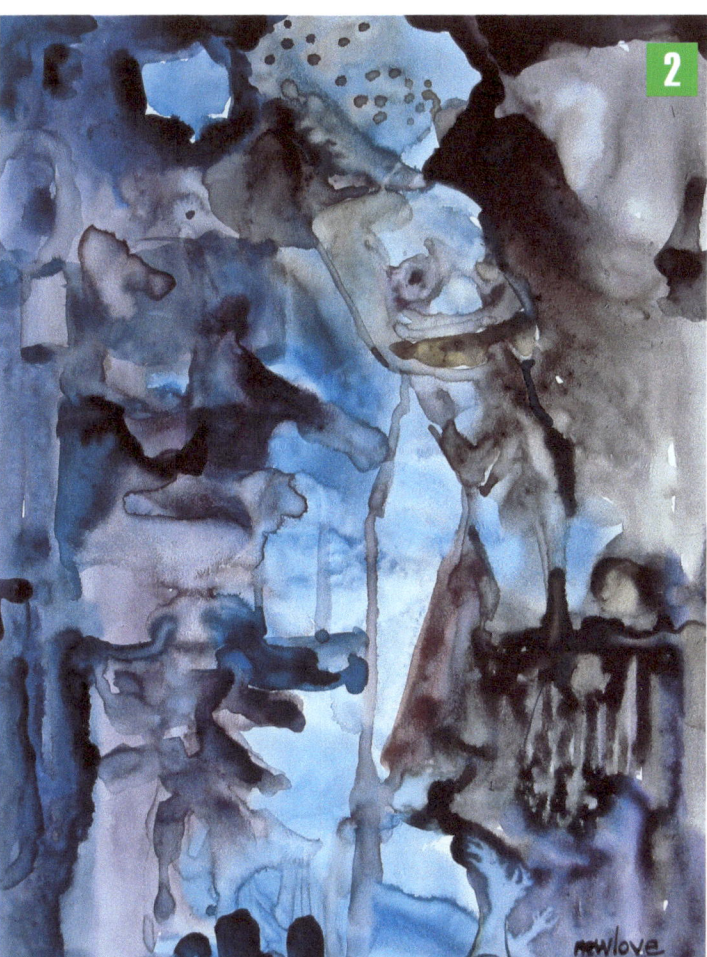

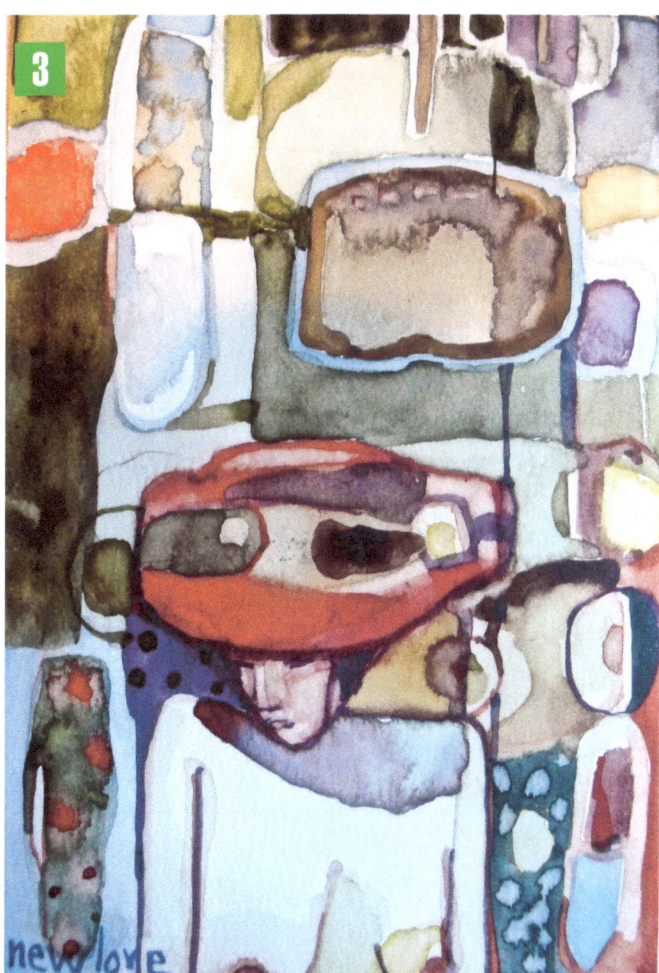

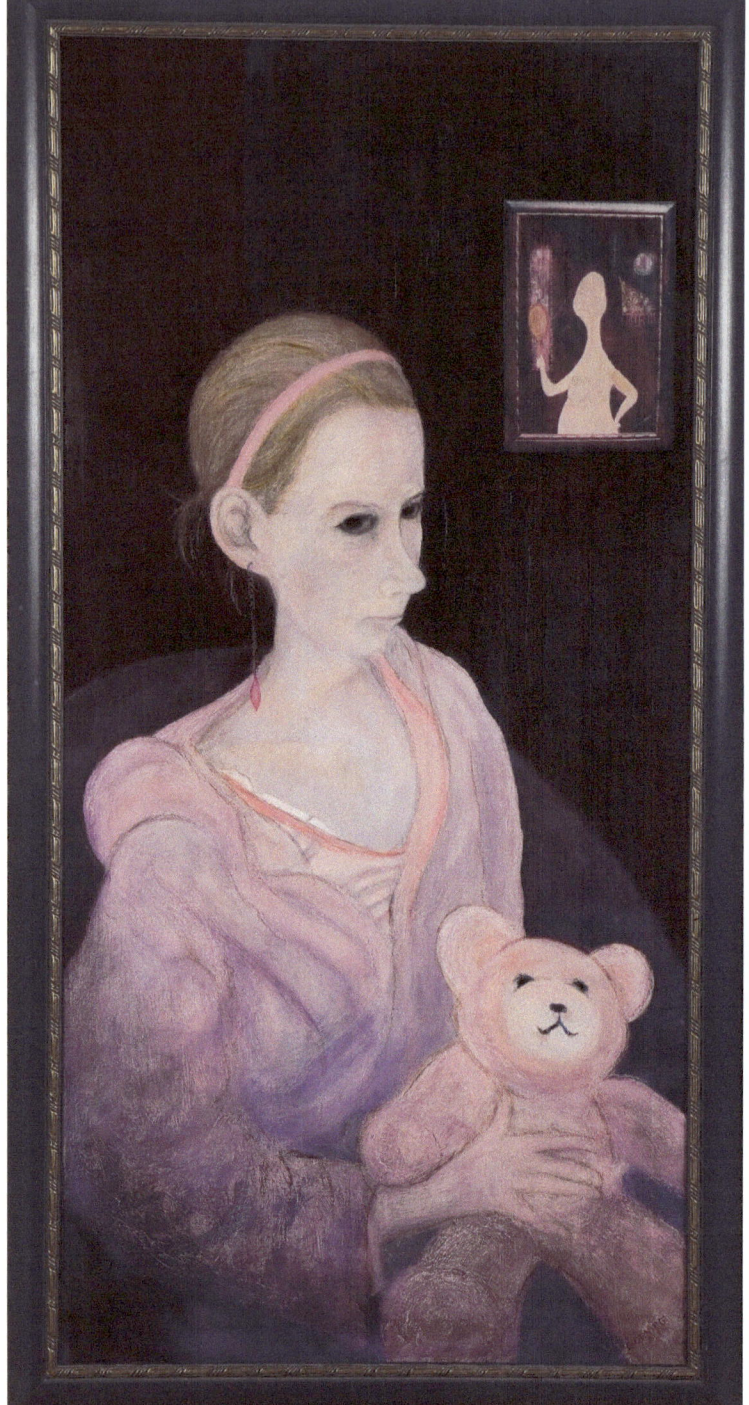

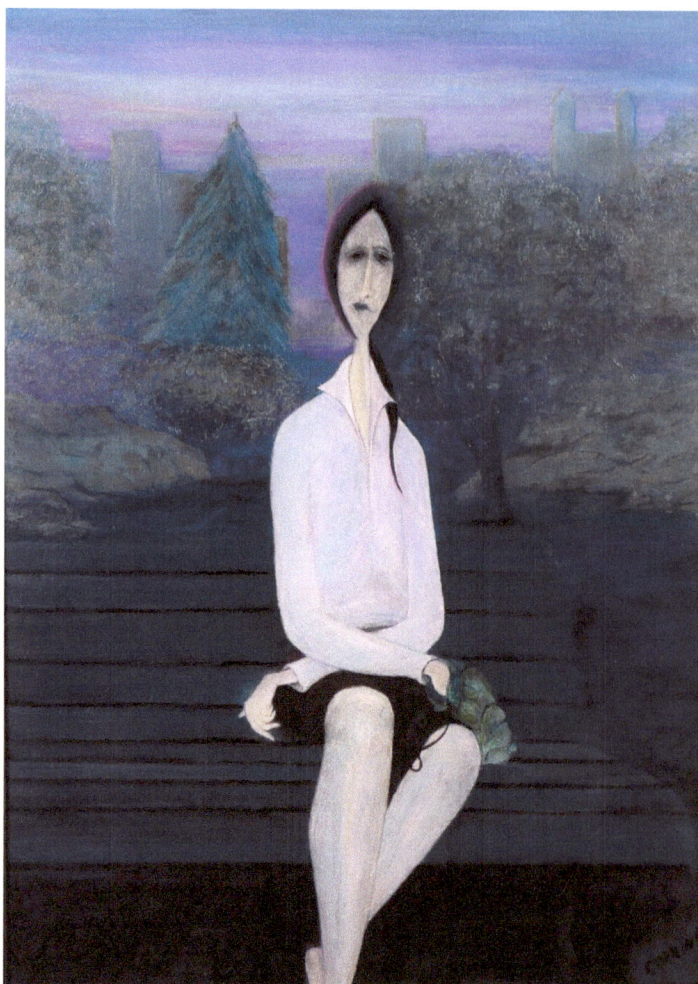

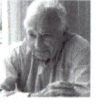

2 Waiting For Central Park
30x40" Oil on canvas.

BILL CORNING

LOCATION: Baden
WEB: corningworksart.com
EMAIL: bill.corning@sympatico.ca

A Left & Right Brain History. My mother tells me that I was producing organized drawings as well as reading by age 5. The artistic side of me led to a summer workshop stipend at the Rochester Art Gallery at age 10 followed in later life by recognition in the U.S. & Canada beginning with my first show entry in the 1967 Greenwich Ct. open show (3rd prize) and 1st prize in the prestigious Western N. Y. Art show in Buffalo (2006). Left brain activities were more complicated: An appetite for knowledge and an interest in neuroscience led to a Ph.D., academia and 75+ research papers and 6 books). I finished left brain stuff with the development and clinical application of digitized EEG data in assessing problematical children. In summary: Art is more fun - trust me.

1 The Pubescent 24x48" Oil on canvas. 1st prize, Western N.Y. Art Group show

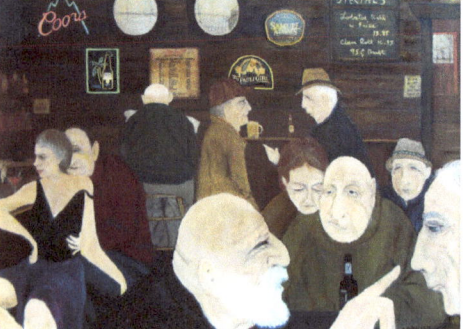

3 Social Intercourses at Capt. Simeon's Bar 40x30" Oil on canvas.

KAREN CUMMINGS

LOCATION: Cambridge
WEB: kCummings.ca
EMAIL: karen@kCummings.ca

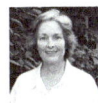

Karen is a contemporary art quilter. Her present work is characterized by bold colors, shapes and dimensions using commercial fabrics, painted surfaces, paper, scraps and embellishments from various venues. Karen pulls out fabrics that work from an idea, a photo, a painting or a scene that captures her imagination and creates an image to represent some aspect of the inspiring theme. The goal of each piece is an abstraction so colors need not represent reality. Freeform organic images are randomly cut and stitched into place working intuitively allowing each piece to add to the story.

1

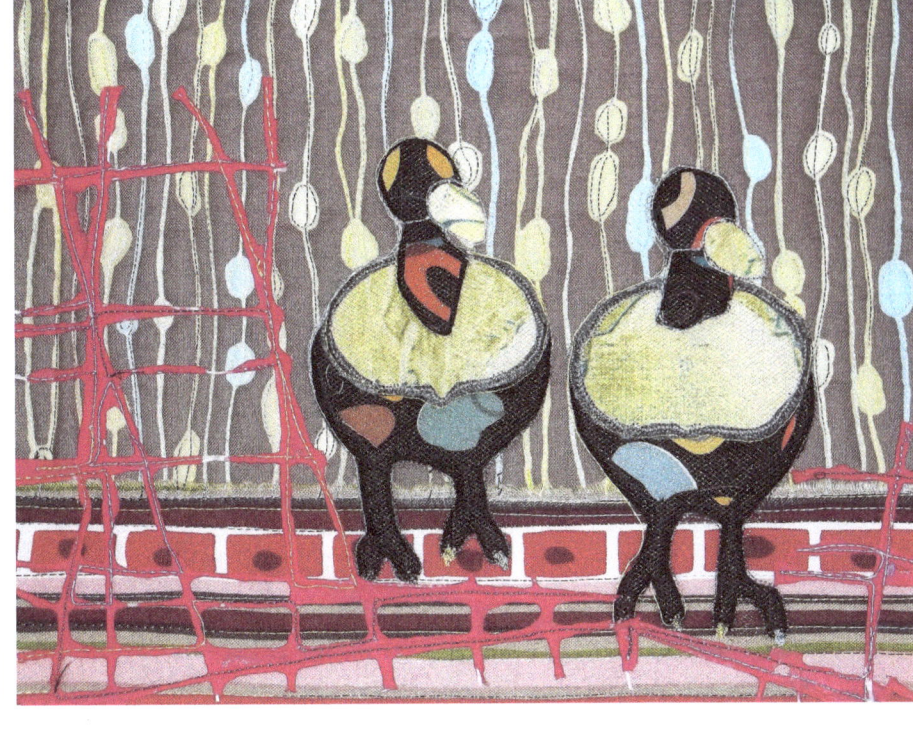

1 Loose Ducks 8x10" Quilting.

2 InSPIREation 36x38" Quilting.

3 Eye Believe 10x25" Quilting.

3

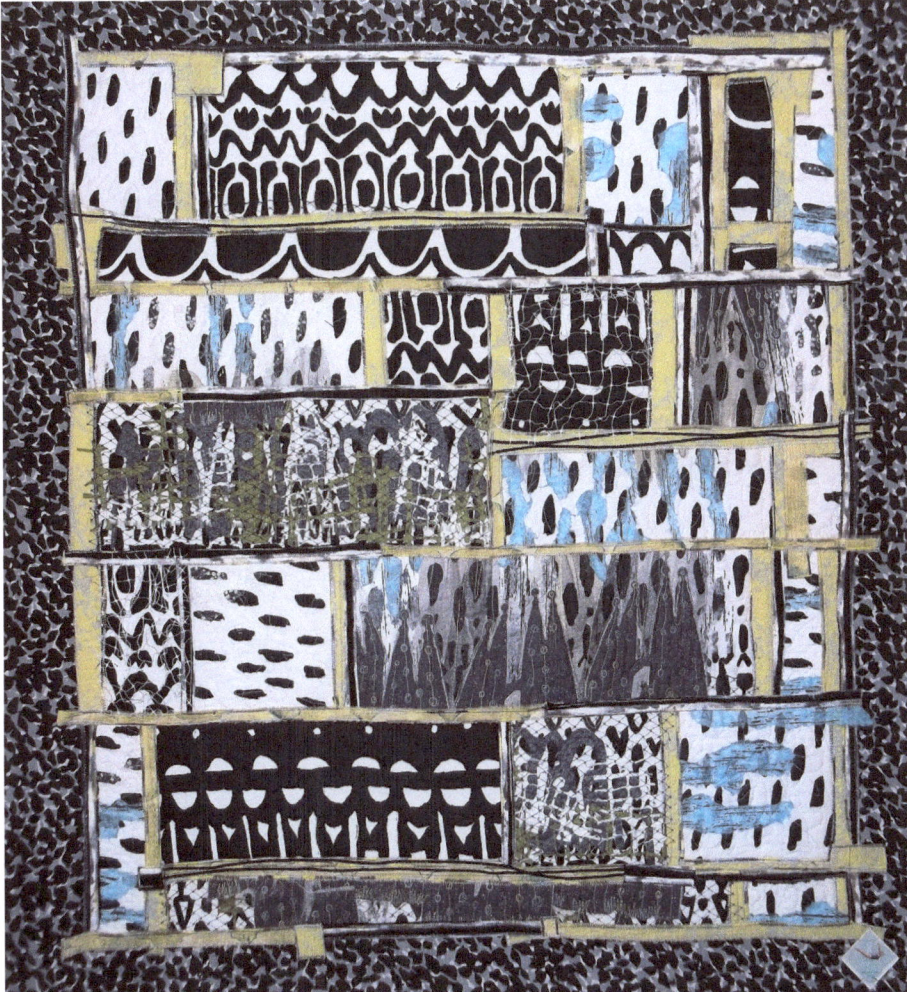

2

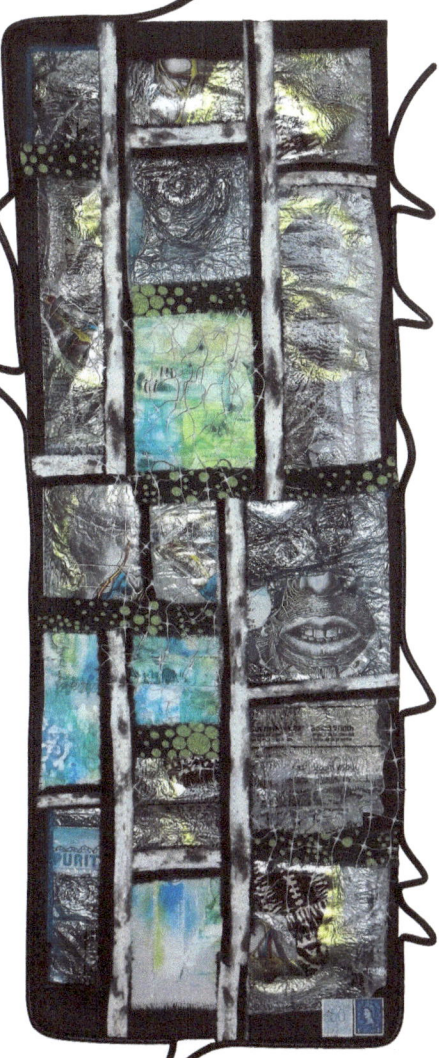

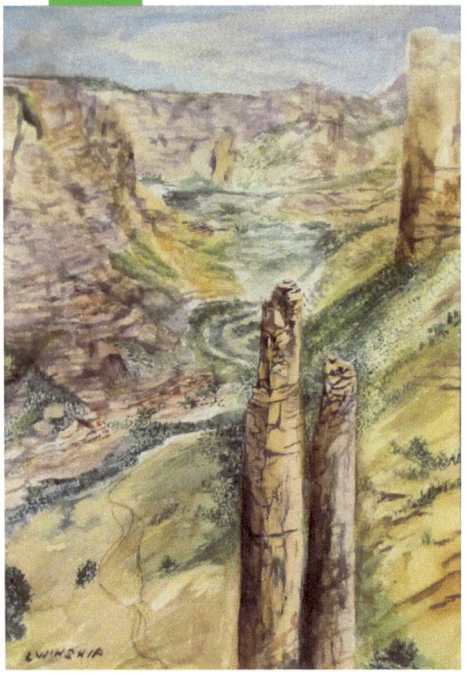

1

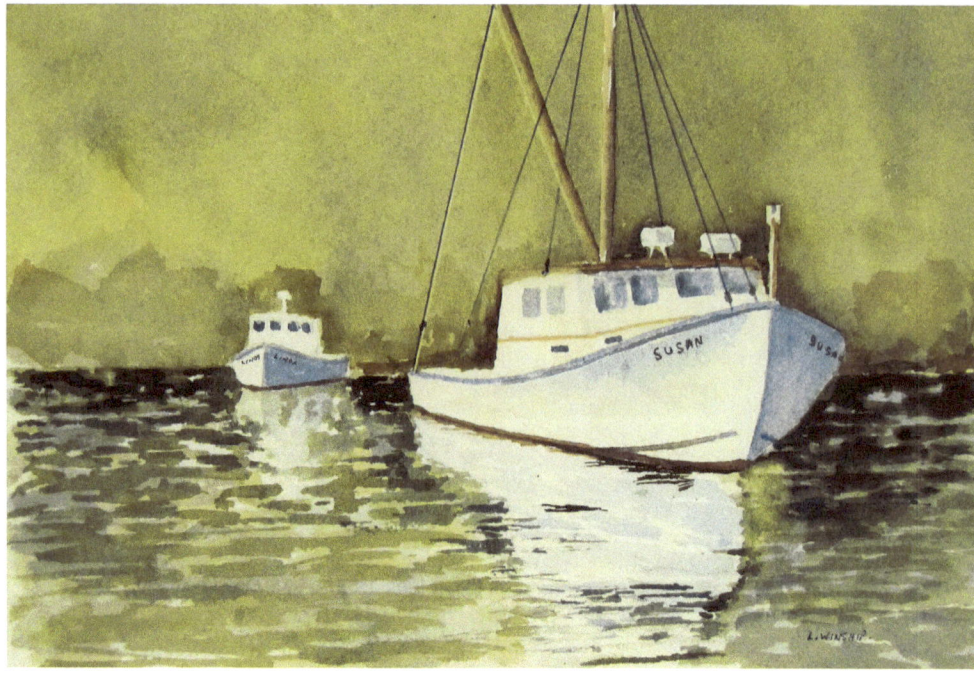

2

LES WINSHIP

LOCATION: Guelph
WEB: (N/A)
EMAIL: artist123@rogers.com

3 **Waterlilies** 8x10" Watercolour.

I have been seriously painting since 1967 starting with oils then with acrylics. I decided to try other mediums, egg tempera, pastel gouache, pen and ink and then watercolour which I paint with to this day. I have taken many workshops with local and some outstanding famous artists around the region.

1 **Spider Rock** 16x20" Watercolour. Canyon de Chelly Arizona

2 **Sleeping Beauty** 8x10" Watercolour.

3

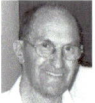

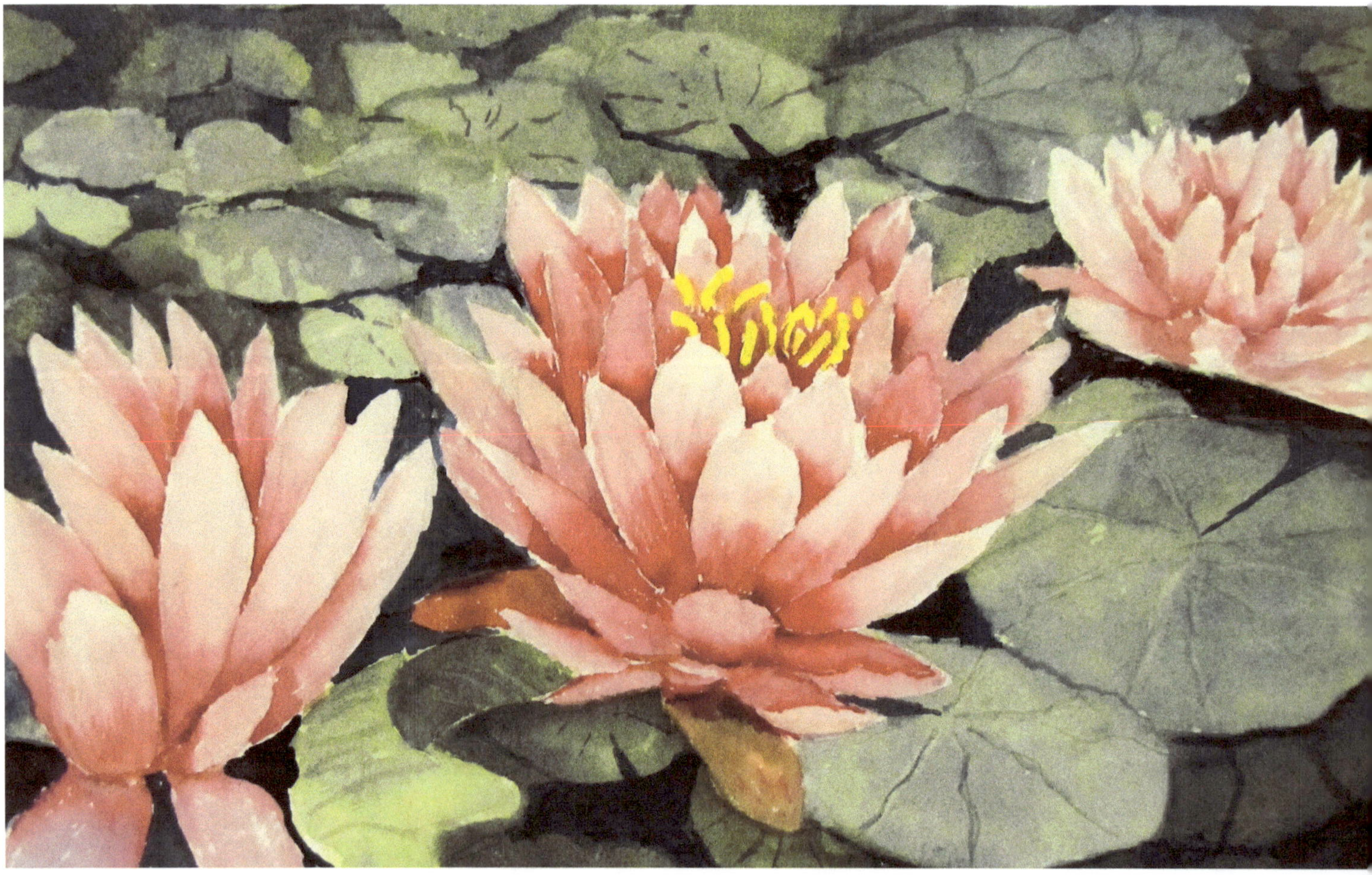

Laura Bauer

LOCATION: Cambridge Guelph
WEB: alphasoupphotography.etsy.com
EMAIL:
alphabetsoupphotography@hotmail.com

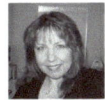

After exploring many other types of media, Laura decided to try photography. Thus Alphabet Soup Photography was born. Capturing the beauty of the Guelph Ont. area, architechural elements are taken to become letters that can spell whatever you desire - the happy couple's name as a unique wedding present, an inspirational word, or any other reason you can think of. Landmarks are also part of the collection - Church of Our Lady and the Cenetaph to name a few. Don't forget Catty Cards - animals with an attitude. Greeting cards that will bring a smile to anyone's face.

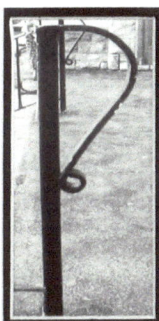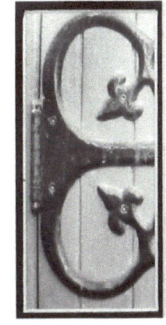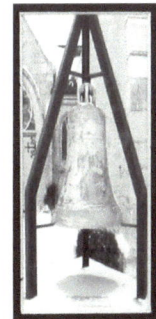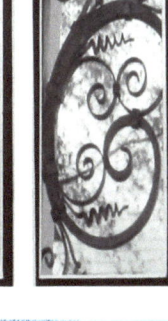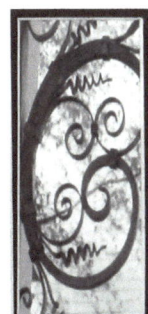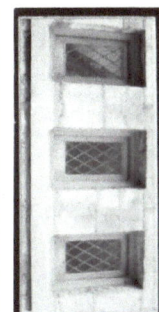

1

1 Peace Photographs.

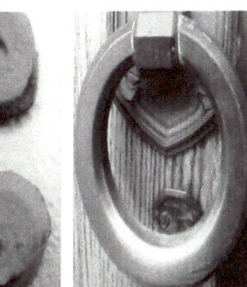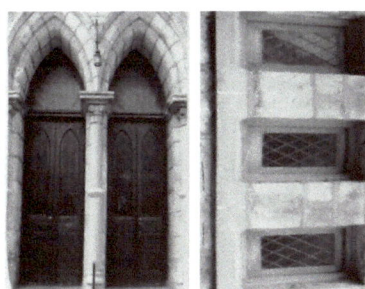

2 Church Photograph.

2

3 Welcome and Guelph Photographs. With over 350 letter pics, there are plenty of choices to make your work unique.

3

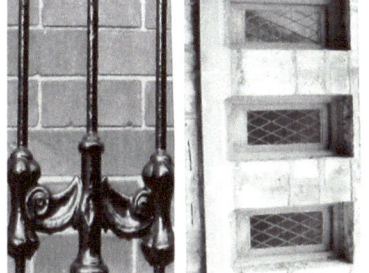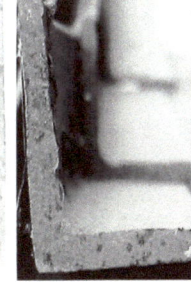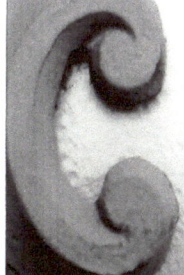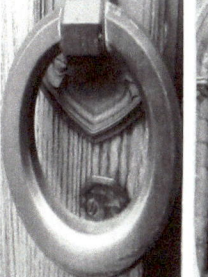

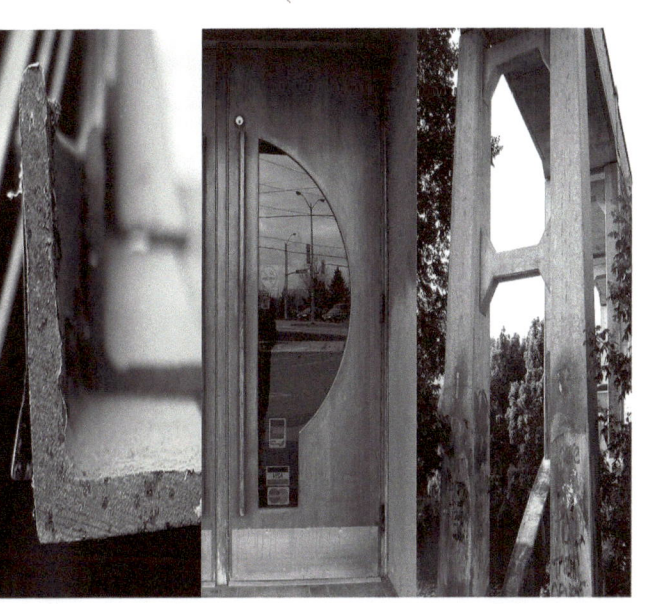

114

SHARON MAILLET

LOCATION: Cambridge
WEB: funkfolkbrokenglass.etsy.com
EMAIL: sharonmaillet@yahoo.ca

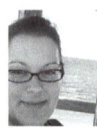

Sharon is an artist at heart. She gets goosebumps when she sees beautiful glass, was giddy at the Van Gogh Museum in Amsterdam, and loves to encourage people to get in touch with their playful side through art. With a BSc in Psychology, her ultimate goal is to create a career where she can blend her love of the arts with her passion for promoting mental health, and like all artists, have some money left over to buy more supplies. She enjoys riding creative waves, is always grateful when they come, and is happy to surrender to them.

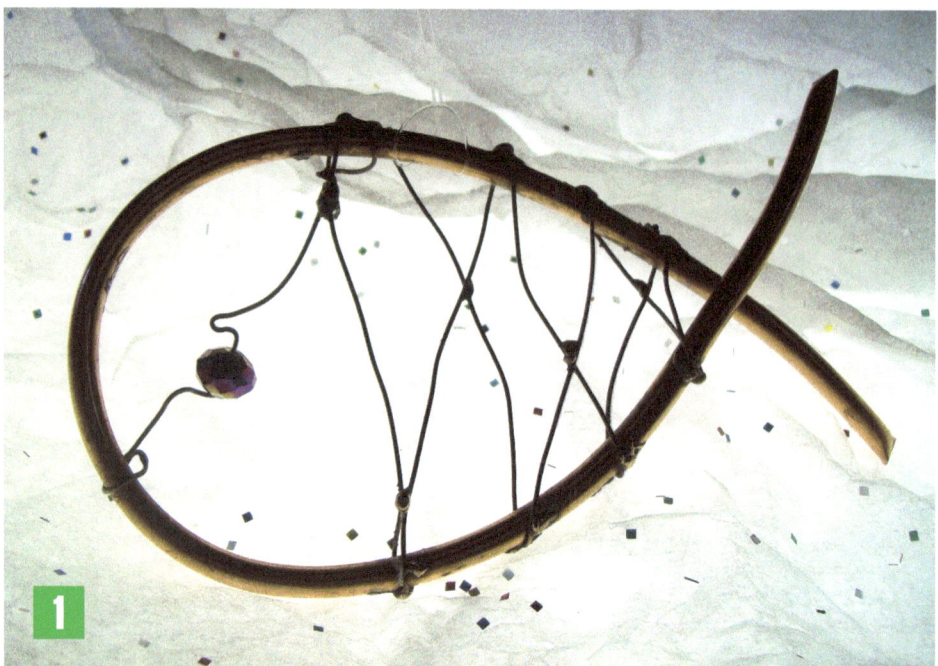

1

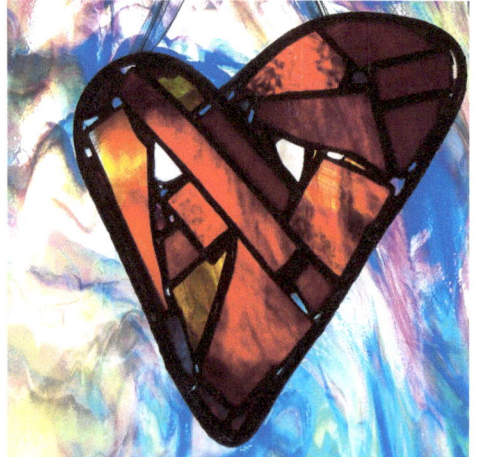

2

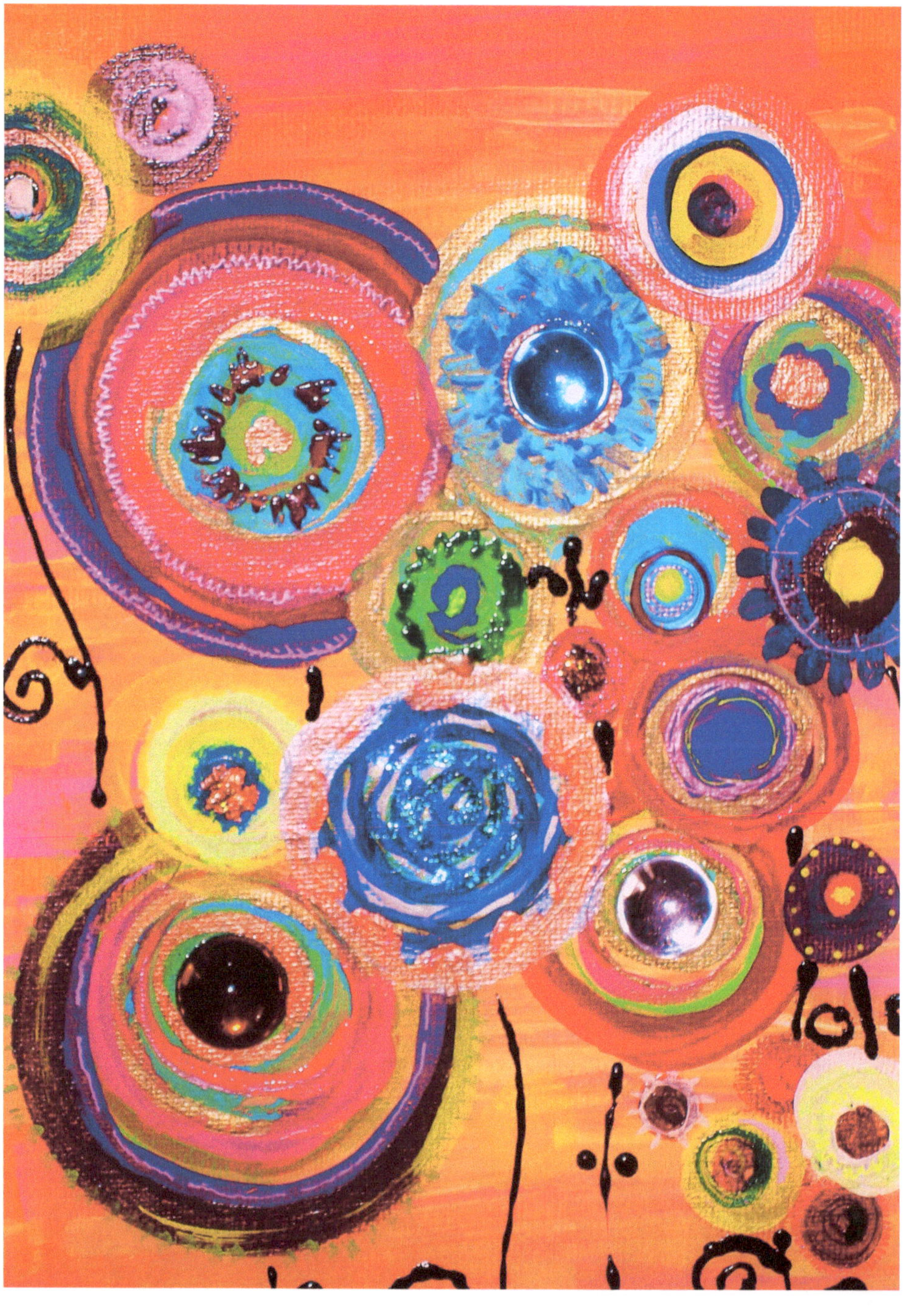

3

1 Copper Fish 9x4" Copper, glass. Guaranteed not to bite.

2 Pieces of My Heart 11x14" Stained glass and copper. Tried to set it free, but it came back. Love is like that.

3 Sol D'Orange 9x12" Acrylic, mixed media on canvas. One of a series of happy experimentations.

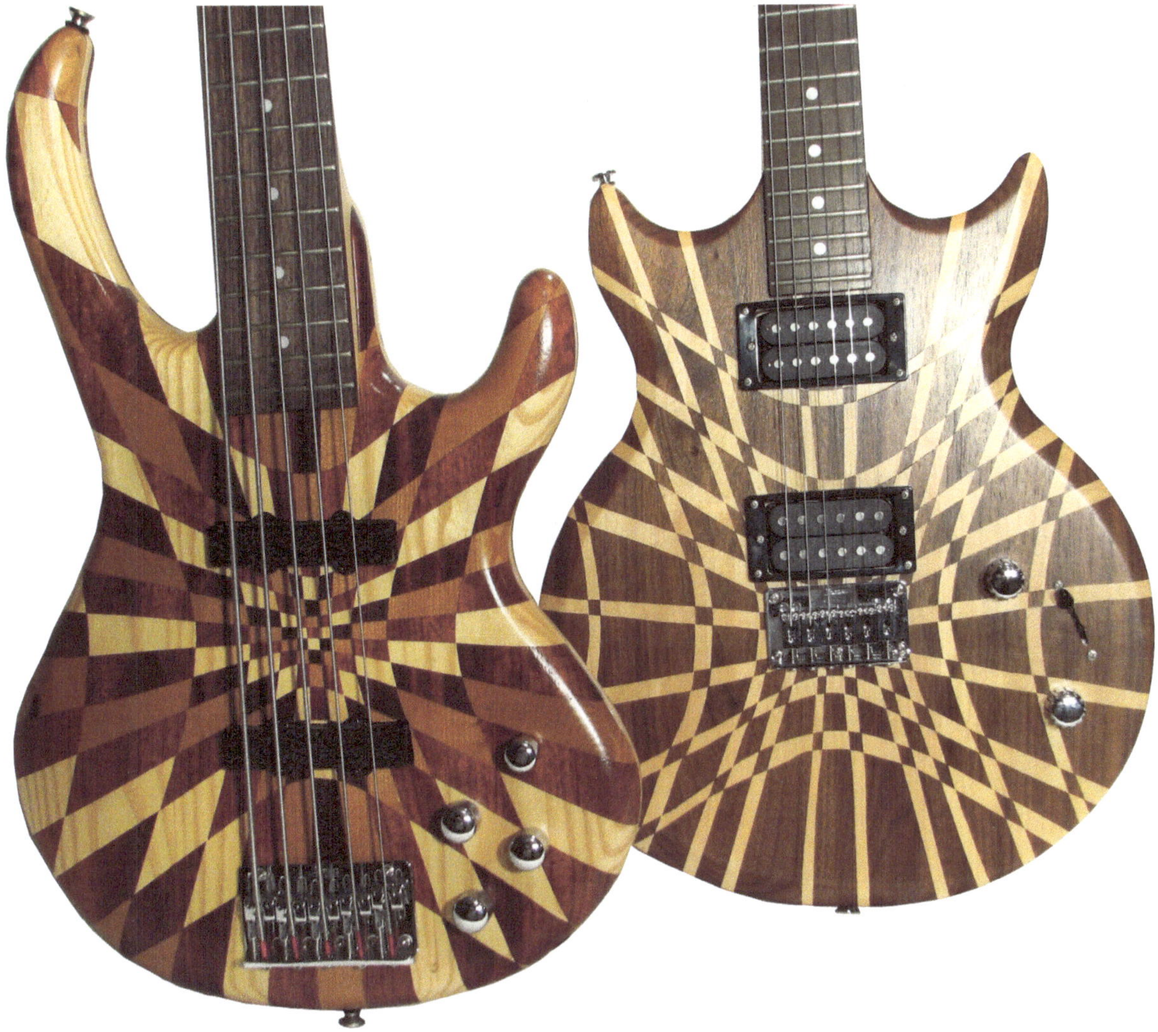

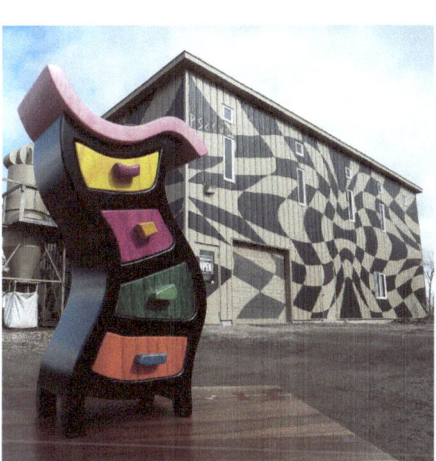

PAUL SZEWC (CHEFS)

LOCATION: Guelph
WEB: masterpiece.on.ca
EMAIL: masterpiece@masterpiece.on.ca

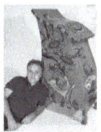

With a degree in Woodworking Technology, Paul Szewc is known as the crazy wood artist. In fact, when it comes to his work, his philosophy is, "the crazier the better". Paul has created mini jewellery boxes which he has affectionately dubbed "wonky". "I like building things that are curvy and crooked". He is also known for his live edge tables with stitching.

1 Crazy Guitars

2 The Gallery (Crazy pattern on the building).

3 Mini Wonky Jewellery Boxes 10x3.5x5" approximately.

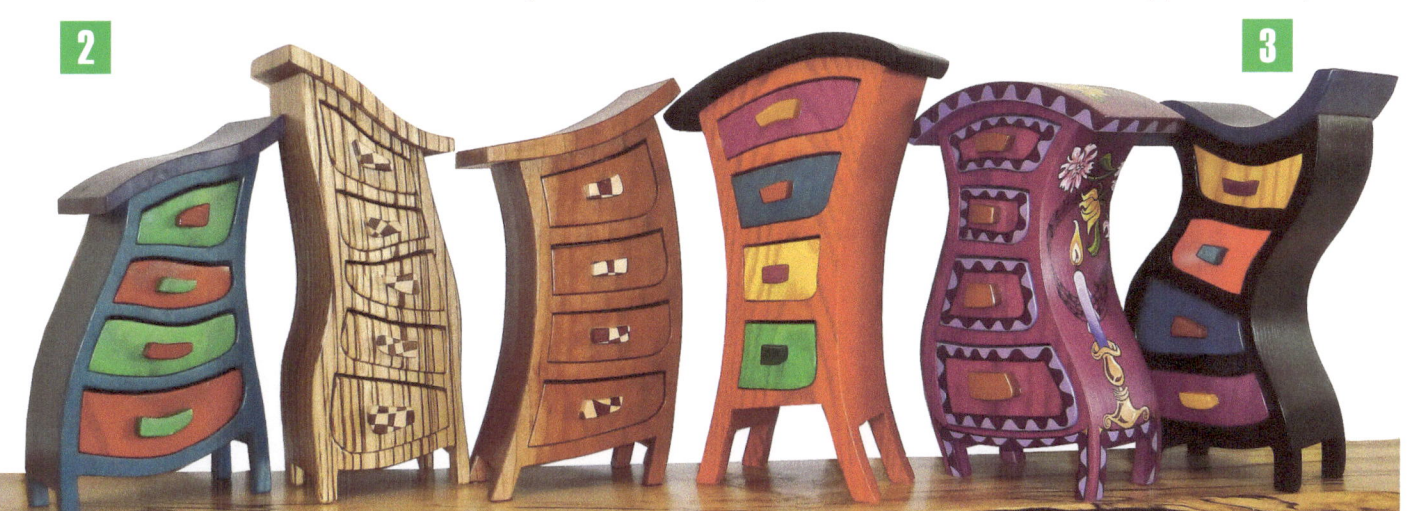

MICHELLE RAMALHO

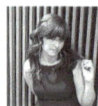

LOCATION: Guelph
WEB: (N/A)
EMAIL: michelleramalho@hotmail.com

Michelle is an up and coming artist who used these pieces in her portfolio to apply to art schools for September 2011 around Canada and are only the beginning of a life time of work she plans to create. She usually works main with acrylics, however, also does some sculpture and recently photography, and is looking forward to learning how to work with new media forms during the school term.

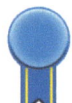

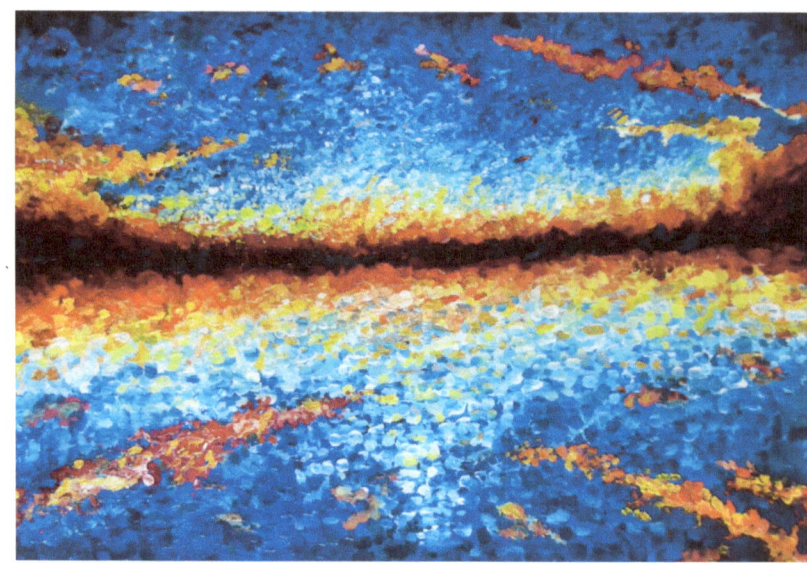

1 Absent 60x45" Acrylic on canvas. An abstract impression of a beautiful sky being reflected onto a calm lake, the two pieces are intentionally asymmetric to capture a different kind of beauty.

2 The Morning After 5x4" Clay Sculpture. The turmoil and suffering the depressed feel after a terrible day, the feeling of not wanting to get out of bed.

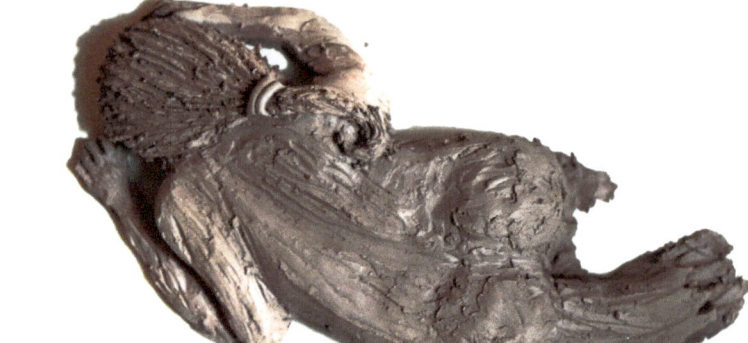

SUE STURDY

LOCATION: Cambridge
WEB: (N/A)
EMAIL: suesturdy@rogers.com

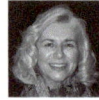

Fibre Artist, Sue sturdy wants to make you smile! Whether it's Janet Jackson's costume malfunction immortalized in knit or pimping your ride with a toque, she creates fun and fascination. Sue wants people to be involved in her art and she recently accomplished that by encasing Cambridge's Main Street Bridge in knit when she was the 2010 Artist-in-Residence.

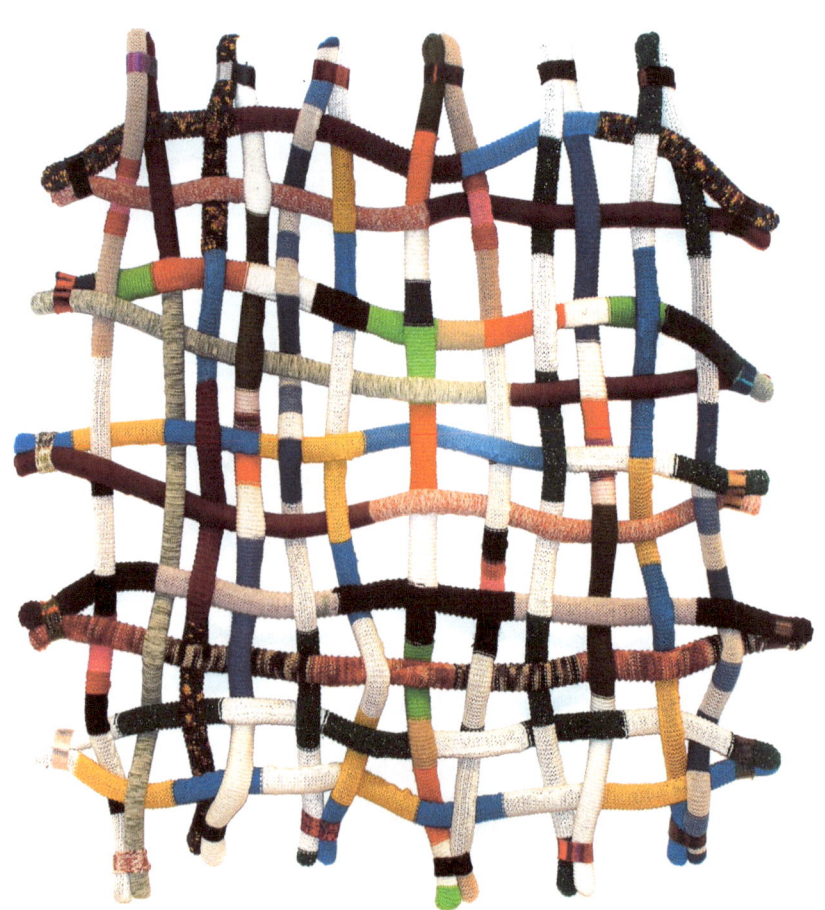

1 Uneven Bridge Weave Knit.

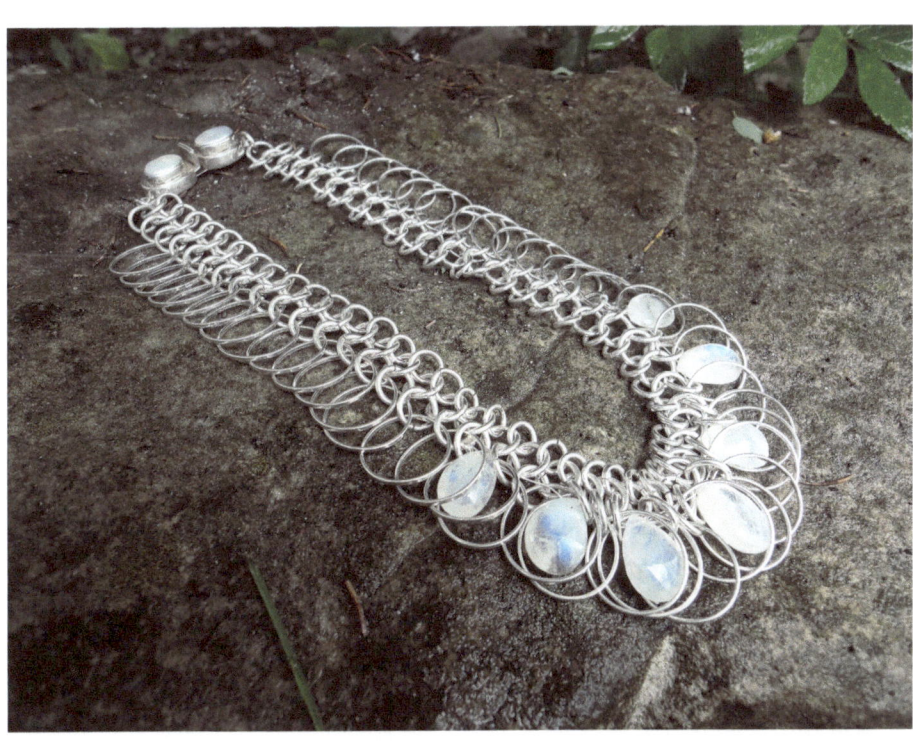

RICHARD PREISS

LOCATION: Guelph
WEB: flickr.com/photos/richiepreiss
EMAIL: dickiepea@gmail.com

Richard is a student at the University of Guelph. He is a biology major but spends a lot of free time taking photos. He gets his best results from film cameras and spontaneity.

1

1 We See What We Want Photograph. Toronto, Ontario..

DARIA LOVE

LOCATION: Eden Mills
WEB: darialovejewelry.com
EMAIL: daria@darialovejewelry.com

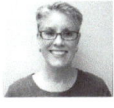

I am a self-taught jewelry artist, seeking to explore the beauty of nature through the art of jewelry. My work features sterling silver, using exceptional clasps and often integrates beaded designs with handmade silver chainmaille. Each piece is designed to reflect movement and light as well as the beauty and individuality of the stones and the person.

1

1 Chainmaille Handmade sterling silver chainmaille, moonstone and double mabe pearl silver clasp.

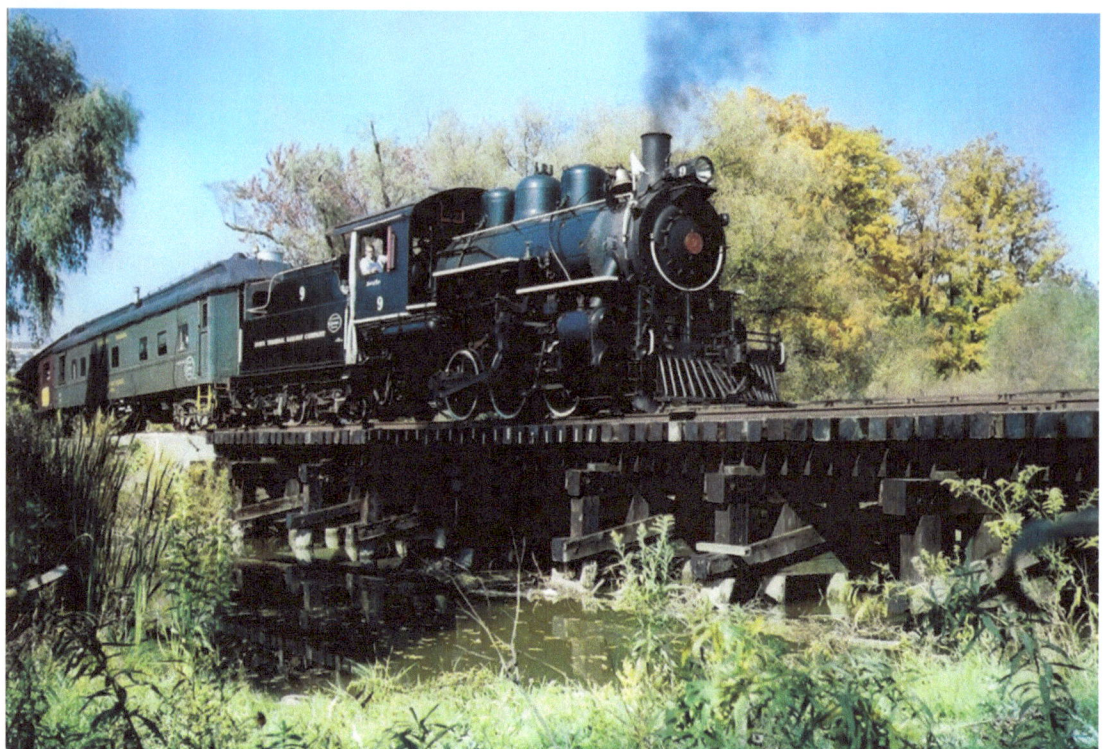

1 Train Photograph (Film).

2 Birds On a Wire Photograph.

3 Pioneer Tower Print.

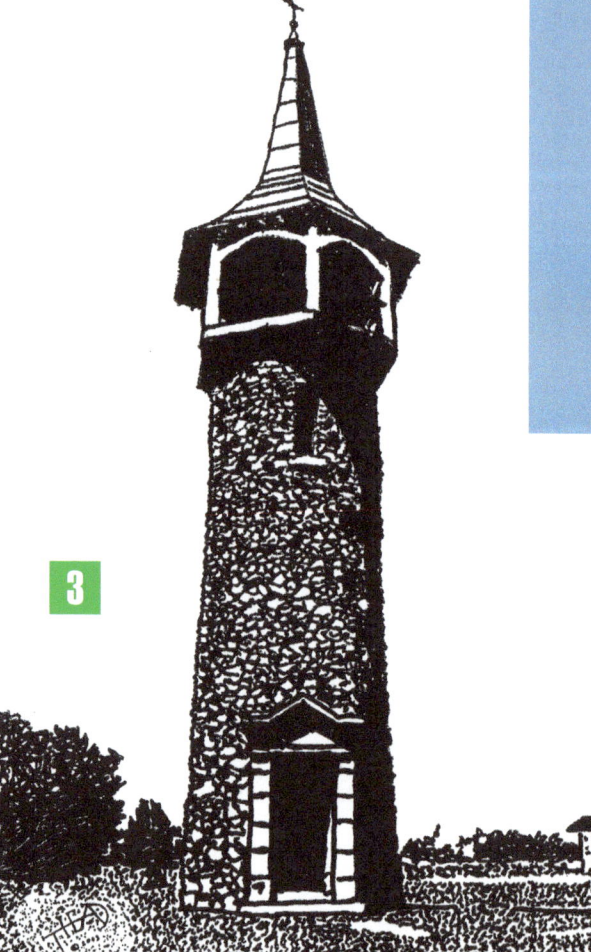

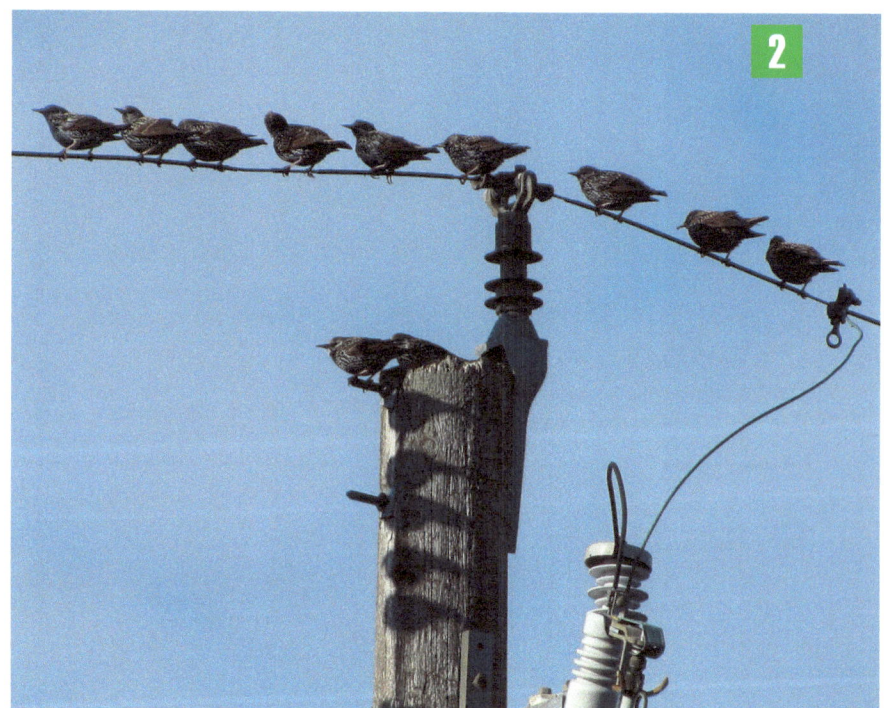

THOMAS HEAD
LOCATION: Kitchener
WEB: (N/A)
EMAIL: (N/A)

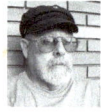

A lifetime of travel in 40 plus countries and several years of working as a newspaper layout artist in the advertising department of a large retail store has enabled me to hone my powers of observation. Working as a mobile portrait photographer in northern Ontario taught me the necessity of patience often required in obtaining a beautiful photograph. You may have seen the postcards I created for the Waterloo Central Railway. I have had memberships in photography associations in both the UK and Waterloo Region.

KEVIN W. KRELLER

LOCATION: Guelph
WEB: wix.com/kreller/kevinkreller
facebook.com/#!/media/set/?set=o.49686242085
EMAIL: krellerdesigns@yahoo.ca

Born in 1973, Kevin W. Kreller was raised in the beautiful northern forests of Haliburton Ontario, relocating and currently residing in Guelph Ontario. Kevin's love for art and design, came at an early age by drawing and recreating the complex skateboard logos and graphics of his youth ,winning countless awards that eventually led to a feature story in a local newspaper at the age of 14, and not long after had a gallery showing of his works. Successfully completeing Graphic Design at Conestoga College in Kitchener Ontario, Kevins main focus is in all forms of print. Kevin has also won a snowboard design contests in 2009 and led to being recognized by Forum snowboards.

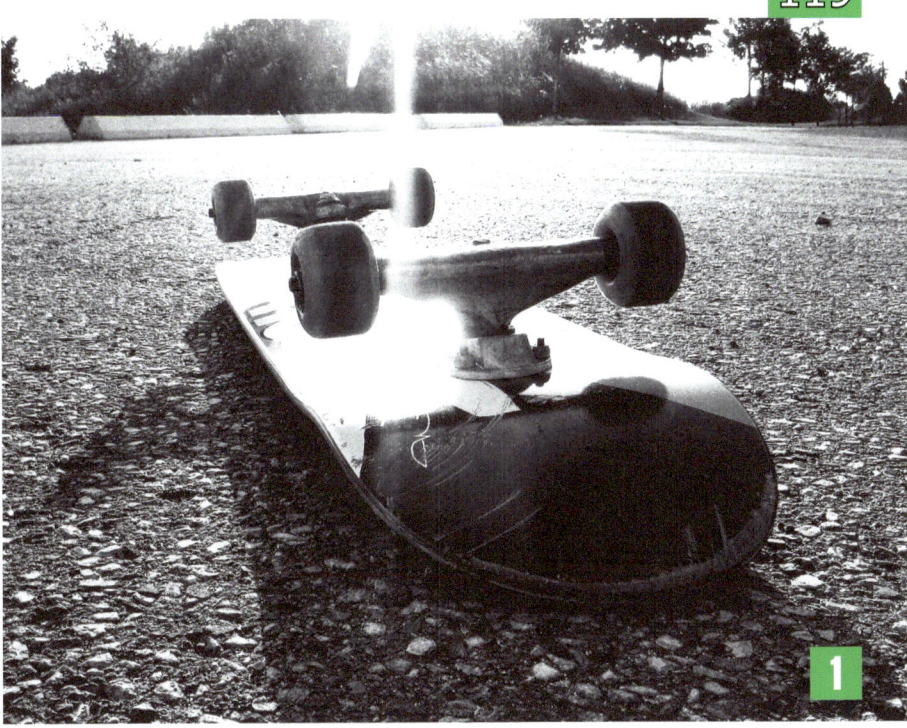

2 Owl Acrylic.

3 Face Ripping Ink on paper illustration.

1 Skating Photograph.

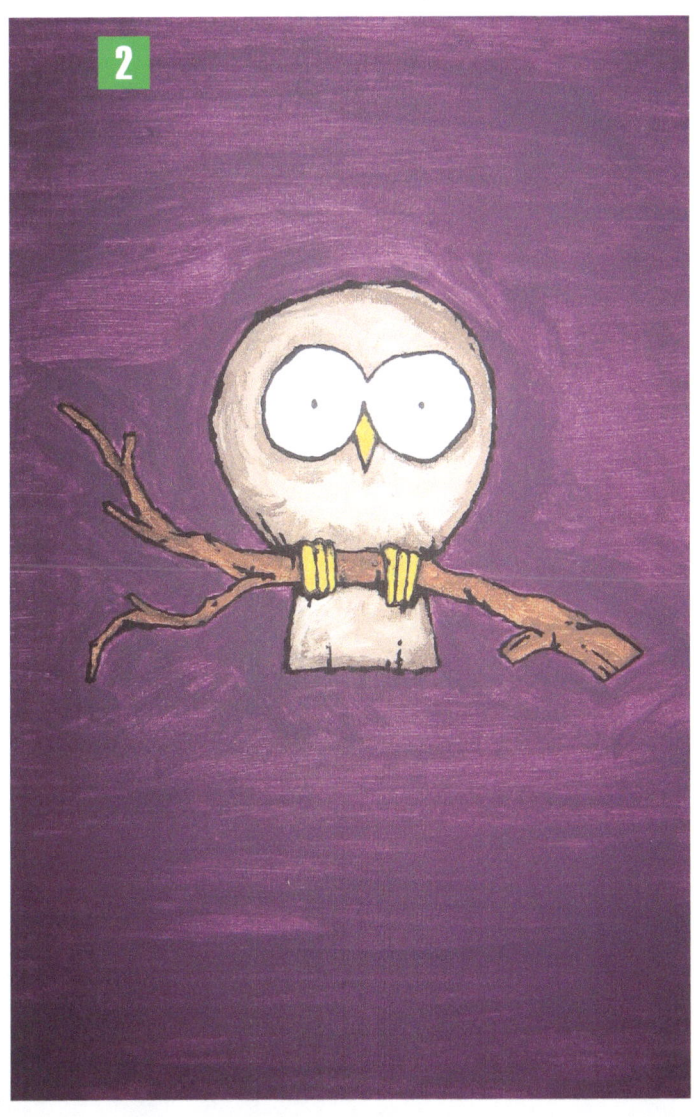

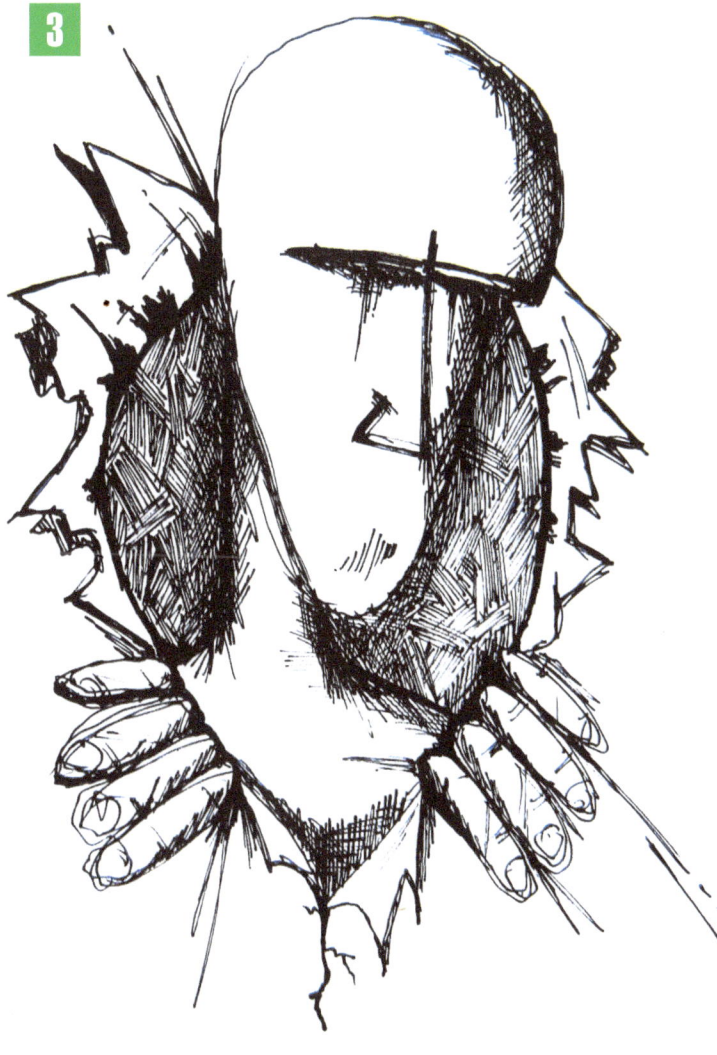

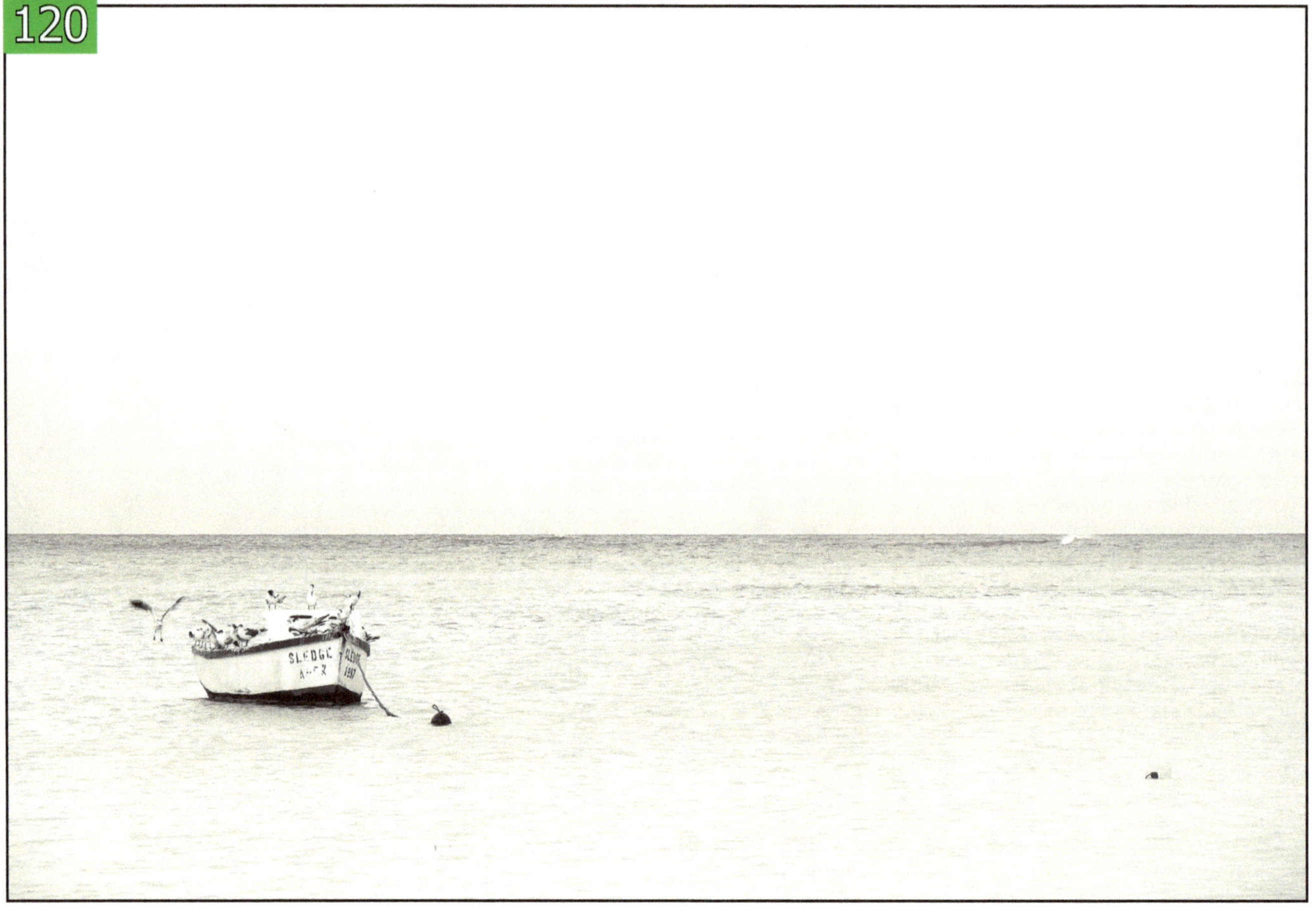

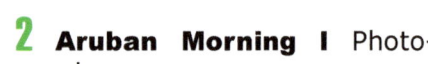

MANDY RESENDES

LOCATION: Cambridge
WEB: (N/A)
EMAIL: mandysimages@gmail.com

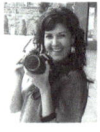

Mandy is a photographer born and raised in Cambridge. She discovered her talent by experimenting with an old film SLR camera while on a very long and ambitious solo trip through Europe. She knew nothing of photography, but upon her return developed her "experiments" and saw she had a definite knack for it. She decided to study the craft at Santa Monica College in California (more out of the need to set a goal than to actually become a photographer!). Mandy recently launched her own business, Studio~M Photography, specializing in what she dubs as "Docu-Travel" (documenting client journeys) as well as Portraiture. Mandy is also passionate about yoga, travel, fundraising for local organizations that help those struggling with addictions and depression, working with the City of Cambridge to organize the youth portion of the annual "Mayor's Celebration of the Arts", as well as performing with her band Delta Grand Speed for whom she plays keys and sings.

1 **Aruban Morning II** Photograph.

1

2 **Aruban Morning I** Photograph.

3 **Hand Abreast** 35mm film, dark room developed and printed by the artist.

3

2

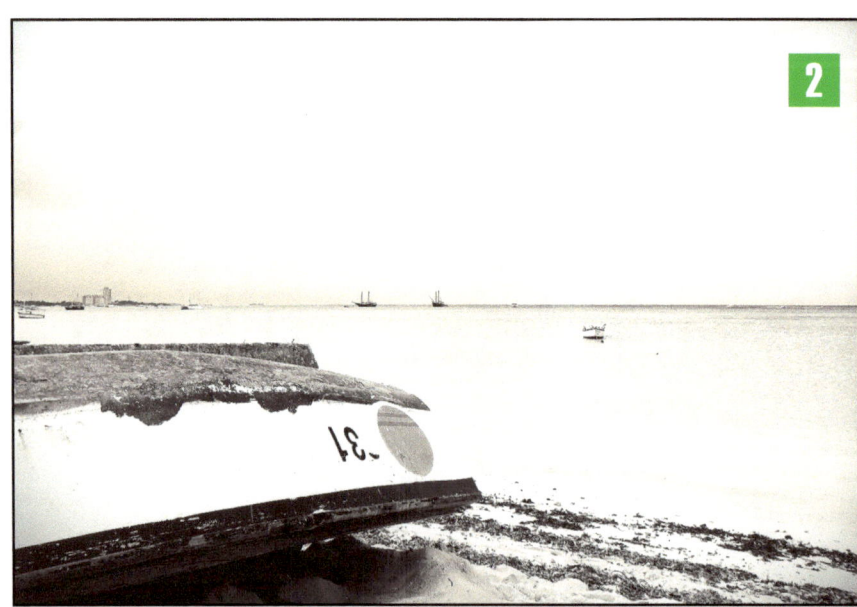

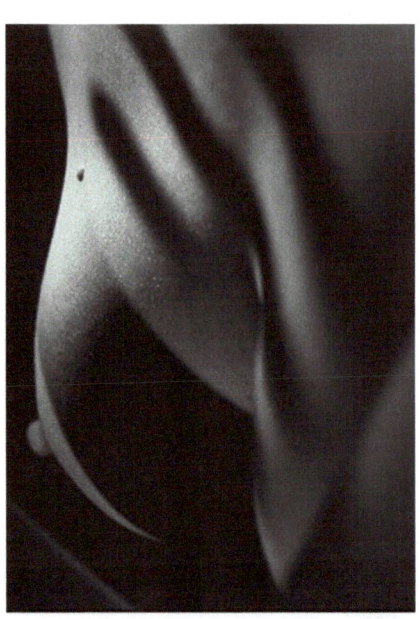

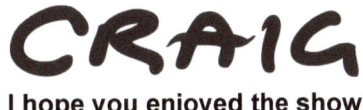

I hope you enjoyed the show!

**I would like to thank the artists who partici-
pated. Whether you got the email right the
first time or the 25th you got it eventually and
that is what matters.**

Index

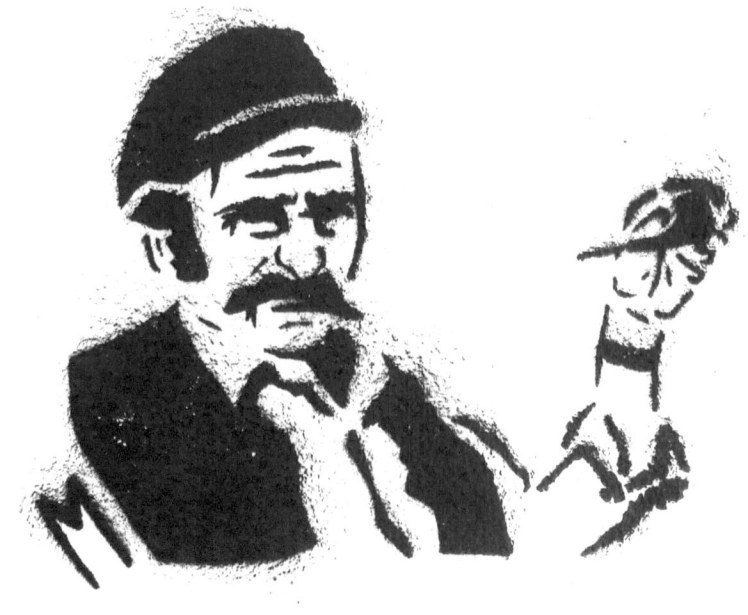

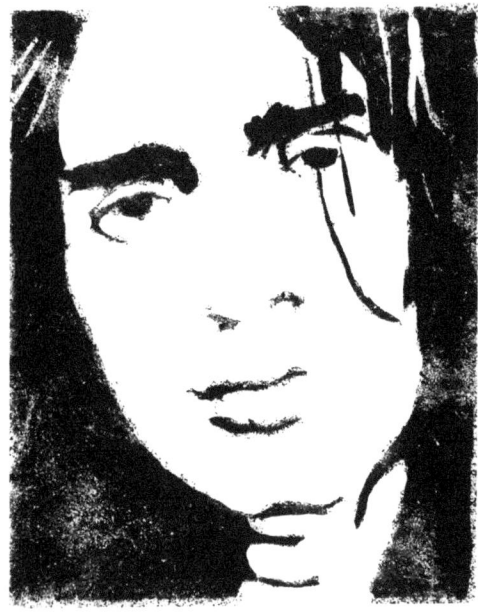

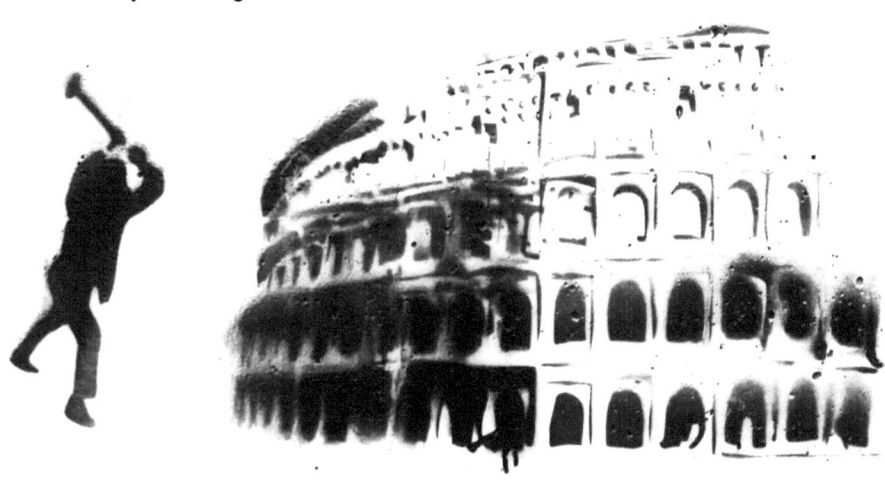

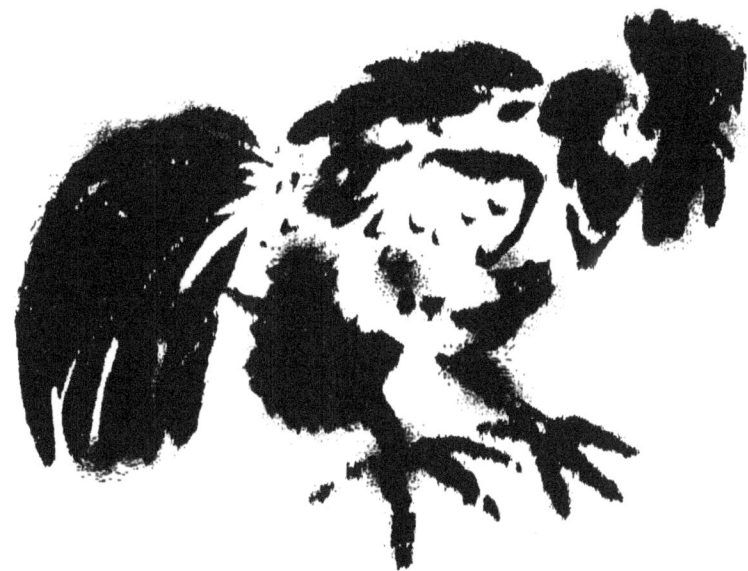
Unauthorized Street Art
Spraypainted vandalism, various places in Cambridge & Guelph.

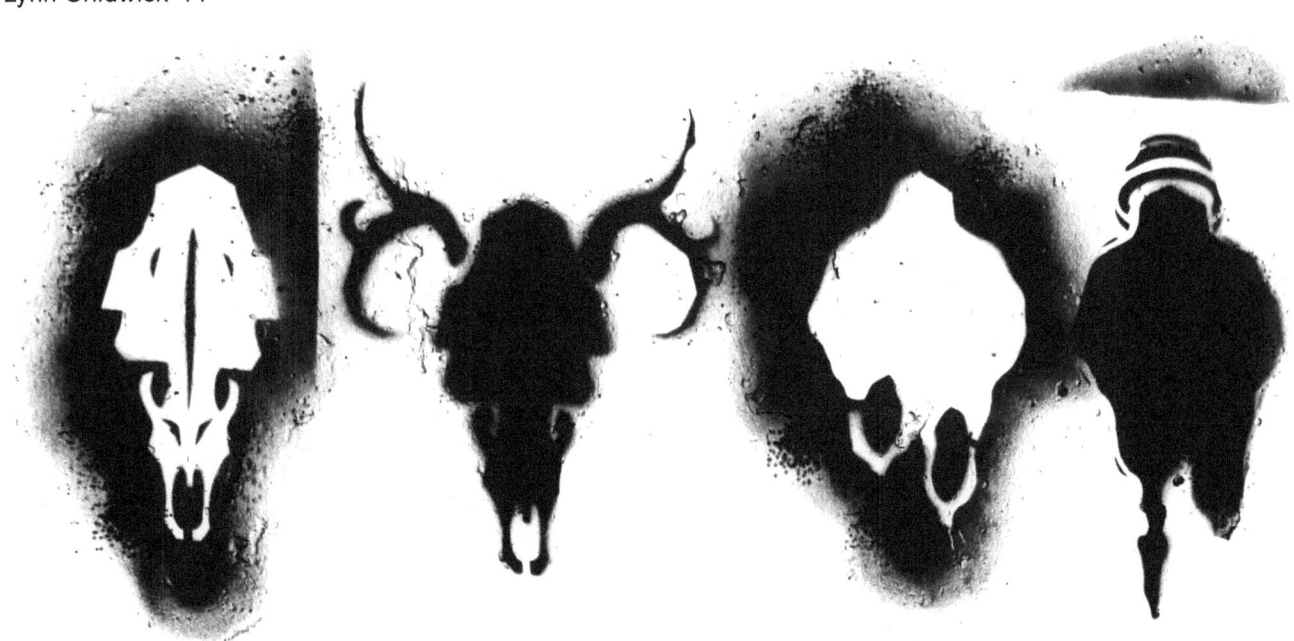

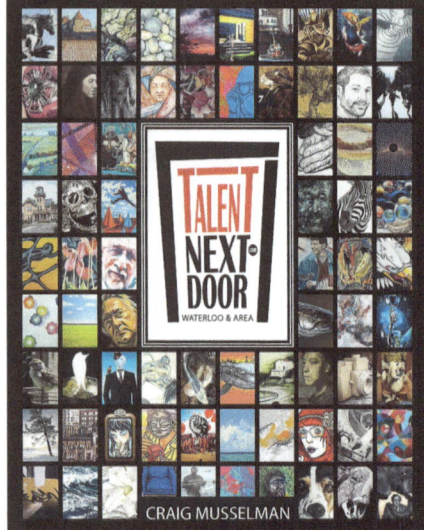

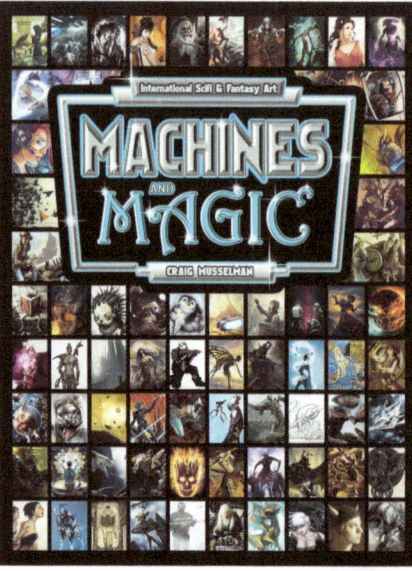

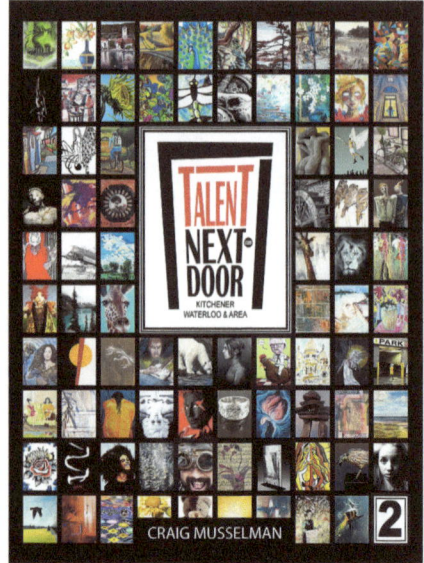

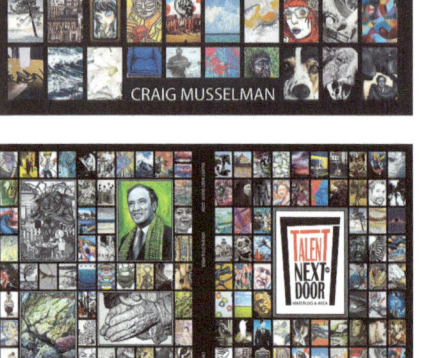

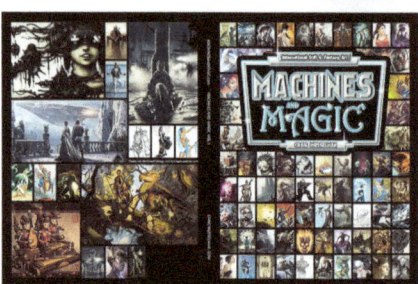

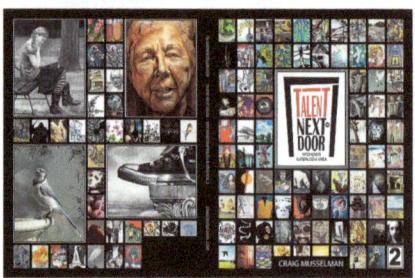

Talent Next Door - Waterloo & Area Volume 1 8x10" Featuring 142 top local artists from the Waterloo to Stratford region on 136 pages (2010) www.TalentNextDoor.com ISBN: 978-1453808061

Machines and Magic Volume 1 8.5x11" Outstanding Fantasy and Sci Fi art from every continent featuring 91 top artists on 156 colour pages. (2011) www.MachinesAndMagic.com ISBN 978-0987789501

Talent Next Door - Waterloo & Area - Volume 2 8.5x11" Featuring 139 top local artists from the Kitchener Waterloo region on 136 pages (2011) www.TalentNextDoor.com ISBN:978-0-9877895-1-8

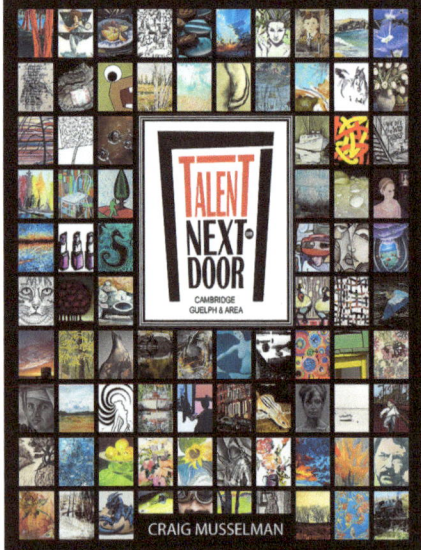

ART BOOKS BY CRAIG MUSSELMAN

By 2011 Craig will have 4 books in print shown here, with several more planned for 2012. If you would like to participate, please visit the appropriate website for details or link through his portal at www.CraigMusselman.com. His books are printed by Createspace.com (an Amazon owned company) & are available through Createspace, Amazon & other online bookstores, but he usually has a few on hand for local pickup. He can be contacted at his business email CraigBMusselman@gmail.com or the email specific to each book.

Steampunk Art The best of steampunk art from around the world. Victorian Splendour of the future! Costumes, props, artefacts, and art. Recruiting submissions for 2012 www.SteampunkArt.org

Flower Reference From my stock photo website a full colour book of hundreds of flower pictures to draw and paint. Featuring leaves, flowers and closeups. (spring 2012) www.ShootItFor.Me

Talent Next Door - Cambridge / Guelph and Area Volume 1 8.5x11" 116 outstanding local artists from the Cambridge / Guelph region on 124 pages (2011) www.TalentNextDoor.com ISBN 978-0-9877895-2-5

Super Real Art and **Black and White Drawings** one on realistic, "Wow how did you do that?" art the other drawings in black and white. Recruiting submissions for 2012/2013. www.RealisticArt.org

Science Fiction / Fantasy Art Reference From my stock photo website a full colour book featuring helpful references for all your fantasy/sci fi art needs. (planned for summer 2012) www.ShootItFor.Me